SYMBOLISM

A Bibliography of Symbolism
as an International
and Multi-Disciplinary
Movement

SYMBOLISM

A Bibliography of Symbolism as an International and Multi-Disciplinary Movement

Compiled and Edited by

DAVID L. ANDERSON
University of Denver

with

Georgia S. Maas

and

Diane-Marie Savoye

Published under the supervision of
Anna Balakian, Director of
Symbolist Research, New York University

New York: New York University Press
1975

Library of Congress Catalog Card Number: 74-17460
ISBN: 0-8147-0555-3

Library of Congress Cataloging in Publication Data

Anderson, David L   1937-
    Symbolism.

    Includes index.
    1.   Symbolism in art—Bibliography.   2.   Arts—
Bibliography.   I.   Title.
Z5936.S9A52   [NX600.S95]   016.7   74-17460
ISBN 0—8147—0555—3

Manufactured in the United States of America

Preface

The basic principle of this bibliography is to provide an international and interdisciplinary cross-listing of works written on Symbolism in the European languages, from 1880 to 1973. No bibliography scanning as many years and englobing as many areas of this nature now exists on the specific subject of Symbolism, and it is felt that the present compilation is long overdue, and will fill a pressing need. At the same time, it must be stated forthrightly that no such undertaking can claim definitiveness, if for no other reason than that scholarly publications continue to roll off the presses while bibliographical compilation must cease arbitrarily at a given moment if any practical result is to be achieved at all. To this fact of humanistic life and endeavor must be added the supernumerary difficulties of compiling a multi-lingual, and multi-disciplinary checklist in an area of study subject to an especially wide range of definitions. In the case of Symbolism (read: Symbolism referring to a specific intellectual movement originating in Paris, *circa* 1880-1885), the number and kind of definitions are almost as varied as the number of scholars, and the number of discrete listings represented here. The thorny question of bibliographical parameters therefore presents itself: does one include such an article as Michael Edwards' "*La nausée*—A Symbolist Novel," in *Adam* 343-45(1970):9-21, with the perfectly obvious realization that Sartre can be considered a "Symbolist" only in the most remote sense of the word (if that)? And if one draws the line on Sartre, what of Valéry? or Poe? or Gauguin? or Wagner? or James Joyce? and so on.

For bibliographical purposes then, this listing *does* include titles such as the above on patently non-Symbolist figures when there is a direct association made (be it "right" or "wrong") with the Symbolist movement, and when the article, essay or monograph is or could be of scholarly interest to the researcher concerned with Symbolism. Not all critics, of course, will agree on what is of scholarly interest, but it is not the function of the bibliographer to decree which scholar's opinion is right, or which is wrong; the very purpose of bibliography is to provide the available data so that scholars might best decide such matters for themselves.

In the same manner also we have included some general works on literature, some anthologies, some bibligraphies, and some general discussions such as Romeo Arbour's *Henri Bergson et les lettres françaises* (Paris: Corti, 1956), where, it is felt, there are specific chapters or sections of interest with regard to the Symbolist movement. In the case of *Festschriften* and other collections of essays, we have recorded both the title of the individual essay and the title of the collection under appropriate headings. Conversely, we have tried to *exclude* the literally countless titles referring to symbolism (lower case "s") as a general term, applicable to anything from archeology to zoology.

Problems of this nature, while common to all bibliographical enterprise, become particularly acute when the deliberate focus of the compilation is multi-disciplinary, reaching into the heterogenous areas of Art, Literature, Music, Philosophy, and so on. As Anna Balakian aptly stated at a recent (March 1974) meeting of the American Comparative Literature Association, to trace the diffusion of a movement such as Symbolism ". . . would entail the collective work of a large team. . . . We have such a team, and although our work will not exhaust the subject, it will reflect into the record of a multifaceted literary expression the response of our own moment in history." The present Bibliography is, in fact, an outgrowth of (and complement to) a forthcoming critical history of Symbolism, which will represent the collective efforts of a team of some seventy-five internationally known scholars, headed by Professor Balakian. The forthcoming volume on Symbolism, in turn, will be part of a multivolumed project on the comparative history of literature in the European languages, sponsored by the International Comparative Literature Association. Those scholars participating in the Symbolism project are well aware of the bibliographical problems we have encountered, and their expert advice and counsel have done much to attenuate the limitations of a single bibliographer or two who might otherwise have foundered in a heavy sea of unfamiliar names, publications and art forms.

Even so, a proper and coherent blend of diverse disciplines and languages is difficult to achieve. Toward that end, and by way or organization, this Bibliography is divided into four principle categories:

I General and Miscellaneous
II National and International Movements
III Forms and Genres
IV Individual Figures

These categories are then further subdivided into boldface headings which are the indices for specific areas, subjects, forms and individual names related to Symbolism. Under each of these boldface headings, bibliographical records are listed alphabetically, while the entire compilation is enumerated consecutively from the beginning of Section I, to the end of Section IV. Further blending has been achieved through the extensive use of cross references which are listed at the end of each alphabetical grouping. Thus, an article on Mallarmé, Debussy and Ravel will be listed alphabetically (by author name) under the heading *Mallarmé* (Item 2131), and at the end of the alphabetical listings for *Debussy* and *Ravel* there are indicators to *"See also* 2131."

It should be noted that the more than 280 individual names represented here in boldface headings are those of men and women, many of whom are of great reknown, and to whom enormous amounts of critical writings have been devoted. In this Bibliography, however, our intent was not to provide an exhaustive listing of works devoted to each of them, but rather to list those titles which signal their connections with Symbolism, with each other, and with the various forms and genres also represented here with the same intent. Along with this important delimitation, the bibliographical records included in our list have been verified as to both content and imprint data, either by means of multiple-reference comparison, or, where possible, by physical inspection. And yet, everyone who has ever dealt with bibliography either as a compiler or as a user knows that it must inevitably be marred by errors, omissions, and perhaps even erroneous inclusions; in this regard, we ask only that such errors be brought to our attention, for in the final analysis, this is only a beginning. This is especially true with regard to the systematic analysis of East European and South American sources, many of which continue to be unknown and/or unavailable to American and European scholars. And in an even broader sense, we have suggested here a wealth of as yet undeveloped bibliographical potential in journals, serials and monographs devoted to nonliterary subjects (Aesthetics, Art, Dance, Music and so on), but which are of great moment in this most non-parochial of intellectual movements. It is hoped, therefore, that the present compilation, in addition to providing a more comprehensive and better organized reference work than any that currently exist on Symbolism, will also provide a solid basis and point of departure for future and more exhaustive compilations, checklists and bibliographical studies on the subject of the Symbolist movement, in all its multifarious associations.

It is appropriate to acknowledge here the generous grant which the National Endowment for the Humanities provided to New York University in support of the project on the Symbolist movement in conjunction with which this Bibliography was launched. Thanks to a subsequent grant from the Pennsylvania State University, I was able to systematize, expand and edit the Bibliography. A debt of gratitude and appreciation is also owed to the French Department of the Pennsylvania State University for its financial and secretarial support of the project, to my editorial assistant, Nancy Mercinko, for her unflagging devotion, and to Harrison T. Meserole of the *Modern Language Association of America International Bibliography* for his encouragement and his expert advice on bibliographical matters.

Denver   *David L. Anderson*

Contents

Preface   v

Introduction   xi

List of Journals and Serials Consulted   xiii

		Items nos.	
I	*General and Miscellaneous*	1-273	1
II	*National and International Movements*	274-717	13
III	*Forms and Genres*	718-1138	33
IV	*Individual Figures*	1139-3182	51
	Author Index		135

Introduction

Plurality of Views and the Bibliographical Spectrum

Although bibliographies and anthologies are wont to be considered among the most objective of research documents relating to literary history, they are nonetheless subject to personal taste, arbitrary decisions, and above all to provincial perspectives. A literary movement as globally infectious and as catalytic of poetic inspiration as the Symbolist Movement has bridged two centuries and penetrated a multitude of countries and their languages; any compilation, therefore, of texts, or references to primary and secondary sources demands imaginative search, detective intuition, a large measure of common sense, and a vision unobstructed by national prejudices or barriers.

To these high virtues must be added, in the case of bibliographers, the unsung but indispensable qualities of patience and persistence. These are indeed the assets of the several researchers who brought to fruition the quest for the references radiated by and responding to that phenomenon designated as the Symbolist Movement. They identified, sorted out, and made their discriminatory choices of what was relevant and significant to this literary trend. Professor David L. Anderson and our N.Y.U. research assistants, Georgia S. Maas and Diane Savoye, who undertook the task, were tireless and intelligently dedicated to this work, which we hope will be a permanent reference tool for many years to come, needing in the future temporal continuation rather than the filling of lacunae.

The Bibliographical activity was a subsidiary of the scholarly research reconstructing the history of the Symbolist Movement. This project is in an advanced state of progress and a publication date is foreseeable in the near future. The international roster of names of symbolists and their critics does not have the character of an international delegation serving vested interests. On the contrary, the multinational bibliography and the ensuing volumes on Symbolism will serve to demonstrate empathy and amalgamation; and the plurality of perspectives that unfolds will sharpen the focus and extend the horizon.

It is interesting to note that in processing these critical writings one discovers the limiting power of standard national bibliographies and of their unconscious selectivity of references caused by a consensus, long left uncontested, concerning what constitutes *major* literatures and *major* literary figures. These figures generally emerge from politically prominent nations, and the chances of entering the bibliographical hall of fame is far greater for those who write in the prominent languages or make the object of their critical scrutiny a work belonging to a large and powerful national unit. The productivity of small national groups is often identified as "minor" when perhaps it should be called simply "unfamiliar." To bring works of "unfamiliar" literature to the awareness of scholars everywhere should well be one of the principal functions of Comparative Literature. This bibliography represents a major effort to make available the internationally unfamiliar in the history of literature.

Justification for the publication of such a reference volume in advance of the projected history of the Symbolist Movement is twofold. If an arbitrary limit must be set for practical reasons for the termination of the bibliography, it must go to print before becoming dated. The second reason is that the bibliography will enable the user to discover many new channels of research into a subject that seems exhausted only because the traffic has proceeded over the same well trodden paths. The new roads opened up by the current bibliography invite a new traffic. To keep these thoroughfares closed when they are ready for circulation would be a self-defeating procedure.

I would like to add my thanks to Professor Anderson's for the financial support we have had in the pursuit of this collaborative research. The grant from the National Endowment of the Humanities made it possible for two students to advance their graduate studies at N.Y.U. while engaged in bibliographical research for the project. They became keen observers and knowledgeable finders; Professor Anderson gave the work organization, direction, discrimination; and he applied to the enormous body of miscellaneous materials the judgments of an experienced and astute bibliographer. We are grateful that he was able to obtain the support of his institution, Pennsylvania State University, to complete the project and give it a definitive destiny in the guise of an independent volume.

New York   Anna Balakian

List of Journals and Serials Consulted

ABI   Accademie e Biblioteche d'Italia
Abside
Academy
Accent
Acropole
Adam
Aesthetics
Aevum
AFLUSM   Annali della Fac. de Filos.
  e Lett. dell'Univ. Stale di Milano
AG   Anglica Germanica
AI   American Imago
Aika
AION   Annali Istituto Universitario
  Orientale, Napoli

AJFS   Australian Journal of French
  Studies (Monash University)
AKML   Abhandlung zur Kunst-
  Music- und Literaturwissenschaft
Akzente
AL   American Literature
ALitASH   Acta Litteraria Academiae
  Scientiarum Hungaricae (Budapest)
AllaB   Alla Botega (Brianza)
American Artist
Anglo-French Review
Annales de la Faculté de Philologie
  (Belgrade)
Annales de la Fondation Maeterlinck
Antaios

AntigR   Antigonish Review
APen   Anima-Pensiero
Apollo
Apollon
Approdo   L'Approdo Letterario (Roma)
Arcadia
L'Arche
Archiv   Archiv für das Studium der
  Neueren Sprachen und Literaturen
Archiv für Musikwissenschaft
Archivio di Filosofia
Arena
ArQ   Arizona Quarterly
L'Art
Art and Artists
Arte Illustrata
Artforum
Arti
Art in America
Art Interior
Art Journal
L'Art moderne
Art News
ArtQ   Art Quarterly
Arts
Arts and Architecture
Artscanada
ASEER   American Slavic and East
  European Review
ASNSP   Annali della Scuola Normale
  Superiore di Pisa
Asomante
AȘUI   Analele Stiințifice ale
  Universității Iasi
Atlantic Monthly
AUA   Annals of the Ukrainian Academy
  of Arts and Sciences in the U.S.
L'aube
AUB-LLR   Analele Universității,
  București, Limbă Literară Română
Audace
AUMLA   Journal of the Australasian
  Universities Language and Literature
  Association
Ausonia
BA   Books Abroad
BAASB   British Association for
  American Studies Bulletin
BADL   Bonner Arbeiten sur Deutschen
  Literatur

Barroco
Bayou
BCB   Boletín Cultural y Bibliográfico
  (Bogotá)
BCCMP   Boletim Cultural, Câmara
  Municipal do Porto
Belfagor
BEPIF   Bulletin des Etudes Portugaises
  et de l'Institut Français au Portugal
BHS   Bulletin of Hispanic Studies
BJRL   Bulletin of the John Rylands
  Library
Blackwood's Magazine
BNL   Beiträge zur Neueren Literaturge-
  schichte (Heidelberg)
Bookman
Brotéria
BSUF   Ball State University Forum
Bulletin Baudelairien
Bulletin de l'Académie de Langue et de
  Littérature Françaises
Bulletin de l'Université de Toulouse
Bulletin des Lettres
BuR   Bucknell Review
Burlington Magazine
CA   Cuadernos Americanos
Cahiers du Nord
Cahiers du Sud
CAIEF   Cahiers de l'Association
  Internationale des Etudes Françaises
Carovana
CCa   Civiltà Cattolica
CCLC   Cuadernos del Congreso por la
  libertad de la cultura
CCU   Cuadernos de la Catedra Unamuno
CdS   Corriere della Sera
CentR   The Centennial Review (Michigan
  State University)
Century Magazine
CHA   Cuadernos Hispanoamericanos
Chesterian
ChiR   Chicago Review
Círculo
CIS   Cahiers internationaux de
  symbolisme
CL   Comparative Literature
CLAJ   College Language Association
  Journal (Morgan State College)
ClaudelS
Clavileño

xiv

CLLA   Cahiers de Littérature et de
  Linguistique Appliquée
CLQ   Colby Library Quarterly
CLS   Comparative Literature Studies
  (University of Illinois)
CMLR   Canadian Modern Language
  Review
Colóquio   Colóquio/Letras
Commercial Advertiser (New York)
Commonweal
CompD   Comparative Drama
Confluences
ConL   Contemporary Literare
ConLit   Convorbiri Literature
ConnArts   Connecticut Arts
Connoisseur
ConnR   Connecticut Review
Contemporanul
ContempR   Contemporary Review
  (London)
Contrepoints
Convivium
Le Correspondant
Cosmopolis
Cosmopolitan
CPe   Castrum Peregrini
Credo:Katolsk Tidskrift (Uppsala)
Criterion
Critic
Criticism
Critique
CSP   Canadian Slavonic Papers
ČsR   Československá rusistika
CSS   Canadian Slavic Studies
Culture française
Current Literature
DA   Dissertation Abstracts
DAI   Dissertation Abstracts
  International
Dansk Udsyn
DBGU   Deutsche Beiträge zur
  Geistigen Überlieferung
Le Décadent
Delos
Derrière Miroir
Deutsche Monatschrift Für Russland
Deutsche Rundschau
Dial (Chicago)
Dialogues
DialogW   Dialog (Warsaw)

Die Welt der Slaven
Dimensioni
Le Divin
DNAL   Diário de Noticias,
  Almanaque (Lisbon)
Dnipro
Domaine Français
DPL   De Propietatibus Literarum
DR   Dalhousie Review
Dramma
DS   Deutsche Studien
DVLG   Deutsche Vierteljahrsschrift
  für Literaturwissenschaft und
  Geistesgeschichte
DWB   Dietsche Warande en Belfort
EA   Etudes Anglaises
L'Echo de Paris
ECl   Etudes Classiques
ECr   L'Esprit Créateur
Edda
EF   Etudes françaises
EFL   Essays in French Literature
  (University of Western Australia)
EFT   English Fiction in Transition
  (1880-1920)
EG   Etudes Germaniques
EIC   Essays in Criticism (Oxford)
ELH   Journal of English Literary
  History
ELT   English Literature in Transition
  (1880-1920)
Encounter
Entretiens politiques et littéraires
EP   Etudes Philosophiques
EPo   Esperienza Poetica
L'Ermitage
ESA   English Studies in Africa
  (Johannesburg)
ESl   Etudes Slaves et Est-Européennes
Esprit
ESPSL   O Estado de São Paulo,
  Suplemento Literário
Ethnomusicology
Etudes d'Art
Etudes Finno-Ougriennes
Euphorion
Europe
L'Express
ExTL   Explicación de Textos Literarios
Extracta   Extracta:Resumeer af

Specialoepgaver fra det Filosofiske
  Fakultet ved Københavns Universitet
FI   Forum Italicum
Filologija
Filosofía y Letras
FK   Filológiai Közlöny
FL   Le Figaro littéraire
FMLS   Forum for Modern Language
  Studies
Fortnightly Review
Fort Hare Papers
ForumH   Forum (Houston)
ForumZ   Forum (Zagreb)
FP   Filološki Pregled (Belgrade)
FR   French Review
France-Illustration
France Libre
FS   French Studies
FUF   Finnisch-ugrische Forschungen:
  Zeitschrift für Finnisch-ugrische
  Sprach- und Volkskunde
Galleria
Gazette des Beaux-Arts
Gazit
GCFI   Giornale Critico della
  Filosofia Italiana
GdB   Giornale de Bordo:Mensile di
  Storia, Letterature ed Arte
GdI   Giornale d'Italia (Roma)
Gegenwart
Gentleman's Magazine
Gids   De Gids
GLit   Gazeta Literară
GL&L   German Life and Letters
GN   Germanic Notes
Goya
GQ   German Quarterly
GR   German Review
Grande Encyclopédie
Grande revue
Grial
La Grive
GRM   Germanisch-Romanische
  Monatschrift
GuG   Gestalt und Gedanke:Ein
  Jahrbuch
Harper's Magazine
Harper's Monthly
HDL   Handbuch der Deutschen
  Literaturgeschichte

Helicon
Hellénisme contemporain
L'Hermitage
Hier et Demain
Hispania
Hispanica
Hispano - Hispanófila
L'Homme (Paris)
Hound and Horn
HR   Hispanic Review
HudR   Hudson Review
Humanitas.   Revista de la Fac. de
  filos. y letras de la Univ. Nacional
  de Tucumán
HumB   Humanitas (Brescia)
HussR   Husson Review
IAN   Izvestija Akademii Nauk S.S.S.R.,
  Serija Literatury i Jazyka (Moscow)
Ibero   Ibero-romania (München)
IH   Ita Humanidades (São José dos
  Campos, Brazil)
IL   L'Information littéraire
L'Information d'histoire de l'art
Insula
International Quarterly
Italica
JAAC   Journal of Aesthetics and Art
  Criticism
Jahrbuch für Philologie
Jardin des arts
JdL   Jornal do Letras
JDSG   Jahrbuch der deutschen
  Schiller-Gesellschaft
JEGP   Journal of English and Germanic
  Philology
JES   Journal of European Studies
JHI   Journal of the History of Ideas
JJQ   James Joyce Quarterly (University
  of Tulsa)
JLA   Jornal de Letras e Artes (Lisboa)
Journal Musical Français
JTR   Journal of Typographic Research
KAL   Kyushu American Litstsyutr
  (Fukuoka)
KDVS   Kongelige Danske Videnskabornes
  Selskab (Copenhagen)
Kenyon Review
KFLQ   now KRQ
KnijiNov   Knijževne Novine (Belgrade)

Konsthist Tidskr
KR   Kenyon Review
KRQ   Kentucky Romance Quarterly
  [formerly KFLQ]
KuL   Kunst und Literatur
Kunstchronik
Kunstwerk
Kwartalnik Neofilologiczny
L&P   Literature and Psychology
  (University of Hartford)
Lang&S   Language and Style
LangQ   Language Quarterly (University
  of South Florida)
Langue et Littérature
LanM   Les Langues Modernes
LATR   Latin American Theater
  Review
LBR   Luso-Brazilian Review
LdProv   Lettore di Provincia
LeS   Lingua e Stile (Bologna)
LetN   Lettres Nouvelles
Letras   Letras:Organo de la Facultad
  de Letras y Ciencias Humanas de la
  Univ. Nacional Mayor de San Marcos
Letteratura
Lettres
Lettres Modernes
Letture
LHB   Lockhaven (Pa.) Bulletin
LHR   Lock Haven (Pa.) Review
Life and Letters Today
LiG   Literatus in der Gesellschaft
LimR   Limbă Romănă (Bucureşti)
Linguistics
Listener
Lit   Littérature (University of Paris)
Das literarischer Echo
Literary World
Literaturas y Literatos
Literaturnoe Nasledstvo
LitR   Literary Review (Fairleigh
  Dickinson)
LM   Language Monographs
LR   Les Lettres Romanes
LS   Le Lingue Straniere (Roma)
LşL   Limbă şi literatură
LT   Levende Talen
Luc   Luceafărul (Bucharest)
Lyrikvännen (Stockholm)
Maatstaf

Magazine Littéraire
M&H   Medievalia et Humanistica
Marsyas
MArt   Mundus Artium
Mastera Slova
Mbk   Maandblad voor beeldende kunsten
  (Amsterdam)
MD   Modern Drama
Meanjin   Meanjin Quarterly
Médiations
Melos
Menestrel
Mens en Melodie
MdF   Mercure de France
Mercurio
Merlyn
Messagero
MfS   Meddelanden från Strind-
  bergssällskapet
MFS   Modern Fiction Studies
MGSL   Minas Gerais, Suplemento
  Literário
Minerve française
Minneapolis Institute Bulletin
MissQ   Mississippi Quarterly
ML   Modern Languages (London)
MLF   Modersmålslärarnas Förening:
  Årsskrift (Lund)
MLJ   Modern Language Journal
M'lle New York
MLN   Modern Language Notes
MLQ   Modern Language Quarterly
MLR   Modern Language Review
Modern Austrian Literature
Moloda Ukrajina
Monatshefte
Monthly Musical Record
Mosaid   Mosaic:A Journal for the
  Comparative Study of Literature
  and Ideas
MP   Modern Philology
MR   Massachusetts Review
MRom   Marche Romane
MSpr   Moderna Språk (Stockholm)
MuK   Maske und Kothurn (Graz-Wien)
Musica
Musica Disques
Musical Times
Music and Letters
Music Review

Musikforschung
NA   Nuova Antologia
N&Q   Notes and Queries
Nation
NATS Bulletin
NC   Nuova Corrente
NCF   Nineteenth-Century Fiction
NCFS   Nineteenth Century French
   Studies
NDH   Neue Deutsche Hefte
Neophil   Neophilologus (Groningen)
NEQ   New England Quarterly
Nerthus   Nerthus:Nordisch-deutsche
   Beiträge
Neue Schweizer
Neue Schweizer Rundschau
Neue Zeitschrift für Musik
Neue Zürcher Zeitung
New Republic
New York Herald
NFS   Nottingham French Studies
NHochland   Neues Hochland
Nineteenth Century and After
Nivel
NL   Nouvelles Littéraires
NLH   New Literary History
   (University of Virginia)
North American Review
Nosotros
La Nouvelle Revue
Nouvelle Revue Canadienne
NovM   Novyi Mir
NovŽ   Novyj Žurnal (New York)
NRF   Nouvelle Revue Française
NRFH   Nueva Revista de Filología
   Hispánica (Mexico)
NRs   Neue Rundschau
NRS   Nuova revista storica (Roma)
NS   Die Neueren Sprachen
NT   Nordisk Tidskrift
NTg   De Nieuwe Taalgids
OB   Ord och Bild
Ocidente
Oeil
Oesterreichische Musikzeitschrift
OGS   Oxford German Studies
Ohioana Quarterly
OJES   Osmania Journal of English
   Studies
OL   Orbis Litterarum

OnsE   Ons Erfdeel (Rekkem)
Opera
O prozie polskiej XX Wieku
Orbis Scriptus
Orizont: Revista a Uniunii Scriitorilor
   din R.S. Romania
Outlook
Paragone
Paris-Théâtre
Parnassus
Parole e il libro
Paru
Paul Valéry
Person   The Personalist
Perspektiv   (Copenhagen)
PhQ   Philosophical Quarterly
PHum Prezgląd Humanistyczny
PIME   Petöfi Irodalmi Múzeum Évkönyve
PJGG   Philosophisches Jahrbuch der
   Görres-Gesellschaft (Freiburg:München)
PL   Pamiętnik Literacki
PLL   Papers on Language and Literature
La Plume
PMLA   Publications of the Modern
   Language Association of America
PN   Poe Newsletter Washington State
   University)
Poetica
Poétique:Revue de théorie et d'analyse
   littéraire
Poetry
PolR   Polish Review (New York)
PP   Philologica Pragensia
PQ   Philological Quarterly (Iowa City)
PR   Partisan Review
Pradalgė
Preussische Jahrbücher
Prisma
Proceedings of the Pacific Northwest
   Conference on Foreign Languages
Prospetti
PSA   Papeles de Son Armadans (Mallorca)
PU   Problemi di Ulisse
PULC   Princeton University Library
   Chronicle
QFSK   Quellen und Forschungen zur
   Sprach- und Kulturgeschichte der
   Germanischen Völker, N.F.
QQ   Queen's Quarterly
Quaderni della Rassegna musicale

La Quinzaine Littéraire
Raam
Rassegna d'Italia
Rassegna Musicale
RCB   Revista de Cultura Brasileña
RCSF   Revista Critica della Storia della
  Filosofia
RD   Rivista Dalmata
RdC   Resto del Carlino
RdE   Rivista di Estetica (Università
  de Padova)
RdL   Revista do Livro
RDM   Revue des Deux Mondes
RdP   Revue de Paris
RdPac   Revista del Pacífico
RE   La Revue d'Esthétique
Renascence
Rep   Republika (Zagreb)
RESl   Revue des Etudes slaves
RevBib   Revista Bibliotecilor
Review of Reviews
Revista Cubana
RevR   Revue Romane
Revue Bleue
Revue Blanche
Revue d'Allemagne
Revue de Belgique
Revue de France
Revue de Genève
Revue de musicologie
Revue des cours et conférences
Revue du Claire
Revue Européenne
Revue franco-belge
Revue indépendante
Revue métapsychique
Revue musicale
Revue nationale
Revue neuve
Revue universitaire
Revue wagnérienne
RF   Romanische Forschungen
RG   Revue générale
RHL   Revue d'Histoire Littéraire de
  la France
RHM   Revista Hispánica Moderna
RHT   Revue d'Histoire du Théâtre
RI   Revista Iberoamericana
RIB   Revista Interamericana de
  Bibliografía

RITL   Revista de istorie şi teorie
  literară
Rivista di Critica
RJŠ   Russkij Jazyk v Škole
RL   Revista de Literatura
RLC   Revue de Littérature Comparée
RLit   Russkaja Literature (Leningrad)
RLM   La Revue des Lettres Modernes
RLMC   Riv. de Letterature Moderne e
  Comparate (Firenze)
RLT   Russian Literature Triquarterly
RLV   Revue des Langues Vivantes
  (Bruxelles)
RLz   Radjans'ke Literaturoznavstvo
  (Kiev)
RMM   Revue de Métaphysique et de
  Morale
RNC   Revista Nacional de Cultura
  (Caracas)
RoLit   România Literară
Romanistica Pragensia
RomN   Romance Notes
RoR   Romanian Review
Royal Music Assn. Proceedings
RUL   Revue de l'Université Laval
RR   Romanic Review
RS   Research Studies (Washington State
  University)
RSH   Revue des Sciences Humaines
RUSP   Revista da Universidade de
  São Paolo
RSV   Revista Signos de Valparaiso
RUCR   Revista de la Universidad de
  Costa Rica
RuchL   Ruch Literacki (Kraków)
Rumo
RusR   Russian Review
Russkaia Mysl
Russkaya filologia
Russkaya literatura
RUO   Revue de l'Université d'Ottawa
RyF   Razón y Fe
SA   Studi Americani (Roma)
Saggi e ricerche di letteratura francese
Samlaren
Samtiden
SAQ   South Atlantic Quarterly
Saturday Review
Savremenik (Belgrade)
La Scala

SCB   South Central Bulletin
Schweizer Monatshefte für Politik,
   Wirtschaft, Kultur
Science and Society
Scribner's
Scrutiny
SDR   South Dakota Review
SEEJ   Slavic and East European Journal
SEER   Slavonic and East European
   Review
SEL   Studies in English Literature,
   1500-1900
SELit   Studies in English Literature
   (English Literary Society of Japan)
Senate
SFr   Studi Francesi
SG   Studium Generale
SGG   Studia Germanica Gandensia
Silarus (Salerno)
Slavonic Yearbook
SlavR   Slavic Review
SLD   Studia Litteraria
SLT   Svensk Litteraturtidskrift
Socialističeskij realizm i klassičeskoe
   nasledie
SocR   Social Research:An International
   Quarterly
SoQ   Southern Quarterly
SoR   Southern Review (Louisiana State
   University)
Southerly
SP   Studies in Philology
SpL   Spiegel der Letteren
SPR   Slavistic Printings and Reprintings
SR   Sewanee Review
SRAZ   Studia Romanica et Anglica
   Zagrabiensia
SSASH   Studia Slavica Academiae
   Scientiarum Hungaricae
SSl   Scando-Slavica (Copenhagen)
Standpunte
StCL   Studii şi Cercetări de Istorie
   Lit. şi Folclor
Steaua
Stil- und Formprobleme
Studien zur Musikwissenschaft
Studies in the Humanities
Studi Germanici
Studii de literatură universală
Studium
Style

SuL   Sprache und Literatur
Survey
SUS   Susquehanna University Studies
   (Selinsgrove, Pa.)
SUSFL   Studi Urbinati di Storia,
   Filosofia e Letteratura
Sustancia
Le Symbolist
Symposium
Symposium Unamuno
Synthèses
La Table Ronde
TCL   Twentieth Century Literature
Telegrafo
TelQ   Tel Quel
Temple Bar
Tempo
Les Temps Modernes
Theoria:A Journal of Studies in the Arts,
   Humanities and Social Sciences
Thesaurus:Boletín del Instituto Caro
   y Cuervo
Threshold
Time and Tide
TLL   Travaux de linguistique et de
   littérature (Université de Strasbourg)
TLOP   The Language of Poetry
   (University of South Carolina)
TLS   London Times Literary Supplement
TNTL   Tijdschr. voor Ned. Taal- en
   Letterkunde (Leiden)
Torre   La Torre
TPr   Tempo Presente
TR   La Table Ronde
Trimestre
TSL   Tennessee Studies in Literature
Tw   Twórczość
TWA   Trans. of the Wisconsin Acad. of
   Sciences, Arts, and Letters
TWAS   Twayne's World Author Series
UCSLL   Univ. of Colorado Studies in
   Language and Literature
UES   Unisa English Studies
Unitas
Universal Review
UR   University Review (Kansas City)
UTQ   University of Toronto Quarterly
UTRFS   University of Toronto French
   Series
UWR   University of Windsor Review
   (Windsor, Ontario)

Veltro

Verri

VidaL   Vida Literaria

Vie des Peuples

Vindrosen

Vinduet

XXe Siècle

ViR   Viaţa Românească (Bucharest)

VJa   Voprosy Jazykoznanija (Moscow)

Vlaanderen

VlG   De Vlaamse Gids

VLit   Voprosy Literatury

VLU   Vestnik Leningradskogo U.
   Ser. Isotorii, Jazyka i Literatury

VMU   Vestnik Moskovskogo U. Ser.
   VII. Filologija, Žurnalistika

VP   Victorian Poetry

VSI A   Vetenskapssocieteten i Lund
   Årsbok

Westminster Reveiw

WHR   Western Humanities Review

Wort und Wahrheit

WSJ   Wiener Slawistisches Jahrbuch

WSl   Die Welt der Slaven (Wiesbaden)

WSLit   Wisconsin Studies in Literature

WUS   Washington University Studies

WW   Wirkendes Wort

YCGL   Yearbook of Comparative and
   General Literature

YES   Yearbook of English Studies

YFS   Yale French Studies

YR   Yale Review

YWMLS   Year's Work in Modern
   Language Studies

ZAAK   Zeitschrift für Ästhetik und
   allgemeines Kunstwissenschaft

ZDP   Zeitschrift für Deutsche Philologie
   (Berlin-Bielefield-München)

Zeitschrift für Philosophie und
   philosophische Kritik

Zeitschrift für Deutschkunde

Zeitwende

ZFSL   Zeitschrift für Französische
   Sprache und Literatur

ŻLit   Życie Literackie (Kraków)

ZRG   Zeitschrift für Religions- und
   Geistesgeschichte

ZS   Zeitschrift für Slawistik (Berlin)

ZED   Zur Erkenntnis der Dichtung
   (München)

SYMBOLISM

A Bibliography of Symbolism
as an International
and Multi-Disciplinary
Movement

I General and Miscellaneous

1. Adam, Paul. "La presse et le Symbolisme." *Le Symboliste* 1(oct 1886): 1-2.

2. Angers, Pierre. "Situation du symbolisme." *Nouvelle Revue Canadienne* 1,vi(fév-mars 1952):10-20.

3. Anon. "Impressionnisme et symbolisme dans la littérature et dans les arts." *CAIEF* 12(1960):103-87.

4. Anon. "The Literary Decadents." *Critic* 23(11 Nov 1893):302-03.

5. Anon. "Symbolism." *Academy* 64(11 Apr 1903):368-69.

6. Apostel, Léo. "Symbolisme et anthropologie philosophique:Vers une herméneutique cybernétique." *CIS* 5(1964):7-31.

7. Arbour, Romeo. *Henri Bergson et les lettres françaises*. Paris: Corti, 1956. 460 pp. [Esp. pp. 219-40, "Bergson et la poésie symboliste."]

8. Arnauld, Michel. "Gustave Kahn: *Symbolistes et Décadents* (Vanier)." *Revue Blanche* 27(1902):559. [Rev. art.]

9. Arnauld, R. "Sur un système des beaux-arts." *NRF* (juin 1920):842-64.

10. Aubéry, Pierre. "The Anarchism of the Literati of the Symbolist Period." *FR* 42(1968-69):39-47.

11. *Autour du symbolisme*. Lille: Corti, 1955.

12. Bacou, Roseline,ed. *Lettres de*

Gauguin, Gide, Huysmans, Jammes, Mallarmé, Vahaeren ... à Odilon Redon. Préf. d'Arî Redon. Paris: Corti, 1960. 314 pp.

13. Baker, Houston A., Jr. "The Idea in Aestheticism, 1886-1899." *DA* 29 (1968):1862A(U.C.L.A.)

14. Balakian, Anna. "Le caractère international du symbolisme," 293-99 in *Actes du Ve Congrès de l'Association Internationale de Littérature Comparée, Belgrade 1967.* Belgrade: Université de Belgrade; Amsterdam: Swets & Zeitlinger, 1969.

15. ———. "The International Character of Symbolism." *Mosaic* 2,iv(1969): 1-8.

16. ———. *The Symbolist Movement:A Critical Appraisal.* New York: Random House, 1967. 208 pp.

17. Barea, José Antonio. "Las modernas tendencias literarias de vanguardia." *Sustancia* 2,vi(Mar 1941):254-61.

18. Barre, André. *Le symbolisme.* Vol. I:*Essai historique sur le mouvement symboliste en France 1885-1900.* Vol. II:*Bibliographie de la poésie symboliste.* (Essays in Lit. and Criticism 8.) New York: Burt Franklin. 414+294 pp. [Repr. Orig. pub. Paris: Jouve, 1911. Also repr. Genève: Slatkine, 1970.]

19. Baruk, Henri. "Les symboles dans les maladies mentales et dans le monde moderne." *CIS* 4(1964):5-2.

20. Bataille, Henry. *Têles et pensées.* Paris: Ollendorff, 1900. [Portraits of Kahn, Mendès, Régnier and Rodenbach *inter alios*.]

21. Baudelaire, Charles P. *L'art romantique, littérature et musique.* Ed. Lloyd J. Austin. Paris: Garnier-Flammarion, 1968. 444 pp.

22. Bays, Gwendolyn. *The Orphic Vision:Seer Poets from Novalis to Rimbaud.* Lincoln: U. of Neb. P., 1964. 303 pp.

23. Beatty, R.C. "The Heritage of Symbolism in Modern Poetry." *YR* 36 (1947):467-77.

24. Beebe, Maurice,ed. *Literary Symbolism.* San Francisco: Wadsworth Pub. Co., 1960. 181 pp.

25. Bell, S.M. and W.M.L. "The Nineteenth Century." *YWMLS* 31(1969): 139-56.

26. Bellot, Etienne. *Notes sur le symbolisme.* Paris: Linard, 1908. 64 pp.

27. Bely, Andrei. *Simvolizm.* Moscow: Mycarerb, 1910. 633 pp.

28. Benamou, Michel,ed. "Symposium on Impressionism." *YCGL* 17(1968): 40-68.

29. Berthelot, Ph. "Symbolisme." *Grande Encyclopédie* 30(1902):75.

30. Boès, A. Karl. "Le parloir aux images." *La Plume* 307(fév 1902):140-46.

31. Bonneau, G. "Symbolisme poétique et symbolisme théâtral," 127-36 in *Mélanges critiques.* (Pubs. de la Fac. des Lettres de l'Univ. d'Ankara.) Ankara: Dil ve Tarih-Cografya Fakültesi, 1956.

32. Bonnefoy, Yves. "Symbolism." Tr. by Stephen Spender, 323-26 in *The Concise Encyclopedia of English and Poetry*, Stephen Spender and Donald Hall,eds. London: Hutchinson, 1963.

33. Borel, Jacques. "D'une expérience de l'impuissance." *Cahiers du Sud* 58 (1964):270-87.

34. Bornecque, Jacques H. "Rêves et réalités du symbolisme." *RSH* 77 (1955):5-23.

35. Bose, Mme Das. *Les thèmes et la prosodie du symbolisme français dans la poésie bengalie moderne* Paris: Univ. Paris Lettres, 1970. [Diss.]

36. Boutique, Alexandre. "A propos du Symbolisme." *La Plume* 43(fév 1891):58.

37. Bouvier, E. *Initiation à la littérature d'aujourd'hui.* Paris: La Renaissance du livre, 1928. 217 pp.

38. Bowra, C. Maurice. *The Creative Experiment*. London: Macmillan, 1949. 255 pp.

39. ———. *The Heritage of Symbolism*. London: Macmillan, 1943. 231 pp.

40. ———. "The Triumph of Symbolism." *Oxford Outlook* 12(1952): 1-25.

41. Bray, René. *La préciosité et les précieux de Thibaut de Champagne à Jean Giraudoux*. Paris: Albin Michel, 1948. 406 pp. [Esp. Part 3, Chaps. V-VI; Part 4, Chaps. I-III.]

42. Brieu, Jacques. "Les suggestions des fleurs." *Revue Blanche* 24(1901): 194-99.

43. Brinkmann, Richard. "Lyrics of Expressionism:End or Transformation of the Symbol," 109-36 in Helmut Rehder,ed. *Literary Symbolism*. Austin: U. of Texas P., 1965.

44. Brown, Calvin S. *Music and Literature:A Comparison of the Arts*. Athens, Ga.: U. of Ga. P., 1948. 287 pp.

45. Brun, J. "Analogie et Anatomie:Le verbe et la chair dans le symbolisme et le surréalisme." *Archivio di Filosofia* 3(1965):43-51.

46. Brunetière, Ferdinand. *Nouvelles questions de critique*. Paris: Calmann-Lévy, 1890.

47. ———. "Symbolistes et Décadents." *RDM* 90(1 nov 1888):213-26.

48. Bury, Yetta Blaze de. *French Literature of Today*. Westminster, 1898.

49. Carlyle, Thomas. "Des symboles." *Entretiens politiques et littéraires* 1(avril 1890):1-4.

50. Carmody, Francis. "Le décadisme." *CAIEF* 12(1960):121-31.

51. Carter, Thomas P. "*Art et critique*." *DAI* 32(1972):5223A(Brown). [Periodical, 1889-92.]

52. Casella, Georges, and Ernest Gaubert. *La nouvelle littérature, 1895-1905:Ecoles et manifestes, la critique, la poésie, le roman, le théâtre, les jeunes en province, dictionnaire bio-bibliographique, documents*. Paris: Sansot, 1908.

53. Cassirer, Ernest. *Philosophie der Symbolischen Formen*. 4 Bde. Berlin: B. Cassirer Verlag, 1923-31.

54. ———. *Wesen und Wirkung des Symbolbegriffs*. Darmstadt: Wissenschaftliche Buchgesellschaft, 1959.

55. Chadwick, Charles. *Symbolism*. London: Methuen, 1971. 71 pp.

56. Chalon, Jean. "L'étrange paradis des symbolistes." *FL* 1314 (23 juillet 1971):8. [Rev. art.]

57. Champigny, Robert. "Trois définitions du symbolisme." *CLS* 4(1967): 127-33.

58. Charpentier, John. *Le Symbolisme*. Paris: Les Arts et le Livre, 1927. 319 pp.

59. Chassé, Charles. *Le mouvement symboliste*. Paris: Librairie Floury, 1947. 215 pp.

60. Chiari, Joseph. "Symbolism and Reality," 109-24 in *Realism and Imagination*. London: Barrie and Rockliff, 1960.

61. ———. *Symbolism from Poe to Mallarmé:The Growth of a Myth*. London: Rockliff, 1956; New York: Macmillan, 1957. 198 pp.

62. Chicoteau, Marcel. *Studies in Symbolist Psychology (Mind, Spirit, Morals, Men)*. Cardiff: Priority Press, Ltd., 1940. 2nd ed., Sydney: Hoertel, 1958. 47 pp.

63. Christophe, Lucien. "Ombres et lumières du symbolisme." *RG* 93(13 mars 1957):28-40.

64. *Cinquantenaire du Symbolisme*. Catalogue de l'exposition de la Bibliothèque Nationale. Paris, 1936.

65. Claretie, Jules. "The Shudder in Literature." *North American Review* 155(Oct 1892):356.

66. Cœuroy, André. *Appels d'Orphée: Nouvelles études de musique et de*

littérature comparée. Paris: Nouvelle revue critique, 1928. 214 pp.

67. Cohn, Robert G. "The Assault on Symbolism." *CLS* 5(1968):69-75.

68. Corbin, Henry. "Mundus imaginalis ou l'imaginaire et l'imaginal." *CIS* 6(1964):3-26.

69. Cornell, Kenneth. *The Symbolist Movement*. New Haven: Yale U.P., 1951. 217 pp.

70. Crispolti, Enrico. "Il surrealismo e la sua lezione." *Ulisse* 76(1973):70-96.

71. Daxhelet, Arthur. *Une crise littéraire:Symbolisme et symbolistes*. Bruxelles: Weissenbruck, 1904.

72. Décaudin, Michel. "Poésie impressioniste et poésie symboliste." *CAIEF* 12(1960):133-42.

73. ———. *Siècle français:Les temps modernes*. Lausanne: Guilde du livre, 1964. 255 pp.

74. Deguy, Michel. "Jusqu'à la dernière minute...." *CIS* 15-16(1967-68): 3-14.

75. Delaroche, Achille. "Les annales du Symbolisme." *La Plume* 41(janv 1891):14-20.

76. De Waelhens, Alphonse. "Note sur le symbolisme dans la pensée et l'expérience schizophrènes." *CIS* 5(2964):33-45.

77. Dinar, André. *La croisade symboliste*. Paris: Mercure de France, 1943. 187 pp.

78. Divoire, Fernand. *Le symbolisme: Son influence sur la poésie d'aujourd'hui*. Paris: Cercle de la librairie, 1924.

79. Dolembreux, Jacques. "Dans le halo du symbolisme." *Audace* 16,i(1970): 136-48.

80. Dresse, Paul. "Que fut le symbolisme?" *Audace* 16, i(1970):3-7.

81. Drieu la Rochelle, Pierre. "L'autre face du symbolisme," 232-41 in *Sur les écrivains. Essais critiques réunis*. Paris: Gallimard, 1964.

82. ———. "Naturalisme et symbolisme," 224-32 in *Sur les écrivains. Essais critiques réunis*. Paris: Gallimard, 1964.

83. Dujardin, Edouard. "La vivante continuité du symbolisme." *MdF* 6(1 juillet 1924):55-73.

84. Dumur, Louis. "Le Symbolisme jugé par un Russe." *MdF* 7(fév 1893): 173-78.

85. Durand, Gilbert. "Les gnoses, structures et symboles archétypes." *CIS* 8(1965):15-34.

86. ———. "Les trois niveaux de la formation du symbolisme." *CIS* 1 (1962).

87. ———. *L'imagination symbolique*. Paris: *PUF* 1964. [2nd ed. 1968.]

88. ———. "L'occident iconclaste." *CIS* 2(1963).

89. Durand, Yves. "Structures de l'imaginaire et comportement." *CIS* 4(1964):61-80.

90. Durgnat, Raymond. "Symbolism and the Underground." *HudR* 22 (1969):457-68.

91. Engel, Claire-Eliane. "L'exotisme dans la littérature anglaise." *Revue de Genève* 21(1930):734-45.

92. Engels, Edouard. "Décadents et symbolistes." *Cosmopolis* 1(mars 1896).

93. Engelson, Moïse. "Introduction au colloque de symbolisme de Paris de mai 1963." *CIS* 4(1964):3-4.

94. Ermite, Pierre L'. "Danses macabre et symboliste." *L'Ermitage* 2(1891): 246-47.

95. *Essais sur la littérature contemporaine*. Paris: Calman-Lévy, 1890.

96. Fagus. "Art et critique:Trois instants du Symbolisme." *La Plume* 353(janv 1904):25-29. [Vicaire, Laforgue, and Viélé-Griffin.]

97. Fausset, Hugh l'Anson. "The Cult of Symbolism," 81-95 in *Poets and Pundits:Essays and Addresses*. London: Cape, 1947.

98. Favre, Robert. "Desnos danse des Esseintes." *Europe* 517-18(1972):

105-12. [On Desnos, Breton and antecedent connection of poetry and dance.]

99. Flam, Léopold. "Symbolisme et philosophie." *CIS* 12(1966):7-18. [German lit. and philosophy.]

100. Fontainas, André. *Mes souvenirs du symbolisme.* Paris: La Nouvelle Revue Critique, 1928. 220 pp.

101. Fontainas, André, and Nina Berberove. *Le symbolisme.* Textes suivis de débats au studio franco-russe. Paris: Cahiers de la Quinzaine, 1931. 67 pp.

102. Formigari, Lia. "Poesia simbolista e poesia realista." *GCFI* 11(1957): 343-59.

103. Fowlie, Wallace. "Legacy of Symbolism." *YFS* 9(1952):20-26.

104. ——. *Love in Literature:Studies in Symbolic Expression.* Bloomington: Indiana U.P., 1965. 155 pp.

105. Fox, E. Inman. "La poesía 'social' y la tradición simbolista." *Torre* 64 (1969):47-62.

106. Frye, N[orthrop]. "Three Meanings of Symbolism." *YFS* 9(1952): 11-19.

107. Fumet, Stanislas. "Symbolisme contemporain," 135-48 in *Polarité du symbole.* Paris, Bruges: Desclée de Brouwer, 1960.

108, Furst, Lilian R. "The Structure of Romantic Agony." *CLS* 10(1973): 125-38. [On Novalis and Huysmans, Romanticism and Decadence.]

109. Gaultier, Jules de. "Péladan, Sar: *La Décadence esthétique. Réponse à Tolstoi.*(Chamuel)." *Revue Blanche* 18(1899):150-51. [Rev. art.]

110. Gengoux, Jacques. "Le symbolisme et les symbolistes." *LR* 5 (1951):3-37.

111. Germain, Alphonse. "L'interprétation symbolique." *L'Ermitage* 15 (nov 1897):335-44.

112. Ghil, René. *Les dates et les oeuvres:Symbolisme et poésie scientifique.* Paris: Crès, 1923. 838 pp.

113. Gide, André. "Le traité du Narcisse:Théorie du symbole." *Entretiens politiques et littéraires* 22(janv 1892):20-28.

114. Gordon, Jan B. "The Imaginary Portrait:Fin-de-Siècle Icon." *UWR* 5 (1969):81-104.

115. Goudeau, Emile. "L'individualisme." *Entretiens politiques et littéraires* 5(août 1890):137-42. [On lit. schools.]

116. Gourmont, Rémy de. *Le livre des masques-portraits symbolistes-gloses et documents sur les écrivains d'hier et d'aujourd'hui.* 2 vols. Paris: Société du Mercure de France, 1896-1898.

117. Grappe, G. "Quelques notes sur le Symbolisme." *MdF* 65(1907):70-77.

118. Grojnowski, D. "Le Symbolisme: Vue d'ensemble." *Critique* 21(1965): 178-85.

119. Guimbretière, André. "Quelques remarques sur la fonction du symbole à propos de l'espace sacralisé." *CIS* 13(1967):33-55.

120. Guiraud, Pierre. *Index du vocabulaire du Symbolisme.* 5 vols. Paris: Klincksieck, 1953-1962.

121. Håkanson, B. "Upproret mot symbolismen." *Vinduet* 21(1967):69-78.

122. Halder, Alois. *Kunst und Kult:Zur Ästhetik und Philosophie der Kunst in der Wende vom 19. zum 20. Jahrhundert.* (Symposion, 15.) Freiburg (i.Br.), München: Alber, 1964. 95 pp.

123. Henel, Heinrich. "Erlebnisdichtung und Symbolismus." *DVLG* 32 (1958):71-99.

124. Hirst, Désirée. "Symbolism and the Changing Climate in Thought:A Problem in Literary Criticism," 132-48 in Joseph P. Strelka,ed. *Anagogic Qualities of Literature.* (Yearbook of Comparative Crit. 4.) University Park: Penn State U.P., 1971. 335 pp.

125. Holm, Søren. *Mythe og symbol.* (Festskrift udgivet af Københavns

Universitet.) Copenhagen, 1971. 167 pp. [See esp. pp. 19-26 on lit. symbolism.]

126. Hubert, J.D. "Symbolism, Correspondence and Memory." *YFS* 9 (1952):46-55.

127. Huon, Y. "Eugène Canseliet, *Alchimie. Etudes diverses de Symbolisme hermétique et de pratique philsophale.* Jean-Jacques Pauvert, 1964, 283 pp., 59 illus." *CIS* 8(1965):97-99. [Rev. art.]

128. Hurley, E.A. *The Continuity of the 'Decadent' Elements of Baudelaire's Poetry in the Poetry of the Decadent Period, 1880-1900.* London: Kings College, 1966-67. [Unpub. diss.]

129. Husain, F.N. Yusuf Jamal. "Edith Sitwell in the Symbolist Tradition." *DA* 26(1965-66):5437(Minn.).

130. Iengo, Francesco. "Benedetto Croce, György Lukács et il problema del decadentismo." *Trimestre* 6 (1972):85-126.

131. Itterbeck, Eugene van. "Van symbolisme tot objectivisme." *DWB* 106 (1961):591-600.

132. Jaloux, Edmond. *Les saisons littéraires, 1896-1903.* Vol. I. Fribourg: Edition de la librairie de l'Université, 1942.

133. Jászi, Andrew O. "In the Realm of Beauty and Anguish:Some Remarks on the Poetry of Aestheticism." *ChiR* 15, ii(1961):57-70.

134. Jollivet de Castelot, F. "Hermétisme et spritualisme:Les chefs de l'occultisme contemporain." *La Plume* 257(janv 1900):107-09.

135. ———. "L'école occultiste contemporaine." *L'aube* (juin 1897): 140-41.

136. Joset, Jacques. "Estudios sobre el modernismo." *NRFH* 21(1972): 100-11.

137, Jullian, Philippe. *The Symbolists.* Tr. Mary Anne Stevens. New York: Phaidon, 1973. 240 pp.

138. Kahn, Gustave. "Les origines du Symbolisme." *Revue Blanche* 26 (1901):321-38.

139. ———. *Symbolistes et décadents.* Paris: Vanier, 1902. 404 pp.

140. ———. *Trente ans de symbolisme.* Paris: Vanier, 1902.

141. Kamerbeek, J. " 'Style de Décadence':Généalogie d'une formule." *RLC* 39,ii(1965):268-86.

142. Kayser, W. "Der Europäische Symbolismus:Versuch einer Einführung," 287-304 in *Die Vortragsreise:Studien zur Literatur.* Bern: Francke, 1958.

143. Klemperer, V. "Christian Morgenstern und der Symbolismus." *Zeitschrift für Deutschkunde* 42(1928): 39-55,124-36.

144. Ko Won. "The Symbolists' Influence on Japanese Poetry." *CLS* 8(1971):254-65.

145. Krawitz, Henry. *A Post-Symbolist Bibliography.* Metuchen, N.J.: Scarecrow Press, 1973. 284 pp.

146. Kugel, James L. *The Techniques of Strangeness in Symbolist Poetry.* New Haven: Yale U. P., 1971. 123 pp.

147. Lavaud, Guy. "Retour au symbolisme." *Acropole* 2,viii(août-sept 1950):2-5.

148. Lazare, Bernard. "Entendonsnous." *Entretiens politiques et littéraires* 15(juin 1891):202-05. [On public misunderstanding of symbolist art.]

149. ———. "Interview." *Entretiens politiques et littéraires* 13(avril 1891): 127-31. [Public opinion and knowledge of various movements and authors incl. Symbolism.]

150. Lebois, André. *Admirable 19e siècle.* Paris: l'Amitié par le livre, 1958. 315 pp.

151. Le Cardonnel, G., and Ch. Vellay. *La littérature contemporaine (1905): Opinions des écrivains de ce temps, accompagnées d'un index des noms*

cités. Paris: Société du Mercure de France, 1905. 331 pp.

152. Lefebve, Maurice-Jean. "L'ambiguïté des symboles de Baudelaire à Nous." *CIS* 5(1964):57-74

153. ———. "Le nu comme symbole." *CIS* 11(1966):3-15.

154. Lehmann, A.G. *The Symbolist Aesthetic in France, 1885-1895*. New York: Blackwell, 1968. 328 pp.

155. ———. "Un aspect de la critique symboliste:Signification et ambïguité dans les beaux-arts." *CAIEF* 12 (1906):161-74.

156. Lejeune, Claire. "Du désir à la parole." *CIS* 15-16(1967-68):29-52.

157. *Le mouvement symboliste*. Exposition organisée dans le cadre de l'accord culturel franco-belge, 31 jan-mars 1957. Bruxelles: Edition de la connaissance, 1957. 139 pp.

158. *Le mouvement symboliste et son expression dans les revues symbolistes majeures*. Genève: Slatkine, 1970.

159. Lesdain, Pierre. "Sur la tombe du Symbolisme." *Synthèses* 18,ccix(Oct 1963):397-412.

160. Lethève, Jacques. "Les batailles du symbolisme." *FL* 11 avril (1959): 6,11.

161. Loudet, René. "Du Mysticisme." *La Plume* 168(avril 1896):240-42.

162. Luzi, Mario. "La strada del simbolismo." *Paragone* 118(Oct 1959): 3-18.

163. ———. *L'idea simbolista*. Milano: Garzanti, 1959. 247 pp.

164. Macrì, Oreste. "Simbolismo e realismo:Intorno all'antologia di Castellet." *Approdo* 9,xxi(1963):71-86.

165. Marcazzan, M. "Decadenza romantica e decadentismo." *HumB* 11(1956):543-57.

166. Marie, Aristide. *La forêt symboliste. Esprits et visages*. Réimp. de l'éd. de Paris, 1936. Genève: Slatkine, 1970. 294 pp.

167. Martino, Pierre. *Parnasse et symbolisme, 1850-1900*. Paris: Colin, 1925. 220 pp.

168. Mayoux, J.J. "At the Sources of Symbolism." *Criticism* 1(1959): 279-97.

169. Mazel, Henri. *Aux beaux temps du symbolisme, 1890-1895*. Paris: Mercure de France, 1943. 2 pp.

170. Merrill, Stuart. "Souvenirs sur le Symbolisme." *La Plume* 352(déc 1903):613-21; 353(janv 1904):2-11; 355 (fév 1904):107-15.

171. Michaud, Guy. *La doctrine symboliste. Documents*. Paris: Nizet, 1947. 119 pp.

172. ———. "Langage poétique et symbole." *EP* 26(1971):343-52.

173. ———. *Message poétique du symbolisme*. Paris: Nizet, 1969. 819 pp.

174. Milner, John. *Symbolists and Decadents*. London: Studio Vista/ Dutton, 1971. 158 pp.

175. Minkowski, Eugène. "Métaphore et symbole." *CIS* 5(1964):47-55.

176. Mitchell, Bonner. "Equivocal Engagement in the 1890's." *RomN* 3,i(1961):1-5.

177. Mittenzwei, Johannes. *Das Musickalische in der Literatur:Ein Überblick von Gottfried von Strassburg bis Brecht*. Halle: Veb Verlag Sprache und Literatur, 1962. 576 pp. [Several chaps. on late 19th cent. lit.]

178. Mitterand, Henri. "De l'écriture artiste ou style décadent," in Karl-Heinz Winzberger,ed. *Romanische Philologie Heute:Festschrift Rita Schober*. Berlin: Humboldt-Universität zu Berlin, 1969.

179. Mockel, Albert. *Esthétique du symbolisme*. Bruxelles: Palais des académies, 1962. 256 pp.

180. Moreau, Pierre. "De la symbolique religieuse à la poésie symboliste." *CLS* 4(1967):5-16.

181. ———. "Symbole, Symbolique, Symbolisme." *CAIEF* 6(1954):123-29.

182. Morgan, Charles. "The Heritage of Symbolism," 60-67 in Charles Morgan, *Reflections in a Mirror*. London: Macmillan, 1944.

183. Morrissette, Bruce A. *Les aspects fondamentaux de l'esthétique symboliste*. Clermont-Ferrand: U. of Clermont-Ferrand, 1933. [Diss.]

184. Mouloud, Noël. "Symboles et désignations dans les langues scientifiques et dans les langues naturelles." *CIS* 22-23(1973):65-77.

185. Munch, Jean. *Stéréotypes et symbolisme des schizophréniques*. Strasbourg: Imp. Alsacienne, 1924.

186. Muner, Mario. *Per il riordinamento sistematico degli studi su simbolismo, decadentismo, ermetismo*. Cremona: Ed. tip. Igep, 1957. 14 pp.

187. Olson, E. "A Dialogue on Symbolism," 576-94 in R. S. Crane,ed. *Critics and Criticism*. Chicago: U. of Chicago P., 1952.

188. Ortigues, Edmond. "Le message en blanc." *CIS* 5(1964):75-93.

189. Pádua, Antônio de. *Aspectos estilísticos da poesia de Castro Alves*. Rio: Livraria Sao José, 1972. [Brazilian symbolist *avant la lettre*.]

190. Une Parisienne. "Symbolist Conference." *New York Herald* 1 June(1893). [Paris ed.]

191. Perry, T.S. "The Latest Literary Fashion in France." *Cosmopolitan* 13(July 1892):359-65.

192. Perticucci Bernardini, Ada. *Simbolisti e decadenti*. Roma, 1935.

192a. Peyre, Henri. *Qu'est-ce que le Symbolisme?* Paris: Presses univs., 1974. 264 pp.

193. Pfannkuch, Karl. "Zeitgeist um die Jahrhundertwende:Methodisches-Philosophisches-Literarisches." *ZRG* 14(1962):98-123.

194. Plowert, Jacques, and Paul Adam. *Petit glossaire pour servir à l'intelligence des auteurs décadents et symbolistes*. Paris: Vanier, 1888.

195. Podraza-Kwiatkowska, Maria. "Symbolistyczna koncepcja poezji." *PL* 61,iv(1970):91-138.

196. Point, Armand. "Primitifs et symbolistes." *L'Ermtiage* 2(1895):11-16.

197. Polak, Bettina Spaanstra. *Symbolism*. Amsterdam: J.M. Meulenhoff, 1967. 24 pp.

198. Pongs, Hermann. *Das Bild in der Dichtung:Voruntersuchungen zum Symbol*. 2 Bde. Marburg: H.G. Elwert'sche Verlagsbuchhandlung, 1939.

199. "Pour clore une polémique." *Entretiens politiques et littéraires* 7(oct 1890):201-12.

200. Praz, Mario. *The Romantic Agony*. Tr. Angus Davidson. London, New York: Oxford U.P., 1933. [2nd ed. 1951.] 454 pp.

201. Pucciani, Oreste. "The Universal Language of Symbolism." *YFS* 9(1952):27-35.

202. Purves, A.C. "Impression, Statistics, and the Experience of Literature." *Style* 5(1971):164-69.

203. Ramnoux, Clémence. "Histoire d'un symbole:Histoire antique de 'la Nuit'." *CIS* 13(1967):57-68.

204. Raymond, Marcel. "L'adieu au symbolisme." *NRF* 140(1972): 15-38.

205. Raynaud, Ernest. "Du symbolisme." *Le Décadent* 7(mars 1888): 9-12.

206. ———. *En marge de la mêlée symboliste*. Paris: Mercure de France, 1936. 286 pp.

207. ———. *La mêlée symboliste*. 3 vols. Paris: La Renaissance du livre, 1918-1922.

208. ——— "Réponse à quelques-uns." *La Plume* 267(avril 1900):225-28.

209. Régnier, Henry de. "Victor Hugo et les symbolistes." *Entretiens politiques et littéraires* 15(juin 1891): 193-97.

210. Retté, Adolphe. "Oripeaux académiques." *La Plume* 147(juin 1895):249-51.

211. Richard, Noel. *Le mouvement décadent. Dandys, esthètes et quintessents*. Paris: Librarie Nizet, 1968. 285 pp.

212. Richtofen, Erich von. "Vigny als philosophischdichterischer Wegbereiter des Symbolismus." *RF* 63(1951): 124-28.

213. Ricœur, Paul "Le symbolisme et l'explication structurale." *CIS* 4 (1964):81-96.

214. Rousset, Lucien. "L'âge hérotique du symbolisme." *Confluences* 2(août 1941):157-66; 3(sept 1941):299-310.

215. Rudler, Madeleine. *Parnassiens, symbolistes et décadents*. Paris: Messein, 1938. 82 pp.

216. Saint-Antoine. "Qu'est-ce que le symbolisme?" *L'Ermitage* 1(1894): 332-37.

217. Scherer, Robert. "Das Symbolische." *PJGG* 48(1935):210-57.

218. Schlesinger, Max. *Geschichte des Symbols*. Berlin: Leonhard Simion N.F. Verlag, 1912.

219. Schmidt, Albert-Marie. *La littérature symboliste (1870-1900)*. Paris: P.U.F., 1967. 128 pp.

220. Schrader, Ludwig. *Sinne und Sinneverknüpfungen:Studien und Materialien zur Vorgeschichte der Synästhesie und zur Bewertung der Sinne in der italienischen, spanischen und französischen Literatur*. Heidelberg: C. Winter, 1969.

221. Secretan, Philibert. "L'Utopie comme symbole." *CIS* 8(1965): 49-58.

222. Ségalen, V. "Les Synesthésies et l'Ecole symboliste." *MdF* 42(1902): 57-90.

223. Severini, G. "Symbolisme plastique et Symbolisme littéraire." *MdF* 113 (1916):466-76.

224. Sommavilla, Guido. "Simbolismo conciliatore." *Letture* 14(1959): 563-70.

225. Somville, Pierre. "Suite à une mythologie de l'eau." *CIS* 21(1972): 79-89.

226. Souriau, Paul. "Le Symbolisme des couleurs." *RdP* (15 avril 1895): 849-70.

227. Spagnoletti, Giacinto. "Du Symbolisme au Futurisme." *XXe Siècle* 36,supp.(1971):161.

228. "The Springs of Symbolism." *TSL* (18 Jan 1957):34.

229. Stählin, Wilhelm. "Was ist ein Symbol?" *Zeitwende* 28(1957):586-94.

230. Stepan, F. "Das Wesen des Symbolismus," 805-10 in D. Gerhardt, et al.,eds. *Orbis Scriptus:Festscrift für Dmitrij Tschizewskij zum 70. Geburtstag*. Munchen: W. Fink 1966.

231. Stephan, Philip. "Naturalist Influence and Symbolist Poetry, 1882-86." *FR* 46(1972):299-311.

232. Strich, Fritz. "Symbol und Wortkunst." *ZAAK* 21(1927):344-58.

233. Stromberg, Roland,ed. *Realism, Naturalism and Symbolism:Modes of Thought and Expression in Europe. 1848-1914*. London: Macmillan, 1968. 296 pp.

234. Subrahmanian, Krishnaswami. "The Theory of 'Suggestion' in Sanskrit Poetics, English Romanticism and French Symbolism." *DA* 30 (1969-70):4957A(Ind.).

235. *Le Symbolisme:1886-1936*. Brochure-programme. Bruxelles: I.N.R., 1938.

236. "Symbolists and After." *RLS* 28 Sept(1967):906.

237. Symons, Arthur. "The Decadent Movement in Literature." *Harper's Magazine* 87(Nov 1893):858-67.

238. ——. *The Symbolist Movement in Literature*. London: Heinemann, 1899. [Repr. New York: Dutton, 1958.] 197 pp.

238a. Tarizzo, Domenico "Forma e simbolismo dopo Freud." *Degrés* 4

(1973):h-h5. [On psychological aspects of Symbolism.]

239. Thibaudet, Albert. "Remarques sur le symbole." *NRF* (1 nov 1912): 893-904.

240. Thieme, Hugo P. *Guide bibliographique de littérature française de 1800 à 1906.* Prosateurs, poètes, auteurs dramatiques et critiques. Paris: Welter, 1907.

241. Thompson, Vance. "Of These Things Paris Talks." *Criterion* 18(11 June 1898):12.

242. ———. "The Technique of the Symbolists." *M'lle New York* 1(1 Nov 1895).

243. Tindall, William Y. *The Literary Symbol.* New York: U. of Columbia P., 1955. 278 pp.

244. Valéry, Paul. "Littérature." *NRF* (1 juin 1926):671-76.

245. ——— "The Existence of Symbolism." *KR* 19(1957):425-47.

246. Valette, Alfred. "Le Symbole." *MdF* 7(mars 1893):229-36.

247. Valsecchi, Marco. "Dalla metafisica al novecento e l'antinovecento." *Ulisse* 76(1973):97-103.

248. Van Bever, Pierre. "Signification du *Décadentisme.*" *RLV* 34(1968): 366-72.

249. Van Roosbroeck, Gustave L. *The Legend of the Decadents.* Lancaster, Pa.: Lancaster Press, Inc., 1927. 126 pp.

250. Vedia, Léonidas de. *La poesía del simbolismo.* Buenos Aires: Kraft, 1961. 113 pp.

250a. Vereno, Matthias. "Tradition und Symbol—Die Bedeutung altüberlieferter Weisheit für den modernen Menschen." *Symbolon* 5(1966):9-24.

251. Vielé-Griffin, Francis. "A l'illetré." *Entretiens politiques et littéraires* 2(mai 1890):56-60.

252. ———. "Elucidations." *Entretiens politiques et littéraires* 14(mai 1891):153-58. [On Bruntière and his criticism of Symbolism.]

253. ———. "Inutilisations." *Entretiens politiques et littéraires* 4(juillet 1890):128-32.

254. ———. "La Phonographie." *Entretiens politiques et littéraires* 3(juin 1890):95-98. [Symbol of combination of science and art.]

255. ———. "Patrie." *Entretiens politiques et littéraires* 13(avril 1891): 121-23. [On Goncourt's opinion that Sym. art was unpatriotic.]

256. ———. "Qu'est-ce que c'est?" *Entretiens politiques et littéraires* 12(mars 1891):65-66.

257. Vigée, Claude. "La théorie du symbole." *Table Ronde* 108(déc 1956):58-70.

258. Visan, Tancrède de. *L'attitude du lyrisme contemporain.* Paris: Mercure de France, 1911. 475 pp.

259. ———. "L'idéal symboliste." *MdF* 68(1907):193-208.

259a. Vonessen, Franz. "Sich selbst bestehlen:Von der symbolischen Natur des Eigentums." *Symbolon* 5(1966):25-38.

260. Vordtriede, Werner. "Die Entstehung des Symbols in der Dichtung." *Deutsche Rundschau* 88(1962):744-49.

261. Wais, Kurt. *An den Grenzen der Nationalliteraturen.* Berlin: de Gruyter, 1958. [Essays on Mallarmé, Valéry, Rilke, Poe, *inter alios.*]

262. Weigand, W. *Essays zur Psychologie der Dekadenz.* München: Merhoff, 1893.

263. Weinberg, Bernard. "Les limites de l'hermétisme, ou l'hermétisme et intelligibilité." *CAIEF* 15(1963):151-61.

264. Weinhandl, Ferdinand. *Über das aufschliessende Symbol.* Berlin: n.p., 1929.

265. Wellek, René. *Confrontations.* Studies in the intellectual and literary relations between Germany, England, and the U.S. during the

19th century. Princeton, N.J.: Princeton U.P., 1965. 221 pp.

266. ———. "The Term and Concept of Symbolism in Literary History," 90-121 in *Discriminations: Further Concepts of Criticism 6*. New Haven: Yale U.P., 1970.

267. Wernaer, Robert M. "Das ästhetische Symbol." *Zeitschrift für Philosophie und philosophische Kritik* 130(1907):47-75.

268. West, Rebecca. "The Post-Symbolists." *Time & Tide* 14(Apr 1943): 272-73.

269. Wheelwright, P. *The Burning Fountain: A Study in the Language of Symbolism*. Bloomington: Indiana U.P., 1954. 406 pp.

269a. Wilson, Edmund. *Axel's Castle: A Study in the Imaginative Literature of 1870-1930*. New York: Scribner, 1931. 319 pp.

270. Wyczynski, Paul. "Perspectives du symbolisme." *RUO* 25(1955):34-58.

271. ———. "Symbolisme et création poétique," 235-52 in *Poésie et symbole*. Montréal: Librairie Déom, 1965.

272. Wyzema, Teodor de. "La littérature wagnérienne." *Revue Wagnérienne* 5(juin 1886):150-71.

273. Zerbe, L. R. "The Symbolists." *Outlook* 51(23 Feb 1895):307-08.

See also 637, 689, 805, 1751, 2219, 2512, 2730, 2982.

II National and
International Movements

Anglo-American

274. Beatty, R.C. "The Heritage of Symbolism in Modern Poetry." *YR* 36(1947):467-77.
275. Bercovitch, Sacvan. "The Image of America: From Hermeneutics to Symbolism." *BuR* 20,ii(1972):3-12.
276. Bergonzi, Bernard. "Aspects of the *fin de siècle*," 364-85 in Arthur Pollard, ed. *The Victorians*. With Introd. Vol. VI of *The Sphere History of Literature in the English Language*. London: Cresset; New York: Bantam, 1969 [1970]. 430 pp.
277. Beyette, Thomas K. "Symbolism and Victorian Literature." *DAI* 30 (1970):5440A(Texas, Austin).
278. Block, Haskell M. "The Impact of French Symbolism on Modern American Poetry," 165-217 in Melvin J. Friedman and John B. Vickery,eds. *The Shaken Realist:Essays in Modern Literature in Honor of Frederick J. Hoffmann*. Baton Rouge: U. of La. P., 1970.
279. Bly, Robert. "American Poetry: On the Way to the Hermetic." *BA* 46(1972):17-24.
280. Bruum, Ursula. "Der neue Symbolismus in Amerika." *NDH* 47(1958): 244-50.
281. *A Catalogue of the Imagist Poets*. With Essays by Wallace Martin and Ian Fletcher. New York: J. Howard Woolmer, 1966. [Wallace Martin, "The Forgotten School of 1909," and "The Origins of Imagism," 7-38;

Ian Fletcher, "Some Anticipations of Imagism," 39-53.]

282. Charlesworth, Barbara. *Dark Passages:The Decadent Consciousness in Victorian Literature*. Madison: U. of Wis. P., 1965. 155 pp.

283. Chisholm. A.-R. "La fortune du symbolisme français en Australie." *MdF* 307(1 Sept 1949):112-16.

284. Christadler, Martin,ed. *Die amerikäische Lyrik von Edgar Allan Poe bis Wallace Stevens*. (Ars Interpretandi 4.) Darmstadt: Wissenschaftliche Buchgesellschaft, 1972. 409 pp. [Rptd. essays with "Einleitung" by ed., pp. ix-xvii.]

285. Colum, Padriac. "The Imagists." *Dial* 62(22 Feb 1917):125-27.

286. Fackler, Herbert V. "The Deirdre Legend in Anglo-Irish Literature, 1834-1937." *DAI* 33(1972):1166A (N.C., Chapel Hill). [Incl. disc. of var. auths. Lady Cregory, W.B. Yeats, J.M. Synge, *inter alios*.]

286a. Farmer, Albert J. *Le mouvement esthétique et décadent en Angleterre (1873-1900)*. Paris: Champion, 1931. 413 pp.

287. Feidelson, Charles. *Symbolism and American Literature*. Chicago: U. of Chicago P., 1953. 355 pp.

288. Fletcher, Ian. "Le symbolisme français en Angleterre (compléments à la bibliographie de G. Ross Roy, *RLC* 34 [1960])." *RLC* 36 (1962): 158-59.

289. Fox, Steven J. "Art and Personality: Browning, Pater, Wilde and Yeats." *DAI* 33(1972):751A(Yale).

290. Gale, A.L. "Symbolism in American Literature." *AION* 2(1959): 167-86.

291. Garbáty, Thomas J. "The French Coterie of the *Savoy*, 1896." *PMLA* 75(1960):609-15.

292. Harding, Brian R. " 'Transcendental Symbolism' in the Works of Emerson, Thoreau, and Whitman." *DAI* 32(1972):5789A(Brown).

293. Harris, Wendell. "Innocent Decadence:The Poetry of the Savoy." *PMLA* 77(1962):629-36.

294. Healey, Eleanor C. "Imagist Dialogue." *DA* 29(1969):3612A (Columbia).

295. Healy, J.J. "*The Dial* and the Revolution in Poetry:1912-1917:A Study in Controversy." *BAASB* 10 (1965):48-60.

296. Henessy, Helen. "*The Dial*:Its Poetry and Poetic Criticism." *NEQ* 31(1958):66-87.

297. Heyen, William. "Toward the Still Point:The Imagist Aesthetic." *BSUF* 9,i(1968):44-48.

298. Hoffman, Frederick J. "Symbolisme and Modern Poetry in the United States." *CLS* 4(1967):193-99.

301. Jackson, Holbrook. *The Eighteen Nineties*. London: Jonathan Cape, 1913.

302. Jean-Aubrey, G[eorges]. "Poètes français d'Angleterre." *MdF* 127 (1918):26-48.

303. Jones, A.R. "Notes Toward a History of Imagism." *SAQ* 60(1961): 262-85.

304. Jones, R.F. "Nationalism and Imagism in Modern American Poetry." *WUS* 11(1923):97-130.

305. Kopp, Karl Caton. "The Origin and Characteristics of 'Decadence' in British Literature of the 1890's." *DA* 24(1963):1604(Calif.)

306. Lester, John A.,Jr. *Journey through Despair, 1880-1914:Transformations in British Literary Culture*. Princeton: Princeton U.P., 1968. 211 pp.

307. Lombardo, Agostino. *La Poesia inglese:Dall'estetismo al simbolismo*. Roma: Edizioni di storia e letteratura, 1950. 301 pp.

308. ———. *Realismo e simbolismo:Saggi di letteratura americana contemporanea*. Roma: Edizioni di storia e letteratura, 1957. 261 pp.

309. MacKendrick, Louis K. "The Life and Times of the *Egoist*:The History

of a British Little Magazine." *DAI* 32(1972):6985A-86A(Toronto).

310. Martin, Wallace. "The Sources of the Imagist Aesthetic." *PMLA* 85(1970):196-204.

311. Mix, Katherine C. *A Study in Yellow*:The Yellow Book *and its Contributors*. Lawrence: U. of Kan. P., 1960.

312. Morrissette, Bruce A. "Early English and American Critics of French Symbolism," 159-80 in *Studies in Honor of Frederick W. Shipley*. St. Louis, Mo.: Washington U.P., 1942.

313. Naremore, James. "The Imagists and the French 'Generation of 1900'." *ConL* 11(1970):354-74.

314. Nelson, James G. *The Early Nineties:A View from the Bodley Head*. Cambridge: Harvard U.P., 1971. 387 pp.

315. Pagnini, Marcello. "Imagism." *SA* 11(1965):181-95.

316. ——. "Struttura semantica del grande simbolismo americano," 29-52 in Mario Praz,ed. *Il simbolismo nella letturatura Nord-Americana*. Firenze, 1965.

317. Paterson, Gary H. "The Place of the Roman Catholic Church in the Literature of the Decadence in England." *DAI* 32(1971):928A(Toronto).

318. Peters, R.L. "Towards an 'Undefinition' of Decadent as Applied to British Literature of the Nineteenth Century." *Aesthetics* 18(Dec 1959):258-64.

319. Ramsey, Warren. "Uses of the Visible:American Imagism, French Symbolism." *CLS* 4(1967):177-91.

320. Ransom, J.C. "Symbolism:American Style." *New Republic* 2,ii (1953):18-20.

321. Reed, John R. "Mixing Memory Concepts of Art, Life and Morality in and Desire in Late Victorian Literature." *ELT* 14(1971):1-15.

322. Rexroth, Kenneth. "L'influence de la poésie française sur la poésie américaine." *Europe* 358-359(1959):43-66.

323. Singh, Brijraj. "A Study of the the Criticism of Five Writers from Pater to Yeats." *DAI* 32(1971):3331A-32A(Yale). [Incl. Lionel Johnson, Arthur Symons, Henry James.]

324. Stanford, Derek. "Sex and Style in the Literature of the '90s." *ContempR* 216(1970):95-100.

325. Starkie, Enid. *From Gautier to Eliot:The Influence of France on English Literature. 1851-1939*. London: Hutchinson, 1960. 236 pp.

326. Taupin, René. "French Symbolism and the English Language." *CL* 5 (1953):312-22.

327. ——. *L'influence du symbolisme français sur la poésie américaine de 1910 à 1920*. Paris: Champion, 1929. 302 pp.

328. Temple, Ruth. *The Critic's Alchemy:A Study of the Introduction of French Symbolism into England*. New Haven: College and University Press, 1953. 345 pp.

329. Weintraub, Stanley,ed. The Savoy: *Nineties Experiment*. With Introd. University Park: Penn. State U.P., 1966. 294 pp.

330. ——. The Yellow Book:*Quintessence of the Nineties*. Garden City, N.Y.: Doubleday, 1964. 373 pp.

331. Wiegner, Kathleen. "French Symbolism in England:1890-1900." *WSLiT* 6(1969):50-57.

332. Winters, Yvor. "The Symbolist Influence." *Hound and Horn* 4(1931):607-18.

333. Yoder, Albert C.,III. "Concepts of Mythology in Victorian England." *DAI* 32(1971):3277A(Fla. State).

See also 491, 497, 856, 980, 999, 1008, 1014, 1050, 1083, 1087, 1236, 1320, 1588, 1858, 2153, 2267, 2747, 3003.

Germanic

334. Albert, Henri. "Le Symbolisme en Allemagne." *La Plume* 32(août 1890):144.
335. Albrecht, Hellmuth. *Tendencias en la literatura alemana desde el naturalismo hasta nuestros días*. Vol. 1, *Del naturalismo al neorromanticismo*. Tucumán: Univ. Nacional de Tucumán, 1954.
336. Balotă, Nicolae. "Un dosar expresionist." *Steaua* 23,xxi(1972):23-24.
337. Barthals, Joseph. "De beweging van Tachtig in beweging." *VlG* 47 (1963):790-92.
338. Bedwell, Carol E.B. "The Parallelism of Artistic and Literary Tendencies in Germany, 1880-1910." *DA* 23(1962):2131(Ind.).
339. Bergstrøm-Nielsen, Carl,ed. *Taarnet:Illustreret Maanedsskrift for Kunst og Literatur*. Copenhagen: Gyldendal, 1966. [Selecs. from Symbolist magazine of Johannes Jørgensen pub. 1890's].
340. Böschenstein, Bernhard. "Wirkungen des französischen Symbolismus auf die deutsche Lyrik der Jahrhundertwende." *Euphorion* 55(1964): 375-95.
341. Brachin, Pierre. "Le 'Mouvement de 1880' aux Pays-Bas et la littérature française." *RLM* 52-53(1960):4-35.
342. Brandt Corstius, Johannes C. *Het poetisch programma van Tachtig*. Amsterdam: Athenaeum-Polak and van Gennep, 1967. 92 pp.
343. Brom, Gerard. "Franse invloed op onze Tachtigers." *Neophil* 23 (1938):278-84.
344. Closset, F. "Aspects et figures de la littérature néerlandaise depuis 1880." *LanM* 51(1957):269-78; 374-84.
345. Dieckmann, Liselotte. "Friedrich Schlegel and the Development of the Concept of Symbolism in German Romanticism." *GR* 34(1959):276-83.
346. Diehl, O. "L'influence de l'art français sur la poésie allemande. A propos du 70e anniversaire de Stefan George." *MdF* 287(1938):340-54. [Tr. M.T. Morgan.]
347. Duthie, Enid Lowry. *L'influence du Symbolisme français dans le renouveau poétique de l'Allemagne. Les "Blätter für die Kunst" de 1892 à 1900*. Paris: Champion, 1933. 571 pp.
348. Ekner, Reidar. *En sällsam gemenskap:Baudelaire, Söderberg, Obstfelder, Rilke:Litteraturhistorika essäer*. Stockholm: Norstedt, 1967. 192 pp.
349. Gellynck, H. "Symbolistische aspecten na het symbolisme." *Vlaanderen* 99(mai-juin 1968):183-88.
350. Goff, Penrith. *Wilhelminisches Zeitalter*. (HDL 10.) Bern: Francke, 1970. 215 pp.
351. Gsteiger, Manfred. *Französische Symbolisten in der deutschen Literatur der Jahrhundertwende (1869-1914)*. Bern: Francke, 1971. 325 pp.
352. Hajek, Edelgard. *Literarischer Jugendstil:Vergleichende Studien zur Dichtung und Malerei um 1900*. (LiG 6.) Düsseldorf: Bertelsmann, 1972. 117 pp.
353. Hamann, Richard, and Jost Hermand. *Deutsche Kunst und Kultur von der Gründerzeit Bis zum Expressionismus*. Bd. 4. Berlin: Akademie-Verlag, 1967.
354. Hermand, Jost. *Der Schein des schönen Lebens:Studien zur Jahrhundertwende*. Frankfurt: Athenäum, 1972. 313 pp. [Some reprs.]
355. Hösle, J. "Die deutsche erzählende und lyrische Dichtung der Jahrhundertwende im Spiegel französischer Zeitschriften von 1900-1914," 135-53 in Fritz Ernst, and Kurt Wais,eds.

Forschungsprobleme der vergleichenden Literaturgeschichte. Tübingen: Niemeyer, 1958.

356. Hoorweg, C.M. "Die Blütezeit der Achtiziger Bewegung in Holland." *CPe* 46(1961):43-83.

357. Jong, Martien J.G. de. *Het Nederlandse gedicht naar 1880:Poëzie-essay-kritiek-stijlleer-tekstverklaring.* Leiden: Sijthoff, 1969. 144 pp.

358. King, A.H. *The Influence of French Literature on German Prose and the Drama between 1880 and 1890.* London: n.p., 1933.

359. Klemperer, V. "Entstehung u. Französ, Neuromantik." *Jahrbuch für Philologie* 2(1927):143-72.

360. Koskimies, Rafael. *Der nordische Dekadent:Eine vergleichende Literaturstudie.* Helsinki: Suomalainen Tiedeakatemia, 1968. 119 pp.

361. Menduini, Augusto. "Sul decadentismo post-nietzschiano." *NA* 518 (1973):224-37.

362. Middleton, J.C. "The Rise of Primitivism and Its Relevance to the Poetry of Expressionism and Dada,". 182-203 in Peter F. Ganz,ed. *The Discontinuous Tradition:Studies in German Literature in Honour of Ernest Ludwig Stahl.* Oxford: Oxford U.P., 1971. 279 pp.

363. Milch, Werner. *Ströme, Formeln, Manifeste:Drei Vorträge zur Geschichte der deutschen Literatur im zwanzigsten Jahrhundert.* Marburg: Simons, 1949. 90 pp.

364. Panizza, Oskar. "Die deutschen Symbolisten." *Gegenwart* 47,xiii(30 März 1895):201-04.

365. Paslick, Robert H. "Ethics Versus Aesthetics at the Turn of the Century." *DA* 24(1964):302(Ind.). [Ger. lit. periodicals 1895-1905.]

366. Paulsen, W.ed. *Das Nachleben der Romantik in der modernen deutschen Literatur.* Heidelberg: Stiehm, 1969. 230 pp.

367. Polak, Bettina Spaanstra. *Het Finde-Siècle in de Nederlandse Schilderkunst.* The Hague: Nijhoff, 1955. 415 pp.

368. Printz-Pahlson, Göran. *Solen i spegeln:Essäer om lyrisk modernism.* Stockholm: Bonnier, 1958. 298 pp.

369. Randall, A.W.G. "French Symbolism and Modern German Poetry." *Anglo-French Review* 3,iv(1920): 314-20.

370. Rapsilber, E. *Recherches sur les rapports artistiques franco-allemands de la fin du XIXe siècle à la première guerre mondiale.* Paris: Univ. de Paris, 1961. [Diss.]

371. Rosenhaupt, Hans W. *Der deutsche Dichter um die Jahrhundertwende und seine Abgelöstheit von der Gesellschaft.* Bern, Leipzig: Haupt, 1939. 287 pp.

372. Ruprecht, Erich. "Die Symbolik der neueren deutschen Dichtung." *SG* 6(1963):348-55.

373. Ruprecht, Erich, and Dieter Bänsch,eds. *Literarische Manifeste der Jahrhundertwende 1890-1910.* Stuttgart: Metzler, 1970. 579 pp.

374. Schwerte, Hans. "Deutsche Literatur im Wilhelminischen Zeitalter." *WW* 14(1964):254-70.

375. Seillière, E. *Le néoromantisme en Allemagne.* 2 vols. Paris, 1928.

376. Sokel, Walter H. *Der literarische Expressionismus:Der Expressionismus in der deutschen Literatur des zwanzigsten Jahrhunderts.* München: A. Langen und G. Muller Verlag, 1960.

377. Stahl, E.L. "The Genesis of Symbolist Theories in Germany." *MLR* 41(1946):306-13.

378. Starr, Doris. *Über den Begriff des Symbols in der deutschen Klassik und Romantik:Unter besonderer Berücksichtigung von Friedrich Schlegel.* Reutlingen: Eugen Hutzler, 1964. 103 pp.

379. Strich, Fritz, *Die Mythologie in der deutschen Literatur von Klopstock bis Wagner*. 2 vols. Halle: Niemeyer, 1910.

380. Thys, Walter. "The Literature of the Netherlands in the Eighteen Nineties:National and European Trends," 505-10 in Vol 1 of François Jost,ed. *Proceedings of the IVth Congress of the International Comparative Literature Association, Fribourg 1964*. 2 vols. The Hague: Mouton, 1966.

381. Valkhoff, P. *L'influence de la littérature française dans les Pays-Bas*. Leyde: n.p., 1918.

382. Žmegač, Viktor. "Zur Poetik des expressionistischen Dramas," 482-515 in Reinhold Grimm,ed. *Deutsche Dramentheorien:Beiträge zu einer historischen Poetik des Dramas in Deutschland*. 2 vols. Frankfurt: Athenaum, 1971. 591 pp.

See also 99, 410, 478, 513, 526, 534, 613, 644, 648, 756, 797, 886, 895, 900, 922, 958, 978, 1003, 1042, 1066, 1115, 1258, 1731, 1812, 2054, 2060, 2066, 2074, 2267, 2929, 2950, 3067.

Romance

383. Ajalbert, Jean. *Mémoires en vrac: Au temps du symbolisme*. Paris: Albin Michel, 1938. 413 pp.

384. Alvim, Tereza C. "Pedro Nava." *ESPSL* 17 Dec(1972):1. [Braz. modernism.]

385. Aman-Jean, François. *L'enfant oublié chronique*. Paris: Buchet/Chastel, 1963. 331 pp.

386. Anderson, R.R. *Spanish American Modernism. A Selected Bibliography*. Tuscon: U. of Ariz. P., 1970. 167 pp.

387. Anon. "The French Symbolists." *TLS* 2532(11 Aug 1950):496. [Rev. art.]

388. Anon. "Significance of the French Symbolist Movement." *Current Literature* 44(June 1908):621-23.

389. Anon. "Symbolism." *Academy* 64(Apr 1903):368-69.

390. Antignani, Gerardo. *Dalla Scapigliatura all'ermetismo*. Salerno-Roma: Di Giacomo, 1949. 120 pp.

391. Antunes, Manuel. "Mundividências da poesia portuguesa desde o romantismo aos anos 60." *Brotéria* 96:631-44.

392. Apetroaie, Ion. "V. Voiculescu, *Vitalité de la mythologie roumaine*." *CIS* 17-18(1969):132-37. [Rev. art.]

393. Apollonio, Mario. *Ermetismo*. Padova: CEDAM, 1945. 136 pp.

394. Araujo, Murillo. *Quadrantes do modernismo brasileiro*. 2nd ed. Rio: Livraria São José, 1972. 53 pp.

395. Aubéry, Pierre. "The Anarchism of the Literati of the Symbolist Period." *FR* 41(1968):39-47.

396. Avila, Affonso. "O artista e o escritor na Semana de 22." *MGSL* 19 Feb(1972):9. [On Modernism in Brazil.]

397. Azevedo, Leodegário A. de,Filho. *Poetas do modernismo*. Brasília: Inst. Nacional do Livro, 1972. [To consist of 6 vols.]

398. Baju, Anatole. "Décadents et Symbolistes." *Le Décadent* 23(nov 1888): 1-2.

399. ———. "Décadisme." *Le Décadent* 33(nov 1886):1.

400. ———. "M. Champsaur et les décadents." *Le Décadent* 28(oct 1886):1.

401. Balakian, Anna. "Studies in French Symbolism, 1945-1955." *RR* 46 (1955):223-30. [Rev. art.]

402. Balasov, Nikolai. "Simbolismul francěz." *StCL* 10(1961):317-44.

403. Bastos, C. Tavares. *O simbolismo no Brasil e outros escritos*. Rio: São José, 1969. 182 pp.

404. Beaujon, Georges. *L'école symboliste*. Basle: n.p., 1900. 43 pp.

405. Beaunier, André. "*Les Parnassiens*

et les symbolistes." *MdF* 37(1901): 375-88.

406. ———. *La poésie nouvelle.* Paris: Mercure de France, 1902. 400 pp.

407. Becker, Carl. "Der Werdegang und die Bilanz des französischen Symbolismus." *GRM* 5(1913):544-52.

408. Bernard, Jean-Marc. *Petits sentiers de la poésie française. Symbolisme et classicisme. Etudes et portraits.* Paris: Le Divan, 1923. 856 pp. [Repr. Genève: Slatkine, 1970.]

409. Bernardelli, Giuseppe. "Giochi tecnici nel simbolismo francese. Sul genere dalla rima." *Aevum* 47(1973): 137-43.

410. Berry, R.M. *The French Symbolist Poets in Germany (Baudelaire, Verlaine, Rimbaud):Criticism and Translations,* 1870-1914. Cambridge, Mass.: Harvard Diss., 1944.

411. Bertrán, P., and Juan Bautista. "Caravana de poetas a Belén. Del simbolismo hasta nuestros dias:España, Francia, Italia." *RyF* 48(1948): 12-36.

412. Bigongiari, Piero. *Poesia francese del novecento.* Firenze: Vallecchi, 1968. 352 pp.

413. Billy, André. *L'époque 1900.* Paris: J. Tallandier, 1951. 484 pp.

414. Binni, Walter. *La poetica del decadentismo.* Firense: G.C. Sansoni, 1949. 141 pp.

415. Bloy, L. *Le symbolisme de l'apparition 1879-1880.* Paris: Lemercier, 1925. 287 pp.

416. Bonneau, Georges. *Le symbolisme dans la poésie française contemporaine.* Paris: Boivin, 1930. 138 pp.

417. Bornecque, Jacques-Henri. "Rêves et réalités du symbolisme." *RSH* 77(1955):5-23.

418. Boschot, Adolphe. *La crise poétique.* Paris: Perrin, 1897. 150 pp.

419. Bote, Lidia,ed. *Antologia poeziei simboliste româneşti.* Bucureşti: Minerva, 1972. 391 pp.

420. Bouhélier, Saint-Georges de. "Inutilité de la calomnie." *La Plume* 229(nov 1898):623-27.

421. Braet, Herman. *L'accueil fait au symbolisme en Belgique.* Bruxelles: Palais des Académies, 1967. 195 pp.

422. Brasil, Assis. "Houve uma estética modernista?" *JdL* 268,Cad.1(1972): 3.

423. ———. "A linguagem do modernismo." *JdL* 274,Cad.1(1973):3.

424. ———. "Modernismo:Novos ângulos." *JdL* 270,Cad.1(1973):3.

425. Brunetière, Ferdinand. *Essai sur la littérature contemporaine.* Paris: Calmann-Lévy, 1893.

426. ———. "Revue littéraire—Le symbolisme contemporain." *RDM* (avril 1891):681-92.

427. Burns, C.A. "The 19th Century (post-romantic-1961)." *YWMLS* 23 (1963):105-20.

428. Caccese, Neusa Pinsard. Festa: *Contribuição para o estudo do Modernismo.* São Paulo: Inst. de Esudos Brasileiros, 1971. 242 pp.

429. Carden, Poe. "Parnassianism, Symbolism, Decadentism—Spanish-American Modernism." *Hispania* 43(1960): 545-51.

430. Carmody, Francis. "Le décadisme." *CAIEF* 12(1960):121-31.

431. Carter, A.E. *The Idea of Decadence in French Literature 1830 to 1900.* Toronto: Toronto U.P., 1958. 154 pp.

432. Carton de Wiart, Henry. *Souvenirs littéraires.* Paris: Lethielleux; Bruxelles: Durendal, 1939. 198 pp.

433. Carvalho, J.G. Herculano de. "Símbolo e conhecimento simbólico." *Rumo* 12(1968):301-10.

434. Cassou, Jean, et al. *Les sources du XXe siècle.* Paris: Editions des deux mondes, 1961. 363 pp.

435. Castelo, J. Aderaldo. "Apontamentos para a historia do simbolismo no Brasil." *RUSP* (1950):111-21.

436. Castex, Pierre-Georges,ed. *Autour*

du symbolisme: Villiers-Mallarmé-Ver-laine-Rimbaud. Lille: Faculté des Lettres, 1955. 319 pp.

437. Castro, E.M. de. *L'influence du symbolisme français dans la poésie portugaise contemporaine*. Paris, 1923.

438. Castro, Sílvio. "Significado da Semana de Arte Moderna." *JdL* 261, Cad.1(1972):3.

439. Celant, Germano. "Futurismo esoterico."*Verri* 33/34(1970):108-17.

440. Chast, Denyse. "Eugénio de Castro et les symbolistes français," 155-61 in *Mélanges d'études portugaises offerts à Georges le Gentil*. Lisboa: Instituto para a Alta Cultura, 1949. 351 pp.

441. Chérix, Robert-Benoit. *L'esthétique symboliste*. Fribourg: Imprimerie de l'Oeuvre de Saint-Paul, 1922. 52 pp.

442. Chiari, Joseph. *The Aesthetics of Modernism*. London:. Vision Press, 1970. 224 pp.

443. Christophe, Lucien. "Ombres et lumières du symbolisme." *RG* 93(1957):28-40.

444. Chrohmălniceanu, Ovid S. *Literatura română si expresionismul*. Bucureşti: Editura Eminescu, 1971. 308 pp.

445. Ciobanu, Valeriu. "Simbolismul francez." *RITL* 1(1965):45-71. [Sum. in Fr.]

446. Cioculescu, Şerban,ed. *Istoria literaturii romane*. Vol. III:*Epoca marilor clasici*. Bucureşti: Ed. Acad. R.S.R., 1973. 1042 pp.

447. Clouard, Henri. *Histoire de la littérature française du symbolisme à nos jours*. Vol. I(1885-1914). Paris: Albin Michel, 1947.

448. Coelho, Jacinto de Prado. "Simbolismo," and "Decadentismo," in *Dicionário de literatura*. 2 vols. Porto: Livraria Figueirinhas, 1969.

449. Coelho, Nelly Novaes. "Do van-guardiamo europeu ao poema-processo." *JdL* 262.Cad.2(1972):8. [Rev. art. of Gilberto M. Teles, *Vanguarda europeia e modernismo brasileiro*.]

450. Cohn, Adolphe. "The French Symbolists." *Bookman* 1(Mar 1895): 89-91; 2(Apr 1895):161-63.

451. Colleville, Vicomte de. "Ephémères." *La Plume* 144(avril 1895): 166-67. [Poems about Verlaine and Moréas.]

452. Cordié. Carlo. "Arrigo Solmi critico dei Parnassiani e dei Simbolisti francesi," 255-77 in *Studi in onore di Italo Siciliano*. (Biblioteca dell'Archivum Romanicum, Serie I, 86.) Firenze: Olschi, 1966.

453. Cornell, Kenneth. "French Symbolism." *ConL* 9(1968):163-39.

454. ——. *Post-Symbolist Period. French Poetic Currents 1900-1920*. New Haven: Yale U.P., 1958. 182 pp.

455. Cortés, René. "Primeros poetas modernistas hispanoamericanos. *Círculo* 8,ii(1970):17-23.

456. Coutuvrat, G. and J. "Petites polémiques mensuelles." *Revue Indépendante* 25(1892):197-201.

457. Crespa, Angel. "Muestrario de poemas simbolistas brasileños." *RCB* 22(1967):217-80.

458. D'Agostino, Nemi. "La fin de siècle francese e la poesia di Pound ed Eliot." *Galleria* 4(1954):327-39.

459. Daxhelet, Arthur. "Une crise littéraire, symbolisme et symbolistes." *Revue de Belgique* 105(1903): 99-116; 106(1904):65-81; 107(1904): 175-93.

460. Décaudin, Michel. *La crise des valeurs symbolistes:Vingt ans de poésie française 1895-1914*. Toulouse: Privat, 1960. 532 pp.

461. ——. "Le mouvement poétique de 1895 à 1914." *IL* 12(1961): 199-203.

462. ——. "La poésie en 1914." *MdF* 1158(fév 1960):248-58.

463. ——. "Poésie impressioniste et poésie symboliste." *CAIEF* 12(1960):133-42.

464. ——. "Pre-symbolisme, symbolisme, post-symbolisme," in *Problèmes de périodisation dans l'histoire littéraire:Colloque organisé par la Section d'Etudes Romanes de l'Université Charles de Prague* (29 nov-1 déc 1966). (Acta Univ. Carolunae Philologica 4, Romanistica Pragensia 5.) Praha: Univ. Karlova, 1968.

465. ——. "Le symbolisme vous connaissez?" *La Quinzaine Littéraire* 122(16-31 July 1971):13. [Rev. art.]

466. Dédéyan, Charles. *Le nouveau mal de Baudelaire à nos jours*. Vol. 1:*Du post-romantisme au symbolisme*. Paris: C.D.U. et S.E.D.E.S. réunis, 1968.

467. Delvaille, Bernard. "Le Paris des Symbolistes." *NL* 8 avril(1971):6.

468. ——. *La poésie symboliste*. Paris: Seghers, 1971. 431 pp.

469. DeMichelis, Euralio. "Delle tradition in ispecie dai simbolisti francesi," 325-32 in *Studi in onore di Vittorio Luglio e Diego Valeri*. Venezia: Pozza, 1962.

470. Denis, Maurice. *Du symbolisme au classicisme:Théories*. Paris: Hermann, 1964. 181 pp.

471. Dérieux, Henry. *La poésie française contemporaine, 1885-1935*. Paris: Mercure de France, 1935. 293 pp.

472. Deschamps, Léon. "La Renaissance Belge:Paul Lacomblez." *La Plume* 52(juin 1891):195-96.

473. Dias, Fernando Correia. "A redescoberta do barroco pelo movimento modernista. *Barroco* 4(1972):7-16.

474. Dornis, Jean. *La sensibilité dans la poésie française(1885-1912)*. Paris: A. Fayard, 1912. 357 pp.

475. Drimba, Ovidiu. "Le style symbolisme français style de culture." *Studii de literaturǎ universalǎ* (1966): 223-37. [Sum. in Fr.]

476. Droguett cz., Iván. "La configuración simbólica en el cuento mundonovista chileno." *RSV* 4,i(1970) 87-102.

477. Dubus, Edouard. "Une conférence décadente en 1886." *La Plume* 34(sept 1890):167.

478. Dyserinck, H. "De Frans schrijvende Vlaamse auteurs van 1880 in de spiegel der Franse en Duitse literaire kritiek." *SpL* 8(1964):9-30.

479. Eguía Ruiz, C. "La crisis del simbolismo en literatura en España." *Literaturas y Literatos* 1(1914):433-56.

480. Engel, Eduard. "Die Französischen Dekadenten und Symbolisten." *Cosmopolis* 1(Mar 1896):879-95.

481. Engelen, Bernard. *Die Synästhesien in der Dichtung Eichendorffs. Mit einem Anhang über die sogenannte "Audition colorée" und über Synästhesien in der Dichtung des französischen Symbolismus*. Köln: U. of Köln, 1966. [Diss.]

482. Escorailles, Albert de. "Sensationnisme." *Le Décadent* 32(nov 1886): 1.

483. Fagus [Georges Faillet]. "Les moralités légendaires." *La Plume* 338(mai 1903):553-59.

484. ——. "Le parloir aux images." *La Plume* 309(mars 1902):340-45; 312(avril 1902):495-501.

485. Faurie, Marie-Josèphe. *Le modernisme hispano-américain et ses sources françaises*. Paris: Centre de Recherches de l'Inst. d'Etudes Hispaniques, 1966. 292 pp.

486. ——. "El modernismo hispano-americano y sus fuentes francesas." *CCLC* 98(1963):66-70.

487. Fehr, A.J.A. *De franse symbolisten en de muziek:Een onderzoek naar de betekenis van het begrip "muziek" in*

de gedachtenwereld van de franse symbolisten van omstreeks 1885. Groningen: Wolters, 1960. 24 pp.

488. Feldman, David. *La revue symboliste* La Plume. *(1889-1899).* Paris: Univ. Paris Lettres, 1954. [Diss.]

489. Fernández Retamar, Roberto. "Modernismo, noventiocho, subdesarrollo," 345-53 in *Actas del Tercer Congreso Internacional de Hispanistas.* Carlos H. Magis,ed. Celebrado en Mexico, D.F., del 26 al 31 agosto de 1968. México: El Colegio de México por la Asociación Internacional de Hispanistas, 1970. 962 pp.

490. Ferreres, Rafael. *Los límites del modernismo y del 98.* Madrid: Taurus Ediciones, S.A., 1964. 186 pp.

491. Fletcher, I. "Le symbolisme français en Angleterre." *RLC* 36(1962): 158-59.

492. Flora, Francesco. *La poesia ermetica.* Bari: G. Laterza, 1936. 214 pp.

493. ———. *Dal romanticismo al futurismo.* Placenza: Porta, 1921.

494. Foreman, Dorothy Z. "Modernism in *El Mundo* (1894-1900)." *DAI* 32(1972):5226A(Mo., Columbia).

495. Fowlie, Wallace. *Climate of Violence:The French Literary Tradition from Baudelaire to the Present.* New York: Macmillan, 1967. 274 pp.

496. ———. *Clowns and Angels:Studies in Modern French Literature.* New York: Sheed & Ward, 1943. 162 pp.

497. ———. *La pureté dans l'art:Le secret du chant, Mallarmé, T.S. Eliot, Gide et le roman français.* Montréal: Editions de l'Arbre, 1941. 149 pp.

498. Frattini, Alberto. *Poesia nuova in Italia:Tra ermetismo e neoavanguardia.* Milano: IPL, 1968. 252 pp.

499. Gabibbe, G. "Significato dell'ermetismo." *Rassegna d'Italia* 2(giugno-agosto 1947):86-93.

500. Gaudefoy-Demombynes, J. "L'influence de la poésie française sur la poésie symboliste." *RUL* 3,viii(1949): 658-67.

501. Ghil, René. "Une réponse." *La Plume* 3(mai 1889):1-2.

502. ———. "Réponse aux décadents." *La Plume* 36(oct 1890):191.

503. Ghypa, Matila. "Of Some French Writers and Their Key Words." *Life and Letters Today* 40(Mar 1944): 162-67.

504. Giannesci, Ferdinando. *Gli ermetici.* Brescia: La Scuola, 1951. 117 pp.

505. Gicovate, Bernardo. *Ensayos sobre poesia hispánica del modernismo a la vanguardia.* Mexico City: Ediciones de Andrea, 1967. 135 pp.

506. Gille, Valère. "Du symbolisme." *Bulletin de l'Académie de Langue et de Littérature Françaises* 19(1940): 21-37.

507. Girard, Marcel. "Naturalisme et symbolisme." *CAIEF* 6(1954): 97-106.

508. Goes, Fernando. "Simbolismo," in *Panorama da poesía brasileira.* Vol. 4. Rio: Civilização Brasileira, 1959.

509. Gorren, Aline. "French Symbolists." *Scribner's* 13(March 1893): 337-52.

510. Gourmont, Rémy de. *Le livre des Masques.* 17th ed. Paris: Mercure de France, 1923. 265 pp. [Also in Eng. as *Book of Masks.* Tr. by Jack Lewis. Freeport, N.Y.: Books for Libraries Press, 1967. 265 pp.]

511. ———. *Le IIe livre des masques.* Paris: Mercure de France, 1898. 289 pp.

512. ———. *Souvenirs du symbolisme,* Vol. 4 in *Promenades littéraires.* Paris: Société du Mercure de France, 1912.

513. Graaf, D.A. de. "Trefpunten tussen het Franse symbolisme en de Duitse romantiek." *VlG* 46(1962):533-54.

514. Gregh, Fernand. *Portrait de la poésie moderne de Rimbaud à Verlaine.* Paris: Librairie Delagrave, 1939. 264 pp.

515. ———. "Symbolistes belges (histoire de la poésie contemporaine XII)." *NL* 713(13 juin 1936):2.

516. Gresset, Michel. "Voyeur et voyant. Essai sur les données et le mécanisme de l'imagination symboliste." *NRF* 14(nov 1966):809-26.

517. Griffiths, R.M. "French Studies: The Nineteenth Century(Post-Romantic)." *YWMLS* 29(1967): 116-29.

518. Gringoire, Pedro. "Apuntes sobre la nota mística en la poesía hispano-americana." *CA* 15,iii(1956):234-49.

519. Guex-Gaslambide. "Avant-propros pour quelques lettres inédites du symbolisme." *Revue Neuve* 3, ix(1950): 14-19.

520. Guggenheim, Susanna. "I symbolisti francesi in veste straniera (Alcune traduz. di Stefan George)." *Lettres Modernes* 2(1951):89-90.

521. Guichard, Léon. "Les symbolistes et la musique." *Bulletin des Lettres* 5(1936):193-99,232-39.

522. Guiette, Robert. "Un cas de symbiose dans le Symbolisme en France." *CLS* 4(1967):103-07.

523. Gullón, Ricardo. "Ideologias del modernismo." *Insula* 26(Feb 1971): 1,2.

524. Hamel, A. van. *Franse Symbolisten*. Amsterdam: Gids, 1902.

525. Hatzfeld, Helmut A. *Der französische Symbolismus*. München, Leipzig: Roel & Cie., 1923. 169 pp.

526. Hina, Horst. "Der deutsche Einfluss Kataloniens im Zeitraum 1895-1920," 299-320 in Johannes Hösle, and Wolfgang Eitel,eds. *Beiträge zur vergleichenden Literaturgeschichte: Festschrift für Kurt Wais zum 65. Geburtstag*. Tübingen: Niemeyer, 1972. 406 pp.

527. Holdsworth, Carole A. "Some Modernist 'manías verbales' and Their Connotations in the *Revista Moderna.*" *Hispania* 55(1972):60-65.

528. Ibels, André. "Invectives amicales." *La Plume* 144(avril 1895): 162-64. [Parnasse, les mallarmistes, le ghilisme.]

529. Johansen, Svend. *Le symbolisme: Etudes des symbolistes français*. Copenhagen: Munksgaard, 1945. 377 pp.

530. Jones, Percy Mansell. *The Background of Modern French Poetry: Essays and Interviews*. Cambridge: Cambridge U.P., 1951. 196 pp.

531. Joset, Jacques. "Estudios sobre el modernismo." *NRFH* 21(1972): 100-11.

532. Juin, Hubert. "Des fanatiques de l'écriture:Les symbolistes. *Magazine Littéraire* 52(mai 1971):330.

533. Kahn, Gustave. "Trente ans de symbolisme:L'escalier de Mallarmé." *NL* (2 mars 1929):4.

534. Kayser, Wolfgang J.,ed. *Gedichte des französischen Symbolismus in deutschen Übersetzungen*. Tübingen: Niemeyer, 1955. 147 pp.

535. Kirby, Michael S. "The History and Theory of Futurist Performances." *DAI* 32(1972):4160A (N.Y.U.).

536. Klemperer, Victor. *Moderne Französische Lyrik:Dekandenz, Symbolismus, Neuromantik. Studie und Kommertierte Texte*. Berlin: Deutscher Verlag der Wissenschaften, 1957. 515 pp.

537. Lafue, Pierre. "Le naturalisme corrigé par le symbolisme." *Hier et Demain* 10(1944):145-55.

538. Lalou, René. *Histoire de la littérature française contemporaine (1870 à nos jours)*. Paris: Crés, 1922.

539. Lanson, Gustave. "L'époque symboliste et l'avant-guerre," 1211-1337 in *Histoire de la littérature française*, Paul Tuffrau,ed. Paris: Hachette, 1938.

540. Lapauze, Henry. "M. Léon Cladel." *La Plume* 36(oct 1890):187-88.

541. Laurent, Emile. *La poésie décadente devant la science psychiatrique*. Paris: Alexandre Maloine, 1897. 122 pp.

542. Lawler, James R. "A Symbolist Dialogue." *EFL* 4(1967):80-105.

543. Le Cardonnel, Louis, and Charles Vellay. *La littérature contemporaine*. Paris: Mercure de France, 1905.

544. Lehmann, A.G. *The Symbolist Aesthetic in France*. Oxford: Blackwell, 1950. [New ed. 1968.] 328 pp.

545. Leite, Lígia C. Moraes. *Modernismo no Rio Grande do sul:Materiais para o seu estudo*. São Paulo: Inst. de Estudos Brasileiros, 1972. 358 pp.

546. Lemaître, Henri. *La poésie depuis Baudelaire*. Paris: Armand Colin, 1966. 372 pp.

547. Le Rouge, Gustave. *Verlainiens et décadents*. Paris: Seheur, 1928. 253 pp.

548. Lethève, Jacques. "Un mot témoin de l'époque *fin de siècle*:Esthète." *RHL* 64(1964):436-46.

549. *Les lettres françaises et la tradition hermétique. (Les Cahiers d'Hermès 1.)* Paris: Edition du Vieux Colombier, 1947.

550. Levin, Harry. "The Poetics of French Symbolism:Introductory Note." *RR* 46(1955):161-63.

551. Litvak de Pérez de la Dehesa, Lily. "Alomar and Marinetti:Catalan and Italian Futurism." *RLV* 38(1972): 585-603.

552. Losereit, Sigrid. *Die Suche nach dem verlorenen Eden in der Lyrik der französischen Symbolisten:Zur Tradition eines mythischen "thème"*. Heidelberg: U. of Heidelberg, 1969. [Diss.]

553. Macrí, Oreste. *Realtà del simbolo: Poeti e critici del novecento italiano*. Firenze: Vallecchi, 1968. 646 pp.

554. Maia, João. "Uma antologia da poesia modernista brasileira." *Brotéria* 97(1973):332-34. [Rev. art.]

555. Marjoux, Jean-Jacques. "At the Sources of Symbolism." *Criticism* 1(1959):279-97.

556. Marzot, Giulio. *Il decadentismo italiano*. Bologna: Capelli, 1971. 304 pp.

557. Mathews, Andrew J. *La Wallonie 1886-1892:The Symbolist Movement in Belgium*. New York: King's Crown Press, 1947. 115 pp.

558. Mauclair, Camille. "Souvenirs sur le mouvement symboliste en France." *Nouvelle Revue* (15 oct 1897):670-93; (1 nov 1897):79-100.

559. ———. "Les symbolistes et leurs musiciens." *RdP* 43,ii(1936): 285-301.

560. Mercier, Alain. *Les sources esotériques et occultes de la poésie symboliste 1870-1914*. Vol. 1:*Le symbolisme français*. Paris: Nizet, 1969. 281 pp.

561. Michaud, Guy. "Symbolique et symbolisme." *CAIEF* 6(1956):75-95.

562. Mockel, Albert. "Le cinquantenaire du symbolisme." *Revue franco-belge* 16(juin 1936):304-11.

563. Moises, Massaud. *O simbolismo (1883-1902)*. São Paulo: Cultrix, 1966. 293 pp.

564. Monférier, Jacques. "Symbolisme et anarchie." *RHL* 65(1965):233-38. [In *Revue Blanche* and *Entretiens politiques et littéraires* 1891-1895]

565. Mor, Antonio. "Il senso del mistero nel decadentismo francese." *Studium* 69(1973):187-200.

566. Morice, C. *La littérature de tout à l'heure*. Paris: Perrin, 1889.

567. Mourey, Gabriel. "Some Notes on Recent Poetry in France." *Fortnightly Review* 118(Nov 1897): 650-65.

568. Muricy, J.C. de Andrade. *Panorama do movimento simbolista brasileiro*. Revisão crit. e organização de bibliog. Aurelio Buarque de Hollanda Ferreira. 3 vols. Rio: Inst. Nacional do Livro, 1951-52.

569. Oblomievskij, D. *Francuzskij simvolism*. Moscow: Nauka, 1973. 301 pp.

570. Olinto, Antônio. "Poesia renascença vocabular e simbolismo." *JdL* 277,Cad. 2(1973):5.

571. Orliac, Antoine. "La cathédrale symboliste," in *Mallarmé tel qu'en lui-même*. Paris: Mercure de France, 1948. 241 pp.

572. Osmont, Anne. *Le mouvement symboliste:Mallarmé-Villiers de l'Isle-Adam-Verlaine-Arthur Rimbaud-Jules Laforgue-René Ghil-Moréas et l'école romane*. Paris: Maison du livre, 1917. 167 pp.

573. Oswaldo, Angelo. "Belo Horizonte:Uma semana de artistas modernos." *MGSL* 19 Feb(1972):12. [On Modernism in Brazil.]

574. Pacheco, Léon. "Una visión del modernismo." *CA* 190(1973):191-200.

575. Pachón Padilla, Eduardo. "El modernismo en Colombia." *BCB* 14, i(1973):33-46. [Bibliog. 44-46.]

576. Pautasso, Sergio. "Geografia dell'ermetismo." *PU* 25,lxxi(1972): 61-69.

577. ——. "Profilo della ermetica," 692-710 in *Critica e storia:Studi offerti a Mario Fubini*, II. Padova: Liviana, 1970.

578. Pellegrini, Carlo. "Il paesaggio interiore nei poeti simbolisti francesi," in *Studi in onore di Vittorio Lugli e Diego Valeri*. 2 vols. Venezia: Neri Pozza, 1961.

579. Pelletier, Abel. "Littérature de cénacle." *Revue Indépendante* 20(août 1891):145-66.

580. Peregrino, João, Junior, "Influencias portuguêses do simbolismo brazileiro." *JdL* 153(1962):3.

581. ——. "Modernismo no Brazil." *JdL* 277,Cad.2(1973):8.

582. Petrini, Enzo. "Posizione dell'ermetismo." *HumB* 3(1948):400-05.

583. Petrucciano, Mario. *La poetica dell'Ermetismo italiano*. Torino, 1965.

584. Picco, F. "Simbolismo francese e simbolismo italiano." *NA* (1 May 1926):82-91.

585. Pilon, Edmond. "Carnet des oeuvres et des hommes." *La Plume* 294(juillet 1901):562-64; 300(oct 1901):790-92; 305(janv 1902):55-59; 321(sept 1902):1066-71. [Verlaine, Retté, Laforgue, P. Adam.]

586. Placer, Xavier. "Balanço do modernismo brasileiro." *JdL* 258,Cad.2 (1972):1.

587. Poizat, Alfred. *Du classicisme au symbolisme*. Paris: Nouvelle revue critique, 1914.

588. ——. *Le symbolisme de Baudelaire à Claudel*. Paris: Renaissance du livre, 1919. 198 pp.

589. Pontiero, Giovanni. "O modernismo brasileiro e a sua crítica," 61-66 in Kurt L. Levy, and Keith Ellis, eds. *El ensayo y la crítica literaria en Iberoamérica.| Memoria del XIV Congreso Internacional de Literatura Iberoamericana. Univ. de Toronto, 24-28 de agosto de 1969. Toronto: U. of Toronto P., 1970. 282 pp.

590. Pozzi, Gianni. *La poesia italiana del Novecento:Da Gozzano agli ermetici*. Torino: Einaudi, 1967. 405 pp.

591. Queiroz, Maria J. de. "O Simbolismo e José Severiano de Resende." *MGSL* 23 Dec(1972):12-14.

592. Ragusa, Olga M. "French Symbolism in Italy." *RR* 46(1955):231-35. [Rev. art.]

593. ——. *Mallarmé in Italy:Literary Influence and Critical Response*. New York: S.F. Vanni, 1957. 238 pp.

594. Raitt, A.W. "French Studies: The 19th Century (Post-romantic)." *YWMLS* 27(1965):117-31.

595. Ramos, Pericles Eugenio de Silva. *Poesia simbolista*. São Paulo: Melhoramentos, 1965. 405 pp.

596. Raynaud, Ernest. "Le symbolisme et les cafés littéraires." *MdF* 268 (1 juin 1936):282-93.

597. Retté, Adolphe. "Arabesques:La jeune littérature." *La Plume* 210(janv 1898):33-37.

598. ———. *Le symbolisme:Anecdotes et souvenirs*. Paris: Messein, 1903. 276 pp.

599. Reverseau, J.P. *Poètes parnassiens, peintres, symbolistes. L'inspiration et les thèmes*. Paris: Ecole du Louvre, 1971. [Diss.]

600. Rewald, John. "Symbolists and Anarchists from Mallarmé to Redon, 1886-1890," 147-84 in *Post-Impressionism:From Van Gogh to Gauguin*. N.Y.: Museum of Modern Art, 1956.

601. Ribeiro, João. *Crítica*. Vol. II. Rio: Academia Brasileira de Letras, 1957.

602. Richard, Noel. *A l'aube du symbolisme:Hydropathes, fumistes et décadents*. Paris: Nizet, 1961. 334 pp.

603. ———. "Du parnasse au symbolisme." *Bull. de l'Univ. de Toulouse* (avril-juin 1965):617-21.

604. Rimanelli, Giose. "Still on Italian Hermeticism." *Italica* 43(1966):285-99.

605. Rod, Edouard. "Present Tendencies of French Literature." *ContempR* 93(1908):406-22. [Repr. in *Living Age* 257(30 May 1908):515-28.]

606. Rodrigues, Urbano Tavares. "Os poetas pre-simbolistas portuguêses: Seu estado de espírito e suas unidades estéticas." *JLA* 4(7 août 1964):2-8.

607. Rolland de Renéville, André. *Univers de la parole*. Paris: Gallimard, 1944. 207 pp.

608. Romani, Bruno. "Futurisme I à Barcelone." *XXe Siècle* 30,supp. (1968):131-32.

609. Romano, Salvatore. *Poetica dell' ermetismo*. Firenze: Biblioteca del Leonardo, 1942. 185 pp.

610. Rubio, D. *Symbolism and Classicism in Modern Literature:Introduction to the Study of Symbolism in Spanish and Spanish American Literature*. Philadelphia: n.p., 1923. 56 pp.

611. Rukalski, Z. "Fin-de-siècle in France and Russia." *ESL* 12(1967): 124-27.

612. Russi, Antonio. *Gli anni della antialienazione:Dall'Ermetismo al Neo-realismo*. Milano: Mursia, 1967. 154 pp.

613. Rutten, M. "Le symbolisme français et le renouveau de la poésie belge d'expression néerlandaise." *EG* 17(1962):328-43.

614. Sáinz y Rodríguez, Pedro. *Evolución de las ideas sobre la decadencia española y otros estudios de crítica literaria*. Madrid: Rialp, 1962. 578 pp.

615. Saix, Guillot de. "Au temps du symbolisme." *NL* (18 sept 1952): 1-2.

616. Santilli, Tommaso. *L'ermetismo (G. Ungaretti, E. Montale, S. Quasimodo:Spunti critice)*. Pescara: Trebi, 1966. 101 pp.

617. Saraiva, Arnaldo. "Para a história do modernismo brasileiro:A 'divisão' dos Andrades (Mário, Oswald e Carlos Drummond)." *Colóquio* 6(1972): 24-29.

618. Schinz, Albert. "Symbolism in France." *PMLA* 18(1903):273-307.

619. Schmidt, Albert-Marie. *La littérature symboliste (1870-1900)*. Paris: Presses univs. de France, 1966. 128 pp.

620. Schneider, Marcel. "Fantastique symboliste et décadent (1884-1913)," 275-76 in *La littérature fantastique en France*. Paris: Arthème Fayard, 1964.

621. Schonthal, Aviva H. "The Symbolist Poetics in the *Mercure de France* (1890-1905)." *DA* 17(1957):1768-69 (Columbia).

622. Schulman, Ivan A. "Reflexiones en torno a la definición del Modernismo." *CA* 147(1966):211-40.

623. Secchi, Giovanni. "L'involuzione dei poeti ermetici." *NC* 15(1959): 21-34.

624. Siebenmann, Gustav. "Reinterpretación del modernismo." *Symposium Unamuno* 65(1966):497-511.

625. Silveira, Tasso da. "A poesia simbolista em Portugal." *Ocidente* 26 (1945):150-58.

626. Silvo, Castro R. "¿Es posible definir el modernismo?" *CA* 24(1965): 172-79.

627. Simões, João G. *História da poesia portuguesa do sécolo XX*. Lisboa: Empresa Nacional de Publicidade, 1959. 844 pp.

628. ———. "No cinquentenário do 'Modernismo' brasileiro: Semana da Arte Moderna de São Paulo." *DNAL* 925(26 oct 1972):18,20.

629. Simón Díaz, José. "La literatura francesa en veinticuatro diarios madrileños de 1830-1900 (Continuación)." *RL* 34(for 1968):113-41.

630. Smith, James M. "Concepts of Decadence in Nineteenth Century French Literature." *SP* 50(1953): 640-51.

631. ———. "The Sphinx, the Chimera and the Pursuit of Novelty in Post-Romantic French Literature." *Symposium* 8(1954):289-308.

632. Spitzer, Leo. "Le innovazione sintattiche del simbolismo francese," 7-81 in *Proust e altri saggi*. Torino: Einaudi, 1959.

633. Stark, Bernice S. "The Presence and Significance of the Indian in Modernism." *DAI* 31(1954):6634A (Pittsburgh).

634. Starkie, Enid. "L'esthétique des symbolistes." *CAIEF* 6(1954):131-38.

635. Steiner, Herbert. "A note on 'Symbolism'." *YFS* 9(1952):36-39.

636. Symons, Arthur. "The Decadent Movement in Literature." *Harper's Magazine* 137(Nov 1893):858-67.

637. Teles, Gilberto Mendonça. *Vanguarda européia e modernismo brasileiro*. Manifestos, prefácios e conferências vanguardistas de 1857 até hoje. Petrópolis: Vozes, 1972.

638. Thompson, Vance. "The Technique of the Symbolists." *M'lle New York* 1(Nov 1895).

639. Thorel, Jean. "Les romantiques allemands et les Symbolistes français." *Entretiens politiques et littéraires* 18(sept 1891):95-109.

640. Tosi, Guy. "Aperçus sur les influences littéraires françaises en Italie dans le dernier tiers du XIXe siècle. *RLMC* 19(1966):165-70.

641. Twart, Koenraad W. *The Sense of Decadence in Nineteenth-Century France*. The Hague: Nijhoff, 1965.

642. Vaida, Mircea. "*Carnetul gri* al lui Ion Vinea." *Steaua* 23,vii(1972):12-14; 23,viii(1972):14-15; 23,ix(1972): 16-17; 23,x(1972):12-13. [Incl. orig. Fr., and Rom. tr. by Rodica Baconsky.]

643. Valeri, Diego. *Il simbolsimo francese da Nerval a de Regnier*. Padova: Ed. Liviana, 1954. 151 pp.

644. Van Nuffel, Robert O. "Polémiques belges autour du Symbolisme." *CLS* 4(1967):91-102.

645. Vanier, Léon,ed. *Les premières armes du symbolisme*. Paris: Vanier, 1889. 50 pp. [Arts. by P. Bourde, J. Moréas and A. France.]

646. Vertpré. "Pour M. Gaston Des-Champs." *La Plume* 312(avril 1902): 465-66.

647. Viazzi, Glauco, and Vanni Scheiwiller,eds. *Poeti simbolisti e libertà in Italia*. 2 vols. Milano: All'insegna del Pesce d'Oro, 1971.

648. Visan, T. de. "Le Romantisme allemand et le Symbolisme français." *MdF* 88(1910):577-91.

649. Vossler, K. "Poesía simbólica y neosimbolista." *Rev. Cubana* 15 (1941):5-45.

650. Wais, Kurt. *Französische Merksteine von Racine bis Saint-John Perse*. Berlin: de Gruyter, 1958. 362 pp. [Essays on Mallarmé, Rimbuad, Saint-John Perse, *inter alios*.]

651. Walzer, Pierre. *La révolution des sept*. Neuchâtel: La Baconnière, 1970. [Corbière, Cros, Laforgue, Lautréamont, Mallarmé, Nouveau,Rimbaud.]

652. Wautier, André. "La tradition symboliste chez les poètes français de Wallonie." *Culture française* 11, v(1962):10-43.

653. Young, Howard T. *The Victorious Expression:A Study of Four Contemporary Spanish Poets:Unamuno, Machado, Jiménez, Lorca*. Madison: U. of Wis. P., 1964. 223 pp.

654. Zamfir, Mihai. "Simbolismul ornamental al lui Macedonski:Analiza sonetului 'Avatar'." *LşL* 28,i(1972): 108-13.

655, Zerbe, L.R. "The Symbolists." *Outlook* 51(23 Feb 1895):307-08.

656. Zérèga-Fombona, A. "Le symbolisme français et la poésie espagnole moderne." *MdF* 135(1919):193-224.

See also 18, 20, 82, 101, 191, 241, 278, 283, 298, 313, 319, 322, 325, 326, 327, 331, 340, 341, 343, 346, 347, 351, 355, 358, 369, 660a, 662, 663, 677, 696, 700, 706, 748, 753a, 805, 857, 932, 939, 953, 986, 1003, 1014, 1016, 1018, 1029, 1030, 1040, 1055, 1073, 1086, 1098, 1115, 1143, 1225, 1320, 1417, 1473, 1490, 1543, 1544, 1588, 1593, 1684, 1685, 1704, 1718, 1720, 1726, 1729, 1730, 1734, 1748, 1775, 1776, 1782, 1811, 1812, 1817, 1821, 1905, 1925, 2017, 2047, 2386, 2395, 2396, 2404, 2446, 2471, 2472, 2498, 2553, 2565, 2776, 2893, 2894, 3033, 3041, 3044, 3057, 3058, 3099, 3155.

Slavic

657. Asmus, V. "Filosofia i estetika russkogo simvolizma." *Literaturnoe Nasledstvo* 27-28(1937):1-53.

658. Blok, Aleksandr. "O svremennom sostojanii russkovo simvolizma." *Apollon* mai-juin (1910):21-30.

659. Briusov, V., and A.L. Miropol'ski. *Russkie simvolisty*. 3 vols. Moscow: n.p., 1894/5.

660. Čiževskij, Dmitrij. "O poèzii russko o futurizma." *NovŽ* 73(1963): 132-69.

660a. De Michelis, Cesare G. *Il futurismo italiano in Russia 1909-1929*. Bari: Di Donato, 1973. 282 pp.

661. Donchin, Georgette. "French Influence on Russian Symbolist Versification." *SEER* 33(1954):161-87.

662. ———. *The Influence of French Symbolism on Russian Poetry*. (SPR, 19) The Hague: Mouton, 1958.

663. ———. "A Russian Symbolist Journal and its Links with France." *RLC* 30(1956):405-19.

664. Eimermacher, Karl, ed. *Literaturnye manifesty:Ot simvolizma k Oktyabryu*. Vol. I (Slavische Propyläen 64.) München: Fink, 1969. 301 pp. [Repr. of work by N.L. Brodsky. Orig. pub. Moscow, 1929.]

665. Gray, Camilla. *The Great Experiment in Russian Art*. London: Thames and Hudson, 1962. 326 pp.

666. Grigor'yan, K. "Berlen i russkij simbolizm." *Russkaya literatura* 14,i(1971):111-20.

667. Gumilev, Nikolai. "Nasledie simvolizma i akmeizm." *Apollon* (Jan 1913):42-45.

668. Hahl-Koch, J. *Marianne Werefkin und der russische Symbolismus: Studien zur Ästhetik und Kunsttheorie*. München: Sagner, 1967. 126 pp.

669. Holthusen, Johannes. *Studien zur Ästhetik und Poetik des russischen Symbolismus*. Göttingen: Vandenhoeck and Ruprecht, 1957. 159 pp.

670. Holthusen, Johannes, and Dmitrij Tschiževskij,eds. *Versdichtung der russichen Symbolisten*. (Heidelberger

slavische Texte, H.5-6.) Wiesbaden: Harrassowitz, 1959.

671. Jechová, Hana. "Le problème des symboles chez les poètes romantiques polonais." *Langue et littérature* 6(1962):377-79.

672. Jensen, Kjeld B. "Marinetti in Russia 1910, 1912, 1913, 1914?" *SSl* 15(1969):21-26. [Russ. futurism.]

673. Jeske-Choinski, Teodor. *Dekadentyzm:Wydanie nowe poprawione i uzupelnione*. Warszawa: Gebethner i Wolff, 1905. 204 pp.

674. Karlinsky, S. "Russian symbolism." *ConL* 13, iv(1972):129-31. [Rev. art.]

675. Kluge, Rolf-Dieter. "Zur Deutung der Musik in der Dichtungstheorie einiger russischer Romantiker und Symbolisten." *Musikforschung* 22,i (Jan-Mar 1969):13-22.

676. Kobylinskij, L. *Russkie Simvolisty: Konstantin Balmont, Valerij Brjusov, Andrej Belyi*. Moscow, 1910.

677. Košutitch, V. "Le Parnasse et le Symbolisme chez les Serbes." *Annales de la Faculté de Philologie* (Belgrade) 2(1962):295.

678. Lam, Andrzej. *Polska awangarda poetycka:Programy lat 1917-1923.* 2 vols. Kraków: Wydawn. Literackie, 1969.

679. Lossky, N.O. "Philosophical Ideas of Poet-Symbolists," 335-45 in *History of Russian Philosophy*. New York: 1951.

680. Mašbic-Nerov, I. *Russkij simvolizmi put' A. Bloka*. Kujbysev: Knižnoe izd-vo, 1969.

681. Maslenikov, Oleg. "Russian Symbolists:The Mirror Theme and Allied Motifs." *RusR* 16(1957):42-52.

682. Matlaw, R.E. "The Manifesto of Russian Symbolism." *SEEJ* 1(1957): 171-91.

683. Mickiewicz, D. "*Apollo* and Modernist Poetics." *RLT* 1(1971): 226-61.

684. Mirvaldová-Janatová, Hana. "Podoby symbolického způsobu označeni v Březinove a Vančurove díle." *CL* 18(1970):30-59. [Sum. in Fr.]

685. Mohrenschildt, D.S. von. "The Russian Symbolist Movement." *PMLA* 53(1938):1193-1209.

686. Nag, Martin. "Den russiske symbolisme:Een modell." *Samtiden* 80 (1971):54-68.

687. Nilsson, Nils Ake. "Russian Imagism and the Noun." *Langue et littérature* [6] (1962):341-42.

688. Podraza-Kwaitkowska, Maria, "U źródel polskiego modernizmu." *RuchL* 4,ii(1963):66-74.

689. Poggioli, Renato. "Simbolismo russo e occidentale." *LM* 11(1961): 586-602.

690. Pollack, Seweryn. "Niektóre problemy symbolizmu rosyjakiego a wiersze rosyjskie Leśmiana." *Tw* 18,xii(1963:69-83.

691. Rose, William J. "The Poets of Young Poland 1890-1903." *Slavonic Yearbook* American Series 1(1941): 185-99.

692. Slonim, Marc. "After the Symbolists," 211-33 in *Chekhov to the Revolution Russian Literature, 1900-1917*. New York: Oxford Press, 1962.

693. ———. "Blok and the Symbolists," 184-210 in *Chekhov to the Revolution. Russian Literature, 1900-1917*. New York: Oxford Press, 1962.

694. Stepun, Fiodor Avgustovich. *Mystische Weltschau:Fünf Gestalten des russischen Symbolismus*. München: Hanser, 1964. 442 pp.

695. Strakhovsky, Leonid I. "The Silver Age of Russian Poetry:Symbolism and Acmeism." *CSP* 4(1959):61-87.

696. Strémoonkhoff, D. "Echos du symbolisme français dans le symbolisme russe." *RSH* 78(1955): 297-319.

698. Suško, Mario. "Simbolična organizacja Segedinova *Svetog vraga.*" *Rep* 26(1970):400-02.

699. Szymański, Wiesław P. "Neosymbolizm–Próba bilansu." *PHum* 15iii (1971):53-81. [On Pol. avant-garde poetry since 1930.]

700. Theile, Wolfgang. "Die Beziehungen René Ghils zu Valerij Brjusov und der Zeitschrift *Vesy*:Ein Beitrag zum Verständnis des französischen Symbolismus in Russland." *Arcadia* 1(1966):174-84.

701. Vəlčev, Veličko. "Bəlgarskite simbolisti i narodnoto tvorčestvo," 410-21 in Pantelej Zarev, Georgi Dimov, and Ilija Konev,eds. *Izsledvanija v čest na akademik Mixail Arnaudov.* Sofija: Bəlgarska akademija na naukite, 1970. 541 pp.

702. Valentinov, Nikolay. *Two Years with the Symbolists.* Gleb Struve,ed. Stanford: Stanford U.P., 1969. 241 pp.

703. Wenguerow, Zinaïde. "Lettres russes:Le symbolisme en France et en Russie &c." *MdF* 24(dec 1897): 955-62.

704. West, James. *Russian Symbolism:A Study of Vyacheslav Ivanov and the Russian Symbolist Aesthetic.* London: Methuen, 1970.

705. Zirmunskij, Viktor M. "Preodolevshie simvolizm." *Russkaia Mysl* 12 (1916):25-56. [Repr. with addenda in *Voprosy Teorii Literatury.* The Hague, 1962.]

See also 101, 436, 611, 812, 1137, 1339, 1341, 1739, 1751, 1881, 2091, 2097, 2457, 2614, 2735, 2928, 2951, 3085.

Other

706. Atal, G. "Turkish and French Symbolism:Ahmet Hashim." *DA* 23 (1962-63):4351-52(Ind.).

707. Barzel, Hillel. "Nussaho Ha-simloni shel A.B. Yehoshua (Iyun ba-sippurim 'Tardemat Hayom', 'Ha-mifkad Ha-aharon') [The Symbolism of A.B. Yehoshua]." *Gazit* (Israel) 27 (Dec 1970-Mar 1971):10-26.

708. Karátson, André. *Le symbolisme en Hongrie:L'influence des poétiques françaises sur la poésie hongroise dans le premier quart du XXe siècle.* Paris: Presses Univs. de France, 1970. 499 pp.

709. Matthews, W.K. "The Background and Poetry of Gustav Suits:A Study in Estonian Symbolism." *ASEER* 9,ii(1950):116-27.

710. Nagy, Péter. "La révolution littéraire en Hongrie au début du siècle." *ALitASH* 12(1970):365-74.

711. Noda, Misashi. "The Concepts of Symbolism in Traditional Japanese Literary Criticism and the Poetics of Emerson." *KAL* 12(1970):45-53. [In Jap.]

712. Panayotopoulos, J.M. "Le symbolisme et les poètes lyriques néogrecs." *Hellénisme contemporain* (mars 1954):99-111.

713. Rantavaara, Irma. "From Realism Towards Symbolism:National and International Elements in Finnish Literature in the 1880's and 1890's," 311-16 in Nikola Banašević,ed. *Actes du Ve Congrès de l'Association Internationale de Littérature Comparée, Belgrade 1967.* Belgrade:U. of Belgrade:Amsterdam:Swets & Zeitlinger, 1969.

714. Stergiopoulos, Kostas. *Apo ton Symbolismo sti nea Poisisi.* Athin: Ekdoseis Vakon, 1967. [Dimakis, Geralis, Themelis, Varvitsiltis.]

715. Szabolcsi, Miklos. "Jozsef Attila és a Francia irodalom," 421-34 in *Eszmei és irodalmi talàlkozàsok: Tanulmanyck a magyar-Francia irodalmi kapcsolatok történététébol.* Budapest: Akadèmiai K., 1970.

716. Won, Yo. "The Symbolists' Influence on Japanese Poetry." *CLS* 8(1971):254-65.
717. Zolnai, Béla. "Hongrie:La vie littéraire." *Revue de Genève* 5(1922): 240-52.

See also 787, 890, 2426, 2593, 2615, 2617, 2638, 3169.

III Forms and Genres

Art

718. Abbatte, F. *L'ottocento in Europa, simbolismo e impressionismo*. Milan, 1966.

719. Alvard, J. "Mauve Europe:Turn of the Century Show in Ostend." *Art News* 66(Oct 67):61.

720. Amaya, Mario. *Art nouveau*. London: Studio Vista, 1966. 168 pp.

721. ———. "Flesh and Filigree Exhibition at Toronto Museum." *Art News* 68(Dec 1969):26-27,59-60.

722. ———. "Sacred and Profane in Symbolist Art." *Artscanada* 26(Oct 1969):45-46.

723. Anon. "Three Inquiries into the Effects of Symbolism." *Art Journal* 23(Winter 1963-64):96-116.

724. Armstrong-Wallis. The "The Symbolist Painter of 1890." *Marsyas* 1(1941):117-52.

725. Ashton, Dore. "Symbolist Legacy." *Arts and Architecture* 81(Sept 1964):10.

726. Aurier, G.–A. "Le symbolisme en peinture." *MdF* 2(mars 1891): 155-65.

727. Barilli, Renato. *Il gruppo dei Nabi in l'arte moderna*. Milan, 1967.

728. ———. *Il simbolismo nella pittura francese dell'Ottocento*. Milano: Fabbri, 1967. 100 pp.

729. Battisti, Eugenio. "Simbolo ed arte figurativa." *RdE* 7(1962):185-97.

730. Bénédite, Léonce. *Notre art, nos maîtres*. Vol. I:*Puvis de Chavannes, Gustave Moreau et Burne Jones, G.F.*

Watts. Vol. II:*J.-F. Millet—G. Courbet, Paul Huet, les grands paysagistes au Louvre, Harpignies.* Paris: Flammarion, 1922, 1923. 236 + 238 pp.

731. ———. *La peinture au XIXe siècle d'après les chefs-d'oeuvre des maîtres et les meilleurs tableaux des principaux artistes.* Paris: Flammarion, n.d. 372 pp.

731a. Benet, Rafael. *Simbolismo.* Con la colaboración de Jorge Benet Aurell. Barcelona: Omega, 1953. 367 pp.

732. Berger, Klaus. *Odilon Redon. Phantasie und Farbe.* Cologne: DuMont Schaubert, 1964. 244 pp.

733. Boissière, Albert. "Transpositions d'art." *La Plume* 263(avril 1900): 237-39.

734. Boutet, Henri. "La route de l'idéal." *La Plume* 188(fév 1897): 166.

735. Bouyer, Raymond. "J. Valadon aux Salons Annuels." *La Plume* 188 (fév 1897):105-06.

736. Buysse, Cyriel. "Frantz-Marie Melchers." *La Plume* 331(fév 1903):192-96.

737. Chassé, Charles. *Les nabis et leur temps.* Lausanne: La Bibliothèque des arts, 1960. 186 pp. [Also in Eng. as *The Nabis and Their Period.* London: Lund Humphries, 1969. 136 pp.]

738. Christophe, Jules. "Soûlez-nous de bleu!" *La Plume* 188(fév 1897): 107-08.

739. Coppée, François. "Préambule." *La Plume* 188(fév 1897):97-88.

740. Courthion, Pierre. "Les grandes étapes de l'art contemporain 1907-1917." *XXe Siècle* 26(1966): 75-87.

741. Cousturier, Edmond. "Notes d'art:Torisième exposition de peintres impressionistes et symbolistes(Le Barc de Bouteville)." *Entretiens politiques et littéraires* 35(janv 1893):77-81.

742. Davray, Henry D. "Valadon tel qu'il me fut." *La Plume* 188(fév 1897):118.

743. Denis, Maurice. "Chronique de peinture." *L'Ermitage* 35(déc 1906):321-26.

744. ———. "L'époque du symbolisme." *Gaz. des Beaux-Arts* 11(mar 1934): 165-79.

745. ———. "La peinture." *L'Ermitage* 32(mai 1905):310-20.

746. ———. *Theories, 1890-1910:Du Symbolisme et de Gauguin vers un nouvel ordre classique.* Paris: Bibliothèque de l'Occident, 1912. 270 pp. [Rééd. Paris: Rouart et Watelin, 1913. Réimpr. 1920.]

747. Devillers, Hippolyte. "Ses natures mortes." *La Plume* 188(fév 1897): 109-10.

748. Dimier, Louis. *Histoire de la peinture française au XIXe siècle (1793-1903).* Paris: Delagrave, 1914. 319 pp.

749. Dorfles, Gillo. "Arte concettuale." *Ulisse* 76(1973):113-19.

750. Dragone, Angelo. "Simbolismo a Torino." *Arti* 6(1969):2-9.

751. Eon, Henry. "Expositions:La Rose+Croix." *La Plume* 190(mars 1897):190.

752. Fagus. "Petites expositions." *La Plume* 319(août 1902):938-39.

753. Fezzi, Elda. "Cubismo e futurismo." *Ulisse* 76(1973):38-42.

753a. Finke, Ulrich,ed. *French 19th Century Painting and Literature.* Dedicated to the memory of Dorothy Lawrence Pilkington. With special reference to the relevance of literary subject-matter to French painting. New York: Harper & Row, 1972. 390 pp. [Illus. Essays on Baudelaire, Mallarmé, Redon, *inter alios*, by var. hands.]

754. Focillon, Henri. *La peinture XIXe et XXe siècles:Du réalisme à nos jours.* Paris: Renouard, 1928. 524 pp.

755. Fontainas, André, et al.,eds. *Histoire générale de l'art francais de la Révolution à nos jours.* 3 vols. Paris: Librairie de France, 1922.

756. Forster-Hahn, Françoise, "German Painting:The Forgotten Century." *Art News* 69(Nov 1970):50-55,86-87.

757. *French Symbolist Painters (Moreau, Puvis de Chavannes, and Their Followers).* Exhibition at the Hayward Gallery, London, 7 June– 23 July 1972. London: Arts Council of Great Britain, 1972. 170 pp.

758. Fuller, F. "Symbolists 1860-1925, Piccadilly Gallery, London Exhibit." *Connoisseur* 175(Sept 1970):73.

759. Gallotti, Minola de. "Lo sagrado y lo profano en el simbolismo." *Goya* 91(July 1969):60-61.

760. Gaultier, Jules de. "Le sentiment de la nature et son apparition tardive." *L'Ermitage* 33(oct 1905): 195-201.

761. Germain, Alphonse. "L'art et l'état." *Entretiens politiques et littéraires* 8(nov 1890):274-76.

762. ———. "L'idéal au salon de la Rose-Croix." *L'Ermitage* 1(1892): 210-16.

763. ———. "Théorie du Symbolisme des teintes." *La Plume* 50(mai 1891):171-72.

764. Gevaert, H. Fiérens. "Chronique des arts." *L'Ermitage* 14(avril 1897):271-75.

765. Grinke, Paul. "The Salons de la Rose/Croix." *Art & Artists* 2(May 1968):12-15.

766. Grojnowski, Daniel. "Le mystère Gustave Moreau." *Critique* (1963): 225-38.

767. Guerrand, Roger H. *L'art nouveau en Europe.* Paris:Plon,1965. 243 pp.

768. Henry, Geritt. "Effete Corps of Imprudent Snobs:Nineteenth Century Symbolist Painters." *Art News* 69 (Dec 1970):34-37.

769. ———. "Spencer A. Samuels & Co. Gallery, New York Exhibit." *Art Interior* 15(Jan 1971):37.

770. Hense, Anton. "Erste Bestandsaufnahme des internationalen Symbolismus:Ausstellung in Turin." *Kunstwerk* 22(Aug 1969):41-42.

771. Hoffmann, E. "Some Sources for Munch's Symbolism." *Apollo* (Feb 1965):87-93.

773. Hofstätter, Hans H. *Geschichte der europäischen Jugendstilmalerei.* Köln: Verlag M. DuMont Schauberg, 1963. 272 pp.

774. ———. *Symbolismus und die Kunst der Jahrhundertwende.* Köln: Du Mont Schauberg, 1965. 274 pp.

775. Humbert, Agnès. *Les Nabis et leur époque, 1880-1900.* Geneva: Pierre Cailler, 1954. 151 pp.

776. Huysmans, J.-K. *"L'art moderne.* Paris: G. Charpentier, 1883. 277 pp.

777. Jullian, Philippe. "Nouveau entre le mythe et l'histoire." *RdP* 76(1969): 65-71.

778. ———. *Esthètes et magiciens:L'art fin de siècle.* Paris: Perrin, 1966. [Eng. ed. *Dreamers of Decadence: Symbolist Painters of the 1890's.* Tr. Robert Baldick. New York: Praeger, 1971. 272 pp.]

779. ———. "Nostalgies fin de siècle." *Gaz. des Beaux Arts* 74(1969):161-74.

780. Kahn, Gustave. "L'art à l'exposition." *La Plume* 270(juillet 1900): 444-48; 273(sept 1900):553-59.

781. Kandinsky, Wassily. *Concerning the Spiritual in Art.* New York: Wittenborn, 1955. 93 pp.

782. Kerbrat, Georges. "Jean Veber." *La Plume* 298(sept 1901):706-13.

783. Klingsor, Tristan. "L'évolution de l'art français depuis vingt ans." *Revue de Genève* 5(1922):230-40.

784. Kotzin, Michael. "Pre-Raphaelitism, Ruskinism and French Symbolism."*Art Journal* 25(1965-66):347-50.

785. Lacaze-Duthiers, Gérard de. "La peinture comtemporaine en Autriche." *La Plume* 276(oct 1900):621-24.

786. Lamberti, M. Mimita. "Lionello Venturi sulla via dell'impressionismo." *ASNSP* N.S. 1(1971):257-77.

787. Lecomte, Georges. "Japon." *Entretiens politiques et littéraires* 3(juin 1890):90-94.

788. Legrand, Francine-Claire. "Il simbolismo en Belgio." *Arte Illustrata* (juillet-sept 1969):55-61.

789. ———. *Le symbolisme en Belgique.* Bruxelles: Laconti, 1971. 251 pp.

790. Lethève, Jacques. *Impressionistes et symbolistes devant la presse.* Paris: Colin, 1959. 302 pp.

791. ———. "Un personnage typique de la fin du XIXe siècle:L'esthète." *Gaz. des Beaux Arts* 65(1965): 181-91.

792. Lichtblau, Charlotte. "Symbolists, Spencer A. Samuels Gallery, New York." *Arts* 45(Dec 1970):60.

793. Loevgren, Sven. *The Genesis of Modernism, Seurat, Gauguin, Van Gogh, and French Symbolism in the 1880's.* Bloomington, Indiana: Indiana U.P., 1971. 241 pp.

794. "Symbolismens genombrott i det franska 1880-talsmaleriet." *Konsthist Tidskr* 26(1957):67-69.

795. Lucie-Smith, Edward. *Symbolist Art.* New York:Praeger,1972. 216pp.

796. Maillard, Léon. "Le dernier gentilhomme." *La Plume* 188(fév 18 97):103-04.

797. Marchiori, Giuseppe. "Espressionismo, expressionisti." *Ulisse* 76 (1973):63-69.

798. ———. "Le rendezvous symboliste." *XXe Siècle* 33(dec 1969):61-68. [Redon, Gauguin, M. Denis, Kandinsky *inter alios*.]

799. *Les mardis, Stéphane Mallarmé and the Artists of His Circle.* Lawrence: U. of Kan. Museum of Art, 1966.

800. Masini, Lara V. "Simbolismo, Nabis, art nouveau." *Ulisse* 76 (1973):27-34.

801. Mauclair, Camille. "Les deux mystères en art." *La Plume* 273(sept 1900):547-48.

802. Messina, Maria G. "L'opera teorica di Adolf Loos."*ASNSP* N.S. 3(1973): 231-300.

803. Millerio, André. *Odilon Redon.* Paris: Secrétariat, 1961. 166 pp.

804. Milner, John. *Symbolists and Decadents.* London: Dutton Press, 1971.

805. Mourey, Gabriel. "J.-L. Forain." *Entretiens politiques et littéraires* 36 (fév 1893):129-34.

806. Muller, Joseph-Emile. "L'expressionisme européen." *XXe Siècle* 35, supp.(1970):161-63.

807. Museus, E. "La Rose+Croix." *La Plume* 62(nov 1891):409-10.

808. Myers, B. "Development of Modern Art:Symbolism." *American Artist* 15 (Nov 1951):65.

809. "Nabis and Their Circle." *Minneapolis Inst. Bull.* 51(Dec 1962):128-34.

810. Nakov, Andrée B. "Balla:La reconstruction futuriste de la peinture." *XXe Siècle* 39,supp.(1972):117-19.

811. Natanson, Thadée. "Notes sur l'art des salons." *Revue Blanche* 16 (1898):147-50,216-20.

812. Orlandini, Marisa V. "Arte d'avanguardia in Russia." *Ulisse* 76(1973): 50-62.

813. Péladan, Joséphin. *L'Art idéalistique et mystique.* Paris, 1894. 280 pp.

815. Pilon, Edmond. "Septième exposition des peintres impressionistes et symbolistes." *La Plume* 128(août 1894):349.

816. Pincus-Witten, Robert. "Iconography of Symbolist Painting." *Artforum* 8(Jan 1970):56-62.

817. ———. "Samuels Gallery New. York." *Artforum* 9(Jan 1971):76.

818. Rambosson, Yvanhoé. "Au Salon

des Cent." *La Plume* 213(mars 1898):157-59.

819. ——. "Deuxième Exposition des peintres impressionistes et symbolistes." *La Plume* 79(août 1892):351-52.

820. ——. "Exposition permanente des peintres impressionistes et symbolistes." *La Plume* 71(avril 1892): 165.

821. ——. "Jules Valadon." *La Plume* 188(fév 1897):100-03; 272(août 1900):523-24.

822. ——. "La promenade de Janus: Causeries d'art." *La Plume* 233(janv 1899):29-30; 235(fév 1899):94-95; 243(juin 1899):282-83. [Gauguin, Puvis de Chavannes.]

823. ——. "Société Nationale des Beaux-Arts:La peinture." *La Plume* 211(juillet 1898):458-60.

824. Raynal, Maurice. *Histoire de la peinture moderne de Baudelaire à Bonnard. Naissance d'une vision nouvelle:L'école de Honfleur, l'impressionisme, le néoimpressionisme, le symbolisme, le post-impressionisme.* 3 vols. Geneva: Skira, 1949.

825. Raynaud, Ernest. " 'Ode Forestière':Au peintre Jules Valadon sur son tableau:'Le Prix de la Danse'." *La Plume* 220(juin 1898):419.

826. Rebell, Hugues. L'érotisme et le mysticisme en art." *L'Ermitage* 1(1894):253-62.

827. Redonnel, Paul. "Jules Valadon: Par Yvanhoé Rambosson." *La Plume* 194(mai 1897):320-21.

828. Retté, Adolphe. "Des artistes indépendants." *L'Ermitage* 2(1891):293-301.

829. Rewald, John. *Post-Impressionism.* New York: Museum of Modern Art, 1948. 151 pp.

830. Rheims, Maurice. *The Age of Art Nouveau.* Tr. Patrick Evans. London: Thames & Hudson, 1966. 450 pp.

831. Richardson, Edgar P. *The Way of Western Art 1776-1914.* Cambridge, Mass.: Harvard U.P., 1939. 204 pp.

832. Riotor, Léon. "Pendant un service funèbre." *La Plume* 188(fév 1897): 107.

833. Roberts, Keith. "Symbolists 1860-1925 at the Picadilly Gallery." *Burlington Magazine* 112(July 1970): 483.

834. Roditi, Edouard. *Dialogues on Art.* New York: Horizon Press, 1960-61. 198 pp.

835. Rookmaaker, H.R. *Synthetist Art Theories: Genesis and Nature of the Ideas on Art of Gauguin and His Circle.* Amsterdam: Swets & Zeitlinger, 1959. 362 pp.

836. Rouge, Gustave Le. "L'Homme." *La Plume* 188(fév 1897):117-18.

837. Rougé, Jean de. "Valadon chez lui." *La Plume* 188(fév 1897):115-16.

838. Sandblad, Nils Gosta. "Sven Sandstrom:*Le monde imaginaire d'Odilon Redon.*" *Konsthist Tidskr* 24(1957): 67-69. [Rev. art.]

839. Saunier, Charles. "Exposition des peintres impressionistes et symbolistes." *La Plume* 66(janv 1892):52.

840. ——. "Jules Valadon au Luxembourg." *La Plume* 188(fév 1897): 106.

841. Schelling, Friedrich W.J. von. *Philosophie der Kunst.* Darmstadt: Wissenschaftliche Buchgesellschaft, 1960. [Repr. of 1895 ed.]

842. Schopfer, Jean. "Voyage idéal en Italie." *Revue Blanche* 16(1898): 561-86. [See esp. pp. 584-85, "La Décadence."]

843. Schultze, Jürgen. *Art of Nineteenth Century Europe.* Tr. Barbara Forryan. New York: Abrams, 1970. 264 pp.

843a. Sells, C. "Esthètes et magiciens Musée Galliera, Paris." *Burlington Magazine* 113(May 1971):171.

844. Selz, Peter. "Art Nouveau—An International Movement." *Art in America* 48,ii(Summer 1960):80-85.

845. Silvestre, Armand. "Quelques mots sur Valadon." *La Plume* 188(fév 1897):98-100.

846. Simon, John. "Torments of Imagination." *Arts* 36(Feb 1962):20-27.

847. Smeets, Albert. "Het symbolism als international kimstbeging." *Vlaanderen* 17(1968):145-48.

848. Sojcher, Jacques. "Le graveur anonyme." *CIS* 21(1972):91-95. [On René De Coninck.]

849. Sutton, Denys. "Note in Yellow." *Apollo* 76(Dec 1962):801-02.

850. ——. "Sources of 20th Century Art." *Connoisseur* 147(1961):34-37.

851. ——. "The Symbolist Exhibition in Paris." *MbK* 26(1950):161-71.

852. "Le symbolisme." *L'art moderne* (3 oct 1886):313-15.

853. Symons, Arthur. *From Toulouse-Lautrec to Rodin:With Some Personal Impressions*. Freeport, N.Y.: Books for Libraries Press, 1968. 242 pp. [Repr. First pub. London: John Lane, 1929.]

854. Tahier-Durand, H. "Le Salon de la Rose+Croix." *La Plume* 70(mars 1892):131-32.

855. Taillandier, Yvon. "De Baudelaire à la sculpture mouvante." *XXe Siècle* 26(1966):53-57.

856. Taylor, John R. *The Art Nouveau Book in Britain*. Cambridge, Mass.: MIT Press, 1967. 175 pp.; London: Methuen, 1967. 176 pp.

857. Taylor, S.W. "Symbolist Art in Toronto:The Development of the Movement in France." *Arts* 44(Nov 1969):40-43.

858. Ténib, Charles. "Le nouvel art décoratif." *La Plume* 157(nov 1895): 481-86.

859. Tomassoni, Italo. "Dall'astrattismo all'informale." *Ulisse* 76(1973): 104-12.

860. Toronto, Art Gallery of Ontario. *Sacred and Profane in Symbolist Art: Exhibition catalogue*. Toronto, 1969. 20 pp.

861. Toscano, Bruno. *Simbolismo e intimiso fine secolo:Saggio introduttivo*. Milano: Fratelli Fabbri, 1966.

862. Trier, Eduard. "Bettina Polak:*Het Fin-de siècle in de nederlandsche schilderkunst:De symbolistische beweging 1890-1900. Agnès Humbert: Les Nabis et leur époque, 1888-1900*." *Kunstchronik* 9(1956):335-38. [Rev. art.]

863. Uzanne, Joseph. "Un peintre." *La Plume* 188(fév 1897):108.

864. Vaillant, Annette. "Les amitiés de la *Revue Blanche*." *Derrière Miroir* 158-59(1966):1-15.

866. "Valadon devant la critique." *La Plume* 188(fév 1897):110-15.

867. "Valadon devant les artistes." *La Plume* 188(fév 1897):119-23.

868. Valin, Pierre. "L'art par le symbole." *L'Ermitage* 2(1891):385-90.

869. Vanor, Georges. *L'art symboliste*. Paris: Chez le bibliophile Vanier, 1889. 43 pp.

870. Vielé-Griffin, Francis. "Les 'Forts'." *Entretiens politiques et littéraires* 5 (août 1890):162-65.

871. "Visionaries and Dreamers:Exhibition of French Symbolist Art at the Corcoran Gallery in Washington." *Arts* 30(May 1956):16-18.

872. Waldemann, Emil. *Die Kunst des Realismus und des Impressionismus im 19. Jahrhundert*. Berlin: Propyläen Verlag, 1927. 653 pp.

873. Warmoes, J. "Le climat esthétique à l'époque de Maeterlinck." *Synthèses* 17(août 1962):24-35.

874. Weston, Neville. *The Reach of Modern Art:A Concise History*. New York: Harper & Row, 1969. 240 pp.

875. Whittet, G.S. "Picadilly Gallery, London Exhibit." *Art & Artists* 5(June 1970):44.

876. Whittick, A. *Symbols, Signs and Their Meanings and Uses in Design*. Newton, Mass: C.T. Branford Co., 1960. 408 pp.

877. Wilenski, R.H. *The Modern Move-*

ment in Art. London: Faber & Gwyer, 1927. 237 pp.

878. Wind, E. "The Eloquence of Symbols." *The Burlington Magazine* (Dec 1950):349-50.

879. Wyzewa, Teodor de. "La peinture wagnérienne." *Revue Wagnérienne* 4(mai 1886):100-13.

880. Zeitler, Rudolf, Fritz Novotny, et al. *Die Kunst des 19. Jahrhunderts*. Berlin: Propyläen Verlag, 1966. 412 pp.

See also 3, 137, 155, 259a, 346, 352, 599, 665, 944, 1068, 1144, 1180, 1181, 1201, 1347, 1384, 1404, 1662, 1963, 2173, 2196, 2312, 2346, 2347, 2350, 2403, 2423, 2426, 2506, 2508, 2512, 2574, 2586, 2726, 2873, 3177.

Dance

See 98, 1017, 3180.

Drama and Theater

881. Arnaud, Noël. "Le théâtre décadent et symboliste." *Paris-Théâtre* 218(1965):21-28.

882. Barbey d'Aurevilly, J.A. *Théâtre contemporain 1870-1883*. Paris: Tresse & Stock, 1892.

883. Beaubourg, Maurice. "Critiques des théâtres." *La Plume* 310(mars 1902):407-09; 315(juin 1902):711-15; 334(mars 1903):366-69; 340(juin 1903):702-07. [Ibsen, Maeterlinck.]

884. Bérenger, Henry. "Le théâtre de M. Henri Mazel." *L'Ermitage* 2(1892):129-35.

885. Canudo, Ricciotto. "Lettre d'Italie." *La Plume* 336(avril 1903):468-71.

886. Chiusano, Italo Alighiero. *Il teatro tedesco del naturalismo all'espressionismo (1889-1925)*. Bologna: Cappelli, 1964. 215 pp.

887. Costaz, G. "Lugné-Poe et le théâtre symboliste belge à la fin du XIXe siècle." *Audace* 16,i(1970):130-35.

888. Got, Maurice. *Théâtre et symbolisme:Recherches sur l'essence et la signification spirituelle de l'art symboliste*. Paris: Le Cercle du livre, 1955. 344 pp.

889. Daniels, May. *The French Drama of the Unspoken*. Edinburgh: U. of Edinburgh P., 1953. [Diss.]

890. Davray, Henry D. "Le théâtre au Japon." *La Plume* 318(juillet 1902):886-88.

891. Evans, Calvin. "Mallarmean Antecedents of the Avant-Garde Theater." *MD* 6(1963):12-19.

892. Guerra, Manuel H. *El teatro de Manuel y Antonio Machado*. Madrid: Editorial Mediterráneo, 1966. 208 pp.

893. Hellens, Franz. "Le théâtre populaire flamand—Deux commémorations: Verhaeren et Charles de Caster." *Revue de Genève* 16(1928):98-107.

894. Henderson, John A. *The First Avant-Garde 1887-1894:Sources of the Modern French Theatre*. London: George G. Harrap & Co., 1971.

895. Hinck, Walter. *Das moderne Drama in Deutschland:Vom expressionistischen zum dokumentarischen Theater*. Göttingen: Vandenhoeck & Ruprecht, 1973. 241 pp.

896. Ireson, John C. "Towards a Theory of the Symbolist Theatre," 135-56 in John C. Ireson, I.D. McFarlane, and Garnet Rees,eds. *Studies in French Literature Presented to H.W. Lawton by Colleagues, Pupils and Friends*. Manchester: Manchester U.P.; New York: Barnes & Noble, 1968.

897. Jasper, Gertrude. *Adventures into Theater:Lugné-Poe and the Théâtre de l'oeuvre to 1889*. New Brunswick, N.J.: Rutgers U.P., 1947.

898. Kahn, Gustave. "Théâtres." *Le Symboliste* 4(nov 1886):1-2.

899. Knowles, Dorothy. *La réaction idéaliste au théâtre depuis 1890*. Paris: Droz, 1934. 558 pp.

900. Rasch, W. "Tanz als Lebenssymbol im Drama um 1900," 58-77 in *Zur deutschen Literatur seit der Jahrhundertwende:Gesammelte Aufsätze*. Stuttgart: Metzler, 1968.

901. Robichez, Jacques. "Le symbolisme au théâtre:Lugné-Poe et les débuts de l'oeuvre." *Il* 7(1955): 143-49.

902. ———. *Le symbolisme au théâtre: Lugné-Poe et les débuts de l'oeuvre*. Paris: Editions de l'Arche, 1957. 568 pp.

903. Rousseau, André. "Maeterlinck et le théâtre symboliste." *France-Illustration* 188(21 mai 1949):528.

904. Saint-Antoine. "Le théâtre symboliste." *L'Ermitage* 2(1894):152-55.

905. Shartar, I. Martin. "The Theater of the Mind:An Analysis of Works by Mallarmé, Yeats, Eliot, and Beckett." *DA* 27(1966):2161A(Emory).

906. Valin, Pierre. "Le symbole au théâtre." *L'Ermitage* 1(1892):25-29.

907. Zillmer, Herman L. "A Study of the Use of the Symbol in the Dramatic Aesthetics of Mallarmé, Maeterlinck, Valéry and Claudel." *DA* 26(1965):5600A(U. of Wis.).

See also 1200, 1656, 1691, 1809, 2028, 2058, 2062, 2065, 2097, 2129, 2168, 2172, 2217, 2759, 2862, 2873, 3053, 3085, 3091, 3095, 3110, 3135.

Folklore

See 379, 3112, 3114, 3139, 3148.

Journals

908. Anon. "Les jeunes revues." *Atlantic Monthly* 76(July 1895):141-43.

909. *Le Centavre* 1(1896):1-130; 2(1896):1-156. [Art and lit. by Gide, Louÿs, Régnier, Rops, Fantin-Latour, *inter alios.*]

910. Jackson, S.B. La Revue Blanche *(1889-1903):Origine, influence, bibliographie*. Paris: Lettre modernes, Minard, 1960.

911. Morino, L. *La Nouvelle revue française dans l'histoire des lettres (1908-1937)*. Paris: Gallimard, 1939.

912. Raynaud, Ernest. "Les Samedis de *La Plume.*" *La Plume* 336(avril 1903):425-40.

913. Retté, Adolphe. "M. Georges Lecomte." *La Plume* 208(déc 1897): 798-99. [Editor of *La Cravache*.]

914. "Revue des Revues françaises." *La Plume* 237(mai 1903:548-51.

See also 51, 158, 339, 488, 494, 564, 621, 642, 864, 2004.

Music

915. Austin, William W. *Music in the Twentieth Century:From Debussy through Stravinsky*. New York: Norton, 1966. 708 pp.

916. Bernac, Pierre. *The Interpretation of French Song*. New York: Praeger, 1970. 326 pp.

917. Boulez, Pierre. "Son et verbe," 57-62 in *Relevés d'Apprenti*. Paris: Editions du Seuil, 1966.

918. Bright, William. "Language and Music:Areas for Cooperation." *Ethnomusicology* 7(1963):26-32.

919. Brown, Calvin. "The Relations between Music and Literature as a Field of Study." *CL* 32,ii(1970):97-107.

920. Coeuroy, André. *Appels d'Orphée: Nouvelles études de musique et de littérature comparées*. Paris: La Nouvelle Revue Critique, 1928.

921. ———. *Musique et littérature*. Paris: Bloud & Gay, 1923. 262 pp.

922. ———. "Petites notes sur les touches musicales de l'impres-

sionisme et du symbolisme allemands," 109-13 in *Mélanges offerts à M. Charles Andler*. Strasbourg, 1924.

923. Cohen, Gustave. "Musique et poésie," 15-19 in *Mélanges d'histoire et d'esthétique musicales offerts à Paul-Marie Masson*. Paris: Richard-Mass-Editeur, 1955.

924. Collaer, Paul. *La musique moderne*. 2e éd. revue et corrigée. Préf. de Claude Rostand. Bruxelles: Elsevier, 1958. 279 pp. [On Music 1880-1957. Tr. Sally Abeles. *A History of Modern Music*. Cleveland and New York: World Pub. Co., 1961. 413 pp.]

925. ———. "Poésie et musique dans la mélodie française contemporaine," 149-62 in *Hommage à Charles van den Borren:Mélanges*. Anvers: De Nederlandsche Boekhandel, 1945. 359 pp.

927. Cone, Edward T. "Words into Music:The Composer's Approach to the Text," 3-15 in Northrop Frye,ed. *Sound and Poetry*. New York: Columbia U.P., 1956.

928. Cooke, Deryck. *The Language of Music*. London: Oxford U.P., 1959.

929. Cooper, Martin. *French Music: From the Death of Berlioz to the Death of Fauré*. London: Oxford U.P., 1951. 239 pp. [Repr. 1969.]

930. Cox, David. "The World of French Song." *Listener* 68(6 Sept 1962): 369.

931. Crist, Bainbridge. *The Art of Setting Words to Music*. New York; Fischer, 1944. 95 pp.

932. Davies, L. "The French Wagnerians" *Opera* 19(May 1968):351-57.

933. Dujardin, E. "Le mouvement symboliste et la musique." *MdF* 72(1908):5-24.

934. Duschak, A.G. "Interrelationship of Impressionism and Symbolism." *NATS Bulletin* 24(1967):18-21.

935. Eckart-Bäcker, Ursula. *Frankreichs Musik zwischen Romantik und Moderne:Die Zeit im Spiegel der Kritik*.

(Studien zur Musikgeschichte des 19. Jahrhunderts, Band 2.) Regensburg: Gustav Bosse Verlag, 1965. 324 pp.

936. Gielen, J.G. "Muziek en literatuur bij Schopenhauer, Mallarmé en Wagner." *Mens en Melodie* 15(Oct. 1960):291-93.

937. Gille, Jean-Charles. "Notions de symbolisme musical." *CIS* 6(1964): 27-48.

938. Guichard, Léon. "Liszt et la littérature française." *Revue de musicologie* 56,i(1970):3-34.

939. ———. *La musique et les lettres en France au temps du Wagnerisme*. Paris: Presses Univs. 1963. 354 pp.

940. Hall, James H. *The Art Song*. Norman: U. of Okla. P., 1953. 310 pp.

941. Kesting, Marianne. "Mallarmé und die Musik." *Melos* 35(Feb 1968): 45-56.

942. Klingsor, Tristan. "Les musiciens et les poètes contemporains." *MdF* 36(Nov 1900):430-44.

943. Lockspeiser, Edward. *The Literary Clef*. London: J. Calder, 1958. 186 pp.

944. ———. "Music and Painting:Chabrier, Debussy and the Impressionists." *Apollo* 83(jan 1966):10-16.

945. Meyer, Leonard D. *Emotion and Meaning in Music*. Chicago: U. of Chicago P., 1953. 307 pp.

946. Meylan, Pierre. *Les écrivains et la musique:Etudes de musique et de littérature comparée*. Lausanne: Editions du Cervin, 1951.

947. Michell, Joyce. *Symbolism in Music and Poetry*. Philadelphia: U. of Pa., 1944. [Diss.]

948. Miller, Philip L. *The Ring of Words*. Garden City, N.Y.: Doubleday, 1963. 518 pp.

949. Myers, Rollo H. "Claude Debussy and Russian Music." *Music and Letters* 39(1958):336-42.

950. ———. *Modern French Music:From Fauré to Boulez*. New York: Praeger, 1971. 210 pp.

951. Noske, Frits. *French Song from Berlioz to Duparc.* 2nd ed. Tr. Rita Benton. New York: Dover, 1970. 454 pp.

952. Piguet, Jean-Claude. "Quelques remarques sur la nature de l'image musicale." *CIS* 8(1965):35-47.

953. Rauhut, F. "Vom Einfluss der französischen Literatur des Symbolismus auf die moderne französische Musik." *GRM* 24(1936):440-60.

954. Salazar, Adolfo. *Music in Our Time:Trends in Music Since the Romantic Era.* Tr. Isabel Pope. New York: Norton, 1946. 367 pp.

955. Scher, Steven. "Notes toward a Theory of Verbal Music." *CL* 32,ii(1970):147-56.

956. Schmidt-Garre, Helmut. "Musique suggérée." *Neue Zeitschrift für Musik* 130,xii(1969):567-75.

957. Schwermer, J. "Jugendstil-Musik in der ästhetischen Enklave." *Neue Zeitschrift für Musik* 126(Jan 1965): 2-5.

958. Suarès, André. *Musique et poésie.* Paris: Editions C. Aveline, 1928.

959. Szabolcsi, Bence. *A History of Melody.* Tr. Cynthia Jolly and Sara Karig. London: Barrie and Rockliff, 1965.

960. Wallon, Simone. "L'alliance franco-russe dans la chanson française de 1890 à 1901," 126-36 in Harald Heckmann,ed. *Mélanges offerts à Vladimir Féderov.* Kassel: Bärenreiter, 1966.

961. Welleck, Albert. "The Relationship between Music and Poetry." *JAAC* 21(1962-1963):149-56.

962. ——. "Über das Verhältnis von Musik und Poesie." *Studien zur Musikwissenschaft* 25(1962):574-85.

963. Whitmore, Donnell R. "Music and Modernist Poetry:A Re-evaluation." *DAI* 33(1972):2957A-58A(N.M.)

See also 6, 66, 177, 487, 487, 521, 559, 675, 968, 1026, 1036, 1044, 1066, 1172, 1280, 1322, 1733, 1749, 1828, 1835, 1896, 1936, 1950, 1959, 1982, 1996, 2051, 2119, 2126, 2127, 2131, 2133, 2137, 2179, 2200, 2217, 2220, 2236, 2371, 2372, 2448, 2455, 2548, 2567, 2570, 2573, 2630, 2655, 2685, 2757, 2822, 2829, 2905, 2906, 2931, 2939, 2959.

Poetry

964. Allard, R. "Poésie et mémoire *NRF* (1 nov 1919):908-15.

965. Anon. "The Poet as Symbolist: Towards a Remade Experience." *TLS* 2065(30 Aug 1941):418,442.

966. Antoine, Emile. "Ballade à Verlaine." *La Plume* 28(juin 1890):104. [Poem.]

967. Arnauld, Michel. "Du vers français." *NRF* (1 janv 1910):429-39.

968. Backès, Jean-Louis. "De la poésie à la musique:Remarques sur le lied romantique et post-romantique." *RLC* 45(1971):465-88.

969. Bandy, L.J. "Trois poètes français." *CMLR* 18(1961-1962):7-12.

970. Beaunier, André. *La poésie nouvelle.* Arthur Rimbaud, Jules Laforgue, Gustave Kahn, Jean Moréas, Emile Verhaeren, Henri de Régnier, Francis Vielé-Griffin, Maurice Maeterlinck, Stuart Merrill, Francis Jammes, Paul Fort, Max Elskamp. Paris: Mercure de France, 1902.

971. Binet, Alfred. "Le problème de l'audition colorée." *RDM* (1 oct 1892):586-614.

972. Block, Haskell M. "The Alleged Parallel of Metaphysical and Symbolist Poetry." *CLS* 4(1967):145-59.

973. ——. "The Impact of French Symbolism on Modern American Poetry," 165-217 in *The Shaken Realist:Essays in Modern Literature in Honor of Frederik J. Hoffman.*

Melvin J. Friedman and John B. Vickery,eds. Baton Rouge: La. State U.P., 1970.

974. ———. "Interpretation of Symbolist Poetry." *CLS* 7(1970):489-503.

975. Blum, Jean. "La philosophie de M. Bergson et la poésie symboliste." *MdF* 63(1906):201-07.

976. Bordeaux, Henry. "Les poètes au commencement du siècle. Souvenirs sur Maurice Maeterlinck, Francis Jammes, C. Guerin. A. de Noailles." *RDM* 21(nov 1952):20-35.

977. Braak, S. *Poètes symbolistes*. Amsterdam, 1924. [Repr. Genève: Slatkine, 1970.]

978. Brinkmann, Richard. "Zur Wortkunst des Sturmkreises:Anmerkungen über Möglichkeiten und Grenzen abstrakter Dichtung," 63-78 in Klaus Lazarowicz, and Wolfgang Kron,eds. *Unterscheidung und Bewahrung: Festschrift für Hermann Kunisch zum 60. Geburtstag*. Berlin: de Gruyter, 1961.

979. Cary, Joseph B.,Jr. "The Theory and Practice of the Vague. A Study in a Mode of 19th Century Poetry." *DA* 27(1967):1367A(N.Y.U.).

980. Cazamian, Louis. *Symbolisme et poésie:L'exemple anglais*. Neuchâtel: Eds. de la Baconnière, 1947. 252 pp.

981. Champigny, Robert. "The *Swan* and the Question of Pure Poetry." *ECr* 1(1961):145-55.

982. Chantovoine, H. "La littérature inquiète. La poésie obscure. Le mallarméisme." *Le Correspondant* 186(10 mars 1897):967-76.

983. Child, Theodore. "Literary Paris— The New Poetry." *Harper's Monthly* 85(Sept 1892):339-40.

984. Cidade, Hernani. *O conceito da poesia como expressão da cultura: Sua evolução através das literaturas portugesa e brasileira*. Coimbra: A. Amado, 1957. 328 pp.

985. Claudel, Paul. "Réflexions et pro-

positions sur le vers français." *NRF* (1 nov 1925):417-46.

986. Davis, Eugene. "The New School of Poetry in France." *Literary World* 23(Oct 1892):356.

987. Davray, Henry D. "Lettres anglaises." *MdF* 277(1937):417-25. [Rev. art. See esp. 421-23 on Laforgue, Péguy and T.S. Eliot.]

988. Davy, Charles. "Symbols and Signs," 32-42 in *Words in the Mind. Exploring Some Effects of Poetry, English and French*. London: Chatto & Windus, 1965.

989. Degron, Henri. "Paysageries littéraires:Klingsor." *La Plume* 351(déc 1903):595-601.

990. Deguy, Michel. "Usages poétiques du Symbole." *CIS* 13(1967):3-18.

991. Delvaille, Bernard. *La poésie symboliste*. Paris: Seghers, 1971. 431 pp.

992. Deschamps, Léon. "La poésie française." *La Plume* 107(oct 1893): 404-05.

993. Dujardin, E. "Les premiers poètes du vers libre." *MdF* 146(1921): 577-621.

994. Durand, Gilbert. " 'Les chats, les rats et les structuralistes':Symbole et structuralisme figuratif." *CIS* 17-18(1969):13-38.

995. Edeline, Francis. "La poésie et les éléments (A propos d'un recueil de Yanette Delétang-Tardif)." *CIS* 8 (1965):75-93.

996. Eliot, T.S. "From Poe to Valéry," 74-86 in *Literary Lectures Presented at the House of Congress*. Wash., D.C.: Lib. of Congress. 602 pp. [Out-of-print lectures prev. pub. by LC.]

997. Elwert, W. Theodor. "Mallarmé entre la tradition et le vers libre:Ce qu'en disent ses vers de circonstance," 123-40 in Monique Parent, ed., *Le vers français au 20e siècle: Colloque organisé par le centre de Philologie et de Littérature Romanes*

de l'Université de Strasbourg du 3 mai au 6 mai 1966. Paris: Klincksieck, 1967.

998. Emerson, Ralph W. "Poésie." *Entretiens politiques et littéraires* 6(sept 1890):169-70.

999. Engelberg, Edward. *The Symbolist Poem*. New York: Dutton, 1967. 350 pp.

1000. Feder, Lillian. *Ancient Myth in Modern Poetry*. Princeton: Princeton U.P., 1972. 432 pp.

1001. Formigari, L. "Poesia simbolista e poesia realista." *GCFI* 11(1957): 343-59.

1002. Formont, Maxime. *Les symbolistes:Choix de poésies et notices*. Paris: Lemerre, 1933.

1003. Frank, Heinz G. *Wechselwirkungen deutsch-französischer Einflüsse in symbolistischer Dichtung*. Manitoba: U. of Manitoba, 1967. [Diss.]

1004. Friedrich, Hugo. *Die Struktur der modernen Lyrik von Baudelaire bis zur Gegenwart*. Hamburg: Rowohlt, 1956. 214 pp. [2nd ed. 1959.]

1005. Ghéon, Henri. ":Une discipline du vers libre." *NRF* (1 avril 1910):452-64.

1006. Gourmont, Rémy de. "La poésie française et la question du muet." *MdF* 42(1902):289-303.

1007. Gossez, A. M. *Poètes du nord, 1880-1902*. Paris: Ollendorff, 1902.

1008. Gross, Harvey S. *Sound and Form in Modern Poetry:A Study of Prosody from Thomas Hardy to Robert Lowell*. Ann Arbor: U. of Mich. P., 1964. 334 pp.

1009. Guimbretière, André. "Symbole et langage dans l'expérience poétique." *CIS* 6(1964):49-67.

1010. Hamburger, Michael. *The Truth of Poetry:Tensions in Modern Poetry from Baudelaire to the 1960's*. New York: Harcourt, Brace & World, 1970. 341 pp.

1011. Hassen, Ihab H. "French Symbolism and Modern British Poetry: With Yeats, Eliot, and Edith Sitwell as Indices." *DA* 13(1953):232-33 (Pa.).

1012. Henel, Heinrich. "Erlebnisdichtung und Symbolismus," 218-54 in Reinhold Grimm,ed. *Zur Lyrik-Diskussion*. Darmstadt: Wissenschaftliche Buchgesellschaft, 1966.

1013. Holthusen, Hans Egon. *Das Schöne und das Wahre in der Poesie: Zur Theorie des Dichterischen bei Eliot und Benn*. Berlin-Friedenau: Wichern Verlag, 1960. 35 pp.

1014. Isaacs, Joseph. *The Background of Modern Poetry*. New York: Dutton, 1958.

1015. Kahn, Gustave. "Albert Samain. *Le chariot d'or.*" *Revue Blanche* 25 (1901):634-35. [Rev. art.]

1016. Kearns, E.J. *L'image dans la poésie symboliste française*. Reading: U. of Reading, 1958-59. [Diss.]

1017. Kermode, Frank. "Poet and Dancer Before Diaghilev." *PR* 28 (1961):48-75. [Loie Fuller and the influence of dance on Symbolist poetry.]

1018. Lanson, Gustave. "The New Poetry in France." *International Quarterly* 4(Oct 1901):433-65. [Tr. Susan H. Taber.]

1019. Le Blond, Maurice. "La parade littéraire." *La Plume* 220(juin 1898):422-25; 226(sept 1898):574-75; 227(oct 1898):597-98. [Jammes, Moréas, Mallarmé.]

1020. ———. "Poésie contemporaine." *La Plume* 205(nov 1897):657-64.

1021. Lefebve, Maurice-Jean. "Le procédé de l'imitation et la mythomanie littéraire." *CIS* 19-20(1970):19-33.

1022. Lescure, Jean. "Du calcul des improbabilités." *CIS* 6(1964):69-87.

1023. Lote, G. "La poétique du symbolisme:Poésie et musique, la synthésie." *Revue des Cours et Conférences* 35(1934):109-26.

1024. McClelland, John. "Fin de siècle, belle époque, and avant-garde." *QQ* 79(1972):301-11.

1025. McLaren, James C. "Criticism and Creativity:Poetic Themes in Mallarmé and Valéry." *ECr* 4(1964): 222-27.

1026. Mallarmé, Stéphane. "Vers et musique en France." *Entretiens politiques et littéraires* 27(juin 18-92):237-41.

1027. Maritain, Jacques. *Frontières de la poésie et autres essais.* Paris: Rouart, 1935. 226 pp.

1028. Martín-Crosa, Ricardo. "Notas de urgencia para una poesía de lo absoluto." *CHA* 61(1965):103-09.

1029. Mendès, Catulle. *Le mouvement poétique français de 1867 à 1900.* Paris: Fasquelle, 1903. 325 pp.

1030. ———. "Recent French Poets." *Gentlemen's Magazine* 247 (Oct-Nov 1879):478-504, 563-88. [Tr. Arthur O'Shaughnessy.]

1031. Merrill, Stuart. "Critiques des poèmes." *La Plume* 282(janv 1901): 39-42; 289(mai 1901):303-05; 291 (juin 1901):404-10; 294(juillet 1901):555-57; 298(sept 1901):736-39; 303(déc 1901):925-28; 339(juin 1903):626-34. [Moréas, Verhaeren, Retté, Samain and Tailhade.]

1032. ———. "Critique des poèmes:Symbolistes, humanistes, naturistes et somptuaires." *La Plume* 330(janv 1903):120-26.

1033. ———. "La poésie symboliste." *L'Ermitage* 1(1893):370-72.

1034. ———. "Le rapport de M. Catulle Mendès sur le mouvement poétique français." *La Plume* 342(juillet 1903):37-50.

1035. Michaud, Guy. *Message poétique du symbolisme.* 3 vols. Paris: Nizet, 1947.

1036. Miller, Philip L. *The Ring of Words:An Anthology of Song Texts.* Orig. texts selected and tr., with introd. New York: Doubleday, 1963. 200 pp. [Incl. texts by Baudelaire, Mallarmé, Rimbaud and Verlaine *inter alios.*]

1037. Moore, A.K. "The Case for Poetic Obscurity." *Neophil* 48(1964):322-40.

1038. Moreau, Pierre. "De la symbolique religieuse à la poésie symboliste." *CLS* 1-2(1967):5-16.

1039. Morier, Henri. *Le rythme du vers libre symboliste et ses relations avec le sens.* 3 vols. Genève: Presses Académiques, 1943-44.

1039a. Mossop, Deryk J. *Pure Poetry: Studies in French Poetic Theory and Practice, 1746-1945.* Oxford: Clarendon, 1971. 254 pp.

1040. Mourey, Gabriel. "Some Notes on Recent Poetry in France." *Fortnightly Review* 68(1897):650-65.

1041. Munier, Roger. "Communément." *CIS* 19-20(1970):45-49.

1042. Naumann, Walter. *Traum und Tradition in der deutschen Lyrik.* Stuttgart: Kohlhammer, 1966. 181 pp.

1043. Nelli, René. "Le temps imaginaire et ses structures dans l'oeuvre poétique." *CIS* 14(1967):53-67.

1044. Nerval, Gérard de. *Notes d'un amateur de musique.* Ed. avec introd. d'André Coeuroy. Paris: Cahiers de Paris, 1926. 103 pp.

1045. Noulet, Emilie. *Etudes littéraires:L'hérmetisme dans la poésie française moderne:Influence d'Edgar Poe sur la poésie française:Exégèse de trois sonnets de Stéphane Mallarmé.* Mexique: Talleres gráficos de la editorial Cultura, 1944. 5 pp.

1046. ———. *Le ton poétique: Mallarmé, Corbière, Verlaine, Rimbaud, Valéry, Saint-John Perse.* Avec un poème inédit de Saint-John Perse. Paris: Corti, 1972. 288 pp.

1047. Nyman, Alf Tor. *Begreppet lyrisk erfarenhet:Kunskapsteoretiska och estetiskt-psykologiska studier:Symbolistisk och realistisk diktning.* Lund: Gleerup, 1958. 423 pp.

1048. Pestalozzi, Karl. *Die Entstehung des lyrischen Ich:Studien zum Motiv der Erhebung in der Lyrik.* Berlin: de Gruyter, 1970. 364 pp.

1049. Pfeiffer, Jean. "La communication poétique." *CIS* 19-20(1970): 51-56.

1050. Pinto, Vivian De S. *Crisis in English Poetry, 1880-1940.* New York: Hutchinson's University Library, 1951. 228 pp.

1051. Radley, Hilton. "The Twilight of the Poets." *Westminster Review* 173 (1910):657-62.

1052. Raymond, Marcel. *De Baudelaire au Surréalisme.* Paris: Corti, 1966. 367 pp.

1053. Raynaud, Ernest. "Les poètes décadents." *La Plume* 352(déc 1903):634-41; 354(janv 1904):65-74.

1054, Rebell, Hugues. "La poésie française." *L'Ermitage* 2(1893):152-60.

1055. Régie, José,ed. *Pequena história da moderna poesia portuguesa.* Lisboa: Inquérito, 1941.

1056. Retté, Adolphe. "Sur le rythme des vers." *MdF* 29(mars 1899):169-32.

1057. ——. "Le vers libre." *MdF* 8(juillet 1893):203-10.

1058. Rieux, Lionel des. "La Magicienne." *L'Ermitage* 14(janv 1897): 39-41.

1059. Roinard, Paul-Napoléon, Victor-Emile Michelet and Guillaume Apollinaire. *La poésie symboliste.* Paris: L'Edition, 1909.

1060. Sauro, Antoine. *La lingua poetica in Francia dal romanticismo al simbolismo.* Bari: Adriatica, 1954. 422 pp.

1061. Sinocim. "Progression wagnérienne." *L'Ermitage* 1(1894):216-20.

1062. Sorrento, Luigi. *Dal parnaso al simbolismo, con particolare studio sulla poesia di Sully Prudhomme e di Francis Jammes.* Milano: Edizioni de "L'Arte," 1952.

1063. Souza, R. de. "Le rôle de l'e muet dans la poésie française." *MdF* 13(janv 1895):3-23.

1064. Spire, A. "La technique du vers français." *MdF* 98(1912):498-503.

1065. ——. "Le vers français d'après la phonétique expérimentale." *MdF* 110(1914):308-21.

1066. Stein, Jack M. *Poem and Music in the German Leid from Gluck to Hugo Wolf.* Cambridge, Mass.: Harvard U.P., 1971. 238 pp.

1067. Stephan, Philip. "Naturalist Influences on Symbolist Poetry, 1882-86." *FR* 45(1972):299-311.

1067a. Suckling, Norman. "Toward a Better Poetic. The Contribution of the Post-Symbolists." *FS* 3(1949): 233-44.

1068. Thompson, Vance. "Wagnerian Poets and Painters." *M'lle New York* 1(23 Aug 1895).

1069. Valéry, Paul. "Difficulté de définir la simulation." *NRF* (1 mai 1927):612-21.

1070. ——. "Questions de poésie." *NRF* (1 janv 1935):53-70.

1071. Vallmy, Jean. *Aspects du silence dans la poésie moderne. Une étude sur Verlaine, Mallarmé, Valéry, Rimbaud, Claudel, René Char, et Francis Ponge.* Zurich: U. of Zurich, 1952. [Diss.]

1072. Verdin, Simone. "La triple voie." *CIS* 19-20(1970):63-76.

1073. Verhaeren, Emile. "French Poetry to-Day." *Fortnightly Review* 75(1901):723-38. [Tr. C. Heywood.]

1074. Vielé-Griffin, Francis. "Le Banquet d'hier." *Entretiens politiques et littéraires* 11(fév 1891):58-62. [With poem about Sym. poets.]

1075. ——. *"Entretiens* sur le mouvement poétique." *Entretiens politiques et littéraires* 45(juin 1893): 529-37; 46(juillet 1893):35-41.

1076. ——. "Le mouvement poétique." *MdF* 26(avril 1898):5-10.

1077. ——. "Le plus grand poète." *Entretiens politiques et littéraires* 8(nov 1890):277-78.

1078. ——. "Poésie." *Entretiens politiques et littéraires* 28(juillet 1892): 35-43.

1079. ——. "A propos du vers libre." *Entretiens politiques et littéraires* (mars 1890):3-11.

1080. Vigée, Claude. "Metamorphosen der modernen Lyrik," 128-72 in Reinhold Grimm,ed. *Zur Lyrik-Diskussion.* Darmstadt: Wissenschaftliche Buchgesellschaft, 1966.

1081. Vigié-Lecocq, E. *La poésie contemporaine, 1884-1896.* Paris: Mercure de France, 1897.

1082. Walch, J. *Anthologie des poètes français contemporains, le Parnasse et les écoles postérieures au Parnasse (1886-1906).* Morceaux choisis accom. de notices bio et bibliographiques. 3 vols. Paris: Delagrave, 1906-07.

1083. Weatherhead, Andrew. *The Edge of the Image:Marianne Moore, William Carlos Williams and Some Other Poets.* Seattle: U. of Wash. P., 1967. 251 pp.

1084. Weber, Jean-Paul. *Genèse de l'oeuvre poétique.* Paris: Gallimard, 1960. 563 pp.

1085. Welleck, Albert. "Die Struktur der modernen Lyrik:Betrachtungen zu dem Buch von Hugo Friedrich und zu Grundsatzfragen einer Literaturästhetik und systematischen Literaturwissenschaft." *SG* 16(1963):36-46.

1086. Wells, Benjamin W. "Contemporary French Poets—II." *SR* 4(Nov 1895):15-37.

1087. Wilson, Jean. "The 'Nineties' Movement in Poetry:Myth or Reality?" *YES* 1(1971):160-74.

See also 18, 78, 98, 127, 231, 234, 278, 307, 347, 357, 391, 405, 410, 437, 530, 550, 583, 621, 662, 942, 957, 963, 1537, 1549, 1910, 1927, 2134, 2282, 2332, 2474, 2518, 2873, 2949, 3095.

Prose Fiction

1088. Bosch, Rafael. *La novela española del siglo XX.* New York: Las Americas, 1970.

1089. Brumm, U. "Symbolism and the Novel." *PR* 25(1958):329-42.

1090. Cellier, Léon. "Le roman initiatique en France au temps du romantisme." *CIS* 4(1964):22-40.

1091. Freedman, Ralph. "Symbol as Terminus:Some Notes on Symbolist Narrative." *CLS* 4(1966):135-43.

1092. Harris, Wendell V. "Identifying the Decadent Fiction of the Eighteen-Nineties." *EFT* 5,v(1962):1-13.

1093. Klingsor, Tristan. "Le roman italien." *La Plume* 266(mai 1900): 298-300. [Capuana, D'Annunzio, Butti.]

1094. Kronegger, M.E. "Impressionist Tendencies in Lyrical Prose:19th and 20th Centuries." *RLC* 43(1969): 528-44.

1095. Mickelsen, David J. "Anti-Realist Directions in the Novel, 1885-1901." *DAI* 32(1971):445A(Ind.). [Eng. and European figures.]

1096. Ronse, Henri. "Le labyrinth, espace significatif." *CIS* 9-10(1965-66):27-43.

1097. Scheffer, Robert. "Critique des romans." *La Plume* 311(avril 1902: 457-59; 314(mai 1902):641-43; 316 (juin 1902):758-60; 331(fév 1903): 254-56; 334(mars 1903):363-65;

337(mai 1903):537-40. [Régnier, Maeterlinck, Bourget, Péladan and Huysmans.]

1098. Swift, Bernard C. "The Hypothesis of the French Symbolist Novel." *MLR* 68(1973):776-87.

1099. Uitti, Karl D. *The Concept of Self in the Symbolist Novel*. The Hague: Mouton, 1961. 66 pp.

See also 2902.

Stylistics

1100. Blanchot, Maurice. "Mallarmé et le langage." *L'Arche* 14(Mar-Apr 1946):134-46.

1101. Buccellato, M. "Il linguaggio e la filosofia delle forme simboliche." *RCSF* 10(1956-57):212-25.

1102. Caussy, Fernand. "Le style et l'émotion." *L'Ermitage* 33(août 1905):77-94.

1103. Coutant, Gaston. "De quelques procédés fantaisistes." *La Plume* 183 (déc 1896):751-54. ·

1104. Cuénot, Claude. *Le style de Paul Verlaine*. 2 vols. Paris: CDU, 1963.

1105. Gourmont, Rémy de. "Du style ou de l'écriture." *MdF* 30(avril 1899):5-31.

1106. Lawler, James R. *The Language of French Symbolism*. Princeton: Princeton U.P., 1970. 270 pp.

1107. Morawska, Ludmilla. *L'adjectif dans la langue des symbolistes français:Rimbaud, Mallarmé, Valéry*. Poznan: Uniwersytet im. Adama Mickiewicza w Posnaniu, 1964. 169 pp.

1108. ———. "Le nom épithéte dans la langue des symbolistes:Essai d'une interprétation." *Kwartalnik Neofilologiczny* 11(1964):70-73.

1109. Mounin, Georges. "Les stylistiques actuelles." *CIS* 15-16(1967-68):53-60.

1110. Paxton, Norman. *The Develop-*

ment of Mallarmé's Prose Style, With the Original Texts of Twenty Articles. Genève: Droz, 1968. 175 pp.

1111. Retté, Adolphe. "Aspects:Préface omise." *La Plume* 167(avril 1896):204.

1112. Vielé-Griffin, Francis. "Objections raisonnées." *Entretiens politiques et littéraires* 16(juillet 1891):18-20. [On grammatical usage in Symbolism.]

See also 194, 201, 527, 529, 687, 1021, 1060, 1234, 1271, 1519, 1647, 1668, 2285, 2470, 2804, 2816, 2902.

Themes, Motifs, and Topoi

1113. Alexander, Paul J. "Byzantium and the Migration of Literary Works and Motifs:The Legend of the Last Roman Emperor." *M&H* N.S. 2(1971):47-68.

1114. Austin, Lloyd J. "Mallarmé et le mythe d'Orphée." *CAIEF* 22(1970): 167-80.

1115. Béguin, Albert. *L'Ame romantique et le Rêve*. 2 vols. Nogent-le-Rotrou: Daupeley-Gouverneur; Marseilles: Eds. des Cahiers du Sud, 1937.

1116. Borel, J. "D'une expérience de l'impuissance." *CdS* 58(1964): 270-87.

1117. Bornstein, Paul. *Die Dichter des Todes in der modernen Literatur*. Berlin: Ebering, 1899. 40 pp.

1118. ———. *Der Tod in der modernen Literatur und andere Essays*. Leipzig: J. Cotta, 1900. 278 pp.

1119. Borowitz, Helen. "Visions of Salome." *Criticism* 14(1972):12-21.

1120. Cansinos Asseüs, Rafael. *Salome en la literatura: Flaubert, Wilde, Mallarmé, Eugênio de Castro, Apollinaire*. Madrid: Editorial-America, 1919. 254 pp.

1121. Chassé, Charles. "Le thème de

Hamlet chez Mallarmé." *RSH* (jan-mars 1955):157-69.

1122. Daemmrich, Horst S. "The Infernal Fairy Tale:Inversion of Archetypal Motifs in Modern European Literature." *Mosaic* 5,iii(1972): 85-95. [On Maeterlinck, T. Mann, Hoffmann, Villiers de l'Isle-Adam, Hofmannsthal, Kafka and Ionesco.]

1123. Daffner, Hugo. *Salome:Ihre Gestalt in Geschichte und Kunst.* München: H. Schmidt, 1912. 406 pp.

1124. Décaudin, Michel. "Un mythe *fin de siècle:*Salomé. *CLS* 4(1967):109-17.

1125. ———. "Salomé dans la littérature et dans l'art à l'époque symboliste." *Bulletin de l'Univ. de Toulouse* (mars 1965):519-25.

1126. Drewska, Hélène. *Quelques interprétations de la légende de Salomé dans les littératures contemporaines* Montpellier: U. of Montpellier, 1912. [Diss.]

1127.Figueiredo, Fidelino de. *Símbolos e mitos*. Lisboa: Publicações Europa-América, 1964. 186 pp.

1128. Lamont, R. "The Hamlet Myth." *YFS* 33(1964):80-92.

1129. Lethève, Jacques. "Le thème de la décadence dans les lettres françaises à la fin du XIXe siècle." *RHL* 62(1963):46-61.

1130. Lohner, Edgar. "Das Bild des Schwans in der neueren Lyrik," 297-322 in Egon Schwarz, Hunter G. Hannum, and Edgar Lohner,eds. *Festschrift für Bernhard Blume: Aufsätze zur deutschen und euro-päischen Literatur.* Göttingen: Vandenhoeck and Ruprecht, 1967.

1131. McClain, William H. "Symbolic Extensions of the Hyperion-Myth," 177-93 in Lieselotte E. Kurth, William H. McClain, and Roger Homann, eds. *Traditions and Transitions: Studies in Honor of Harold Jantz*. München: Delp'sche Verlagsbuchhandlung K.G., 1972. 262 pp. [On Stefan George, et al.]

1132. Michaud, Guy. "Le thème du miroir dans le symbolisme français." *CAIEF* 11(1959):199-216.

1133. Rose, Marilyn Gaddis. "The Daughters of Herodias in 'Hérodiade,' 'Salomé,' and 'A Full Moon in March'." *CompD* 1(1967):172-81.

1134. Senior, John. *The Way Down and Out:The Occult in Symbolist Literature*. Ithaca, N.Y.: Cornell U.P., 1959. 217 pp.

1135. Taupin, René. "The Myth of Hamlet in France in Mallarmé's Generation." *MLQ* 14(1953):432-47.

1136. Vaucaire, Maurice. "Salomé à travers l'art et la littérature." *Nouvelle Revue* (15 mai 1907): 145-51.

1137. Vitaletti, G. *Salome nella leggenda e nell'arte*. Roma: n.p. 1908.

1138. Wais, Kurt. "Die Errettung aus dem Schiffbruch:Melville, Mallarmé und einige deutsche Voraussetzungen." *DVLG* 34(1960):21-45.

See also 286, 1660, 1752, 2263, 2547, 2555, 2562, 2588, 2912, 3069, 3072, 3160, 3176.

IV Individual Figures

Adam, Paul

1139. Deschamps, Léon. "Le Banquet Paul Adam (7 décembre 1899)." *La Plume* 256(déc 1899):789-95.

1140. Saint-Jacques, Louis de. "Expertises:'L'année de Clarisse' de Paul Adam." *La Plume* 193(mai 1897): 266-71.

1141. Segard, Achille. "Notre banquet préparatoire." *La Plume* 254(déc 1899):748-50.

See also 585.

Ady

1142. Gömöri, George. "Two Hungarian Poets." *Mosaic* 5,i(1971):145-51. [Ady and F. Juhász. Rev. art.]

1143. Kiss, S. "Ady's Translations from the French." *SLD* 3(1965):59-72.

1144. Varga, József. "Ady képzőmu-vészeti érdaklődése," 315-31 in B. Kőpeczi, and István Sőter,eds. *Eszmei és irodalmi találkozások: Tanulmányok a magyar-francia iro-dalmi kopcsolatok történetéből,* Budapest: Akadémiai K., 1970.

1145. Vezér, Erzsébet. "Ady és Fran-ciaország," 289-313 in B. Kőpeczi, and István Sőtér,eds. *Eszmei és iro-dalmi találkozások:Tanulmányok a magyar-francia irodalmi kapcsolatok történetéből.* Budapest: Akadémiai K., 1970.

See also 1495.

Alain-Fournier

1146. Giannoni, Robert. "Les traductions italiennes du *Grand Meaulnes.*" *RLMC* 23(1970):57-53.

Aldington

1147. Gates, Norman T. "Richard Aldington and F.S. Flint:Poet's Dialogue." *PLL* 8(1972):63-69.

Andrade, M. de

1148. Barata, Mário. "Crítica de arte e estética no Brasil." *MGSL* 21 Oct(1972):2-3.

1149. Duarte, Paulo. *Mário de Andrade por êle mesmo.* Pref. Antônio Cândido. São Paulo: Edart, 1971.

1150. Lopes, João A. "Uma introdução a Mário de Andrade." *IH* 7(1971):87-122.

1151. López, Telê Porto Ancona. *Mário de Andrade:Ramais e caminho.* São Paulo: Inst. de Estudos Brasileiros, 1972.

1152. Lucas, Fábio. *"Amar, verbo intransitivo."* *LBR* 8,i(1971):69-77.

1153. Morais, Frederico. "O crítico de arte." *MGSL* 19 Feb(1972):4-5.

André, Marius

1154. Czerny, Zygmunt. "Le félibrige symboliste, ésotérique et wagnérien: *Monserrat*, roman mystique et féerique de Marius André," 637-82 in *Mélanges de philologie romane dédiés à la mémoire de Jean Boutière.* 2 vols. Liège: Soledi, 1971.

Andrian

1155. Perl, Walter H.ed. *Leopold Andrian und die Blätter für die Kunst.* Hamburg: Hauswedell, 1960. 136 pp.

1156. ——. *Leopold von Andrian:Ein vergessener Dichter des Symbolismus, Freund Georges und Hofmannsthals.* Hamburg: Hauswedell, 1958. 309 pp.

Anghel

1157. Cioculescu, Serban. "Un nou portret al lui D. Anghel." *RoLit* 21 Sept(1972):7. [Rev. of new biog. of A by Georgeta Horodinca.]

1158. Dragomirescu, M.I. "Colaborarea literara D. Anghel–St.O. Iosif." *Luc* 15 July(1972):7.

1159. "Pseudonimele lui D. Anghel." *AUB-LLR* 19,i(1970):53-68.

1160. Georgescu, Paul. "Farmecul exegezei." *Contemporanul* 17 Nov (1972):3.

1161. Horodincă, Georgeta. "Centenar Dimitrie Anghel:Portret speculativ." *Luc* 15 July(1972):7.

1162. ——. "De ce Dimitrie Anghel?" *Luc* 29 Jan(1972):4.

1163. ——. "Dimitrie Anghel în oglinda poeziei." *ViR* 25,iii(1972):82-91.

1164. ——. "Dimitrie Anghel şi mitul floral." *Luc* 25(Mar(1972):10.

1165. ——. "Mitul grădinii în opera lui Anghel." *ConLit* 30 May(1972):3,11.

1166. Micu, Dumitru. "Un simbolist baroc:100 de ani de la naşterea lui Dimitrie Anghel." *ViR* 25,vii(1972): 61-71.

1167. Papu, Edgar. "Cutezanţa de a gîndi." *Contemporanul* 18 Aug-(1972):3.

1168. Piru, Alexandru. "Verlaine, Anghel, Iosif." *RoLit* 13 July(1972):16-17.

1169. Radian, Sanda. "Dimitrie Anghel." *RevBib* 25,vii(1972):431-32.

1170. Vaida, Mircea. "D. Anghel in trei oglinzi." *Luc* 16 Dec(1972):6.

Anjos, A. dos

1171. Buss, Alcides. "A poesia pessoal de Augusto dos Anjos (VI):Cosmovisão ou visão cósmica?" *JdL*

247,Cad. 2(1971):7; 248,Cad. 2 (1971):4.

Apollinaire

1172. Décaudin, Michel. *Apollinaire et la musique.* Actes du Colloque tenu à Stavelot, 27-29 août 1965. Stavelot: Eds. "Les amis de G. Apollinaire," 1967. 104 pp.

1173. Décaudin, Michel, and Pierre M. Adéma. *Album Apollinaire.* Paris: Gallimard, 1971. 315 pp.

1174. Décaudin, Michel, ed. *Le dossier d' "Alcools".* Genève: Droz, 1965. 242 pp.

1175. ——. *Lettres à Lou.* Paris: Gallimard, 1969. 530 pp.

1176. ——. *Le poète assassiné.* Paris: Club du Meilleur Livre, 1959.

1177. *ECr* 10(1970). [Spec. Apollinaire issue. Octavio Paz, " 'The Musician of Saint-Merry' by Apollinaire: A Translation and a Study," 269-84; Laurence M. Porter, "The Fragmented Self of Apollinaire's 'Zone'," 285-95; Anne Hyde Greet, "Wordplay in Apollinaire's *Calligrammes*," 296-307; Dolly S. Rieder, "Time and Emptiness in Apollinaire's Poetry," 308-18; Richard L. Admussen, "Apollinaire and *SIC*," 319-28.]

1178. Gothot-Mersch, Claudine. "Apollinaire et le symbolisme:*Le Larron.*" *RHL* 67(1967):590-600.

1179. Lockerbie, S.I. "*Alcools* et le symbolisme." *RLM* 85-89(1963): 5-40.

1180. Noszlopy, George T. "Apollinaire, Allegorical Imagery and the Visual Arts." *FMLS* 9(1973):49-74.

1181. Valeton, D. *Lexicologie:L'espace et le temps d'après un texte critique d'Apollinaire sur la peinture moderne.* Paris: Nizet, 1973. 62 pp.

See also 1120, 2520.

Aurier

1182. Coulon, M. *Une minute de l'heure symboliste, Albert Aurier, 1865-1892.* Paris: Mercure de France, 1921. 46 pp.

Azorín

1183. Blanco Aguinaga, Carlos. "Escepticismo, paisajismo y los clásicos: Azoríno la mistificación de la realidad." *Insula* 22(June 1967):3-5.

1184. Romero, Hector R. "Simbolismo e impresionismo en la trilogía a *Antonio Azorin.*" *RomN* 15(1973): 30-36.

1185. Stimson, Frederick S. "Lo invisible:Azorín's Debt to Maeterlinck." *HR* 26(1958):64-70.

Bachelard

1186. Durand, Gilbert. "Science objective et conscience symbolique dans l'oeuvre de Gaston Bachelard." *CIS* 4(1964):41-59.

See also 203.

Bacovia

1187. Baltag, Cezar. "The Poet's Privilege." *RoR* 26,i(1972):39-40.

1188. Cioculescu, Barbu. "Dualitetea ris-plîns în poezia lui Bacovia." *RITL* 21(1972):207-11.

1189. Cristea, Dan. " 'Temele' lui Bacovia." *Luc* 17 June(1972):9.

1190. Dimov, Leonid. "Nu numai plumbul." *Luc* 17 June(1972):9.

1191. Hanganu, George. "Climatul verlainian în lirica lui George Bacovia." *AUB-LLR* 20(1971):137-44.

1192. Manu, Emil. "Introducere în cromatica lui Bacovia." *RITL* 21(1972): 219-22.

1193. Mioc, Simion. "Poezia lui Baco-via:Timbru unic." *Orizont* 21[22], ix(1971):25-29.

1194. Mitescu, Adriana. "Imagine şi materie în poetica bacoviană." *RITL* 21(1972):213-18.

1195. Petroveanu, Mihail. "Gh.V. Baco-via, destinul poetului." *RoLit* 1 June(1972):4.

1196. Saramandu, N. "Despre technica realizarii sugestiei cromatice (alb, negru) în poezia lui Bacovia," 809-14 în *Omagiu lui Alexandru Rosetti la 70 de ani*. Bucharest: Editura Academiei Republicii Socialiste Romania, 1965.

1197. Vornicu, Mihai. "Masca poetica a lui George Bacovia." *RITL* 21(1972): 223-27.

Balmont

1198. Markov, Vladimir. "Balmont:A Reappraisal." *SlavR* 28(1969): 221-64.

1199. Schmidt, Tatyana. "K. Balmont: Escapism as a Form of Revolt." *SEER* 47(1969):323-43.

See also 676.

Bang

1200. Amsinck, Hanne. *Sceneinstruk-tøren Herman Bang og det franske symbolistiske teater*. (SSO 282). Copenhagen: Gad, 1972. 125 pp.

1201. Gravier, Maurice. "Herman Bang *Växelverkan mellan skönlitteratur-enoch andra konstarter:Sixth International Study Conference on Scandinavian Literature*. Uppsala 12/8-16/8 1966. Uppsala: Student Service, 1966.

1202. Simonsen, Sofus E. "Herman Bang:Life and Theme." *GN* 3,v (1972):34-37.

1203. Winge, Mette,ed. *Omkring Haab-løse Slaegter*. (Vaerkserien [7].)

Copenhagen: Hans Reitzel, 1972. 333 pp.

See also 1440.

Barbu

1204. Nicolescu, Basarab. "A Poetic Method." *RoR* 26,iii(1972):68-71.

1205. Pavel, Toma. "O cercetare ling-vistică a poeziei Lui Ion Barbu." *StCL* 18(1967):79-89.

1206. Petroveanu, Mihail. "A Brief Survey of Ion Barbu's Poetry." *RoR* 26, iii(1972):31-33.

1207. Pillat, Dinu. "Din tinereţea de poem dionisiac a lui Ion Barbu." *Luc* 19 Feb(1972):4.

1208. ———. "Etapele vietii si ale ideatiei lui Ion Barbu." *GLit* 13(6 Oct 1966): 1.

1209. Vianu, Tudor. "Ion Barbu's Poetry:The Degrees of Vision." *RoR* 26,iii(1972):65-68.

Baudelaire

1210. Aarnes, Asbjorn. "Malaise et nostalgie chez Baudelaire." *RMM* 76 (1971):466-74.

1211. Adriani, Bruno. *Baudelaire und George*. Berlin: Riemerschmidt, 1939. 67 pp.

1212. Aggeler, William F. *Baudelaire Judged by His Spanish Critics*. Athens, Ga.: U. of Ga. P., 1971. 128 pp.

1213. Arnold, Paul. *Esoterisme de Baudelaire*. Paris: Vrin, 1972. 192 pp.

1214. Austin, Lloyd J. "Baudelaire Poet or Prophet?" 18-34 in Lloyd James Austin, Garnet Rees, and Eugène Vinaver,eds. *Studies in Modern French Literature Presented to Percy Mansell Jones by Pupils, Colleagues and Friends*. Manchester: Manchester U.P., 1961.

1215. ———. *L'univers poétique de Baudelaire:Symbolisme et symbolique*.

Paris: Mercure de France, 1956. 354 pp.

1216. Axelrod, Steven. "Baudelaire and the Poetry of Robert Lowell." *TCL* 17(1971):257-74.

1217. Bachrach, A.G.H. "Baudelaire en T.S. Eliot." *Maatstaf* 5(1957): 304-16.

1218. Bandy, William T. *Baudelaire:An Exhibition Commemorating the Centennial of* Les fleurs du mal. Madison: U. of Wis. P., 1957. 32 pp.

1219. ———. "Baudelaire et Edgar Poe: Vue rétrospective." *RLC* 41(1967): 180-94.

1220. ———. "Baudelaire et Poe:Vers une nouvelle mise au point." *RHL* 67(1967):329-34.

1221. ———. *Baudelaire Judged by His Contemporaries (1845-1867).* Nashville, 1933. 188 pp. [Tr. as *Baudelaire devant ses contemporains.* Monaco: Eds. du Rocher, 1957. 347 pp. Repr.: Paris: U.G.E., 1967. 311 pp.]

1222. ———. "Recensement bibliographique:1970." *Bull. Baudelairien* 7,i (1971):16-30.

1223. Banjanin, Milica E. "The City Poetry of Baudelaire and Blok." *DAI* 31(1971):4110A(Wash. U.).

1224. Barth, E. "Die Langeweile:Ein Versuch über Baudelaire." *NDH* 7 (1960-61):321-35.

1225. Bertocci, Angelo. *From Symbolism to Baudelaire.* Carbondale: Southern Ill. U.P., 1964. 223 pp.

1226. Betz, Dorothy K.M. "Baudelairian Imagery and Rhetoric in the Works of Several Later Nineteenth Century Poets." *DA* 28(1967-68):4163A(Cornell).

1227. Bonfantini, Mario. *Baudelaire.* Turin: Giapichelli, 1970. [4th ed. with five new essays.]

1228. Brench, Angela D., and Henri de Briel. "The Marriage of Heaven and Hell:An Insight into the Duality of Baudelaire's Metaphysical Vision in *Les Fleurs du Mal.*" *Le Français au Nigeria.* 8,iii(1973):26-33.

1229. Brown, Eleanor G. "Baudelaire, Proust, and the Artistic Ideal:A Comparative Study of Thematic Relationships." *DAI* 32(1971):4602A(Ill., Urbana-Champaign.).

1230. Brunnemann, Anna. "Baudelaire und sein Übersetzer Stefan George." *NS* 26(1919):338-57.

1231. Bruyr, José. "Baudelaire et ses musiciens:Chant d'automne, de Gabriel Fauré." *Musica Disques* 41 (1957):33-35.

1231a. Cargo, Robert T. "Baudelaire's 'Chant d'automne'," 27-44 in Robert T. Cargo, and Emanuel J. Mickel, Jr.,eds. *Studies in Honor of Alfred G. Engstrom.* (UNCSRLL 124.) Chapel Hill: U. of N.C. Press, 1972. 229 pp. N.C. Press, 1972. 229 pp.

1232. Carrier, Warren. "Baudelaire y Silva." *RI* 7,xiii(1943):39-47.

1233. Cattaui, Georges. *Orphisme et prophétie chez les poètes 1850-1950: Hugo - Nerval - Baudelaire -Mallarmé-Rimbaud-Valéry-Claudel.* Paris: Plon 1965. 140 pp.

1234. Cellier, Léon. "D'une rhétorique profonde:Baudelaire et l'oxymoron." *CIS* 8(1965):3-14.

1235. "Charles Baudelaire." *La Plume* 338,supp(mai 1903); 340(juin 1903): 3-96. [Incl. facsims. of mss. and sketches.]

1236. Charpentier, J. "La poésie britannique et Baudelaire." *MdF* 147 (1921)298:332; 635-75.

1237. Cladel, Léon. "La tombe de Baudelaire." *La Plume* 36(oct 1890):183.

1238. Clark, Philip F. "Répertoire de thèses canadiennes sur Baudelaire." *Bull. Baudelairien* 7,i(1971):13-15.

1239. Cook, Douglas B. "The Introduction of Baudelaire into Italy." *DAI* 34(1973):308A-09A(N.C., Chapel Hill).

1240. Crepet, Jacques. "Charles Baudelaire et Jeanne Duval." *La Plume* 216(avril 1898):242-44.

1241. Decker, Henry. "Baudelaire and the Valéryan Concept of Pure Poetry." *Symposium* 19(1965): 155-61.

1242. Delattre, Floris. "Charles Baudelaire et le jeune A.C. Swinburne (1861-1867)," 199-214 in *Mélanges d'histoire littéraire générale et comparée offerts à F. Baldensperger.* Paris: Champion, 1930.

1243. Dérieux, H. "La plasticité de Baudelaire et ses rapports avec Théophile Gautier." *MdF* 123(1917):416-31.

1244. Doucet, J. "'Harmonie du soir' de Charles Baudelaire." *ECL* 11 (1942):100-07.

1245. DuBos, Charles. "Méditation sur Baudelaire." *Revue de Genève* 4 (1922):342-58,426-52.

1246. Eliot, T.S. "*Baudelaire and the Symbolists:Five Essays*, by Peter Quennell:A Review." *Criterion* 9(Jan 1930):357-59.

1247. Fauconnier, Jean. *La marche à l'idéal:Baudelaire, Verlaine, Mallarmé.* Jumet: Imprimerie Mornard, 1950.

1248. Ferran, André. "Baudelaire et la musique," 387-93 in *Mélanges de philosophie et d'histoire littéraire offerts à Edmond Huguet.* Paris: Boivin, 1940.

1249. Feuerlicht, Ignace. "Baudelaire's 'Harmonie du soir'." *FR* 33(1959-1960):17-26.

1250. Fontainas, A. "Baudelaire." *MdF* 147(1921):5-27.

1251. Fowlie, Wallace. "Baudelaire and Eliot:Interpreters of Their Age." *SR* 74,i(1965):293-300.

1252. Frandon, I.-M. "Le structuralisme et les caractères de l'oeuvre littéraire, à propos des 'Chats' de Baudelaire." *RHL* 72(1972):101-16.

1253. Gallico, Claudio. "Baudelaire e la musica." *Convivium* 23(1955):68-81.

1254. Gautier, F. "La vie amoureuse de Baudelaire." *MdF* 45(1903):46-86.

1255. Gide, André. "Baudelaire et M. Faguet." *NRF* (1 nov 1910): 499-518.

1256. Graaf, Daniel A. de "Een sleutel tot Baudelaire's Dandysme." *RLV* 24(1958):428-30.

1257. Grandpré, Daruty de. "Baudelaire et Jeanne Duval." *La Plume* 103(août 1893):329-33.

1258. Gsteiger, Manfred. "Baudelaire in der deutschen Literatur:Ein Umriss." *Neue Zürcher Zeitung* (27 Aug 1967):5.

1259. ———. "*Die Blumen des Bösen*: George als Uebersetzer Baudelaires," 49-91 in *Literatur des Uebergangs: Essays.* Bern and Munich: Francke, 1963.

1260. Haasan, I.H. "Baudelaire's Correspondances:The Dialectic of a Poetic Affinity." *FR* 27(1954):437-45.

1261. Hambly, Peter S. "The Structure of *Les fleurs du mal*:Yet Another Suggestion," 203-04 in J.R. Ellis,ed. *Australasian Univs. Lang. and Lit. Assn.:Proceedings and Papers of the Thirteenth Congress Held at Monash Univ. 12-18 August 1970.* Melbourne: AULLA and Monash U., 1971. 493 pp.

1262. Hauser, O. "Baudelaire in deutscher Übersetzung." *Das literarische Echo* 4(1901-02):1253-55.

1263. Hittle, Gervasse G. "Arthur Symons' Translation of Baudelaire's *Petits poèmes en prose*:A Collision of Styles." *DAI* 32(1971):2690A(Ohio).

1264. Hubert, Judd D. "Baudelaire's Revolutionary Poetics." *RR* 46 (1955):164-77.

1265. ———. "Symbolism, Correspondence, and Memory." *YFS* 9(1952): 46-55.

1265a. Hyslop, Lois B. "Baudelaire: 'Madame Bovary, c'est moi'?" *KRQ* 20(1973):343-58.

1265b. ——. "Baudelaire on *Les misér-ables." FR* 41(1967):23-29.

1265c. ——. "Baudelaire's *Elévation* and E.T.A. Hoffmann." *FR* 46(1973) 951-59.

1265d. Hyslop, Lois B., and Francis E., Jr., trs. and eds. *Baudelaire:A Self-Portrait.* Selected letters tr. and ed. with a running commentary. London, New York, Toronto: Oxford U.P., 1957. 259 pp.

1265e. ——. *Baudelaire As a Literary Critic.* Univ. Park, Pa.: Penn State U.P., 1964. 387 pp.

1265f. Hyslop, Lois B., ed. *Baudelaire As A Love Poet and Other Essays.* Univ. Park, Pa.: Penn State U.P., 1969. 130 pp. Essays by Henri Peyre, Marcel Ruff, Lois B. Hyslop and Francis E. Hyslop.

1266. Jean-Aubry, G. "Baudelaire et Swinburne." *MdF* 124(1917):265-81.

1267. Johnson, Lee M. "Art Criticism as a Genre of Literature:Baudelaire, Ruskin and Pater." *DAI* 31(1971): 4123A(Stanford).

1268. Jones, P.M. "Baudelaire, Verlaine and Verhaeren." *MLR* 21(1926): 288-99.

1269. ——. "The Uses of Nature in the Poems of Baudelaire," 151-64 in *Gallica:Essays Presented to Heywood Thomas by Colleagues, Pupils and Friends.* Philip F. Butler,ed. Cardiff: U. of Wales P., 1969. 271 pp.

1270. Juden, Brian. "Que la théorie des correspondances ne dérive pas de Swedenborg." *TLL* 11,ii(1973): 33-46.

1271. Kaire, Alexandre. "Charles Baudelaire." *La Plume* 139(fév 1893): 72-74.

1272. Kies, A. "Baudelaire et Valéry." *LR* 10(1956):51-63.

1273. King, William W. "Baudelaire and Mallarmé:Metaphysics or Aesthetics?" *JAAC* 26(1967):115-23.

1274. Köhler, Hartmut. "Valéry und Baudelaire," 209-24 in Johannes Hösle, and Wolfgang Eitel,eds. *Beiträge zur vergleichenden Literaturgeschichte:Festschrift für Kurt Wais zum 65. Geburtstag.* Tübingen: Niemeyer, 1972. 406 pp.

1275. Kzocsa, Sándor. *Baudelaire Magyarorzágon/Baudelaire en Hongrie* (Bibliografiak/Bibliographies 2.) Univ. L. Eötvös de Budapest. Inst. de langue et littérature françaises. Budapest, 1969.

1276. Laforgue, Jules. "Notes sur Baudealire, Corbière, Mallarmé, Rimbaud." *Entretiens Politiques et littéraires* 1,ii(1891):97-104.

1277. Lemonnier, Léon. "Baudelaire et Mallarmé, traducteurs d'Edgar Poe." *LanM* 43(1949):25-46.

1278. Le Petit, Jules. "Notes sur Baudelaire." *La Plume* 101(juillet 1893): 287-88. [Incl. facsim. of ms by B.]

1279. Luszeznski, Walter R. "La symbolique des couleurs dans l'oeuvre de Baudelaire." *DA* 28(1967):1081A-82A(Wayne State).

1280. Macchia, Giovanni. "Baudelaire e la musica." *Mercurio* 3,xxii(1946): 103-09.

1281. Magliola, Robert R. "Phenomenological Criticism:Its Theory and Methodology, with Practical Applications to the Poetry of Hart Crane and Charles Baudelaire." *DAI* 31(1971): 4127A-28A(Princeton).

1282. Maire, G. "Un essai de classification des 'Fleurs du Mal'." *MdF* 65(1907):260-80.

1283. Mary, André. "Méditations sur Charles Baudelaire." *L'Ermitage* 28(oct 1903):122-42.

1284. Maurice-Amour, Lila. "Musiques inspirées par les *Fleurs du mal." RSH* 89(1958):167-80.

1285. Mein, Margaret. "Baudelaire and Symbolism." *ECr* 13(1973):154-65. 13(1973):154-65.

1286. Michaud, Régis. "Baudelaire et Edgar Allan Poe:Une mise au point." *RLC* 18(1938):666-83.

1287. Mickel, Emanuel. "Concerning the Source and Date of Baudelaire's 'La Beauté'." *RomN* 14(1972): 299-303.

1288. "Notes inédites de Laforgue sur Baudelaire." *Entretiens politiques et littéraires* 13(1891):97-120.

1289. "Notes pour une iconographie du poète Charles Baudelaire." *La Plume* 180(oct 1896):634-41.

1290. Nugent, R. "Baudelaire and the Criticism of Decadence, 1882-1886." *PhQ* 36(1957):234-43.

1291. Osborn, Catherine B. "Mystic Fusion:Baudelaire and *le sentiment du beau*." *PMLA* 88(1973):1127-35.

1292. Ourousof, Prince A. "Baudelairiana:Les 'Errata' incorrigés des 'Fleurs du Mal'." *La Plume* 236(fév 1899):99.

1293. ———. "Iconographie baudelairienne." *La Plume* 174(juillet 1896): 533-34.

1294. ———. "Le tombeau de Charles Baudelaire." *La Plume* 148(juin 1895):267-69 [Inédits.]

1295. Oxenhandler, Neal. "The Balcony of Charles Baudelaire." *YFS* 9 (1952):56-62.

1296. Platz, Hermann. "Baudelaire und die Ursprünge des französischen Symbolismus." *DVLG* 10(1932): 687-718.

1297. Poirion, Daniel. "Baudelaire et l'allégorie." *Bull. d'information du service de documentation* (Univ. de Grenoble) Supp. 19-20(oct-déc 1968):10-17.

1298. Polanšćak, Antun. "Le Mal de Baudelaire." *SRAZ* 24(1967):23-32.

1299. Poulet, Georges. *Qui était Baudelaire?* Précédé de notices documentaires par Robert Kopp. Genève: Shira, 1969, 188 pp.

1299a. Prete, Antonio. "Baudelaire critico: La dialettica parzialità-apertura." *Degrés* 2(1973):h-h6.

1300. Proust, M. "A propos de Baudelaire." *NRF* (1 juin 1921):641-63.

1301. Quennell, Peter. *Baudelaire and the Symbolists*. London: Weidenfeld and Nicolson, 1954. 164 pp.

1302. Raynaud, E. "Baudelaire et Théophile Gautier." *MdF* 123(1917): 577-606.

1303. Rees, Garnet. "Baudelaire and the Imagination," 203-15 in *Modern Miscellany Presented to Eugene Vinaver by Pupils, Colleagues and Friends*, T.E. Lawrenson, F.E. Sutcliffe and G.F. Gadoffre,eds. Manchester: Manchester U.P., 1969. 314 pp.

1304. Régnier, Henri de. "Charles Baudelaire." *Entretiens politiques et littéraires* 37(fév 1893):145-50.

1305. "Rencensement bibliographique: Supplément 1966." *Bull. Baudelairien* 7,ii(1972):13-20.

1306. Reynold, Gonzague de. *Charles Baudelaire*. Paris: G. Crès, 1920. 417 pp.

1307. Rivière, Jacques. "Baudelaire." *NRF* (1 déc 1910):721-40.

1308. Roache, J. "Baudelaire and Symons:Symbolism and Decadence." *RLC* 41(1967):351-66.

1309. Roedig, Ch.F. "Baudelaire and Synesthesia." *KRQ* 5(1958):128-35.

1310. Royère, J. "L'érotologie de Baudelaire." *MdF* 140(1920):618-37.

1311. Schaeffner, André. "Corrispondenze Baudelairiane." *Quaderni della Rassegna musicale* 1,iv(1968):97-104.

1312. Seguin, M. *Aux sources vivantes du symbolisme:Génie des* Fleurs du Mal. Paris, 1938. [Repr. Genève: Slatkine, 1970.]

1313. Spire, A. "Baudelaire:Esthéticien et précurseur du symbolisme." *Europe* 456-57(Apr-May 1967):79-99.

1314. Starkie, Enid. *Baudelaire*. Londen: Faber and Faber, 1957; Norfolk, Conn: New Directions, 1958. 622 pp.

1315. Stäuble, Michele, and Lippman Wulf. "De Quincey, Baudelaire e i paradisi artificiali," *NA* 514(1972): 245-54.

1316. Stuart, Esmè [Leroy, Amélie Claire]. "Charles Baudelaire and Edgar Poe: A Literary Affinity." *Nineteenth Century and After* 34 (1893):65-80.

1317. Sugar, Charlotte de. *Baudelaire et R.M. Rilke*. Paris: Nouvelles Editions Latines, 1954.

1318. Tiedemann-Bartels, Hella. *Versuch über das artistische Gedicht: Baudelaire, Mallarmé, George*. München: Rogner & Bernhard, 1971. 159 pp.

1319. Turnell, Martin. "Charles Baudelaire." *SoR* 6(1970):104-36. [Also on J. Laforgue and T.S. Eliot.]

1320. Turquet-Milnes, Gladys R. *The Influence of Baudelaire on France and England*. London: Constable, 1913. 300 pp.

1321. Vergniol, Camille. "Cinquante ans après Baudelaire." *RdP* (15 août 1917):673-709.

1322. Vestdijk, S. "Baudelaire en de muziek." *Maatstaf* 5(1957):248-64.

1323. Welch, Cyril and Liliane. *Emergence: Baudelaire, Mallarmé, Rimbaud*. State College, Pa.: Bald Eagle Press, 1973. 134 pp.

See also 21,128, 152, 348, 753a, 824, 855, 957, 994, 1048, 1084, 1360, 1433, 1458, 1580, 1600, 1612, 1617, 1696, 1697, 2116, 2181, 2295, 2450, 2456, 2458, 2459, 2460, 2468, 2469, 2470, 2471, 2676, 2799, 2855, 2970, 3023, 3038, 3043.

Beardsley

1324. Barnett, Pat. "Some Aspects of Symbolism in the Work of Aubrey Beardsley." *AntigR* 1,iv(1971): 33-45.

1325. Davray, Henry D. "Aubrey Vincent Beardsley." *La Plume* 246(juillet 1899):447-51. [Incl. bibliog. on B.]

1326. Mattenklott, Gert. *Bilderdienst: Ästhetische Opposition bei Beardsley und George*. München: Rogner & Bernhard, 1970. 385 pp.

1327. Reade, Brian E. *Aubrey Beardsley*. New York: Viking Press, 1967; London: Studio Vista, 1967. 372 pp.

1328. Rambosson, Yvanhoé. "Aubrey Beardsley." *La Plume* 215(avril 1898):218-19.

1329. Weintraub, Stanley. *Beardsley: A Biography*. New York: George Braziller, 1967. 285 pp.

See also 2778.

Beer-Hoffmann

1330. Oberholzer, Otto. *Richard Beer-Hofmann: Werk und Weltbild eines Dichters*. Bern: Francke, 1947. 272 pp.

Bely

1331. Belyj, Andrej. *Simvolizm*. Moscow, 1910.

1332. Burkhart, Gagmar. "Leitmotivik und Symbolik in A. Belyjs Roman *Peterburg*." *Die Welt der Slaven* 9(1964):277-323.

1333. Cioran, Samuel. "The Apocalyptic Symbolism of Andrey Bely." *DAI* 30(1970):5441A(Toronto).

1334. ———. "The Eternal Return: Andrej Belyj's *Kotik Lataev*." *SEEJ* 15 (1971):22-23.

1335. ———. "In the Imitation of Christ: A Study of Andrej Bely's *Zapiski Chudaka*." *CSS* 4(1970):74-92.

1336. Hart, Pierre R. "Andrej Belyj's *Petersburg*." *DAI* 30(1969):2023A-24A(Wis.).

1337. Keuchel, Ernst. "A. Bjely und der

russische Symbolismus." *Deutsche Monatschrift für Russland* 56,iii (1914):195-202.

1338. Malmstad, John Earl. "The Poetry of Andrej Belyj:A Variorum Edition." *DAI* 30(1969):2031A (Princeton). [Rus. text with Eng. Introd.]

1339. Maslenikov, Oleg. *The Frenzied Poets:Andrey Biely and the Russian Symbolists.* Berkeley: U. of Calif. P., 1952. 234 pp.

1340. Monas, Sidney. "Unreal City." *ChiR* 13,iii(1959):102-12. [Rev. art.]

1341. Pflanzl, Jutta. *Weltbild und Kunstschau des russischen Symbolismus in der theoretischen Gestaltung durch A. Belys.* Wien: U. of Wien, 1946. [Diss.]

1342. Reeve, F.D. "A Geometry of Prose." *KR* 25(1963):9-25.

1343. Specovius, Günther. "Wiederentdeckung des Andrey Belyj." *Deutsche Rundschau* 86(1960):376-78.

1344. Steffensen, Eigil. "Symbol og vision:Om Andrej Belyj og hans forfatterskab." *Dansk Udsyn* 50(1970): 114-26.

1345. Struve, Gleb. "Andrej Belyj's Experiments with Novel Technique." *Stil- und Formprobleme* 4(1959): 459-67.

1346. Tschizewskij, Dmytro. "A. Bely," 8-14 in *Versdichtung der Russischen Symbolisten.* Wiesbaden: O. Harrassowitz, 1959.

See also 676.

Benn *See* 1013, 1591, 1693.

Berdyayev *See* 694.

Besnard

1347. Adam, Paul. "Le symbolisme dans l'oeuvre d'Albert Besnard."

Gaz. des Beaux-Arts 6(Dec 1911): 437-54.

Biegas

1348. Basler, Adolphie. "Boleslas Biegas." *La Plume* 317(juillet 1902): 817.

1349. "Biegas." *La Plume* 320(août 1902):1004-08. [Extraits de journaux.]

1350. Fontainas, André. "Boleslas Biegas." *La Plume* 320(août 1902): 995-97.

1351. Gierszynski, Stanislas. "Un sculpteur polonais." *La Plume* 317(juillet 1902):827-32.

1352. Jaudon, Pierre. "La sculpture de M. Boleslas Biegas." *La Plume* 317(juillet 1902):823-26.

1353. Josez, Virgile. "Biegas." *La Plume* 320(août 1902):1000-03.

1354. Morice, Charles. "A propos du statuaire Biegas." *La Plume* 320(août 1902):993-94.

1355. Réja, Marcel. "Biegas, sculpteur." *La Plume* 320(août 1902):998-99.

Bjørnson *See* 2790.

Blaga

1356. Cioculescu, Serban. "Metafora inorogului in poezia lui Lucian Blaga." *RoLit* 31 Aug(1972):8.

1357. Gáldi, L. "Le vers libre est-il libre? Réflexions sur la versification de Lucian Blaga," 265-70 in *Omagiu lui Alexandru Rosetti la 70 de ani.* Bucharest: Editura Academiei Republicii Socialiste România, 1965.

1358. Todoran, Eugene. "Preliminarii la opera lui Lucian Blaga." *RITL* 16(1967):101-17.

1359. Vultur, Smaranda. "Virtuţile limbajului in Asfinţit marin de Lucian Blaga." *LimR* 21(1972):455-62.

See also 336.

Bloem

1360. Kamerbeek, J., Jr. *De Poëzie van J.C. Bloem in Europees perspectief.* Amsterdam: Polak and van Gennep, 1967. 128 pp.

Blok

1361. Blok, Alexandre. "La vocation du poète." *Table Ronde* 185(1963): 37-44. [On Pushkin. Tr. Jean Gauvain.]

1362. Christa, Boris. "Metrical Innovations in Blok's Lyrical Verse." *AUMLA* 17(1962):44-52.

1363. Eršov, P. "Simvoličeskaja lirika na scene:'Balagančik' Al. Bloka." *NovŽ* 67(1962):98-117.

1364. Futrell, Michael. "Alexander Blok." *Survey* 36(1961):119-20.

1365. Gerasimov, Ju.K. "Teatr i drama v kritike A. Bloka v period pervoj russkoj revoljucii." *VLU* 17, xx,(1962):73-85.

1366. Gzovskaja, O. "A.A. Blok v Moskovkom Xudožestvennom teatre." *RLit* 3(1961):197-205.

1367. Jur'eva, Zoja. *"Aleksandr Blok: Between Image and Idea." NovŽ* 71(1963):276-81. [Rev. art.]

1368. Kisch, Sir Cecil. *Alexander Blok: Prophet of Revolution.* New York: Roy Pubs., 1961.

1369. Kruk, I. "Blok i Gogol." *RLit* 1(1961):85-103.

1370. Laffitte, Sophie. "Le symbolisme occidental et Alexander Blok." *RESl* 34(1958):88-94.

1371. Levin, V.I. "Poèma Aleksandr Bloka 'Dvenadcat' glazami sovetskogo i amerikanskogo issledovatelja." *IAN* 22(1963):386-96.

1372. Mašbic-Verov, I. *Russkij simvolizm i put' Aleksandra Bloka.* Kujbyšev: Knižnoe izd-vo, 1969.

1373. Masing, I. "H.Ch. Andersen and A. Blok's Poetic Cycle *The Snow Mask,"* 122-29 in A.P. Treweek,ed. *Australasian Univs. Lang. and Lit. Assn.:Proceed. and Papers of the Twelfth Cong. Held at the Univ. of West Australia, 5-11 Feb. 1969.* [Sydney]: AULLA, 1970. 504 pp.

1374. Medvedev, P.N. *V laboratorii pisatelja.* Moscow: Sovetskij pisatel', 1960.

1375. Pajman, A. "Aleksander Blok v Anglii." *RLit* 1(1961):214-20.

1376. Reeve, F.D. *Aleksandr Blok: Between Image and Idea.* New York: Columbia U.P., 1962.

1377. ———. "Structure and Symbol in Blok's *The Twelve." ASEER* 19(1960):275.

1378. Šarykin, D.M. "Blok i Strindberg." *VLU* 28,i(1963):82-91.

1379. Taranovsky, Kiril. "Certain Aspects of Blok's Symbolism," 249-60 in R. Magidoff et al.,eds. *Studies in Slavic Linguistics and Poetics in Honor of Boris O. Unbegaun.* New York: N.Y.U. Press, 1968.

1380. Timofeev, L. "Poèma Bloka 'Dvenadcat' i eë tolkovateli." *VLit* 7(1960):116-27.

1381. ———. "Poétika kontrasta v poèzii Aleksandra Bloka." *RLit* 5(1961): 98-107.

1382. Vejdle, V. "Poxorony Bloka." *NovŽ* 65(1961):270-76.

1383. Vogel, Lucy. "A Symbolist's Inferno:Blok and Dante." *RusR* 29(1970):38-51.

See also 680, 693, 694, 1223.

Böcklin

1384. Roberts, K. "Hayward Gallery, London Exhibit." *Burlington Magazine* 113(July 1971):419.

Bois, Jules

1385. Saint-Jacques, Louis de. "Ex-

pertises: 'L'Eve nouvelle' de M. Jules
Bois." *La Plume* 187(fév 1897):
85-89.

Boissière

1386. Mazel, Henri. "Albert Boissière."
La Plume 237(mars 1899):146-50.

Bouchor

1387. Vérola, Paul. "Maurice Bouchor
et 'les symboles'." *La Plume* 136(déc
1894):511.

Bourges

1388. Lebois, André. *Les tendences du
Symbolisme à travers l'oeuvre
d'Elémir Bourges.* Paris: L'Amitié par
le livre, 1952. 414 pp.

Bourget

1389. Labat, Louis. "Les origines de M.
Paul Bourget d'après son oeuvre
poétique." *La Plume* 192(avril
1897):230-33.
1390. Pouilliart, R. "Paul Bourget et
la naissance du symbolisme." *LR*
18(1964):215-39; 315-28.

See also 1097, 1103, 1986.

Brandão, Raul

1391. Coelho, Jacinto do Prado. "Entre
le symbolisme et l'existentialisme:
Humus(1917) de Raoul Brandao,"
335-61 in Nikola Banašević,ed.
*Actes du Ve Congrès de l'Association
Internationale de Littérature Comparée, Belgrade 1967.* Belgrade: U.
de Belgrade; Amsterdam: Swets &
Zeitlinger, 1969.
1392. Ferro, Tulio R. "Raul Brandão et
le Symbolisme portugais." *BEPIF*
13(1949):21-28.
1393. Malpique Cruz. "Raul Brandão, o

obsessivo da vida, da morte, do
sonho e da dor." *BCCMP* 22(1969):
272-338.

Brennan, Christopher

1394. Kirsop, Wallace. "The Greatest
Renewal, The Greatest Revelation:
Brennan's Commentary on Mal-
larmé." *Meanjin* 29(1970):303-11.

See also 2146, 2153.

Brjusov

1395. Berkov, P.N. "Pervye Brjusovskie
čtenija v Erevane." *IAN* 22(1963):
255-56.
1396. Gindin, S.I. "Vzgljady V.Ja. Brjusova na jazykovuju priemlemost'
stixovyx sistem i sud'by russkoj sil-
labiki (po rukopisjam 90-x godov)."
VJa 19,ii(1970):99-104.
1397. Grossman, L. "Brjusovi fran-
cuzskie simvolisty." *Mastera Slova*
1928):261-69.
1398. Markovitch, Milan. "Venise dans
l'oeuvre d'un symboliste russe,"
212-18 in Carlo Pellegrini,ed. *Venezia nelle letterature moderne.* Atti
del primo congresso dell'Associa-
zione internazionale di letteratura
comparata, Venezia, 25-30 settembre
1955. Venezia-Roma: Instituto per la
collaborazione culturale, 1961.
1399. Močul'skij, K. *Valerij Brjusov.*
Paris: n.p., 1962.
1400. Reeve, F.D. "Dobroljubov and
Brjusov:Symbolist Extremists." *SEEJ*
8(1964):292-301.
1401. Rice, Martin P. "Valery Briusov
and the Rise of Russian Symbolism."
DAI 32(1972):4020A(Vanderbilt).
1402. Tukh, B. "K istorii polemiki
vokur 'Russkix simbolistov' V.Ja.
Brjusova." *Russkaya filologia*
3(1971):76-86.

See also 676, 700, 1739.

Bugayev *See* 694.

Carreras, R. de las

1403. Russell, Dora Isella. "Roberto de las Carreras, iniciador del simbolismo en el Uruguay." *CHA* 73(1968): 333-55.

Carrière, E.

1404. Batilliat, Marcel. "Une famille d'artistes." *La Plume* 291(juin 1901):369-73.
1405. Kahn, Gustave. "Critiques des romans." *La Plume* 300(oct 1901):829-31.
1406. Leclère, Tristan. "Les Expositions." *La Plume* 334(mars 1903): 369-70.
1407. Séailles, Gabriel. *Eugène Carrière*. Paris: A Colin, 1911. 270 pp.

Castro, Eugénio de

1408. Fein, John M. "Eugénio de Castro and the Introduction of *Modernism* to Spain." *PMLA* 73(1958):556-61.
1409. "Eugénio de Castro and the Reaction to Symbolism in Portugal." *MLJ* 34(1962):268-71.
1410. Ramos, Feliciano. *Eugénio de Castro e a poesia nova*. Lisboa, 1943. 184 pp.

See also 437, 440, 1120, 2144.

Celan, *See* 2218.

Chekhov

1411. Harrison, John Wm. "Symbolic Action in Chekhov's 'Peasants' and 'In the Ravine'." *MFS* 7(1961): 369-72.
1412. Kjetsaa, Geir. "Den symbolske struktur i Tjekhovs *Tre søstre*." *Edda* 70(1970):215-21.

See also 1883.

Claudel

1413. Bancroft, David. "Claudel on Wagner." *Music and Letters* 50 (1969):439-52.
1414. Becker, Aimé. "*Tête d'or* et *Cébès*, ou le drame de l'adolescence." *RLM* 271-75(1971):53-67.
1415. Berchan, Richard. "Paul Claudel's *Ode to the Muses*:Reflections on the Role of a Poem in the Creation of Its Author." *Claudel S* 1,i(1972):28-35.
1416. Brodeur, Leo A. *Le corps-sphère, clef de la symbolique claudienne*. Paris: Nizet, 1970.
1417. Dubarle, Father."Paul Claudel y el española."*CHA* 37(1957):29-50.
1418. Erwin, John F., Jr. "Claudel and the Lesson of Mallarmé:The Theme of Absence." *ECr* 13(1973):44-54.
1419. Fowlie, Wallace. *Paul Claudel*. London: Bowes & Bowes; New York: Hillary House, 1957. 111 pp.
1420. Halévy, Daniel. "Claudel à Berlin." *Revue de Genève* 21(1930): 234-50.
1421. Horry, Ruth N. *Paul Claudel and Saint-John Perse*. Chapel Hill: U. of N.C. Press, 1971.
1422. Kaech, René. "Le symbolisme de l'eau chez Claudel." *CIS* 21(1972): 27-38.
1423. Lawler, James R. "Claudel and Symbolism." *RNL* 6,ii(1973):34-46.
1424. Lioure, Michel. *L'esthétique dramatique de Paul Claudel*. Paris: Colin, 1971. 674 pp.
1425. MacCombie, John. *The Prince and the Genie: A Study of Rimbaud's Influence on Claudel*. Amherst: U. of Mass. P., 1972. 197 pp.
1426. Oeuel, Mildred. "A Study of the Dramatic Structure of *Partage de midi* from 1905-1949." *FR* 45 (1972):964-70.
1427. Oswald, Werner. "Die symbolischen Bezüge in P. Claudels *Tête d'Or*:Versuch einer Deutung." *NS* (1963):61-72.

1428. Petit, Jacques,ed. "Paul Claudel 7:La poésie de la nuit." *RLM* 245-48(1970):1-126.
1429. Pollmann, Leo. "Paul Claudel und Stéphane Mallarmé:Interpretation von Paul Claudel *Jour d'automne*." *ZFSL* 76(1966):1-9.
1430. Schmidt, Albert-Marie. "L'itinéraire symboliste de Paul Claudel." *Table Ronde* 88(1955):24-26.
1431. Vargas, Maria F. "O simbolo nas 'Cinq grandes odes' de Paul Claudel." *Colóquio* 3(1971):17-24.
1432. Vial, Fernand. "Symbols and Symbolism in Paul Claudel." *YFS* 9(1952):93-102.
1433. Watson, Harold. "Baudelairian Realism in Claudel's Early Drama." *ECr* 13(1973):55-65.

See also 107, 907, 1084, 1233, 2167, 2212, 2650, 2893, 3133.

Claussen

1434. Andersen, Harry. "Nogle allusioner i Sophus Claussens digtning." *DS* 57(1962):118-25.
1435. ——. "Sophus Claussen." *NT* 41 (1965):328-44.
1436. ——. *Studies i Sophus Claussens Lyrik*. Copenhagen: Universitets Kassererkonter, 1967. 324 pp.
1437. Brandt, Torben. "Sophus Claussen og Eros:En undersøgelse af drømmen og desillusioneringen i Sophus Claussens forfatterskab 1887-1896." *Extracta* 2(1969):41-52.
1438. Bresson, Leo. "Pan-motivet hos Sophus Claussen:Studier i Sophus Claussens digtning fra *Valfart* til *Heroica*." *Extracta* 2(1969):53-59. [Abst.]
1439. Brostrøm, Torben. "Digteren på trampolineme." *Vindrosen* 13,iv (1966):39-47.
1440. Petersen, Lise B. "Sophus Claussen og Hermann Bang:Digtermodet i Paris og dets litteraere eftervirkninger." *Extracta* 1(1953):224-31. [Abstr.]

See also 2764.

Conrad

1441. Karl, Frederick R. "Joseph Conrad:A *fin de siècle* Novelist:A Study in Style and Method." *LitR* 2(1959): 565-76.
1442. Yelton, Donald C. *"Mimesis and Metaphor:An Inquiry into the Genesis and Scope of Conrad's Symbolic Imagery*. s'-Gravenhage: Mouton, 1967. 336 pp.

Corbière

1443. Arnoux, Alexandre. *Une âme et pas de violon:Tristan Corbière*. Paris: Grasset, 1930.
1444. Burch, Francis F. *Tristan Corbière:L'originalité des Amours jaunes et leur influence sur T.S. Eliot*. Paris, Nizet, 1970. 352 pp.
1445. Grin, Micha. *Tristan Corbière poète maudit*. Evian: Ed. du Nant d'Enfer, 1971. 238 pp.
1446. Sonnenfeld, Albert. "Tristan Corbière:The Beatific Malediction." *ECr* 9(1969):37-45.
1447. Thomas, Henri. *Tristan le dépossédé*. Paris: Gallimard, 1972. 192 pp.

See also 651, 1276, 1986.

Couperus

1448. Blok, W. *Verhael en lezer:Een onderzoek naar enige structuuraspecten van* Van oude mensen, de dingen die vorbij gaan *van Louis Couperus*. Groningen:Wolters-Noordhoff, 1969.
1449. Eliassen-De Kat, Martha H. "Nog eens stijlverschijnselen bij Couperus." *NTg* 65(1972):287-302.

1450. Kooij, J.G. "Couperus en Engeland." *Marlyn* 2,v(1964):11-28.

1451. Stuiveling, Garmt. "Op zoek naar Louis Couperus." *Gids* 127(1963):357-70.

1452. Tricht, H.W. van. *Louis Couperus:Een verkenning*. 's-Gravenhage: Daamen, 1960.

1453. Woudenberg, Gerda van. "Fin di Secolo in Olanda:Louis Couperus." *RLMC* 10(1957):31-43.

Crane

1454. Anderson, David D. "Journey Through Time:The Poetic Vision of Hart Crane." *Ohioana Quart*. (Columbus, Ohio.) 15(1972):59-64.

1455. Coffman, Stanley K., Jr. "Symbolism in 'The Bridge'." *PMLA* 66 (1951)65-77.

1456. Guiguet, Jean. *L'univers poétique de Hart Crane*. Paris: Lettres modernes, 1965. 149 pp.

1457. Hinz, Evelyn J. "Hart Crane's 'Voyages' Reconsidered." *ConL* 13 (1972):315-53.

1458. Holton, Milne. " 'A Baudelairesque Thing':The Directions of Hart Crane's 'Black Tambourine'." *Criticism* 9(1967):215-28.

1459. Houston, Robert W. "Hart Crane and Arthur Rimbaud:A Comparison," 13-19 in Howard Creed,ed. *Essays in Honor of Richebourg Gaillard McWilliams*. With pref. Birmingham, Ala.: Birmingham-Southern Coll., 1970.

1460. Yannella, Philip R. "Voyages Out and Back:A Study of Hart Crane's Major Poetry." *DAI* 32(1972):4032A(Wis., Milwaukee).

See also 1611, 1994.

Cros

1461. Forestier, Louis. *Charles Cros*. Paris: Seghers, 1972. 175 pp.

1462. ———. *Charles Cros, L'homme et l'oeuvre*. Paris: Minard (Lettres Modernes), 1969. 587 pp.

1463. Renna, Pamela S. "Aux pays lointains:The Poetry of Charles Cros." *DAI* 33(1972):5243A(Brown.).

See also 651.

Cruz e Souza

1464. Franzbach, Martin. "Brasilianischer Beitrag zu einer Geschichte des Lachens:Des Symbolismus des Cruz e Sousa." *Ibero* 2(1970):158-61.

1464a. Montenegro, Abelardo F. *Cruz e Sousa e o movimiento simbolista no Brasil*. Fortaleza, 1954.

1465. Muricy, Andrade. "O cisne negro Cruz e Souza (1861-1961)." *RIB* 12 (1962):15-38.

D'Annunzio

1466. Aprea, Vincenzo. "La tragedia dannunziana." *Silarus* 7(1971): 14-15.

1467. Bo, Carlo. "D'Annunzio e la letteratura del novecento," 69-79 in *L'arte di Gabrielle D'Annunzio Atti del convegno internazionale di studio:Venezia-Gardone Riviera Pescara 7-13 ottobre 1963*. Emilio Mariano, ed. Milano: Mondadori, 1968.

1468. Bonomo, Dario. "Noterelle su Gabriele D'Annunzio." *APen* 8 (1972):60-66.

1469. Cataro, Atanasio. "Parole oscure in una lirica di D'Annunzio." *GdI* 21-22(agosto 1972):3.

1470. Ciaffi, Gesualdo. "Incontri con Gabriele D'Annunzio." *GdB* 3 (1970):491-94.

1471. Cigada, Sergio. "Flaubert, Verlaine e la formazione poetica di Gabriele D'Annunzio." *RLMC* 12 (1959):18-35.

1472. De Montera, V., and G. Tosi. *D'Annunzio, Montesquiou, Matilde*

Serão. Documents inédits. Roma: Storia e letteratura, 1972. 432 pp.

1473. Gullace, Giovanni G. *Gabriele D'Annunzio in France:A Study in Cultural Relations*. Syracuse, N.Y.: Syracuse U.P., 1966. 243 pp.

1474. Jullian, Philippe. *D'Annunzio*. Paris: Fayard, 1971. 370 pp.

1475. ———. "D'Annunzio the Decadent." *ForumH* 10,i(1972):12-16. [From Chap. 4 of *D'Annunzio*; tr. Eugène M. Decker,III.]

1476. Lobner, Coriana del Greco. "James Joyce's 'Tilly' and Gabriele D'Annunzio's 'I Pastori d'Abruzzio'." *JJQ* 9(1972):383-89.

1477. Mariano, Emilio,ed. *L'arte di Gabriele D'Annunzio. Atti del convegno internationale di studio (Venezia-Gardone Riviera-Pescara 7-13 ottobre 1963)*. Milano: Mondadori, 1968.

1478. Paolazzi, G.V. "Presenze dannunziane nel novecento." *Ausonia* 26,iv (1971):69-71.

1479. Paratore, Ettore. "Il ritorno di D'Annunzio." *Tempo* 7(luglio 1972):3.

1480. Revel, Jean-François. "D'Annunzio ressuscité." *L'Express* 1026 (8-14 mars 1971):65.

1481. Rota, V. *Decadentismo morale e decadentismo estetico*. Bologna: Patron, 1966.

1482. Roussel, Georges. "Théâtres." *La Plume* 211(fév 1898):91.

1483. Tosi, Guy. "Gabriele D'Annunzio et Paul Valéry," 225-41 in *Scritti vari dedicati a Marino Parenti per il suo sessantesimo anniversario*. Firenze: Sansoni, 1958.

1484. ———. La tentation symboliste chez d'Annunzio." *RSH* 78(1955): 285-96.

1485. Traverso, Leone. "Nell'anniversario di D'Annunzio:Hofmannsthal e D'Annunzio." *SUSFL* 45(1971): 201-07

1486. Valeri, Diego. "Posizione di D'Annunzio nel simbolismo europeo." *Approdo* 9,xxii(1963):6-19.

1487. Vecchioni, Mario. "Le immagini dannunziane." *GdI* 22-23(agosto 1972):3.

1488. Vettori, Vittorio. "Romanzo wagneriano." *Telegrafo* 2(giugno 1972):3. [Trionfo della morte.]

See also 885, 2235.

Darío

1489. Aguado-Andreut, Salvador. "La Luz en el mundo poético de Rubén Darío," 36-58 in Vol. I of *Saggi e ricerche in memoria de Ettore Gotti*. (Centro di studi filologici e linguistici siciliani. Bollettino 6.) Palermo, 1962.

1490. Alonso, Amado. *Rubén Darío y los escritores españoles de su tiempo*. Madrid: C.S.I.C., 1967.

1491. Argüello, Santiago. *Rubén Darío: La encarnación del modernismo*, Vol. I in *Modernismo y modernistas*. Guatemala: C.A. Tipografía nacional, 1935.

1492. Ashmurst, A. W. "Clarín y Darío: Una guerrilla literaria del modernismo." *CHA* 260(1972):324-30.

1493. Balseiro, José A. "Presencia de Wagner y casi ausencia de Debussy en Rubén Darío." *Abside* 31(1967): 174-89.

1494. Belmás, Antonio O. *Este otro Rubén Darío*. Madrid: Estudios literarios Aguilar, 1968. 583 pp.

1495. Bocsi, J. Peter. "Cuatro notas sobre Rubén Darío y el poeta hungaro Endre Ady." *RL* 28(1965):75-86.

1496. Bus, L.M.R. "La 'Marcha Triunfa' y 'El Cortejo nocturne' (Comparación entre Rubén Darío y Paul van Ostaijen)." *Thesaurus* 22(1967):369-77.

1497. Campos, Mário M. *Rubén Darío e o modernismo hispano-americano.* Belo Horizonte: Imprensa Universitária, 1968. 117 pp.

1498. Çarreño, Mada. "Rubén Darío:El Cisne." *VidaL* 24(1972):13-16.

1499. Chamorro, Alejandro H. *La mitología griega en Rubén Darío.* Avila: Editorial la Muralla, 1967. 248 pp.

1500. Chasca, Edmundo de. "El 'Reino interior' de Rubén Darío y 'Crimen Amoris' de Verlaine." *RI* 21(1956): 309-17.

1501. Costanzo, Luigi. "Il mondo di Rubén Darío." *AllaB* 6,iii(1968): 14-16.

1502. Darroch, Ann B. "Rubén Darío's 'Sinfonía en gris mayor':A New Interpretation." *Hispania* 53(1970): 46-52.

1503. De Tommaso, Vincenzo. "Rubén Darío e il rinnovamento della poesia spagnola." *Carovana* 14(1964): 91-94.

1504. Durand, René L. "Rubén Darío et les lettres françaises." *RIB* 17 (1967):157-64.

1505. Fiber, L.A. "Rubén Darío's Debt to Paul Verlaine in 'El reino interior'." *RomN* 14(1972):92-95.

1506. Fogelquist, Donald F. *Rubén Darío and Juan Ramón Jiménez: Their Literary and Personal Relations.* Coral Gables, Fla: U. of Miami P., 1956.

1507. Forcadas, Alberto. "Más sobre el gongorismo de Rubén Darío." *PSA* 66(1972):41-55.

1508. García-Abrines, Luis. "Una curiosa aliteración simbolista de Rubén Darío." *RHM* 28(1962):45-48.

1509. Glendinning, Nigel. "En torno a *Sonetina*," 165-74 in *Homenaje a Arturo Marasso 1890-1970.* (Cuadernos del Sur.) Bahia Blanca: Inst. de Humanidades, Univ. Nacional del Sur, 1972. 466 pp.

1510. Goić, Cedomil. "Generación de Darío." *RdPac* 4,iv(1967):17-35.

1511. González-Gerth, Miguel, and George D. Schade,eds. *Rubén Darío Centennial Studies.* Austin: Dept. of Span. and Port., Inst. of Lat. Amer. Studies, U. of Texas, 1970.

1512. González Rodas, Rubio. "Rubén Darío y el Conde de Lautréamont." *RI* 37(1971):375-89.

1513. Greiff, Otto de. *La poesia de Rubén Darío.* Bogotá: Kelly, 1967. 171 pp.

1514. Gullón, Ricardo. "Del Darío sonoro al Rubén interior," 241-50 in Rizel Pincus Sigele, and Gonzalo Sobejano,eds. *Homenaje a Casalduero:Critica y poesía. Ofrecido por sus amigos y discípulos.* Madrid: Gredos, 1972. 510 pp.

1515. Horányi, Mátyá. "Rubén Darío a századvégi Spanyolorzágról és a spanyol modernizmusról." *FK* 15(1969):246-55.

1516. Ibáñez, Roberto. *Páginas desconocidas de Rubén Darío.* Montevideo; Biblioteca de Marcha, 1970. 229 pp.

1517. Litz, Norman. "El dualismo en Darío y Unamuno." *CA* 25(1966): 186-204.

1518. Lozano, Carlos. *Rubén Darío y el modernismo en España (1888-1920):Ensayo de bibliografía comentada.* New York: Las Américas, 1968. 158 pp.

1519. Mayor, Avelino H. *Rubén Darío: Gramática y misterio en su poesía, con otras amenidades estilísticas.* Buenos Aires: Editorial Pleamoar, 1968. 198 pp.

1520. Monuio, Luis. "En torno a 'El reino interior,' de Rubén Darío," 721-28 in *RHM* 34(1968). [*Homenaje a Federico de Onis(1885-1966).*]

1521. Neapes, Erwin. *L'influence française dans l'oeuvre de Rubén Darío.* Paris: Champion, 1921.

1522. Oliveros-Delgado, Rafael. "Darío y Nervo:Su Culto por Francia." *Abside* 34(1970):35-44.

1523. Rull, Enrique. "El símbolo de Psique en la poesía de Rubén Darío." *RL* 27(1965)33-50.

1524. Salinas, Pedro. *La poesía de Rubén Darío.* Buenos Aires: Ed. Losada, 1948. 294 pp.

1525. Sánchez, Ernesto M. *Estudios sobre Rubén Darío:Lengua y estudios literarios.* Mexico City: Fondo de Cultura Económica, 1968. 629 pp.

1526. Schrader, Ludwig. "Rubén Darío, crítico literario en *Los raros,*" 95-99 in Kurt L. Levy, and Keith Ellis,eds. *El ensayo y la crítica literaria en Iberoamérica.* Memoria del XIV Congreso Internacional de Literatura Iberoamericana. Univ. de Toronto, 24-28 de agosto de 1969. Toronto: U. of Toronto P., 1970. 282 pp.

1527. Serra-Lima, Federico. "Rubén Darío y Gérard de Nerval." *RHM* 32 (1966):25-32.

1528. Skyrme, Raymond. "Darío's *Azul* ...:A Note on the Derivation of the Title." *RomN* 10(1968):73-76.

1529. Tamayo Vargas, Augusto. "La muerte de Darío y el Modernismo en el Perú." *Letras* 76/77(1966):15-30.

1530. Torres Bodet, Jaime. *Rubén Darío:Abismo y cima.* Mexico City: Fondo de Cultura Economica, 1966. Univ. Nacional de México, 361 pp.

1531. Trueblood, Alan S. "Rubén Darío:The Sea and the Jungle." *CLS* 4(1967):425-56.

1532. Valente, José A. "Darío o la innovación." *Insula* (July 1967):5-27.

See also 1783, 1854, 1901, 2031, 2801, 2891.

Debussy

1533. Bathari, Jane. *Sur l'interprétation des mélodies de Claude Debussy.* Paris, 1953.

1534. Brody, Elaine. "La famille Men-

dès:A Literary Link between Wagner and Debussy." *Music Review* 33,iii (Aug 1972):177-89.

1535. Ghéon, Henri. "Notes sur une renaissance dramatique." *L'Ermitage* 25(juillet 1902):5-14.

1536. Henderson, Robert. "Debussy and Schönberg." *Musical Times* 108 (Mar 1967):222-26.

1537. Kolatschewsky, Valerius. *Claude Debussy und das Poetische.* Bern: Francke, 1943.

1538. Lockspeiser, Edward. *Debussy.* London: J.M. Dent; New York: Dutton, 1936. 291 pp. [Repr.: New York: Pellegrini, 1951. 304 pp.]

1539. ——. "Debussy and Swinburne." *Monthly Musical Record* 89(1959): 49-53.

1540. ——. *Debussy et Edgar Poe: Manuscrits et documents.* Pref. André Schaeffner. Monaco:Rocher, 1962. 97 pp.

1541. ——. *Debussy—His Life and Mind.* 2 vols. London: Cassell, 1962-65.

1542. ——. "Debussy's Concept of the Dream." *Royal Music Assn. Proceedings* 89(1962-63):49-61.

1543. ——. "Les Symbolistes et Claude Debussy." *Menestrel* (7 and 14 August 1936):241-42.

1544. Philips, C. Henry. "The Symbolists and Debussy." *Music and Letters* 13(1932):298-311.

1545. Schmidt-Garre, Helmut. "Debussy und Maeterlinck—Die Kongruenz ihres Empfindens und die Inkongruenz ihrer Wirkung." *Neue Zeitschrift für Musik* 130(Feb 1969): 85-88.

1546. ——. "Rimbaud-Mallarmé-Debussy: Parallelen zwischen Dichtung und Musik." *Neue Zeitschrift für Musik* 125(1964):290-97.

1547. Terenzio, Vincenzo. "Debussy e Mallarmé." *Rassegna Musicale* 17 (1947):132-36.

1548. Vallas, Léon. *The Theories of*

Claude Debussy, Musicien Français.
Tr. Maire O'Brien. New York: Dover,
1967.

1549. Wenk, Arthur B. "Claude Debussy and the Poets." *DA* 31(1970):
2964A(Cornell).

See also 944, 949, 1493, 2131, 2211,
2213, 2217, 2767, 2987, 3049.

Denis, Maurice

1550. [*Exposition*] *Maurice Denis.*
Orangerie des Tuileries, 3 juin- 31
août 1970. Préf. de Louis Hautecoeur. Paris: Réunion des Musées
Nationaux, 1970. 127 pp. [Incl. illus.
catalog of works, autobiog. statements on art and Symbolism, and
critical bibliog. of works on D.]

1551. Jamot, P. *Maurice Denis.* Paris:
Plon, 1945.

1552. Retté, Adolphe. "Maurice Denis."
La Plume 57(sept 1891):301.

See also 798.

Doolitte

1553. Bianchi, Ruggero. "Saffo in
America." *SA* 11(1965):197-211.

1554. Gibbons, K.G. "The Art of H.D."
MissQ 15(1962):152-60.

1555. Gregory, Horace. "A Poet's
Poet." *Commonweal* 48(1958):
82-83.

1556. Kaufman, J. Lee. "Theme and
Meaning in the Poetry of H.D." *DA*
20(1959):1790(Ind.).

1557. Milicia, Joseph,Jr. "The Fiction
of H.D." *DAI* 33(1972):320A
(Columbia).

Dostoevski

1558. Burssow, B. "Dostojewski und
der Modernismus." *KuL* 14(1966):
155-74,256-64.

1559. Sommavilla, Guido. "Il simbolismo de *L'idiota* di F. Dostoevskij."
Letture 14(1959):748-52.

Dowson

1560. Dakin, Laurence. *Ernest Dowson,
the Swan of Lee.* New York: Papyrus
Books, 1972. 86 pp.

1561. Duffy, John J. "Ernest Dowson
and the Failure of Decadence." *UR*
34(1967):45-49.

1562. Goldfarb, Russell M. "The Dowson Legend Today." *SEL* 4(1964):
653-62.

1563. ——. "Ernest Dowson Reconsidered." *TSL* 14(1969):61-74.

1564. Gordon, Jan B. "Poetic Pilgrimage of Dowson." *Renascence* 20
(1967):3-10,55.

1565. Hönnighausen, Lothar. "Dowsons
Seraphita-Gedichte." *Archiv* 204
(1967):192-201.

1566. Munro, John M. "A Previously
Unpublished Letter from Ernest
Dowson to Arthur Symons." *EA* 17
(1964):284-87.

Dujardin

1567. Collet, G.-P. "Edouard Dujardin
et le symbolisme." *SCB* 20,i(1960):
18.

1568. Régnier, Henri de. "Le chevalier
du passé." *Entretiens politiques et
littéraires* 28(juillet 1892):31-34.

1569. Vielé-Griffin, Francis. "Une préface." *Entretiens politiques et littéraires* 14(mai 1891):159-62.

See also 436, 3023.

Eeden, F. van

1570. Buurman, Henk. "Van Eeden en
Dèr Mouw." *OnsE* 15,ii(1972):
93-97.

1571. Dam, C.F. van. "Van de koele

meren des doods." *NTg* 59(1966): 111-17.

1572. Rümke, Henricus C. *Over Frederik van Eeden's Van de koele meren des doods*. Amsterdam: Scheltema en Holkema, 1964. 191 pp.

1573. Vanderpÿl, Fritz. "Essai sur Frederik van Eeden." *La Plume* 331(fév 1903):203-06.

Ekelund, V.

1574. Kärnell, Karl-Åke. "Vilhelm Ekelund om August Strindberg." *MfS* 35 (May 1964):17-26.

1575. Valdén, Nils Gösta. "Vilhelm Ekelund och världs-litteraturen." *VSLÅ* (1971):142-56.

1576. Wijkmark, Carl-Henning. "Symbolistinfluenser hos Vilhelm Ekelund:Tre Studier." *Samlaren* 89 (1968):7-36.

Eliot, T.S.

1577. Abel, Richard O. "The Relationship Between the Poetry of T.S. Eliot and Saint-John Perse." *DAI* 31 (1971):6041A(So. Calif.).

1578. Ames, Russell. "Decadence in the Art of T.S. Eliot." *Science and Society* 16(1952):193-221.

1579. Antrim, Harry T. *T.S. Eliot's Concept of Language*. (UFMH 35.) Gainesville: U. of Fla. P., 1971. 75 pp.

1580. Beery, Judith A. "The Relevance of Baudelaire to T.S. Eliot's *The Waste Land*." *SUS* 7,v(1966):283-302.

1581. Bergsten, Staffan. *Time and Eternity:A Study in the Structure and Symbolism of T.S. Eliot's "Four Quartets."* Stockholm: Svenskabokforlaget, 1960. 258 pp.

1582. Bollier, E.P. "La Poésie Pure:The Ghostly Dialogue Between T.S. Eliot and Paul Valéry." *ForumH* 8,i (1970):54-59.

1583. Brotman, D. Bosley. "T.S. Eliot: 'The Music of Ideas'." *UTQ* 18, (1948):20-29.

1584. Cambon, Glanco. *"The Waste Land* as Work in Progress." *Mosaic* 6,i(1972):191-200.

1585. Chairi, Joseph. *T.S. Eliot:Poet and Dramatist*. London: Vision Press, 1972. 167 pp.

1586. Davidson, Arthur. *The Eliot Enigma:A Critical Examination of* The Waste Land. London, 1959.

1587. DeLaura, David J. "Pater and Eliot:The Origin of the 'Objective Correlative'." *MLQ* 26(1965):426-31.

1588. Donoghue, Denis. "La parola nella parola." *Paragone* 280(1973): 5-24. [Tr. Giovanna Morsiani.]

1589. Eliot, Valerie,ed. The Waste Land:*A Facsimile and Transcript of the Original Drafts Including the Annotations of Ezra Pound*. New York: Harcourt, 1971. 149 pp.

1590. Empson, William. "My God Man There's Bears on It." *EIC* 22(1972): 417-29. [Rev. art. on Valerie Eliot's facsim. ed. of the drafts of *The Waste Land*.]

1591. Fiumi, Annamaria B. "G. Benn e T.S. Eliot:Poetiche a confronto." *SA* 16(1970):301-51.

1592. Fussell, Paul. "The Gestic Symbolism of T.S. Eliot." *ELH* 22 (1955):194-211.

1593. Greene, Edward J.H. *T.S. Eliot et la France*. Paris: Boivin, 1951. 248 pp.

1594. Hargrove, Nancy D. "Landscape as Symbol in the Poetry of T.S. Eliot." *DAI* 31(1971):3548A(So. Carolina).

1595. Heller, Erich. "T.S. Eliot:Die Tradition und das Moderne." *GuG* 11 (1966):98-137.

1596. Howarth, Herbert. "Eliot and Hofmannsthal." *SAQ* 59(1960):500-09.

1597. ———. *Notes on Some Figures Be-*

hind T.S. Eliot. Boston: Houghton Mifflin, 1964. 396 pp.

1598. Lawler, James R. "T.S.Eliot et Paul Valéry. *MdF* 1169(1961): 76-101.

1599. Little, Roger. "T.S. Eliot and Saint-John Perse." *ArtQ* 2,ii(1969): 5-17.

1600. Marshall, Robert. "T.S. Eliot et le *Baudelaire* de Swinburne." *Bayou* 70 (1957):432-38.

1601. Martin, Mildred. *A Half-Century of Eliot Criticism:An Annotated Bibliography of Books and Articles in English, 1916-1965*. Lewisburg, Pa.: Bucknell U.P., 1972. 361 pp.

1602. Meckier, Jerome. "T.S. Eliot in 1920:The Quatrain Poems and *The Sacred Wood*." *FMLS* 5(1969): 350-76.

1603. Pearson, Gabriel. "Eliot:An American Use of Symbolism," 83-101 in Graham Martin,ed. *Eliot in Perspective:A Symposium*. London: Macmillan; New York: Humanities, 1970.

1605. Praz, Mario. "T.S. Eliot e il Simbolismo," 1-27 in Mario Praz et al, eds. *Il Simbolismo nella letteratura Nord-Americana:Atti del Symposium tenuto a Firenze 27-29 novembre 1964*. (Publicazioni dell'Inst. di Studi Americani, Il. degli Studi di Firenze, 1.) Firenze: La Nuova Italia, 1965.

1606. Rees, Thomas R. "T.S. Eliot's Early Poetry as an Extension of the Symbolist Technique of Jules Laforgue." *ForumH* 8,i(1970):46-52.

1607. Schuchard, Ronald. "Eliot and Hulme in 1916:Toward A Revaluation of Eliot's Critical and Spiritual Development." *PMLA* 88(1973): 1083-94.

1608. Sen, Jyoti P. *The Progress of T.S. Eliot as Poet and Critic*. New Delhi: Orient Longman, 1971.

1609. Sheppard, Richard. "Cultivating *The Waste Land*." *JES* 2(1972):183-89. [Rev. art.]

1610. Smith, Grover. "The Making of *The Waste Land*." *Mosaic* 6,i(1972): 127-41.

1611. Spinucci, Pietro. "T.S. Eliot e Hart Crane." *SA* 11(1965):213-50.

1612. Stéphane, N. "T.S. Eliot et Baudelaire." *Europe* 456-57(1967):244-46.

1613. Stormon, E.J. "Some Notes on T.S. Eliot and Jules Laforgue." *EFL* 2(1965)103-14.

1614. Tate, Allen,ed. "T.S. Eliot (1888-1965)." *SR* 74,i(Jan-Mar 1966).

1615. Torrens, James. "T.S. Eliot and the Austere Poetics of Valéry." *CL* 23(1971):1-17.

1616. Weber, Alfred. *Der Symbolismus T.S. Eliots:Versuch einer neuen Annäherung an moderne Lyrik*. Tübingen: n.p., 1954.

1617. Weinberg, Kerry. *T.S. Eliot and Charles Baudelaire*. (Studies in Gen. and Comp. Lit. 5.) The Hague: Mouton, 1969. 84 pp.

1618. Wimsatt, W.K. "Prufrock and Maud:From Plot to Symbol." *YFS* 9 (1952):84-92.

1619. Wright, N. "Source for T.S. Eliot's Objective Correlative?" *AL* 41(1970:589-91.

See also 458, 497, 905, 1000, 1011, 1013, 1050, 1217, 1251, 1319, 1444, 1762, 1766, 1773, 1847, 1977, 2378, 2427, 2575, 2587, 2789, 3042.

Elskamp

1620. Davignon, Henri. *L'amitié de Max Elskamp et d'Albert Mockel*. Bruxelles: Palais des académies, 1955. 76 pp.

Emerson, Ralph W. *See* 998.

Eminescu

1621. Rusu, Liviu. "La perspective de la

profondeur dans l'étude des influences littéraires et de l'originalité illustrée par le rapport entre le poète Eminescu et Schopenhauer," 1031-35 in Vol. 2 of François Jost,ed. *Proceedings of the IVth Congress of the International Comparative Literature Association.* Fribourg, 1964. 2 vols. The Hague: Mouton, 1966.

Fantin-Latour

1622. Bouyer, Raymond. "Fantin-Latour." *L'Ermitage* 1(1895):281-91.

1623. D'Udine, Jean. "L'oeuvre de Fantin-Latour." *La Plume* 246(juillet 1899):469-70.

1624. Fagus. "Notes sur des dessins de Fantin-Latour." *La Plume* 305(janv 1902):61-62.

1625. Hédiard, Germain. *Les maîtres de la lithographie:Fantin-Latour.* Etude suivie du catalogue de son oeuvre. Paris: E. Sagot, 1892. 46 pp.

1626. Jullien, Adolphe. *Fantin-Latour: Sa vie et ses amitiés.* Lettres inédites et souvenirs personnels. Paris: Lucien Laveur, 1909. 214 pp.

1627. Saunier, Charles. "Dessins de Fantin-Latour." *Revue Blanche* 27 (1902):63-64.

Fargue

1628. Ramsey, Warren. " 'Words of Light' and 'Somber Leaves':The Poetry of Léon-Paul Fargue." *YFS* 9(1952):112-22.

Fauré

1629. Fortassier, Pierre. "Rythme verbal et rythme musical:A propos de la prosodie de Gabriel Fauré," 29-37 in *Mélanges d'histoire et d'esthétique musicales offerts à Paul-Marie Masson.* Paris: Richard-Mass-Editeur, 1955.

1630. Sommers, P.B. "Faure and His Songs:The Relationship of Text, Melody, and Accompaniment." *DA* 31 (1970):791A(Ill.).

Flaubert

1631. Rebell, Hugues. "Histoire de l'esprit français:Gustave Flaubert ou l'artiste impeccable." *La Plume* 317 (juillet 1902):779-83.

See also 1471.

Fletcher

1632. Behrens, Ralph. "John Gould Fletcher and Rimbaud's 'Alchimie du Verbe'." *CL* 8(1956):46-62.

1633. Brown, C. "The Color Symphony Before and After Gautier." *CL* 5(1963):289-309.

See also 2024.

Flint, F.S. *See* 1147.

Floupette

1634. Juin, Hubert. "La vie, l'oeuvre l'influence d'Adoré Floupette." *Magazine littéraire* 32(sept 1969):34-37.

Franko

1635. Jarema, Ja.Ja. "Ivan Franko i tvorcist' Henrixa Hejne." *RLz* 1 (1960):23-32.

1636. Kurylenko, J.M. "Z arxivnyx materialiv pro I. Franko." *RLz* 6,iv (1962):128-29.

1637. Ovcharenko, Maria. "Stress in Ivan Franko's Poetry." *AUA* 8(1960):121-40.

1638. Slavutych, Yar. *Ivan Franko and Russia.* Winnipeg: *UVAN*, 1959.

1639. Vizyr, M.P. "Lysty Ivana Franka do Yu. Yavor'skoho." *RLz* 3(1960): 119-24.

1640. Wytrzens, G. "Ivan Franko als Student und Doktor der Wiener Universität." *WSJ* 8(1960):228-41.

Fröding

1641. Lappalainen, Pekka. *Gustaf Fröding ja Ruotsin runouden uudistus: Kaunokirjallisuuden henkilöm ja aatehistoriallinen tutkimus.* (Jyväskylä Studies in the Arts 1.) Jyväskylä: Jyväskylän yliopistoyhdistys, 1967. 195 pp. [Sum. in Ger.]

1642. Lindström, Göran. "Gustaf Fröding." *Samtiden* 49(1960:413-29.

1643. Michanek, Germuud. *"En morgondröm":Studier kring Frödings ariska dikt.* Stockholm: Bonnier, 1962. [Sum. in Eng.]

1644. Vendelfelt, Erik. "Fröding och Poe:Några anteckningar." *SLT* 39 (1966):56-66.

1645. ———. "Frödings dikt om Edgar Allan Poe." *Samlaren* 40(1959): 77-87.

1646. ———. "Fröding upptäcker Poe." *OB* 49(1960):302-06.

García Lorca

1647. Allen, Rubert C. "An Analysis of Narrative and Symbol in Lorca's *Romance sonámbulo*." *HR* 36(19-68):338-52.

1648. ———. "Una explicación simbológica de 'iglesia abandonada' de Lorca." *Hispano* 26(1963):33-44.

1649. ———. *The Symbolic World of García Lorca.* Albuquerque: U. of N.M. Press, 1972. 205 pp.

1650. Bayón, Damian C. "García Lorca en Francia." *Asomante* 18,i(1962): 94-101.

1651. Correa, Gustavo. *La poesía mítica de Federico García Lorca.* Eugene, Ore.: U. of Ore. Pubs., 1956. 174 pp.

1652. ———. "El simbolismo del sol en la poesía de Federico García Lorca." *NRFH* 14(1960):110-19.

1653. ———. "El simbolismo religioso en la poesía de Federico García Lorca." *Hispania* 39(1956):41-48.

1654. Dickson, Ronald J. "Archetypal Symbolism in Lorca's *Bodas de Sangre*." *L&P* 10(1960):76-79.

1655. Havard, Robert G. "The Symbolic Ambivalence of 'Green' in García Lorca and Dylan Thomas." *MLR* 67(1972):810-19.

1656. Higginbotham, Virginia. "Lorca and Twentieth-Century Theater: Three Precursors." *MD* 15(1971): 164-74.

1657. ———. "Reflejos de Lautréamont en *Poeta en Nueva York*." *Hispano* 46(1972):59-68.

1658. Laubenthal, Penne J. "Prometheus, Prophet and Priest: An Interpretation of García Lorca's *Poet in New York* in Relationship to Walt Whitman's *Leaves of Grass*." *DAI* 33(1972):1973A(Geo. Peabody).

1659. Predmore, Richard L. "Simbolismo ambiguo en la poesía de García Lorca." *PSA* 64(1971):229-40.

1660. Zimbardo, R.A. "The Mythic Pattern in Lorca's *Blood Wedding.*" *MD* 10(1966):364-71.

See also 653, 1774, 1900.

Gauguin

1661. Aurier, G.-A. "Paul Gauguin." *La Plume* 57(sept 1891):300.

1662. Fagus, Félicien. *"Paul Gauguin et Charles Morice:'Noa-Noa' (La Plume).*" *Revue Blanche* 25(1901): 637-38. [Rev. art.]

1663. Guérin, Joseph. "Les arts." *L'Ermitage* 28(nov 1903):232-34.

1664. Jaworska, Wladyslava. *Gauguin and the Pont-Aven School.* With 250 illus. Tr. Patrick Evans. Greenwich, Conn.: New York Graphic Society, Ltd., 1972. 264 pp. [First pub. Neuchâtel: Eds. Ides et Calendes, 1971.]

1665. Perruchot, Henri. *Gauguin.* London: Perpetua Books, 1963. 398 pp. [Tr. by Humphrey Hare.]

See also 746, 793, 822, 834.

Gautier *See* 2165, 2653, 1302.

George

1666. Allinger, Erich. *Stefan George und Hugo von Hofmannsthal.* Wien: U. of Wien, 1950. [Diss.]

1667. Angelloz, J. "Stefan George et son cénacle." *MdF* 314(1952):713-16.

1668. Arbogast, Hubert. *Die Erneuerung der deutschen Dichtersprache in den Frühwerken Stefan Georges:Eine stilgeschichtliche Untersuchung.* Cologne:Böhlau, 1967. 175 pp.

1669. Becker, W. "Die Kunstanschauung Stefan Georges." *Preussische Jahrbücher* 178(1919):443-64.

1670. Binder, Alois. *Die Sprachkunst Georges in seinen Frühwerken.* Frankfurt a.M.: U. of Frankfurt, 1933. [Diss.]

1671. Blank, Bernhard. "Stefan George: Symbolische deutsche Dichtung um 1900." *ZDP* 61(1936):167-209.

1672. Bornmann, Bianca M. "Due note sull'*Algabal* di Stefan George." *RLMC* 9(1956):147-48.

1673. ———. "Interp. Georghiane: 'L'Algabal' e le sue fonti storiche antiche." *Studi Germanici* 8(1970): 251-68.

1674. Breugelmans, René. "Stefan George and Oscar Wilde:A Confrontation." *Proceedings of the Pacific Northwest Conference on Foreign Languages* 15(1964):40-59.

1675. ———. "Stefan George and Oscar Wilde. Part II of a Confrontation: Their Aesthetic-Religious Views." *Proceedings of the Pacific Northwest Conference on Foreign Languages* 17(1966):60-74.

1676. Dahmen, Hans. *Lehren über*

Kunst und Weltanschauung im Kreise um Stefan George. Marburg: Elwert, 1926. 70 pp.

1677. David, Claude. *Stefan George:Son oeuvre poétique.* Lyons: I.A.C., 1952. 409 pp.

1678. ———. "Stefan George und der Jugendstil," 211-28 in *Formkräfte der deutschen Dichtung vom Barock bis zur Gegenwart.* Göttingen: Vandenhoeck & Ruprecht, 1963.

1679. Durzak, Manfred. *Die Algabal-Dichtung und die Kunsttheorie des frühen Stefan George.* Berlin: U. of Berlin, 1963. [Diss.]

1680. ———. "Epigonenlyrik:Zur Dichtung des George-Kreises." *JDSG* 13(1969):482-529.

1681. ———. *Der junge Stefan George: Kunsttheorie und Dichtung.* (ZED 3.) München: Fink, 1968. 294 pp.

1682. ——— "Die Kunsttheoretische Ausgangsposition Stefan Georges: Zur Wirkung Edgar Allan Poes." *Arcadia* 4(1969):164-78.

1683. ———. "Nachwirkungen Stefan Georges im Expressionismus." *GQ* 42(1969):393-417.

1684. Duthie, Enid L. "Some References to the French Symbolist Movement in the Correspondence of Stefan George and Hugo von Hofmannsthal." *CIS* 9 (1943):15-18.

1685. Faber du Faur, Curt von. "Stefan George et le symbolisme français." *CL* 5(1953):151-66.

1686. Frommel, G. "Stefan George:Drei Maximen über Dichtung." *CPe* 89(1969):6-41.

1687. Gerhard, Melitta. "Wirklichkeitsstoff und Mythos:Zum Werk Stefan Georges." *CPe* 101(1972):49-61.

1688. Glur, Guido. *Kunstlehre und Kunstanschauung des George-Kreises und die Aesthetik Oscar Wildes.* (Sprache und Dichtung, NF 3.) Bern: Haupt, 1957. 112 pp.

1689. Goldsmith, Ulrich K. *Stefan*

George. (Columbia Essays on Modern Writers, 50.) New York: Columbia U.P., 1970. 48 pp.

1690. ——. *Stefan George:A Study of His Early Work*. (UCSLL 7.) Boulder: U. of Colo. P., 1959. 172 pp.

1691. ——. "Stefan George and the Theatre." *PMLA* 66(1951):85-95.

1692. Gottschalk, Hilde. *Wesen und Form der Gespräche aus dem Kreis der Blätter für die Kunst*. Frankfurt: U. of Frankfurt, 1932. [Diss.]

1693. Hannum, H. G. "George and Benn:The Autumnal Vision." *PMLA* 78(1963):271-79.

1694. Hermann, Friedrich. *Stefan George und Hugo von Hofmannsthal:Dichtung und Briefwechsel*. Zürich: Classen, 1947. 94 pp.

1695. Hildebrandt, Kurt. *Das Werk Stefan Georges*. Hamburg: Hauswedell, 1960. 473 pp.

1696. Hobohm, Freya. *Die Bedeutung französischer Dichter im Werk und Weltbild Stefan Georges (Baudelaire, Verlaine, Mallarmé)*. Marburg a. Lahn: N.G. Elwert'sche Verlagsbuchhandlung, 1931. 155 pp.

1697. ——. *Stefan George: Baudelaire, Verlaine, Mallarmé:Ein Vergleich*. Marburg: C. Schulze, 1931. 31 pp.

1698. Jaeger, Hans. "Stefan Georges französische Gedichte und deutsche Übertragungen." *PMLA* 51(1936): 563-93.

1699. Jolles, F. "Die Entwicklung der wissenschaftlichen Grundsätze des George-Kreises." *EG* 22(1967):346-58.

1700. Jost, Dominik. *Stefan George und sein Elite:Studie zur Geschichte des Eliten*. Zürich: n.p., 1949.

1701. Just, Klaus G. *Studien zum Ästhetizismus bei Stefan George und seinem Kreis*. Würzburg: U. of Würzburg, 1948. [Diss.]

1702. Klussmann, Paul Gerhard. *Stefan George:Zum Selbstverständnis der Kunst und des Dichters in der Moderne*. Mit einer George-Bibliographie. (BADL, I.) Bonn: Bouvier, 1961. 181 pp.

1703. Landmann, Georg P. *Stefan George und sein Kreis:Eine Bibliographie*. Hamburg: Hauswedell, 1960. 314 pp.

1704. Langer, W. "Stefan George und die französische Lyrik" *NS* 41, (1933):74-77.

1705. Lehmann, Peter L. *Meditationen um Stephan George:Sieben Essays*. Düsseldorf: H. Küpper, 1965.

1706. Linke, Hansjürgen. *Das Kultische in der Dichtung Stefan Georges und seiner Schule*. 2 vols. München, Düsseldorf: Küpper, 1960.

1707. Maier, Hans A. *Stefan George und Thomas Mann:Zwei Formen des dritten Humanismus in kritischem Vergleich*. Zürich: Speer-Verlag, 1946. 192 pp.

1708. Maione, Italo. *Trittico neoromantico:George, Hofmannsthal, Rilke*. Messina: Casa Editrice G. D'Anna, 1950. 184 pp.

1709. Meessen, Hubert J. "Stefan Georges *Algabal* und die französische Dekadenz." *Monatshefte* 39(1947): 304-21.

1710. Metzger, Michael M. and Erika A. *Stefan George*. (TWAS 182.) New York: Twayne, 1972. 208 pp.

1712. "Numéro consacré à Stefan George." *Revue d'Allemagne* 13-14 (nov-déc 1928):385-505.

1713. Ockenden, Raymond C. " 'Komm in den totgesagten park und schau': Some Aspects of Nature and Nature Imagery in Stefan George's Poetry." *OGS* 2(1967):87-109.

1714. ——. "Stefan George:Grundworte seiner Dichtung." *CPe* 81 (1968):5-29.

1715. Oswald, V.A. "The Historical Content of Stefan George's *Algabal*." *GR* 23(1948):193-205.

1716. ——. "Oscar Wilde, Stefan

George, Heliogabalus." *MLQ* 10 (1949):517-25.

1717. Pensa, Mario. "Stefan George e l'Italia." *Veltro* 6(1962):227-42.

1718. Pollak, I. *"Die Einwirkung der französischen Parnassiens and Symbolisten auf Stefan George und seinen Kreis."* Wien: U. of Wien, 1931. [Diss.]

1719. Rasch, Wolfdietrich. "Stefan Georges *Algabal:* Ästhetizismus und gesellschaftliches Engagement," 579-89 in Victor Lange, and Hans-Gert Roloff,eds. *Dichtung, Sprache, Gesellschaft:Akten des IV. Internationalen Germanisten-Kongresses 1970 in Princeton.* Frankfurt: Athenäum, 1971.

1720. Saint-Paul, Albert. "Stefan George et le Symbolisme français." *Revue d'Allemagne* 2(1928):397-405.

1721. San Lazzaro, Clementina di. "Stefan George als Uebersetzer." *GRM* 28(1940):203-11.

1722. Santoli, Vittorio. "Estetismo e bizantinismo di Stefan George," 481-93 in *Studi sulla lett. dell'Ottocento in onore di Pietro Paolo Trompeo.* Napoli: Ed. Scient. Ital., 1959.

1723. Schmidt, A. M. "Stefan George ou du mythe au mythe." *Table Ronde* 63(1953):149-51.

1724. Schmitz, Victor A. "Das Ethos der Kunst bei George und Rilke." *DBGÜ* 6(1970):98-119.

1725. Schonauer, Fritz. "Stefan George und sein Kreis." *Deutsche Rundschau* 86,vii(1961):615-26.

1726. Schultz. H. Stefan. "Französisches und Deutsches bei Stefan George." *DBGÜ* 6(1970):120-39.

1727. ——. "Stefan George u. die Antike." *DBGÜ* 5(1965):204-38.

1728. Sengle, Friedrich. "George:Vom Algabalgarten zum Land der Gnade," 308-17 in H.O. Burger,ed. *Gedicht und Gedanke*. Halle:Niemeyer, 1942.

1729. Sior, Marie-Louise. *Stefan George und der französische Symbolismus.* Giessen: U. of Giessen, 1932. [Diss.]

1730. Spenlé, Jean-Edouard. "Stefan George et les poètes symbolistes français." *Helicon* 2,ii(1939):9-23.

1731. Steffensen, Steffen. "Stefan George und seine Wirkungen in Skandanavien." *Nerthus* 2(1969):52-78.

1732. Strauss, George. "Entzauberung einer Kunstbewegung:Stefan George und seine Gefolgschaft," 128-46 *In Irrlichter und Leitgestirne:Essays über Probleme der Kunst.* Zürich, Stuttgart: Classen, 1966.

1733. Urban, George R. *Kinesis and Stasis:A Study in the Attitude of Stefan George and His Circle to the Musical Arts.* (AC2.) 's Gravenhage: Mouton, 1962. 209 pp.

1734. Vortriede, Werner. "Direct Echoes of French Poetry in Stefan George's Work." *MLN* 60,iv(1945):461-468.

1735. ——. "Zu einem George-Gedicht." *Monatshefte* 43(1951):39-43.

1736. Winkler, Michael. *Stefan George.* Stuttgart: Metzler, 1970.

1737. Wolters, Friedrich. *Stefan George und die Blätter für die Kunst: Deutsche Geistesgeschichte seit 1890.* Berlin: Bondi, 1930.

1738. Zabeltitz, Max Zobel von. "Die Natur bei Stefan George," 469-509 in *Festschrift für Berthold Litzmann.* Bonn, 1920.

See also 347, 520, 635, 1048, 1131, 1155, 1156, 1211, 1230, 1259, 1318, 1326, 1805, 1829, 2228, 2277, 2722, 2723, 2994, 2995, 2996, 2007, 3061, 3065, 3066, 3107.

Ghil

1739. Theile, Wolfgang. "Die Beziehungen Ghils zu Valerij Brjusov und der Zeitschrift 'Vesy':Ein Beitrag zum Verständnis des französischen Symbolismus in Russland." *Arcadia* 1(1966):174-84.

1740. ——. *Ghil:Eine Analyse seiner Dichtungen und theoretischen Schriften.* Tübingen: U. of Tübingen, 1965. [Diss.]

See also 572, 700.

Gide

1741. Boisdeffre, Pierre de. "Les débuts d'un homme de lettres (1891-1892)." *Adam* 337-339(1970):29-47.

1742. Bulgin, Kathleen. "Swamp Imagery and the Moral-Esthetic Problem in Gide's Early Works." *FR* 45 (1972):813-18.

1743. Edwards, Michael. "Gide and the Symbol." *Adam* 337-339(1971):62-64.

1744. Last, Jef. "Gide en de invloed van Wilde." *Maatstaf* 17(1971):386-93.

1745. Lindsay, Marshall. "Time in Gide's Early Fiction." *Symposium* 26(1972):39-56.

1746. Noguez, Dominique. *"Des Esseintes* et Nathanaël." *RLM* 280-84(1971):63-85.

1747. Peyre, Henri. "Gide and Literary Influences." *AJFS* 7(1970):171-88.

1748. Savage, Catherine. "Gide's Criticism of Symbolism." *MLR* 71 (1966):601-09

See also 497,650, 2071, 2251, 2566, 3068.

Gogol

1749. Keefer, Lubov. "Gogol' and Music." *SEEJ* 14(1970):160-81.

Gómez Carillo

1750. Ulner, Arnold R. "Enrique Gómez Carillo en el Modernismo:

1889-1896." *DAI* 34(1973):1297A(Mo., Columbia).

Gorki

1751. Weil, Irwin. "Gor'kij's Relations with the Bolsheviks and Symbolists." *SEEJ* 4(1960):201-19.

Gorter

1752. Eliassen-De Kat, Martha H. "Gorters *Mei* en de mythe van Amor en Psyche." *SpL* 13(1972):1-16.

1753. Es, G. van. "De compositie van Gorters *Mei.*" *TNTL* 77 (1960):263-83.

1754. Jansonius, F. "Impressionistische en andere aspecten van *Mei.*" *NTg* 52(1959):157-61.

1755. Klomp, Henri. *"Alastor, Endymion* and Gorter's *Mei."* *KFLQ* 6 (1959):38-47.

1756. Linssen, H. "Einge opmerkingen over Gorters *Mei.*" *LT* 268-(1970):357-61.

1757. Meeuwesse, Karl. "De structuur van Gorters *Mei.*" *DWB* 113(1968):90-106,194-210.

1758. ——. "Het verhall van *Mei* en Balder:Een hoogleid." *Gids* 130,vi/vii(1967):121-29.

See also 2993.

Gourmont

1759. Brulez, Raymond. "Rémy de Gourmont en de Symbolisten." *VIG* 48-(1964):568-92.

1760. Burne, Glenn S."Rémy de Gourmont and the Aesthetics of Symbolism." *CLS* 4(1967):161-75.

1761. Caramaschi, E. "Simbolismo e critica alla fine dell'Ottocento: I 'Masques' di Gourmont." *Saggi e ricerche di letteratura francesa* 2 (1961):201-65.

1762. Rees, T.R. "T.S. Eliot, Rémy de

Gourmont, and Dissociation of Sensibility." *CL* (1962):186-98.

1763. Rondault, Jean. "La passion critique de Rémy de Gourmont." *Critique* 23(1967):335-43.

1764. Taupin, René. "The Example of Rémy de Gourmont (in England)." *Criterion* (July 1931):614-25.

1765. Uitti, Karl D. *La passion littéraire de Rémy de Gourmont*. Paris: Presses univs. de France, 1962. 326 pp.

1766. Yamada, Shoi chi. "T.S. Eliot and Rémy de Gourmont on Personality." *SELit* Eng. No.(1971):163-64.

See also 3023.

Grasset

1767. "Eugène Grasset et son oeuvre." *La Plume* 260(fév 1900):114-79. [Reprs., plates, essays by var. hands.]

1768. Thévenin, Léon. "L'ésthétique de Grasset." *La Plume* 306(janv 1902): 81-88.

Guénon

1769. Asfar, Gabriel V. "René Guénon: A Chapter of French Symbolist Thought in the Twentieth Century." *DAI* 33(1973):3571A-72A(Princeton).

Guérin

1770. Boussard, Léon. "Le centenaire d'un grand poète, Charles Guérin." *RDM* déc(1973):590-95.

See also 1894.

Guillén

1771. Ciplijauskaité, Biruté. "Jorge Guillén y Paul Valéry, al despertar." *PSA* 33(1964):267-94.

1772. Debicki, Andrew P. "Esquemas

formales y significado intimo en *Cántico*." *Hispania* 55(1972):471-79.

1773. Fowlie, Wallace. "Jorge Guillén, Marianne Moore, T.S. Eliot:Some Recollections." *Poetry* 90(1957): 103-09.

1774. González, Muela Joaquín. *El lenguaje poético de la generación Guillén-Lorca*. Madrid: Insula, 1954.

1775. Vigée, Claude. "Jorge Guillén et les poètes symbolistes français," 139-97 in *Révolte et louanges:Essais sur la poésie moderne*, Paris: Corti, 1962.

1776. ———. "Jorge Guillén et l'esthétique du Symbolisme français," 270-92 in Daniel A. Fineman, ed. *Studies in Western Literature*. Jerusalem: Magnes Press; London: Oxford U.P., 1962.

1777. ———. "Jorge Guillén y la tradición simbolista francesa." *CCLC* 45 (Nov-Dec 1960):53-59.

1778. ———. "Le message poétique de Jorge Guillén." *Critique* 154(1966): 195-221.

1779. Zardoya, Concha. "Jorge Guillén y Paul Valéry." *Asomante* 20(1964): 22-32.

See also 2035.

Guimaraens, A.

1780. Lisboa, Henriqueta. "Alphonsus e Severiano." *Colóquio* 6(1972):27-34.

1781. Silva, Wilson Melo da. *O Simbolismo e Alphonsus Guimaraens*. Belo Horizonte: Imprensa Official, 1971.

Güiraldes

1782. Previtali Morrow, Giovanni. "*Don Segundo Sombra* y los simbolistas franceses." *CHA* 235(1969):222-31.

Gutiérrez Nájera

1783. Carter Boyd G. "Manuel Gutiérrez Nájera y Rubén Darío." *Nivel* 108(1971):1-2,8,10,11,12.

1784. Kester, Garyl. "The Poetry of Manuel Gutiérrez Nájera." *DAI* 31 (1970):2923A(Kan.).

1785. Taylor, Terry O. "A Study of Symbolic Expression in the Work of Manuel Gutiérrez Nájera." *DAI* 32 (1971):3334A(Mich. State.).

Hardy

1786. Finn, Kay. "Archetypal Symbolism in the Major Novels of Thomas Hardy." *DAI* 31(1971): 3545A(Wayne State).

Hauptmann

1787. Albert, Henri. "La base historique des 'Tisserands'." *Entretiens politiques et littéraires* 45(juin 1893): 564-70.

1788. Eustachiewicz, Leslaw. "Symboliczne dramaty Hauptmanna." *DialogW* 3,ii(1962):102-07.

Heidenstam

1789. Wangson, Otto. "Litterät allehanda:Heidenstam och Hans Dhejne." *SLT* 35,i(1972):29-31.

Heine

1790. Weinberg, Kurt. *Henri Heine, "romantique défroqué," heraut du symbolisme français.* New Haven: Yale U.P., 1954. 303 pp.

Henry

1791. Mercier, Alain. "Charles Henry et l'esthétique symboliste." *RSH* 138 (1970):251-72

Herrera y Reissig

1792. Camurati, Mireya. "Notas a la obra de Julio Herrera y Reissig." *CHA* 269(1972):303-16.

1793. Gicovate, B. *J. Herrera y Reissig and the Symbolists.* Berkeley: U. of Calif. P., 1957. 106 pp.

1794. ———. "The Poetry of Julio Herrera y Reissig and French Symbolism." *PMLA* 68(1953):935-42.

1795. González-Gerth, Miguel. "A Probable Source of Julio Herrera y Reissig's 'Ciles alucinada'." *RomN* 12(1970):110-21.

1796. Ibarra, Fernando. "Los *Sonetos vascos* de Julio Herrera Reissig." *Hispano* 44(1972):65-78.

1797. Michalski, André S., and David S. Díaz. "El soneto 'Otoño' de Julio Herrera y Reissig." *RomN* 12(1970): 122-27.

Hippius

1798. Kirillova, Irina. "Zinaida Gippius:A Russian Decadent Poet. A Short Introduction to Her Early Verse," 179-94 in R. Auty, L.R. Lewitter, and A.P. Vlasto,eds. *Gorski vijenac:A Garland of Essays Offered to Professor Elizabeth Mary Hill.* Cambridge: Mod. Humanities Research Assn., 1970. 321 pp.

1799. Maslenikov, Oleg A. "Spectre of Nothingness:The Privative Element in the Poetry of Zinaida Hippius." *SEEJ* n.s.4,xviii(1960):299-311.

1800. ———. "The Symbolic Epithet in the Poetry of Zinaida Hippius." *Langue et littérature* [6] (1962):355.

1801. Matich, Olga. "The Religious Poetry of Zinaida Gippius." *DAI* 30 (1970):4992A(U.C.L.A.).

1802. Pachmuss, Temira. *Zinaida Hippius:An Intellectual Profile.* Carbondale and Edwardsville: So. Ill. U.P., 1971. 491 pp.

Hoffman

1803. Kalfus, Richard M. "The Func-

tion of the Dream in the Works of
E.T.A. Hoffman." *DAI* 34(1973):
1915A-16A(Wash. U.).

1804. Peković, Slobodanka. "Hofman-
ovska i Poovska fantastika." *Savremenik* 37(1973):428-38.

See also 1122, 2453.

Hofmannsthal

1805. Albrecht, Helmuth F.G. " 'Fin de
siècle' y 'décadence' y superación en
H.v. Hofmannsthal, R.M. Rilke y St.
George." *Humanitas. Revista de la
Fac. de filos. y letras de la Univ.
Nacional de Tucumán* 7,ii(1959):
99-130.

1806. Alewyn, Richard. "Der Tod des
Ästheten," 64-77 in *Über Hugo von
Hofmannsthal*. Göttingen: Vanden-
hoeck & Ruprecht, 1963.

1807. Berendsohn, Walter A. *Der Impressionismus Hofmannsthals als
Zeiterscheinung:Eine stilkritische
Studie*. Hamburg: W. Gente, 1920.
52 pp.

1808. Bianquis, Geneviève. "Hofmannsthal et la France." *RLC* 27(1953):
301-18.

1809. Block, Haskell M. "Hugo von
Hofmannsthal and the Symbolist
Drama." *TWA* 48(1959):161-78.

1810. Brückler, Silke. *Hugo von Hof-
mannsthal und Maurice Maeterlinck*.
Würzburg; U. of Würzburg, 1953.
[Diss.]

1811. Burger, Hilde. "French Influences
on Hugo von Hofmannsthal." *CL*
2(1960):691-97.

1812. ———. "Hofmannsthal:Ses relations avec la Belgique et la Suisse."
RLC 37(1962):369-76.

1813. ———. "Hugo von Hofmannsthal—Maurice Maeterlinck:Zwei veröf-
fentlichte Briefe." *NRS* 73(1962):
314-19.

1814. Derungs, Werner. *Form und Weltbild der Gedichte Hugo von Hofmannsthals in ihrer Entwicklung*.
Zurich: Juris, 1960. 216 pp.

1815. Evans, Calvin H. "Hofmannsthal's
Kleine Dramen as Seen in the Focus
of Maeterlinck's 'Static Drama'." *DA*
20(1959):1785(Ore.).

1816. Fiechtner, H.A. "Hofmannsthal
et la France." *Culture Française*
6,v(déc 1957):32-35.

1817. Foldenauer, Karl. *Hugo von Hofmannsthal und die französische Literatur des neunzehnten und zwanzigsten Jahrhunderts*. Tübingen: U. of
Tübingen, 1958. [Diss.]

1818. Goff, Penrith. "Hugo von Hofmannsthal and Walter Pater." *CLS*
7(1970):1-11

1819. ———. "Hugo von Hofmannsthal
and the Aesthetic Experience." *PLL*
4(1968):414-19.

1820. ———. "Hugo von Hofmannsthal:
The Symbol as Experience." *KRQ*
7(1960):196-200.

1821. Grey, M.A.R. *Hofmannsthal and
Nineteenth Century French Symbolism*. Dublin: U. of Dublin, 1950-
1951. [Diss.]

1822. Hahn, Erika. *Leben, Traum und
Tod:Ihr symbolische Gestaltung in
den Gedichten Hugo von Hofmannsthals*. Erlangen-Nürnberg: U. of Erlangen-Nürnberg, 1962. [Diss.]

1823. Hofmannsthal, Hugo von. "En-
counters." *YFS* 9(1952):162-65.
[Tr. Tanya and James Stern.]

1824. Hoope, Manfred. *Literatentum,
Magie und Mystik im Frühwerk Hugo
von Hofmannsthals*. (QFSK 28.) Berlin: de Gruyter, 1968. 140 pp.

1825. Kern, Peter C. *Zur Gedankenwelt
des späten Hofmannsthal:Die Idee
einer schöpferischen Restauration*.
Heidelberg: Winter, 1969. 129 pp.

1826. Kobel, Erwin. *Hugo von Hofmannsthal*. Berlin: de Gruyter, 1970.
377 pp.

1827. Mistry, Freny. "Hofmannsthal's
Oriental Library." *JEGP* 71(1972):
177-97.

1828. Mühlher, Robert. "Hugo von Hofmannsthals Oper *Ariadne auf Naxos,"*
63-79 in *Interpretationen zur öster-
reichischen Literatur*. Hrsg. vom Institut für Österreichkunde. Wien:
Hirt, 1971.

1829. Niebuhr, Walter. *Das Problem der
Einsamkeit im Werke von Hugo von
Hofmannsthal und Stefan George.*
Kiel: U. of Kiel, 1949. [Diss.]

1830. Norton, R.C. "Hofmannsthal's
Garden Image." *GQ* 31(1958):94-
103.

1831. Porter, Michael. "Hugo von Hof-
mannsthal's *Der Tor und der Tod:*
The Poet as Fool." *Modern Austrian
Literature* 5,i(1972):14-29.

1832. Rey, William H. "Die Drohung
der Zeit in Hofmannsthals Frühwerk," 165-206 in Sibylle Bauer,ed.
Hugo von Hofmannsthal. Darmstadt:
Wissenschaftliche Buchgesellschaft,
1968.

1833. Rieger, Erwin. "Hofmannsthal,
l'autrichien." *Revue de Genève* 20
(1930):368-75.

1834. St. Aubyn, F.C. "Hérodiade:Eine
Frau mit Schatten?" *RLC* 33(1959):
40-49.

1835. Schmid, Martin E. *Symbol und
Funktion der Musik im Werk Hugo
von Hofmannsthals*. (BNL 4.) Heidelberg: Winter, 1968. 179 pp.

1836. Schnitzler, O. "Der junge Hofmannsthal." *NRs* 65(1954):514-34.

1837. Schüssler, Margarethe. *Symbol
und Wirklichkeit bei Hugo von Hofmannsthal*. Basel: U. of Basel, 1969.
[Diss.]

1838. Seeba, Hinrich C. *Kritik des
ästhetischen Menschen:Hermeneutik
und Moral in Hofmannsthals* Der Tor
und der Tod. Bad Homburg: Gehlen,
1970. 208 pp.

1839. Siefken, H. "Hugo von Hof-
mannsthal's *Der Tor und der Tod*:
The Paradox of the 'Nahe Ferne'."
GL&L 24(1970):78-88.

1840. Steffen, Hans. "Hofmannsthals

Übernahme der symbolistischen
Technik," 271-79 in Reinhold
Grimm, and Conrad Wiedemann,eds.
*Literatur und Geistesgeschichte:Fest-
gabe für Heinz Otto Burger*. Berlin:
Schmidt, 1968.

1841. Warnach, W. "Hugo von Hof-
mannsthal:Sein Weg von Mythos und
Magie zur Wirklichkeit der
Geschichte." *Wort und Wahrheit*
9(1954):360-77.

1842. Weber, Horst. *Hugo von Hof-
mannsthal:Bibliographie des Schrift-
tums 1892-1963*. Berlin: de Gruyter,
1966. 254 pp.

1843. Wunberg, Gotthart. *Der frühe
Hofmannsthal:Schizophrenie als
dichterische Struktur*. (SuL 25.)
Stuttgart: Kohlhammer, 1965.

See also 635, 1048, 1122, 1156,
1485, 1596, 1666, 1684, 1694,
1708, 1869, 2235, 2571, 3066.

Hopkins

1844. Boyle, Robert, S.J. "Hopkins'
Use of 'Fancy'." *VP* 10(1972):17-27.

1845. Gardner, W.H. "Gerard Manley
Hopkins and the Poetry of Inscape."
Theoria 33(1969):1-16.

1846. Gunter, Richard. "Grammar,
Semantics, and the Poetry of Gerard
Manley Hopkins." *TLOP* 1,i(1972):
2-12. [Comment by N.B. Albers,
TLOP 1,iii(1972):16.]

1847. Joshi, B.N. "Hopkins and T.S.
Eliot:A Study in Linguistic Innova-
tion." *OJES* 1(1961):13-16.

1848. Sulloway, Alison G. *Gerard Manley Hopkins and the Victorian Temper*. New York: Columbia U.P.,
1972. 245 pp.

Housman *See*1360.

Huysmans

1849. Babcock, James C. "The Portrait

of the Contemporary Era in Huysmans' Fiction:Its Nature and Development." *DAI* 32(1972):3942A (Vanderbilt).

1850. Baldick, Robert. *The Life of J.K. Huysmans*. Fair Lawn, New Jersey: Clarendon Press, 1955. 425 pp.

1851. Buet, Charles. "Un livre sincère: *En route* de J.K. Huysmans." *La Plume* 142(mars 1895):137-38. [Rev. art.]

1852. Cevasco, G.A. "*A rebours* and Poe's Reputation in France." *RomN* 13(1971):255-61.

1853. Cressot, Marcel. *La phrase et le vocabulaire de J.-K. Huysmans:Contribution à l'histoire de la langue française pendant le dernier quart du XIXe siècle*. Paris: Droz, 1938. 604 pp.

1854. D'Entremont, Elène. "The Influence of Huysmans' *A rebours* on Rubén Darïo." *RomN* 5,i(1963):37-39.

1855. Duployé, Pie. *Huysmans*. Bruges: Desclée De Brouwer, 1968.

1856. Erickson, John D. "Huysmans' *Là-bas:*A Metaphor of Search." *FR* 43(1970):418-25.

1857. Fixler, M. "The Affinities Between Huysmans and the 'Rosicrucian' Stories of W.B. Yeats." *PMLA* 74(1959):464-69.

1858. Hanighen, F.C. "Huysmans' Influence in America." *RLC* 13(1933):173-86.

1859. Huysmans, J.K. *Certains*. Paris: Tresse and Stock, 1889. 230 pp.

1860. Issacharoff, Michael. *J.-K. Huysmans devant la critique en France*. Paris: Klincksieck, 1969.

1861. Laver, James. *The First Decadent (J.K. Huysmans)*. Oxford: Faber and Faber, 1954. 238 pp.

1862. Liui, François. *J.-K. Huysmans:*A rebours *et l'esprit décadent*. Paris: Nizet, 1972. 200 pp.

1863. Meier, Peter P. "The Circular Structure of *A rebours*." *DAI* 32(19-72):4623A(Case Western Reserve).

1864. Mintcheff, Kina. "Les images de J.K. Huysmans." *DAI* 32(1972): 5239A (Cornell).

1865. Régnier, Henri de. "Portraits (J.K. Huysmans)." *Entretiens politiques et littéraires* 29(août 1892): 85-88.

1866. Retté, Adolphe. "Chronique des livres:Huysmans, *En route*." *La Plume* 144(avril 1895):173-74. [Rev. art.]

See also 108, 607, 799, 1097, 1746, 2923, 2942, 3071.

Ibsen

1867. Albert, Henri. " 'Solness le Constructeur' ou la confession d'un poète." *Entretiens politiques et littéraires* 48(août 1893):103-12.

1868. Ancey, Georges,et al. "Les Français et Ibsen en 1898." *RHT* 1-2 (1957):39-43. [Replies to an enquête organized by the Danish newspaper *Politiken* in 1898 on Mallarmé et al.]

1869. Bigley, B.M. "Perspectivism in Ibsen, Synge, and Hofmannsthal." *DAI* 33(1972):2361 A(Yale).

1870. Clancy, James H. "*Hedda Gabler:* Poetry in Action and Object," 64-72 in Oscar G. Brockett,ed. *Studies in Theatre and Drama: Essays in Honor of Hubert C. Heffner*. (DPL, Ser. maior 23.) The Hague: Mouton, 1972. 217 pp.

1871. Desmoineaux, Auguste. "Le nouveau drame d'Ibsen:Epilogue dramatique en trois actes." *La Plume* 257(janv 1900):97-99.

1872. Drougard, E. "Ibsen et Villiers de l'Isle-Adam." *RLC* 21(1947):230-42.

1873. Ewbank, Inga-Stina. "Ibsen's Dramatic Language as a Link Between His *Realism* and His *Symbolism*," 96-123 in *Ibsen Yearbook Vol. 8:Con-*

temporary Approaches to Ibsen, Daniel Haakonsen,ed. Oslo: Universitetsforl., 1965.

1874. Gaskell, Ronald. "Ibsen:*Peer Gynt* and *Rosmersholm*," 75-93 in *Drama and Reality*. London: Routledge and K. Paul, 1972.

1875. Harmer, Ruth. "Character, Conflict, and Meaning in *The Wild Duck*." *MD* 12(1970):419-27.

1876. Joyce, James, "Inedito su Ibsen." *Dramma* (Torino) 44,iii(1969):4-13. [On *When We Dead Awaken*.]

1877. Paul, Fritz. *Symbol und Mythos: Studien zum Spätwerk Henrik Ibsens*. München: Fink, 1969. 150 pp.

1878. Prunier, Francis. "Ibsen et le mariage du réalisme et du symbolisme." *RLM* 30(1958):73-411.

1879. Régnier, Henri de. "Notes dramatiques:*La dame de la mer* de H. Ibsen." *Entretiens politiques et littéraires* 34(janv 1893):36-38.

1880. Syre, Sivert. " 'Den trettende mann til bords'." *Samtiden* 81(1972): 52-62. [On *The Wild Duck*.]

See also 883, 2790, 3106.

Iosif, S.O. *See* 1158, 1168.

Ivanov, V.

1881. Ivanov, Vyacheslav. "Symbolism." *RusR* 25(1966):24-34. [Tr. from Russ. Thomas E. Bird.]

1882. Stacy, Robert H. "A Study of Vjacheslav Ivanov, *Cor Ardens* (Part I)." *DA* 26(1966):6053(Syracuse).

See also 694.

James, Henry

1883. Stowell, H. Peter. "The Prismatic Sensibility:Henry James and Anton Čexov as Impressionists." *DAI* 34 (1973):288A-89A (U. of Wash.).

Jammes

1884. Arland, M. "Francis Jammes et la poésie." *NRF* (1 fév 1929):253-59.

1885. Borel, Jacques. "De l'Angélus de l'aube à l'Angélus du soir." *NRF* (mars 1971):21-29.

1886. Ghéon, Henri. "Les géorgiques chrétiennes de Francis Jammes." *NRF* (1 oct 1912):692-706.

1887. ———. "Le naturisme en danger ou comment les symbolistes inventèrent Francis Jammes." *L'Ermitage* 17(1898):123-29.

1888. Jammes, F. "Le jammisme." *MdF* 21(mars 1897):492-93.

1889. Leblond, M.A. "Francis Jammes." *MdF* 46(1903):324-46.

1890. Le Breton, A. "L'oeuvre de M. Francis Jammes." *RdP* (15 mai 1907):341-54.

1891. Merlet, J.-F. Louis. "Poèmes pour Francis Jammes." *L'Ermitage* 23(nov 1901):369-72.

1892. Moulin, L. "Sur l'oeuvre de Francis Jammes." *MdF* 14(1920):5-50.

1893. Pilon, E. "Francis Jammes." *MdF* 68(1907):5-29.

1894. Quillard, R. "Fr. Jammes et Ch. Guérin." *MdF* 39(1901):5-19.

1895. Touny-Lérys. "Lettre à Francis Jammes." *L'Ermitage* 24(mars 1902):191-94.

See also 976, 1019.

Janin

1896. Bailbé, Joseph-Marc. "Berlioz, Janin et les 'Impressions d'Italie'." *RLC* 45(1971):489-513.

Jiménez, J.R.

1897. Albornoz, Aurora de. "El 'collage-anuncio' en Juan Ramón Jiménez." *RD* 37(1972):212-20.

1898. Allen, Rupert. "Juan Ramón and the World Tree:A Symbological

Analysis of Mysticism in the Poetry of Juan Ramón Jiménez." *RHM* 35 (1969):306-22.

1899. Bo, Carlo. *La poesia con Juan Ramón*. Firenze: Edizioni di rivoluzioni, 1941. 106 pp.

1900. Carreter, Fernando-Lázaro. "Juan Ramón, Antonio Machado y García Lorca."*Insula* 128-129(1957):1,5,21.

1901. Díaz-Plaja, Guillermo. "Juan Ramón Jiménez y Rubén Darío." *Clavileño* 7,x1ii(1956):9-16.

1902. Garfias, Francisco,ed. *Juan Ramón Jiménez*. Madrid: Taurus Ediciones, S.A., 1958. 263 pp.

1903. Gicovate, Bernardo. "La poesía de Juan Ramón Jiménez en el simbolismo." *CLS* 4(1967):119-26.

1904. Gullón, Ricardo. *Estudios sobre Juan Ramón Jiménez*. Buenos Aires: Losada, 1960. 241 pp.

1905. Jiménez, Juan R. *El modernismo*. México: Aguilar, 1962. 369 pp.

1906. Lira Osvaldo,SS.CC. *Poesía y mística en Juan Ramón Jiménez*. Santiago: Centro de Investigaciones Estéticas, 1969. 248 pp.

1907. Money, Agnes T. "Juan Ramón Jiménez y el modernismo." *Torre* 9(1963):167-74.

1908. Neddermann, Emmy. "Juan R. Jiménez:Sus vivencias y sus tendencias simbolistas." *Nosotros* 1-3(abril-dic 1936):16-25.

1909. ——. *Die symbolistischen Stilelemente im Werke von Juan Ramón Jiménez*. (Hamburger Studien zu Volkstum und Kultur der Romanen,20.) Seminar für romanische Sprachen und Kultur. Hamburg: U. of Hamburg, 1935. 145 pp.

1910. Olson, Paul R. "Structure and Symbol in a Poem of Juan Ramón Jiménez." *MLN* 76(1961):636-47.

1911. ——. "Time and Essence in a Symbol of Juan R. Jiménez." *MLN* 78(1963):169-93.

1912. Predmore, Michael P. "The Struc-

ture of the *Diario de un poeta reciéncasada*:A Study of Hermetic Poetry." *ConL* 13(1972):53-105.

1913. Ulibarri, Sabine R. *El mundo poética de Juan Ramón:Estudio estilístico de la lengua poética y de los símbolos.* Madrid: Edhigar, 1962, 285 pp.

1914. Ynduráin, Francisco. "De la sinestesia en la poesía de Juan Ramón." *Insula* 128-129(1957):1, 6.

See also 653, 1506, 2032, 2036, 2037.

Jørgensen

1915. Frederiksen, Emil. "Johannes Jørgensen:Fragment af en utrykt Studie." *Dansk Udsyn* 46 (1966):317-29.

1916. ——. "Léon Bloy et Johannes Jørgensen." *OL* 22(1967):283-93.

1917. Jones, W. Glynn. *Johannes Jörgensen.* (TWAS 70.) New York: Twayne. 1969.

1918. ——. "Parallelle traek i Sigrid Undsets og Johannes Jørgensens tidlige romaner." *NT* 47(1971):357-77.

1919. Larsen, Finn Stein. "Delen og tegnet," 96-133 in *Prosaens mønstre: Naerlæsninger of danske litteraere prosatekster [fra Edwald til Højholt med udgangspunkt i vaerkernes mønsterdannelser].* Copenhagen: Berlingske, 1971. 210 pp.

1920. Melin, Lars. "Johannes Jørgensen—100 år." *Credo* 48(1967):74-77.

1921. Vinding, Ole. "Johannes Jørgensen." *Perspektiv*(Copenhagen) 9,vii (1961-62):43-46.

Joyce

1922. Edel, Léon. *James Joyce:The Last Journey*. New York: Gotham Book Mart, 1947. 44 pp.

1923. Fox, Charles J. "James Joyce and

Arthur Symons in Transition." *DAI* 32(1972):4609A(Purdue).

1924. Hayman, David. *Joyce et Mallarmé*. 2 vols. Paris: Lettres modernes, 1956.

1925. Kronegger, M.E. "Joyce's Debt to Poe and the French Symbolists." *RLC* 39(1965):243-54.

1926. Tindall, William Y. "James Joyce and the Hermetic Tradition." *JHI* 15(1954):23-39.

1926a. Wolff-Windegg, Philipp. "Auf der Suche nach dem Symbol— J. Joyce und W.B. Yeats." *Symbolon* 5(1966):39-52.

See also 1476, 1876.

Kahn

1927. Carmody, Francis. "La doctrine du vers libre de Gustave Kahn(juillet 1886-décembre 1916)." *CAIEF* 21 (1969):37-50.

1928. Ireson, John C. *L'oeuvre poétique de Gustave Kahn*. Paris: Nizet, 1962. 683 pp.

1929. Pilon, Edmond. "Gustave Kahn." *L'Ermitage* 1(1896):72-86.

Kandinsky

1930. Albers, Josef. "La pensée + le sentiment." *XXe Siècle* 27(1966):99.

1931. Argan, Giulio C. "La libération du mythe." *XXe Siècle* 27(1966): 96-97.

1932. Boulez, Pierre. "Parallèles." *XXe Siècle* 27(1966):98.

1933. Bucarelli, Palma. "Une nouvelle poétique." *XXe Siècle* 27(1966):97.

1934. Cassou, Jean. "Kandinsky et la vie spirituelle." *XXe Siècle* 27(1966): 53-54.

1935. Clay, Julien. "L'année Kandinsky." *XXe Siècle* 39(1972):14-26.

1936. Deutsch, Max. "La rencontre avec Schoenberg." *XXe Siècle* 27(1966): 29-30.

1937. Dorazio, Piero. "Le créateur du XXe siècle." *XXe Siècle* 27(1966)103.

1938. Dupin, Jacques. "L'univers plastique de Kandinsky." *XXe Siècle* 27(1966):67-71.

1939. Estienne, Charles. "Le voyageur." *XXe Siècle* 27(1966):75-77.

1940. Gallwitz, Klaus. "Kandinsky à Baden-Baden." *XXe Siècle* 36(1971): 21-29.

1941. Giedion-Welcker. "L'élan vers le monumental." *XXe Siècle* 27(1966): 41-45.

1942. "Huit lettres de Kandinsky à Klee." *XXe Siècle* 27(1966):78-82.

1943. Kandinsky, Nina. "Kandinsky vivant." *XXe Siècle* 27(1966):83-88.

1944. Kojève, A. "Pourquoi concret." *XXe Siècle* 27(1966):63-66.

1945. Lankheit, Klaus. "Kandinsky et Franz Marc." *XXe Siècle* 27(1966): 31-32.

1946. Leppien, Jean. "La leçon de Kandinsky." *XXe Siècle* 27(1966):100.

1947. Lindsay, Kenneth C. "Les thèmes de l'inconscient." *XXe Siècle* 27 (1966):46-52.

1948. Marchiori, Giuseppe. "Kandinsky en Italie." *XXe Siècle* 27(1966): 104-06.

1949. Messer, Thomas M. "Kandinsky en Amérique." *XXe Siècle* 27(1966): 111-17.

1950. Meyer, Franz. "Le Kandinsky du centenaire." *XXe Siècle* 27(1966): 94. [Notes to K from Stravinsky and Leopold Stokowski.]

1951. Muche, Georg. "L'année 1913 à Munich." *XXe Siècle* 27(1966):33.

1952. Nishida, Hideho. "Genèse du cavalier bleu." *XXe Siècle* 27(1966): 18-24.

1953. "Notes biographiques et bibliographiques." *XXe Siècle* 27(1966): 118-20.

1954. Picon, Gaëtan. "La féerie du premier jour." *XXe Siècle* 27(1966):93.

1955. Read, Herbert. "Magie et raison." *XXe Siècle* 27(1966):95.

1956. Schneider, G. "Le premier lyrique de l'abstraction." *XXe Siècle* 27 (1966):101-02.

1957. Segui, Shinichi. "Kandinsky et l'Orient." *XXe Siècle* 27(1966): 107-10.

1958. Soupault-Niemeyer, R. "Du cheval au cercle." *XXe Siècle* 27(1966):34-40.

1959. Stuckenschmidt, H.H. "Kandinsky et la musique." *XXe Siècle* 27 (1966):25-28.

1960. Vallier, Dora. "Son fil d'Ariane, la couleur." *XXe Siècle* 17(1966): 72-74.

1961. Vieillard, Roger. "L'imagier des steppes." *XXe Siècle* 27(1966):102.

1962. Volboudt, Pierre. "Philosophie de Kandinsky." *XXe Siècle* 27(1966): 55-62.

See also 798.

Khnopff

1963. Legrand, F.C. "Fernand K. Khnopff:Perfect Symbolist." *Apollo* 85(Apr 1967):278.

Kilkerry

1964. Campos, Augusto de. "Kilkerry, Millarmé e o mau leitor." *MGSL* 26 Aug(1972):5.

1965. Martins, Heitor. "Kilkerry:Mallarmé . . . ou Alberto de Oliveira?" *MGSL* 15 July(1972):1-3; 22 July (1972):8-9; 29 July(1972):5.

Konevskoi

1966. Maumoff, Alice R. "Ivan Konevskoj:Mystical Symbolist Poet of Nature." *DAI* 31(1970):128A(N.Y.U.). [Portions of text in Rus.]

Korolenko

1967. Negru, Svetlana. "Semnificaţia simbolului şi locui în creaţia lui Korolenko." *AŞUI* 17(1971):153-57.

Krag

1968. Eide, Roar. "Vilhelm Krag-Rytmeskvulp." *Samtiden* 81(1972): 288-89.

1969. Engelstad, Carl F. "Vilhelm Krag." *Samtiden* 80(1971):645-60.

Krysinska

1970. Delior, Paul. "Les romans:*La force du désir* par Marie Krysinska." *La Plume* 374(juin 1905):635-36.

Kuzmin

1971. Field, Andrew. "Mikhail Kuzmin: Notes on a Decadent's Prose." *RusR* 22(1963):289-300.

Laforgue

1972. Bajomée, Danielle. "Hamlet, une moralité oubliée de Jules Laforgue." *RLV* 33(1967):386-405.

1973. Benamou, Michel. "Jules Laforgue and Wallace Stevens." *RR* 50(1970):107-17.

1974. Champigny, Robert. "Situation of Jules Laforgue." *YFS* 9(1952): 63-73.

1975. Collie, Michael. *Laforgue*. Edinburgh and London: Oliver & Boyd, 1963.

1976. Debauve, J.-L. *Laforgue en son temps*. Boudry: La Baconnière, 1972. 304 pp.

1977. Greene, E.J.H. "Jules Laforgue et T.S. Eliot." *RLC* 22(1948):363-97.

1978. Grojnowski, D. "La poétique de Laforgue." *Critique* 23(1967):254-65.

1979. ———. "Sur quelques comptes-rendus oubliés des *Complaintes* et de *L'imitation de Notre Dame de la lune* de Jules Laforgue." *RHL* 70(1970): 108-13.

1980. Guichard, Léon. *Jules Laforgue et ses poésies*. Paris: Presses Univs. de France, 1950.

1981. Hays, H.R. "Laforgue and Wallace Stevens." *RR* 25(1934):242-48.

1982. Jean-Aubry, G. "Jules Laforgue et la musique." *Revue de Genève* 3(1921):443-59.

1983. Kahn, G. "Jules Laforgue." *MdF* 160(1922):289-313.

1984. Mauclair, Camille. "Essai sur Jules Laforgue." *MdF* 17(fév 1896): 159-78; (mars 1896):302-29.

1985. Miomandre, Francis de. "Jules Laforgue." *MdF* 45(1903):289-316.

1986. "Notes inédites de Laforgue sur Corbière et sur Bourget." *Entretiens politiques et littéraires* 16(juillet 1891):1-17.

1987. Peyre, Henri. "Laforgue Among the Symbolists," 39-51 in *Laforgue: Essays on a Poet's Life and Work,* Warren Ramsey,ed. Carbondale & Edwardsville: So. Ill. U.P., 1969. 194 pp.

1988. Pilon, Edmond. "Jules La-Forgue." *L'Ermitage* 2(1895): 157-67.

1989. Ramsey, Warren. *Jules Laforgue and the Ironic Inheritance*. New York: Oxford U.P. 1953. 302 pp.

1990. ——,ed. *Jules Laforgue:Essays on a Poet's Life and Work*. Pref. Harry T. Moore. Carbondale: So. Ill. U.P., 1969. 194 pp.

1991. Ruchon, François. *Jules Laforgue, sa vie-son oeuvre*. Genève: A. Ciana, 1924. 283 pp.

1992. Saint-Jacques, Louis de. "Pour Jules Laforgue." *La Plume* 177(août 1896):588-90.

1993. Sonnenfeld, Albert. "Hamlet the German and Jules Laforgue." *YFS* 33(1964):92-100.

1994. Wheat, Linda R. "A Comparative Study of Jules Laforgue and Hart Crane." *DAI* 31(1970):1245A (Vanderbilt).

See also 572, 585, 651, 1226, 1319, 1606, 1613.

Larbaud

1995. Delvaille, Bernard. *Essai sur Valéry Larbaud*. Paris: Segher, 1963. 218 pp.

1996. Poÿlo, Anne. "Valéry Larbaud et Ricardo Viñes dans la pénombre d'Elche." *RLC* 46(1972):401-14.

La Tailhède, R. de

1997. De Brousse, J.-R. "Ode à Raymond de La Tailhède." *La Plume* 141(mars 1895):115-16.

1998. Retté, Adolphe. "Chronique des livres:M. Raymond de La Tailhède, *De la métamophose des fontaines.*" *La Plume* 146(mai 1895):234-35. [Rev. art.]

Lautréamont

1999. Jean-Nesmy, Claude. "Lautréamont et Rimbaud." *NL* 27(août 1970):11.

2000. Rousselot, Jean. "Ce mort sans sépulture." *Adam* 349-51(1971): 64-66.

2001. Zweig, Paul. *Lautréamont:The Violent Narcissus*. Port Washington, N.Y.: Kennikat, 192. 122 pp.

See also 549, 651, 1512.

Le Cardonnel

2002. Coulon, Marcel. *Louis Le Cardonnel, poète et prêtre*. Uzès en Languedoc: Editions de la Cigale, 1937. 98 pp.

2003. Lattard, François. "Louis Le Cardonnel." *La Plume* 171(juin 1896): 338-41.

2004. Richard, Noël. *Louis Le Cardonnel et les revues symbolistes*. Paris: Didier-Privat, 1946.
2005. Souchon, Paul. "Louis Le Cardonnel." *La Plume* 272(août 1900): 525-26.

See also 2714.

Leopold

2006. Calis, Piet. "Topkonferentie:J.H. Leopold:Variaties op een stilte." *Maatstaf* 10(1962):159-67.
2007. Donkersloot, N.A. "J.H. Leopold." *Maatstaf* 13(1965):263-71.
2008. Groot, Maria de. "Een interpretatie van 'De Molen' van J.H. Leopold." *LT* 273(1970):746-53.
2009. Jacobsen, R. "Leopold, zoals ik me hem herinner." *Gids* 120,v(1957): 308-24.
2010. Jalink, J.M. *Nieuwe varianten van enkele Leopold-gedichten*. Amsterdam: De Beuk, 1958.
2011. Jong, Martien J.G. de. *Leopolds "Cheops":Een interpreterend essay met tekstuitgave*. Leiden: Sijthoff, 1966.
2012. Kamerbeek, J.,Jr. "Op zoek naar een definitie van het symbolisme." *LT* 273(1970):767-77.
2013. Sötomann, A.L. "Leopold en Chrysippus." *NTg* 60(1967):158-64.
2014. ———. "Leopold en Dionysius van Halicarnassus." *NTg* 61(1968):145-56.

Lerberghe

2015. Davignon, Henri. *Charles Van Lerberghe et ses amis*. Bruxelles: Palais des Académies, 1952. 181 pp.
2016. Piemme, Michèle. "Du circulaire au linéaire:Analyse structurale d'un fragment de *La chanson d'Eve* de Charles Lerberghe." *Linguistics* 62(1970):34-43.

Leroux

2017. Bonfantini, M. "Pierre Leroux e le origini del simbolismo in Francia," 85-96 in *Studi in onore de Italo Siciliano*. (Biblioteca dell'Archivum Romanicum, Série I, 86.) Firenze: Olschki, 1966.

Levertin

2018. Hultman-Boye, Hans. " 'Sommarkväll' av Oscar Levertin." *Lyrikvännen* 14,i(1967):15-16.
2019. Julén Björn. *Hjartats landsflykt: En Levertinstudie*. Stockholm: Bonnier, 1961. [Sum. in Eng.]
2020. Paulin, Hillewi. "Levertin och Bergsons idévärld." *Edda* 72(1972): 201-19.

Levi

2021. Bukáček, Josef. "L'evoluzione di Carlo Levi:Dal decandentismo alla letteratura impegnata," 35-43 in J.O. Fischer and J. Sabršula,eds. *Acta Universitatis Carolinae* (Romanistica Pragensia IV.) Praha: Univ. Karlova 1966. 121 pp.

López, Rafael

2022. Castro Leal, Antonio. "Modernista arrepentido." *VidaL* 27(1972): 7-9.

López Velarde

2023. Fuente, Carmen de la. "El simbolismo y Ramón López Velarde." *CA* 170(1970):175-90.

Lowell, A.

2024. Bianchi, Ruggero. "La poetica del secondo imagismo:Amy Lowell e J.G. Fletcher." *RdE* 9(1964):214-47.

2025. Carlson, E.W. "The Range of Symbolism in Poetry." *SAQ* 48 (1949):442-51.

2026. Fletcher, J.G. "Herald of Imagism." *SoR* 1(1936):813-27.

Lucini

2027. Romani, Bruno. "Lucini e la via italiana al simbolismo." *Prospetti* 7,xxv-xxvi(1972):42-53.

Lugné-Poe

2028. Robichez, Jacques. "Lugné-Poe, le symbolisme et le théâtre." *Table Ronde* 127-128(juillet-août 1958): 116-20.

Macedonski

2029. Drimba, Ovidiu. "Al. Macedonski et le symbolisme français." *Studii de literatură universală* 11(1968): 87-102. [In Rom., sum. in Fr.]

Machado, Antonio

2030. Aguirre, J.M. *Antonio Machado, poeta simbolista*. Madrid: Taurus, 1973. 388 pp.

2031. Carilla, Emilio. "Antonio Machado y Rubén Darío," 150-64 in *Homenaje a Arturo Marasso 1890-1970*. (Cuadernos del Sur.) Bahia Blanca: Inst. de Humanidades, Univ. Nacional del Sur, 1972. 466 pp.

2032. Cobb, Carl W. "The Echo of a Lyrical Moment in Jiménez in a Sonnet of Antonio Machado." *RomN* 14(1972):34-40.

2033. Cobos, Pablo de A. *Humor y pensamiento de Antonio Machado en la metafísica poética*. Madrid: Insula, 1963. 175 pp.

2034. Cuadrado, Eduardo G. *El mar en la poesía de Antonio Machado*. Madrid: Atheo, 1966. 40 pp.

2035. Darmangeat, Pierre. *Antonio Machado, Pedro Salinas, Jorge Guillén*. Madrid: Insula, 1969. 392 pp.

2036. Gullón, Ricardo. "Machado visto por Juan Ramón." *Insula* 15,clxiii-(1960):3-10.

2037. ——. "Mágicos lagos de Antonio Machado:Machado y Juan Ramón." *PSA* 24(1962):26-61.

2038. ——. "Simbolismo en la poesía de Antonio Machado." *Clavileño* 4,xxii(1953):44-50.

2039. Gutierrez-Girardot, R. *Poesía y prosa en Antonio Machado*. Madrid: Ediciones Guadarrama, 1969. 241 pp.

2040. "Homenaje a Antonio Machado." *Torre* 12(1964):11-553. [Arts. by var. hands.]

2041. Pino, Frank,Jr. "El simbolismo en la poesía de Antonio Machado." *DAI* 32(1971):3325A(Northwestern).

2042. Ribbans, Geoffrey. "La influencia de Verlaine en Antonio Machado." *CHA* 31(1957):180-201.

2043. Ricardo, Guillan. "Simbolismo y modernismo en Antonio Machado." *Torre* 12(1964):329-47. [*Homenaje a Antonio Machado*.]

2044. Yndurain, Domingo. "Tres símbolos en la poesía de Machado." *CHA* 75(1968):117-49.

2045. Zubiria, Romón de. *La poesía de Antonio Machado*. Madrid: Editorial Gredos, 1966. 267 pp.

See also 653, 892, 1900, 2580, 2800, 2802, 2930.

Machado, Manuel

2046. Brotherston, Gordon. *Manuel Machado:A Revelation*. London: Cambridge U.P., 1968. 162 pp.
See also 892.

MacLeish

2047. McKulick, Benjamin Max. "Archibald MacLeish and the French Symbolist Tradition." *DA* 30(1969-70): 3950A(South Carolina).

Maeterlinck

2048. Bazalgette, Léon. "La Nature juste." *La Plume* 331(fév 1903):145-50.

2049. Blanchart, Paul. "Maeterlinck et nous." *Europe* 399-400(1962): 94-105.

2050. Bodart, Roger. *Maurice Maeterlinck*. Paris: Segher, 1962.

2051. Bruyr, José. "Maurice Maeterlinck et ses musiciens." *Musica* 105(Dec 1962):29-36.

2052. Carré, Jean-Marie. "Maeterlinck et les littératures étrangères." *RLC* 6(1926):449-501.

2053. Décaudin, Michel. "Maeterlinck et le symbolisme." *Europe* 399-400 (July-Aug 1962):105-14.

2054. Demedts, A. "Maurice Maeterlinck et la littérature flamande." *DWB* 108(1963):830-31.

2055. Doneux, Guy. "Maurice Maeterlinck ou la nudité de l'être." *Synthèses* 289-290(juillet-août 1970): 65-68.

2056. Doumic, R. "Les deux manières de M. Maeterlinck." *RDM* (15 août 1902):924-35.

2057. Dumont-Wilden, Louis. "Maurice Maeterlinck." *NRF* (1912):428-49.

2058. Evans, Calvin. "Maeterlinck and the Quest for a Mystic Tragedy in the Twentieth Century." *MD* 4(1961): 54-59.

2059. Gailliard, J.-J. "Un portrait nouveau de Maeterlinck." *Annales de la Fondation Maeterlinck* 14(1968): 31-38.

2060. Grimm, Reinhold. "Zur Wirkungsgeschichte Maurice Maeterlincks in der deutschen Literatur." *RLC* 33,iv(1959):535-44.

2061. Hadar, Tayitta. "L'angoisse méta-physique dans *Les aveugles* de Maeterlinck." *NCFS* 2(1973-74):68-74.

2062. Kesting, Marianne. "Maeterlincks Revolutionierung der Dramaturgie." *Akzente* 10(1963):527-44.

2063. Lazare, Bernard. *"Les sept princesses* par Maurice Maeterlinck." *Entretiens politiques et littéraires* 22 (janv 1892):32-37. [Rev. art.]

2064. Nardis, L. de. "Simbolismo minore: Maeterlinck." *AFLUSM* 16 (1963):103-10.

2065. Ousterhout, Polly B. "Maeterlinck's Early Plays and the Symbolist Aesthetic." *DAI* 31(1971): 3559A(Wash. U.).

2066. Palleske, Siegwalt O. *Maurice Maeterlinck en Allemagne*. Strasbourg: La Nouvelle imprimerie, 1938. 188 pp.

2067. Pérez de la Dehesa, Rafael. "Maeterlinck en España." **CHA** 255(1971):572-81.

2068. Pilon, Edmond. "Maurice Maeterlinck." *La Plume* 313(mai 1902): 529-32.

2069. Postic, Marcel. *Maeterlinck et le symbolisme*. Paris: Nizet, 1970. 255 pp.

2070. Romains, Willy P. *Maurice Maeterlinck*. Bruxelles: P. de Meyère, 1963. 86 pp.

2071. Saint-Jacques, Louis de. "Expertises: Les 'Douze chansons' de M. Maeterlinck et le 'Voyage d'Urien suivi de Paludes' de M. Gide." *La Plume* 189(mars 1897):150-54.

2072. Saix, Guillot de. "Oscar Wilde chez Maeterlinck: Souvenirs de Georgette LeBlanc recueillis par Guillot de Saix." *NL* 951(25 oct 1945):1-2.

2073. Vidal, Hernán. *"Esa luna que empieza* y Maeterlinck: La contemporaneidad modernista." *LATR* 6,ii(1973):5-11.

2074. Wais, Kurt. "Maeterlinck initiateur des poètes allemands. *Synthèses* 195(août 1962):129-49.

2075. ———. *Serta romantica*. Tübingen: Niemeyer, 1968. 330 pp. [Maeterlinck, Valéry.]

See also 873, 883, 903, 907, 976, 1097, 1122, 1185, 1545, 1810, 1813, 1815, 2781, 2920, 3125, 3129.

Maiakovski

2076. Abramov, A. "Uroki Majakovskojo." *VLit* 7,ix(1963)205-09. [Rev. art.]

2077. Blake, Patricia,ed. *Klop, stixi, poèmy—The Bedbug and Selected Poetry*. Tr. Max Hayward and George Reavey. New York: Meridan Books, 1960.

2078. Bočarov, M.D. "K polemike o knige A.I. Metčenko 'Tvorčestvo Majakovskogo 1925-1930 gg'." *VMU* 18,i(1963):88-92.

2079. Campos, Haroldo de. "Majakóvski em português:Roteiro de uma traduçao." *RdL* 6(Jul-Dez 1961):23-50. [Study of poem "A Sierguéi lessiênin" foll. by tr.]

2080. Čeremin, G. "Ot fevralja k oktjabru (Majakovski j v 1917 godu)." *RLit* 1(1960):26-47.

2081. Duvakin, V.D. "Neizvestnye teksty 'okon' Majakovskogo." *VMU* 18,iv(1963):52-62.

2082. Folejewski, Zbigniew. "Mayakovsky and Futurism." *CLS* Spec. Advance Issue (1963):71-77.

2083. Gorbunov, V.D. "O jazyke i stile stixotvorenija V.V. Majakovskogo 'Neobyčajnoe priključenie'." *RJŠ* 23, v(1962):30-32.

2084. Goriély, Benjamin. "Le théâtre de Maïakovski. A l'occasion du 31e anniversaire de sa mort." *Esprit* 9(1961):222-36.

2085. Guerra, E. Carrera,tr. and ed. *Antologia poética de Vladimir Maiacovski*. Com introd. Rio: Leitura, 1962.

2086. Juin, Hubert. "Maiakovski." *Critique* 137(1958):838-54. [Rev. art.]

2087. Kalitin, N. *Slovo i mysl':O poètičeskom masterstve V. Majakovskogo*. Moscow: Sov. pisatel,' 1959.

2088. Kolmogorov, A.N. "K izučeniju ritmiki Majakovskogo." *VJa* 12,iv (1963):64-71.

2089. Kondratov, A.M. "Evoljucija ritmiki V.V. Majakovskogo." *VJa*, 11,v (1962):101-08.

2090. Lavrenёv, B.,et al. "Sovremenniki o Majakovskogo." *NovM* 39,vii(1963):229-43.

2091. Levcenko, Myxajlo. "Majakovs'kyj ta ukrains'kyj futuryzm." *RLz* 15,vi(1971):19-29.

2092. Mathauser, Zdněk. "Majakovskij 1963." *ČsR* 8(1963):113-18.

2093. Mondrone, Domenico. "Vladimir Maiakovski poeta del mandato sociale." *CCa* 110,ii(1959):248-63.

2094. Moser, Charles A. "Mayakovsky's Unsentimental Journeys." *ASEER* 19(1960):85-100.

2095. Pasternak, Boris. "Premières rencontres avec Maïakovsky." *LetN* 68 (1959):213-24.

2096. Popov, R.N. "Jazykovye osobennosti 'Stixov o sovetskom pasporte' V.V. Majakovskogo." *RJŠ* 22,v(1961):69-73.

2097. Ripellino, Angelo Mario. *Majakovskij e il teatro russo*. Torino: Einaudi, 1959.

2098. Schaumann, G. "Majakovskij und der deutsche Expressionismus." *ZS* 15(1970):517-20.

2099. ———. "Zum Problem des positiven Helden in der sozialistischen satirischen Komödie (Dargestellt an Majakovskijs Komödien 'Klop' und 'Banja')." *ZS* 8(1963): 54-67.

2100. Skvoznikov, V.D. "Osobennosti raskrytija xaraktera v lirike Majakovskogo." *Socialisticeskij realizm i klassiceskoe nasledie* 49(1961):221-70.

2101. Smorodin, A. "Majakovskij vo Francii:Po stranicam progressivnoj pečati." *RLit* 5,iv(1962):199-218.

2102. ——. "Metaforičeskij stil' Majakovskogo." *RLit* 2(1960):82-110.

2103. Sokolsky, Anatole A. "Vladimir Mayakovsky, 1839-1930." *LangQ* 10,i-ii(1971):54-56.

2104. Timofeeva, V.V. *Jazyk poèta i vremja:Poètičeskij jazyk Majakovskogo*. Moscow: ANSSSR, 1962.

2105. ——. "Jazyk poèta i vremja." *RLit* 2(1960):64-81.

2106. Vecchi, Vittorio. "Vladimir Maiakovski." *Dramma* 35,iii(for 1958): 27-42.

2107. Vomperskij, V.P. "Priëmy ispol'zovanija frazeologičeskix oborotov v proiẑedenijax V.V. Majakovskogo." *RJS* 24,iii(1963):18-25.

2108. Zajcev, V.A. "Tradicii revoljucionnogo poètičeskogo slova." *VMU* 18,iv(1963):41-51.

Mallarmé

2109. Abastado, Claude. "Lecture inverse d'un sonnet nul." *Lit* 6(1972): 78-85.

2110. Agosti, Stefano. *Il cigno di Mallarmé*. Roma: Silva, 1969.

2111. Anon. "The Poet as a Symbolist: Toward a Remade Experience." *TLS* (30 Aug 1941):418-21.

2112. Audard, Jean, and Pierre Missac,eds. *Stéphane Mallarmé (1842-1898). Inédits, hors-texte, études*. Paris: Librairie "Les Lettres," 1948.

2113. Auriant. "Sur des vers retrouvés de Stéphane Mallarmé." *NRF* (1 mai 1933):836-39.

2114. Austin, Lloyd J. "*L'après-midi d'un faune* de Stéphane Mallarmé: Lexique comparé des trois états du poème." *Langue et Littérature* 6(19-62):279-89.

2115. ——. "Mallarmé and the 'Prose pour des Esseintes'." *FMLS* 2(19-66):197-213.

2116. ——. "Mallarmé disciple de Baudelaire:*Le Parnasse contemporain*." *RHL* 67(1967):437-49.

2117. ——. "Mallarmé et la critique biographique." *CLS* 4(1967):27-34.

2118. ——. "Mallarmé et le réel, "12-24 in *Modern Miscellany Presented to Eugene Vinaver by Pupils, Colleagues and Friends*, T.E. Lawrenson, F.E. Sutcliff and G.F. Gadoffre,eds. Manchester: Manchester U.P., 1969. 314 pp.

2119. ——. "Mallarmé on Music and Letters." *BJRL* 42(1959):19-39.

2120. ——. "Les moyens du mystère chez Mallarmé et chez Valéry." *CAIEF* 15(1963):103-17.

2121. ——. "The Mystery of a Name." *ECr* 1(1961):130-38.

2122. Ayda, A. "Les sources d'Hérodiade." *Dialogues* 4(Feb. 1956):97-113.

2123. Barbier, Carl,ed. *Documents Stéphane Mallarmé*. Tome II. Paris: Nizet, 1969.

2124. Beausire, Pierre. *Essai sur la poésie et la poétique de Mallarmé*. Lausanne: Roth, 1942. 212 pp.

2125. Benamou, Michel. "Recent French Poetics & the Spirit of Mallarmé." *ConL* 11(1970):217-25.

2126. Benda, Julien. "Mallarmé et Wagner." *Domaine Français* (1943): 353-59.

2127. Bernard, Suzanne. *Mallarmé et la musique*. Paris: Nizet, 1959. 184 pp.

2128. Bird, Edward A. *L'univers poétique de Stéphane Mallarmé*. Paris: Nizet, 1962. 224 pp.

2129. Block, Haskell M. *Mallarmé and the Symbolist Drama*. Detroit: Wayne State U.P., 1963. 164 pp.

2130. ——. "Mallarmé the Alchemist." *AJFS* 6(1969):163-79.

2131. Bohmer, Helga. "Alchemie der Töne:Die Mallarmé Vertonungen von Debussy und Ravel." *Musica* 32,ii (Mar-Apr 1968):83-85.

2132. Bonnet, Henri. "Le symbolism:

Mallarmé," 96-107 in *De Malherbe à Sartre:Essais sur le progrès de la conscience esthétique*. Paris: Nizet, 1964.

2133. Boschot, Adolphe. "Le wagnérisme de Stéphane Mallarmé." *L'Echo de Paris* (4 Oct 1923):4.

2134. Bounoure, Gabriel. "Destin et poésie chez Mallarmé." *Revue du Claire* 8(juin 1943):103-11.

2135. Brasil, Assis,ed. *Coletânea-2*. Rio: GRD, 1965. [5 essays by Mário Faustino on Mallarmé, *Concretismo*, and poetry in general.]

2136. Brie, Hartmut. "Die Theorie des poetischen effekts bei Poe und Mallarmé." *NS* 21(1972):473-81.

2137. Brown, Calvin S. "The Musical Analogies in Mallarmé's *Un coup de dés.*" *CLS* 4(1967):67-79.

2138. Bruns, Gerald L. "Mallarmé:The Transcendence of Language and the Aesthetics of the Book." *JTR* 3(1969):219-34.

2139. Butor, Michel. "Mallarmé selon Boulez." *Melos* 28(Nov 1961):356-59.

2140. Campos, C.L. "Symbolism and Mallarmé," 132-53 in *French Literature and Its Background*, John Cruickshank,ed. Vol. 5: *The Late Nineteenth Century*. London: Oxford U.P., 1969.

2141. Carrel, F. "Stéphane Mallarmé." *Fortnightly Review* 68(1895):446-55.

2142. Cattaui, Georges. "Mallarmé et les mystiques." *Lettres* 1,iii(1943):51-63.

2143. Chadwick, Charles. *Mallarmé, sa pensée dans sa poésie*. Paris: Corti, 1962. 156 pp.

2144. Chast, Denyse. "Eugénio de Castro et Stéphane Mallarmé." *RLC* 21 (1947):243-53.

2145. Chastel, André. "Vuillard et Mallarmé." *Letteratura* 9,iii(maggio-guigno 1947):22-30.

2146. Chisholm, A.R. "Brennan and Mallarmé." *Southerly* 21,iv(1962):23-35.

2147. ——. "Mallarmé and the Act of Creation." *ECr* 1(1961):111-16.

2148. ——. *Mallarmé* l'Après-midi d'un faune:*An Exegetical and Critical Study*. Carlton: Melbourne U.P., 1959. 35 pp.

2149. ——. "Mallarmé's Dream of Self-Creation." *AUMLA* 38(1972):137-42.

2150. ——. *Mallarmé's 'Grand Oeuvre'*. Manchester, Eng.: Manchester U.P., 1962. 139 pp.

2151. ——. "The Role of Consciousness in the Poetry of Mallarmé and Valery." *CLS* 4(1967):81-89.

2152. ——. "Substance and Symbol in Mallarmé." *FS* 5(1951):36-39.

2153. ——. "Le symbolisme français en Australie: Mallarmé et Brennan." *RLC* 18(1938):354-59.

2154. ——. "Two Exegetical Studies (Mallarmé, Rimbaud)." *ECr* 9(1969):28-36.

2155. Cohen, J. "L'obscurité de Mallarmé." *RE* 15(1962):64-72.

2156. Cohn, Robert G. "Keats and Mallarmé." *CLS* 7(1970):195-203.

2157. ——. "Mallarmé and the Greeks," 81-88 in Walter G. Langlois,ed. *The Persistent Voice:Essays on Hellenism in French Literature Since the 18th Century in Honor of Professor Henri M. Peyre*. Foreward Victor H. Brombert. Pref. by contribs. Epilogue. New York: N.Y.U. Press, 1971. 217 pp. [Introds. by ed.]

2158. ——. *Mallarmé's Masterwork: New Findings*. The Hague: Mouton, 1967. 86 pp.

2159. ——. *Toward the Poems of Mallarmé*. Berkeley: U. of Calif. P., 1965. 284 pp.

2160. Cooperman, Hasye. *The Aesthetics of Stéphane Mallarmé*. New York: Koffern Press, 1933. 301 pp.

2161. Corrèa, Manuel T. "Mallarmé e

Fernando Pessoa perante o 'Corvo' de Edgar Allan Poe." *Occidente* 65 (1963):4-20.

2162. Davies, Gardner. "Paradox and Denouement in Mallarmé's Poetry." *FS* 17(1963):351-57.

2163. Delfel, Guy. *L'esthétique de Stéphane Mallarmé.* Paris: Flammarion, 1951. 209 pp.

2164. Delior, P. "La femme et le sentiment de l'amour chez Stéphane Mallarmé." *MdF* 86(1910):193-207.

2165. Epstein, Edna S. "The Entanglement of Sexuality and Aesthetics in Gautier and Mallarmé." *NCFS* 1,i(1972):5-20.

2166. Ernoult, C. "Mallarmé et l'occultisme." *Revue métapsychique* (janvmars 1952):35-50.

2167. Erwin, John F.,Jr. "Mallarmé and Claudel:An Intellectual Encounter." *DAI* 32(1971):42A (Columbia).

2168. Evans, C. "Mallarméen Antecedents of the Avant-garde Theater." *MD* 6(1963-64):12-19.

2169. Fongaro, Antonio. "Chantre, Palais Annie et Mallarmé." *SFr* 46 (1972):82-87.

2170. Fontainas, André. *De Stéphane Mallarmé à Paul Valéry:Notes d'un témoin (1894-1922).* Paris: Bernard, 1928. 59 pp.

2171. Fowlie, Wallace. *Mallarmé.* Chicago: U. of Chicago P., and London: Dennis Dobson, 1953. [Repr. U. of Chicago P., 1962.´ 299 pp.

2172. ———. "Mallarmé and the Aesthetics of the Theater," 265-76 in *Dionysius in Paris.* New York: Meridian, 1960.

2173. ———. "Mallarmé and the Painters of His Age." *SoR* 2(1966):542-58.

2174. ———. *Mallarmé as Hamlet:A Study of Igitur.* Yonkers, New York: Alicat Bookshop Press, 1949. 22 pp.

2175. ———. "Mallarmé as Ritualist." *SR* 59(1951):228-53.

2176. Fretet, Jean. *L'aliénation poéti-
que:Rimbaud. Mallarmé, Proust.* Paris: J.B. Janin, 1946. 332 pp.

2177. Gaede, Edouard. "Le problème du language chez Mallarmé." *RHL* 68(1968):45-65.

2178. Gengoux, Jacques. *Le symbolisme de Mallarmé.* Paris: Nizet, 1950. 269 pp.

2179. Gielen, J.G. "Mallarmé's 'Unvollendete' en de Serialisten." *Mens en Melodie* 16(Mar 1961):70-22.

2180. Gill, Austin. "Mallarmé et l'antiquité." *CAIEF* 10(1958):158-73.

2181. ———. "Mallarmé on Baudelaire," 89-114 in J.C. Ireson,ed. *Currents of Thought in French Literature:Essays in Memory of Professor C.T. Clapton.* Oxford: Blackwell, 1965.

2182. ———. *Mallarmé's Poem "La chevelure vol d'une flamme."* Glasgow: U. of Glasgow P., 1971. 27 pp.

2183. ———. " 'Le tombeau de Charles Baudelaire' de Mallarmé." *CLS* 4(1967):45-65.

2184. Goldsmith, Ulrich R. "On Translating Mallarmé into German." *RLC* 35(1961):474-86.

2185. Gosse, Edmund. "Symbolism and M. Stéphane Mallarmé." *Academy* 43(7 Jan 1893).

2186. Graaf, Daniel A. de. "De doolhof van Stéphane Mallarmé of gedichten als sterrenbeelden." *VIG* 49(1965): 789-93.

2187. Grassi, Ernesto. "Der Tod Gottes: Zu einer These von Mallarmé," 195-214 in Konrad Gaiser,ed. *Das Altertum und jedes Gute:Für Wolfgang Schadewaldt zum 15. März 1970.* Stuttgart: Kohlhammer, 1970.

2188. Hagen, Frédéric. "Mallarmé et l'Allemagne," 225-29 in *Stéphane Mallarmé (1842-98).* Inédits, horstexte, études, réunis par Jean Audard et Pierre Missac. Paris: Librairie "Les Lettres," 1948.

2189. "Hommage à Stéphane Mallarmé." *NRF* (1 nov 1926):517-61.

2190. Horodincă, Georgeta. "Homo aestheticus." *Luc* 20 oct(1973):10.

2191. Ilsley, Marjorie H. "Four Unpublished Letters of Stéphane Mallarmé to Stuart Merrill." *YFS* 9(1952): 155-61.

2192. Jaudon, Pierre. "Hugoliens et mallarméens." *La Plume* 311(avril 1902):417-20.

2193. Jones, Rhys S. "Mallarmé and Valéry:Imitation or Continuation?" 201-17 in *Gallica:Essays Presented to Heywood Thomas by Colleagues, Pupils and Friends.* Philip F. Butler,ed. Cardiff: U. of Wales P., 1969. 271 pp.

2194. ——. "The Selection and Usage of Symbols by Mallarmé and Valéry." *FMLS* 2(1966):180-91.

2195. Jourdain, Louis. "Le concept psychique de Mallarmé." *Cahiers du Sud* 378-79(1964):9-28.

2196. Kahnweiler, Daniel-Henry. "Mallarmé et la peinture," 63-68 in *Stéphane Mallarmé (1842-1898).* Inédits, hors-texte, études, réunis par Jean Audard et Pierre Missac. Paris: Librairie "Les Lettres," 1948.

2197. Kristeva, Julia. "Sémanalyse et production de sens, quelques problèmes de sémiotique littéraire à propos d'un texte de Mallarmé:*Un coup de dés . . .*," 207-34 in Algirdas J. Greimas,ed. *Essais de sémiotique poétique.* Paris: Larousse, 1972. 239 pp.

2198. Lannes, Roger. "Mallarmé, poète de la poésie." *Synthèses* 3,i(1948): 77-81.

2199. Lanson, Gustave. "La poésie contemporaine de Stéphane Mallarmé." *Revue Universitaire* 2(1893):97-104.

2200. Lockspeiser, Edward. "Mallarmé and Music." *Musical Times* 107(Mar 1966):212-13.

2201. Lund, Hans P. "Les *Noces d'Hérodiade, mystère*—Et résumé de l'oeuvre mallarméenne." *RevR* 4(19-69):28-50.

2202. ——. "Une trahison de la lettre. Essai sur *La gloire* de Mallarmé." *RevR* 7(1972):254-80.

2203. Luzi, Mario. "Mallarmé e la poesia moderna." *Rassegna d'Italia* 4,ix(Sept 1949):899-910.

2204. Mannoni, O. "Mallarmé relu." *Temps Modernes* 198(nov 1962): 864-83.

2205. Manston, Augustus. "M. Stéphane Mallarmé." *Temple Bar* 109(Oct 18-96):242-53.

2206. McLuhan, Marshall. "Joyce and Mallarmé," in *The Interior Landscape.* New York: McGraw Hill, 1969. 239 pp.

2207. Michaud, Guy. *Mallarmé.* New York: New York University Press, 1965. 180 pp. [Repr. Paris: Hatier, 1971, 223 pp.]

2208. ——. *Mallarmé, l'homme et l'oeuvre.* Paris: Hatier-Boivin, 1953. 192 pp.

2209. Missac, P. "Stéphane Mallarmé et Walter Benjamin." *RLC* 43(1969): 233-48.

2210. Mondor, Henri. *Autres précisions sur Mallarmé et inédits.* Paris: Gallimard, 1961.

2211. ——. "Mallarmé, Debussy et l'Après-midi d'un faune." *Cahiers du Nord* 21(1948):117-22.

2212. ——. "Mallarmé et Paul Claudel." *RDM* (déc 1948):395-418.

2213. ——. "Stéphane Mallarmé et Claude Debussy." *Journal Musical Français* 1(1951):1,8.

2214. ——. *Vie de Mallarmé.* Paris: Gallimard, 1941. 2 vols. 827 pp.

2215. Moréas, Jean. "Stéphane Mallarmé." *La Plume* 228(oct 1898): 609-12.

2216. Morice, Charles. "Stéphane Mallarmé." *La Plume* 166(mars 1896): 172-76. [Facsim. autographe inédit de M.]

2217. Munro, T. "The *Afternoon of a Faun* and the Interrelation of the Arts." *JAAC* 10(1951):95-111.

2218. Neumann, Gerhard. "Die 'absolute' Metapher:Ein Abgrenzungsversuch am Beispiel Stephane Mallarmés und Paul Celans." *Poetica* 3(1970):188-225.

2219. Nicholas, Henry. *Mallarmé et le symbolisme:Auteurs et oeuvres*. Paris: Larousse, 1963.

2220. Noulet, Emilie. "Mallarmé et la musique." *Cahiers du Sud* 357(1960):297-301.

2221. ———. *L'oeuvre poétique de Stéphane Mallarmé*. Paris: Droz, 1940.

2222. ———. *Stéphane Mallarmé*. Paris Droz, 1940.

2223. ———, ed. "Stéphane Mallarmé: Dix-neuf études inédites." *Synthèses* 22(déc 1967-jan 1968):18-118. [Arts. by var. hands.]

2224. ———. *Suites:Mallarméennes, rimbaldiennes, valéryennes*. Paris: Nizet, 1964. 267 pp.

2225. Oxenhandler, Neal. "The Quest for Pure Consciousness in Husserl and Mallarmé," 149-66 in *The Quest for Imagination:Essays in Twentieth-Century Aesthetic Criticism*, O.B. Hardison,Jr.,ed. Cleveland and London: The Press of Case Western Reserve U., 1971. 286 pp.

2226. Patri, Aimé. "Mallarmé et la littérature." *Paru* 48(nov 1948):7-13.

2227. ———. "Mallarmé et la musique de silence." *Revue musicale* 210 (1952):101-11.

2228. Paxton, N. "Stéphane Mallarmé und Stefan George." *ML* 54(1964): 102-04.

2229. Paz, Octavio. "Stéphane Mallarmé:'Sonnet in *ix*'." *Delos* 4(1970):14-15. [Tr. Agnes Money. Foll. by "Commentary," 16-28.]

2230. Petrucciani, Mario. "Stéphane Mallarmé precursore dell'ermetismo italiano." *Rivista di Critica* l,i(genn-febb 1950):19-26.

2231. Pevel, H. "Résonances mallarméennes du nouveau roman." *Médiations* 7(1964): 95-113.

2232. Philippide, Al. "Stéphane Mallarmé." *RoLit* 13(Jan 1972):26-27.

2233. Philonenko, Monique. "Sur le langage, et Mallarmé." *RMM* 77 (1972):329-38.

2234. Piselli, Francesco. *Mallarmé e l'estetica*. Milano: U. of Mursia, 1969. 299 pp.

2235. Poggioli, R. "Decadence in Miniature." *MR* 4(1963):531-62.

2236. Popo, E. "Mallarmé en de muziek." *VIG* 52,xii(1968):33-37.

2237. Pradal-Rodriguez, G. "La técnica poética y el caso Góngora-Mallarmé." *CL* 3(1950):269-80.

2238. Rabbin, Marcelle. "*Le pitre châtié* ou la société comme cirque." *FR* 45(1972):980-87.

2239. Ramsey, Warren. "A View of Mallarmé's Poetics." *RR* 46(1955): 178-91.

2240. Régnier, Henri de. "Hamlet et Mallarmé." *MdF* 17(1896):289-92.

2241. ———. "Stéphane Mallarmé." *MdF* 28(oct 1898):5-9.

2242. Retté, Adolphe. "Arabesques: Apologie." *La Plume* 209(janv 1898):5-11.

2243. ———. "Aspects:Le décadent." *La Plume* 169(mai 1896):272-77.

2244. ———. "M. Stéphane Mallarmé, *La musique et les lettres*." *La Plume* 138(janv 1895):64-65 [Rev. art.]

2245. ———. "Tribune Libre." *La Plume* 185(janv 1897):62-63.

2246. Reyes, Alfonso. "Mallarmé en espagnol." *RLC* 12 (1932): 546-68.

2247. ———. *Mallarmé entre nosotros*. Buenos Aires:Ed. Destiempo, 1938. 94 pp.

2248. Richardson, Barbara A. "Mallarmé's *Prose pour des Esseintes*." 12(1970):87-92.

2249. Richard, Jean-Pierre. *L'univers imaginaire de Mallarmé*. Paris: Editions du Seuil, 1961. 653 pp.

2250. St. Aubyn, Frederick G. *Stéphane Mallarmé*. New York:Twayne, 1969. 175 pp.

2251. Saint-Jacques, Louis de. "Expertises:La 'Protestation mallarmophile' de M. Gide et Les 'Divagations' de M. Mallarmé." *La Plume* 190(mars 1897):179-86.

2252. Saurat, D. "La Nuit d'Idumée: Mallarmé et la Cabale." *NRF* (1 déc 1931):920-22.

2253. Schérer, Jacques. *L'expression littéraire dans l'oeuvre de Mallarmé.* Paris: Droz, 1947. 289 pp.

2254. Schmidt-Garre, Helmut. "Dichtung, die Musik sein wollte." *NHochland* 60(1968):624-35.

2255. Schwartz, Paul J. "Les noces d'Hérodiade." *NCFS* 1,i(1972): 33-42.

2256. Sherard, Robert H. "Paris Letter." *Bookman* 3(1896):150-51.

2257. Siciliano, I. "Mallarmé:Il narcismo della parola." *Lettres Modernes* 6(1956):7-21,156-75.

2258. Simons, Henri. "Wallace Stevens and Mallarmé." *MP* 43(1947):235-59.

2259. Smith, Harold J. "Mallarmé's Dramatic Lyric." *DAI* 31(1970): 1813A-14A(Calif., Berkeley.)

2260. Smith, M.H. "Mallarmé and the Chimères." *YFS* 11(1952):59-72.

2261. Soulairol, Jean. "Mallarmé et la création poétique." *Le Divin* 238 (avril-juin 1941):71-85.

2262. Steland, Dieter. *Dialektische Gedanken in Stéphane Mallarmés* 'Divagations.' (Freiburger Schriften zur romanischen Philologie 7.) München: Wilhelm Fink Verlag, 1965. 86 pp.

2263. Strauss, W.A. "Mallarmé:Orpheus and the Néant," 81-139 in *Descent and Return:The Orphic Theme in Modern Literature.* Cambridge: Harvard U.P., 1971.

2264. Swift, Bernard. "Mallarmé and the Novel," 254-75 in *Modern Miscellany Presented to Eugene Vinaver by Pupils, Colleagues Friends*, T.C. Lawrenson, F.E. Sutcliffe and G.F. Gadoffre,eds. Manchester; Manchester U.P., 1969. 314 pp.

2265. Symons, Arthur. "Mallarmé's *Divagations.*" *Saturday Review* 83(30 Jan 1897):109-10.

2266. Thibaudet, A. "Deux poèmes de Mallarmé." *NRF* (1 juin 1933): 865-72.

2267. ———. "Mallarmé en Angleterre et en Allemagne." *NRF* (1 janv 1928): 95-101.

2268. ———. "Mallarmé et Rimbaud." *NRF* (1 fév 1922):199-206.

2269. ———. *La poésie de Stéphane Mallarmé.* Paris: Gallimard, 1926. 470 pp.

2270. ———. "La rareté et le dehors." *NRF* (1 août 1927):235-43.

2271. Tortel, Jean. "Note brève sur le regard de Mallarmé." *Cahiers du Sud* 378-79(1964):3-8.

2272. Ungaretti, Giuseppe. *Da Góngora e da Mallarmé.* Milano: Mondadori, 1958.

2273. Valéry, Paul. "Je disais quelquefois à Mallarmé." *NRF* (1 mai 1932):824-43.

2274. Verhoeff, J.P. "Anciens et modernes devant la "Prose pour des Esseintes'." *RomN* 12(1970):87-92.

2275. Vielé-Griffin, Francis. "Mallarmé." *Entretiens politiques et littéraires* 17(août 1891):67-72. [A propos de "Pages."]

2276. ———. "Stéphane Mallarmé." *MdF* 170(1924):22-36.

2277. Vordtriede, Werner. *The Conception of the Poet in the Works of Stéphane Mallarmé and Stefan George.* Evanston, Ill.: Northwestern U., 1944. [Diss.]

2278. ———. "The Mirror as Symbol and Theme in the Works of Stéphane Mallarmé and Stefan George." *MLF* 32,i(1947):1-12.

2279. ———. "Novalis und Mallarmé. *Antaios* 5(1963):64-78.

2280. Wais, Kurt. "Igitur, Begegnungen Mallarmés mit seinen Vorgängern." *CLS* 4(1967):35-43.

2281. ———. *Mallarmé:Dichtung, Weis-*

heit, Haltung. Munich: C.H. Beck, 1938. 800 pp. [2nd ed., 1952.]

2282. Welch, Liliane. "Mallarmé:A New Concept of Poetry." *DR* 48(1968-69):523-29.

2283. ———. "Mallarmé and the Experience of Art." *JAAC* 30(1972):369-75.

2284. Williams, Thomas A. "Affirmation and Negation in Mallarmé." *RomN* 10(1969):247-48.

2285. ———. *Mallarmé and the Language of Mysticism.* Athens: U. of Ga. P., 1970. 99 pp.

2286. Winkel, Joseph. *Mallarmé–Wagner–Wagnerismus.* Bückeburg: H. Prinz, 1935. 73 pp.

2287. Woolley, Grange. "Comments on Mallarmé's Cubism and Preciosity." *ECr* 1(1961):139-44.

2288. Zayed, Georges. "Reflexions sur les variantes d'*Aumone* et l'hermétisme mallarméen." *RHL* 72(1972): 85-100.

2289. Zimmerman, E.M. "Mallarmé et Poe, précisions et aperçus." *CL* 6,iv (1954):304-15.

2290. Zuckerkandi, Frédéric. "L'absent chez Mallarmé." *Synthèses* 285(mars 1970):20-25.

See also 61, 74, 107, 179, 261, 436, 497, 503, 533, 571, 572, 593, 607, 650, 651, 753a, 799, 891, 905, 907. 936, 941, 981, 982, 997, 1019, 1025, 1045, 1048, 1072, 1084, 1107, 1110, 1114, 1120, 1121, 1133, 1135, 1138, 1226, 1233, 1247, 1273, 1276, 1277, 1318, 1323, 1394, 1418, 1429, 1546, 1547, 1696, 1697, 1834, 1924, 1964, 1965, 2319, 2402, 2447, 2451, 2459, 2460, 2483, 2543, 2581, 2853, 2606, 2635, 2641, 2644, 2673, 2707, 2750, 2756, 2766, 2775, 2780, 2809, 2823, 2847, 2852, 2858, 2902, 2920, 3019, 3020, 3023, 3032, 3033, 3038, 3070, 3082, 3100, 3107, 3133, 3160.

Mann, T.

2291. Geiser, Christoph. *Naturalismus und Symbolismus im Frühwerk Thomas Manns.* Bern: Francke, 1972. 87 pp.

See also 1122, 1707, 2571.

Marinetti *See* 672.

Martí

2292. Broderman, Ramón E. "El pensamiento litérario de José Martí:Sus mocedades." *DAI* 33(1972):1136A (Fla. State).

2293. Marinello, Juan. *José Martí.* Madrid: Júcar, 1972. 228 pp.

2294. Schulman, Ivan A. "Martí y el modernismo." *Nivel* 91(1970): 5,10-11.

Matoš

2295. Tomić, Josip. "Baudelaire i A.G. Matoš." *Filologija* 2(1969):175-88. [Sum. in Fr.]

Mauclair

2296. Fontainas, A. "Camille Mauclair." *MdF* 10(avril 1894):338-41.

2297. Miomandre, F. de. "Camille Mauclair." *MdF* 41(1902):641-54.

See also 558.

Melville *See 1138, 2611.*

Mendès

2298. Hanson, Howard L.,Jr. "The *Revue Fantaisiste* of Catulle Mendès." *DAI* 31(1971):3403A(Ky.)

Merrill, Stuart

2299. Henry, Marjorie L. *La contribution d'un Américain au symbolisme français.* Paris: Champion, 1927. 290 pp.

2300. Saint-Jacques, Louis de. "Stuart Merrill." *La Plume* 141(mars 1895): 108-09.

See also 2191.

Meunier

2301. Degron, Henri. "Dauphin Meunier." *La Plume* 156(oct 1895): 463-65.

Michaux

2302. Hoog, Armand. "Henri Michaux, or Mythic Symbolism." *YFS* 9 (1952):143-54.

Micinski, Tadeusz

2303. Rzewuska, E. "Elementy teatralne w powieściach Tadeusza Micińskego." *O prozie polskiej XX Wieku* (1971):39-55.

Mikhaël

2304. Coulon, M. "Le Symbolisme d'Ephraïm Mikhaël." *MdF* 101 (1913):476-500.
2305. Perrin, Henri. "Entre Parnasse et Symbolisme:Ephraïm Mikhael." *RHL* 56(jan-mars 1956):96-107.

Milosz

2306. Bellemin Noël, Jean. "Milosz aux limites du poème." *Poétique* 2 (1970):202-23.
2307. Richer, Jean. "Milosz kabbaliste: Lecture du *Psaume du Roi de Beauté*," 113-24 in *Approches:Essais sur la poésie moderne de langue française.* (Annales de la Fac. des Lettres et Sciences Humaines de Nice 15.) Paris: Les Belles Lettres. 1971. 171 pp.
2308. Vėbrienė, Genovaitė. "Oskaras Vladislovas Milosz-Milašius." *Pradalgė algė* 7(1970):411-35.

Mockel

2309. Champagne, Paul. *Essai sur Albert Mockel. Contribution à l'histoire du symbolisme en France et en Belgique.* Paris: Champion, 1922. 54 pp.
2310. Otten, Michel. *Albert Mockel. Esthétique du symbolisme.* Bruxelles: Palais des Académies, 1962. 256 pp.
2311. Vivier, Robert. "Albert Mockel et le symbolisme." *MRom* 16(1966): 87-92.

Montale *See* 616.

Montesquiou

2312. Jullian, Philippe. "Ce que l'art nouveau doit à la curiosité fantastique de Robert de Montesquiou." *ConnArts* 161(1965):60-65.
2313. ——. *Robert de Montesquiou, un prince 1900.* Paris: Librairie académique Perrin, 1965. 394 pp.

See also 1472.

Moore, George

2314. Blissett, William F. "George Moore and Literary Wagnerism." *CL* 13(1961):52-71.
2315. Burkhart, Charles J. "The Letters of George Moore to Edmund Gosse, W.B. Yeats, R.I. Best, Miss Nancy Cunard, and Mrs. Mary Hutchinson." *DA* 19(1958):131(Md.).
2316. Collet, Georges-Paul. *George Moore et la France.* Geneva: Droz, 1958. 281 pp.
2317. Halévy, Daniel. "George Moore à Paris et son initiation à la littérature française." *Minerve française* 5,xxiv (1 juin 1920):588-96.

99

2318. Hough, Graham. "George Moore and the Nineties," 1-27 in Richard Ellmann,ed. *Edwardians and Late Victorians*. New York: Columbia U.P., 1960.

2319. Noël, Jean. "George Moore et Mallarmé." *RLC* 32(1958):363-76.

2320. Nozick, Martin. *George Moore and French Symbolism*. New York: Columbia U., 1942. [Master's Essay.]

2321. Sinfelt, Frederick W. "Wagnerian Elements in the Writing of George Moore." *Studies in the Humanities* (Ind. U. of Pa.) 1,i(1969):38-49.

2322. White, Clyde P. "George Moore: From Naturalism to Pure Art." *DAI* 31(1971):4800A(Va.).

Moore, M.

2323. Fowlie, Wallace. "Marianne Moore." *SR* 50(1952):537-47.

2324. Guillory, Daniel L. "A Place for the Genuine:The Poetics of Marianne Moore." *DAI* 33(1972):1168A (Tulane).

2325. Wasserstrom, William. "Marianne Moore, *The Dial*, and Kenneth Burke." *WHR* 17(1964):249-62.

See also 1083, 1773.

Moréas

2326. Barrès, Maurice. "Jean Moréas: Symboliste." *La Plume* 41(janv 1891): 7-13.

2327. Butler, John D. "Jean Moréas and *Les Stances*:The Making of a Poet." *DA* 24(1963):1168-69(Stanford).

2328. Coulon, Marcel. *Au chevet de Moréas*. Paris: Eds. du siècle, 1926. 124 pp.

2329. ———. "Moréas 'dévoilé'." *MdF* 90(1911):5-24; 277-99.

2330. ———. "L'unité de Jean Moréas." *MdF* 84(1910):193-216; 431-50.

2331. Delior, Paul. "Les romans." *La Plume* 367(fév 1905):113-14. [Rev. art.]

2332. France, Anatole. "La poésie nouvelle:Jean Moréas." *La Plume* 41 (janv 1891):2-4.

2333. Georgin, René. *Jean Moréas*. Paris: La Nouvelle revue critique, 1930. 255 pp.

2334. Ghéon, Henri. "Le classicisme et M. Moréas." *NRF* (1 juillet 1909): 492-503.

2335. Gillouin, René. "Jean Moréas, poète tragique." *NRF* (1 mai 1912): 731-45.

2336. Gourmont, J. de. "Jean Moréas." *MdF* 51(1904):636-58.

2337. Jouanny, Robert A. *Jean Moréas, écrivain français*. Préf. de Michel Décaudin. Paris: Lettre modernes, Minard, 1969. 852 pp.

2337a. ———. "La carrière de Jean Moréas (1856-1910)."*IL* 21(1969):32-38.

2338. Kahn, Gustave. "Jean Moréas:*Les Stances, IIIe, IVe, Ve, VIe livres* (Editions de *La Plume*)." *Revue Blanche* 24(1901):478. [Rev. art.]

2339. Meunier, Dauphin. " 'Iphigénie' et Jean Moréas." *La Plume* 345(sept 1903):230-34. [Rev. art.]

2340. Noisay, M. de. "L'esprit de Jean Moréas." *MdF* 89(1911):47-62.

2341. Palmiery, R. "Le manifeste symboliste." *Culture française* 10 (1963):45-46.

2342. Quillard, P. "Jean Moréas." *MdF* 37(1901):289-98; 84(1910):577-82.

2343. Schlumberger, J. "Jean Moréas." *NRF* (1 mai 1910):543-50.

2344. Vielé-Griffin, Francis. "Pourquoi pas?" *Entretiens politiques et littéraires* 10(janv 1891):26-28

See also 451, 572, 1019, 1031, 1058, 1360, 2111, 2523, 2942.

Moreau

2345. D'Udine, Jean. "Les Gustave

Moreau du Musée du Luxembourg."
La Plume 236(fév 1899):102-04.

2346. Holten, Ragnar von. *L'art fantas-tique de Gustave Moreau*. Paris: J.J. Pauvert, 1960. 95 pp.

2347. ———. "Le personnage de Salomé à travers les dessins de Gustave Moreau." *Oeil* 79-80(juillet-août 1961): 44-51.

2349. Laran, Jean. *Gustave Moreau.* Paris: Librairie centrale des beaux-arts, 1916. 114 pp.

2350. Mathieu, Pierre-Louis. "Gustave Moreau et la création du tableau." *Information d'histoire de l'art* 10 (1965):91-92.

2351. Paladilhe, Jean, and José Pierre. *Gustave Moreau*. Paris: F. Hazan, 1971. 171 pp.

2352. Péladan, Sor. "Gustave Moreau." *L'Ermitage* 1(1895):29-34.

2353. Saunier, Charles. "Le Musée Gustave Moreau." *Revue Blanche* 27 (1902):153-55.

See also 766, 730, 757, 2503.

Morice

2354. Clerget, Fernand. "Littérature de tout à l'heure par Charles Morice." *La Plume* 4(juin 1889):37-38.

2355. Coursange, Emile. "Charles Morice." *La Plume* 7(juillet 1889): 61-62.

2356. Delsemme, Paul. *Un théoricien du symbolisme:Charles Morice*. Paris: Nizet, 1958. 276 pp.

2357. Leiris, Alan de. "Charles Morice and His Times." *CLS* 4(1967): 371-95.

2358. Maurras, Edouard. "Défense du système des poètes romans." *La Plume* 149(juillet 1895):289-92.

See also 1662.

Mouw, J.A. der *See* 1570.

Munch

2359. Hodin, J.P. *Edvard Munch*. New York: Praeger, 1972; London: Thames and Hudson, 1972. 216 pp.

Nelligan

2360. Bonenfant, Jean-Charles. "Le Canada français à la fin du XIXe siècle." *EF* 3(1967):263-74.

2361. "Chronologie d'Emile Nelligan." *EF* 3(1967):260.

2362. "Documents." *EF* 3(1967): 277-84.

2363. Gagnon, Lysiane. "Emile Nelligan." *Québec* 67(fév 1967):73-81.

2364. Grandmont, Eloi de,ed. *Poèmes choisis ... précédés d'une chronologie, d'une bibliographie et de jugements critiques*. Montréal: Fides, 1966.

2365. Pontaut, Alain. "Un devoir de 'sagesse patriotique'." *Québec* 67(fév 1967):81-83.

2366. Samson, Jean Noël. *Emile Nelligan*. Montréal: Fides, 1968. 103 pp.

2367. Stanic, Sharman Elsa. *French Canada Studies:The Dimensions of Emile Nelligan*. Univ. Park, Pa.: Penn. State, 1973. [MA thesis.]

2368. "Témoignages d'écrivains." *EF* 3(1967):301-07.

2369. Vachon, G.-André. "L'ère du silence et l'âge de la parole." *EF* 3(1967):309-21.

2370. Wyczynski, Paul. "L'influence de Verlaine sur Nelligan." *RHL* 69 (1969):776-94.

2371. ———. *"Nelligan et la musique."* Ottawa: Eds. de l'Univ. d'Ottawa, 1971. 145 pp.

2372. ———. "Nelligan et la musique." *RUO* 39(1969):513-32.

2373. Wyczynski, Paul, and P. Burger. "Bibliographie d'Emile Nelligan." *EF* 3(1967):285-98.

Nerval *See* 1233, 1527.

Nervo

2374. Monterde, Francisco. "Amado Nervo, en su centenario." *RIB* 21 (1971):3-15.

Nijhoff

2375. Calis, Piet. "Topkonferentie VI:M. Nijhoff en de plastiek van het gedicht." *Maatstaf* 10(1962):510-19.

2376. Spies, Lina. "Droom en Dagbreek:'n Interpretasie van Nijhoff se sonnettesiklus *Voor Dag en Dauw* binne historiese verbanden ruimer literere konteks (vervolg)." *Standpunte* 97(1971):34-46.

2377. Spillebeen, Willy. "De sluitsteen van Nijhoffs evolutie." *Raam* 85 (1972):21-36.

2378. Wenseleers, Lucas. *Het wonderbaarlijk lichaam:Martinus Nijhoff en de moderne Westerse poëzie*. s'Gravenhage: Bakker-Daamen, 1966. 288 pp.

Nordau

2379. A., J. "Max Nordau's *Degeneration*." *SR* 3(1895):503-12. [Rev. art.]

2380. Anon. "Imbeciles All." *Nation* 60(25 Apr 1895):327-28. [Rev. art.]

2381. Anon. "A Teuton Come to Judgement." *Saturday Review* 74(9 Mar 1895):323-24. [Rev. art.]

2382. Flower, B.O. "Max Nordau's *Degeneration*." *Arena* 15(Dec 1895): 147-52. [Rev. art.]

2383. Hale, Edward E. "The Dusk of Nations." *Dial* 18(16 Apr 1895): 236-39.

2384. Hogarth, Janet E. "Literary Degenerates." *Fortnightly Review* 63(Apr 1895):586-92.

2385. Lombroso, Cesare. "Nordau's *Degeneration*:Its Values and Its Er-

rors." *Century Magazine* 50(Oct 1895):936-40. [Condensed in *Review of Reviews* 12(Oct 1895): 479-80.]

2386. Nicoletti, G. "Max Nordau e i primi critici del Symbolismo in Italia." *SFr* 3(1939):433-38.

2387. Nordau, Max. *Degeneration*. Tr. from 2nd German ed. London and New York: Appleton, 1912. 566 pp.

2388. Saintsbury, George. "Degeneration." *Bookman* 1(Apr 1895): 178-80.

2389. Stutfield, Hugh E. "Tommyrotics." *Blackwood's Magazine* 157 (June 1895):833-45.

See also 3047.

Norwid

2390. Domaradzki, Théodore F. "Un message symboliste oublié:A l'occasion du centenaire de la parution du poème 'De la liberté de la parole' de C. Norwid." *ES1* 14(1969):49-82. [With appendix containing trs. of six of N's poems, bibliog., notes.]

2391. Fauchereau, Serge. "Zutiste et mendiant." *Quinzaine littéraire* 120(30 juin 1971):10. [Rev. art.]

Nouveau

2392. Forestier, Louis. *Germain Nouveau*. Paris: Seghers, 1971. 169 pp.

2393. ———. "Germain Nouveau et le mouvement décadent." *ECr* 9(1969): 3-8.

2394. ———. "Germain Nouveau: L'image de la mère." *NL* (31 déc 1970):7.

See also 651.

Novalis

2395. Braak, S. "Novalis et le symbolisme français." *Neophil* 7(1922): 243-58.

2396. Vordtriede, Werner. *Novalis und die französischen Symbolisten:zur Entstehungsgeschichte des dichterischen Symbols*. Stuttgart: Kohlhammer, 1963. 196 pp.

Obstfelder

2397. Bjørnsen, Johan F. *Sigbjørn Obstfelder:Mennesket, poeten og grubleren*. Oslo: Gyldendal, 1959. 288 pp.

2398. Hannevik, Arne. *Obstfelder og Mystikken:En Studie:Sigbjørn Obstfelders Forfatterskap*. Oslo: Gyldendal, 1960. 302 pp.

2399. McFarlane, James W. "Sigbjørn Obstfelder," 104-13 in *Ibsen and the Temper of Norwegian Literature*. London: Oxford U.P., 1960.

2400. Rian, Eivind. "Om Sigbjørn Obstfelders *Heimskringla. Edda* 55 (1968):339-42.

2401. Schoolfield, C.C. "Sigbjørn Obstfelder:A Study in Idealism." *Edda* 57 (1975):163.

See also 2554, 2560.

Onofri

2402. Ragusa, Olga. "*La Voce*, Mallarmé e *Tendenze* di Onofri." *EPo* 9-11(1957):54-60.

Osbert

2403. Degron, Henri. "Alphonse Osbert." *La Plume* 165(mars 1896): 138-45.

Ostaijen *See* 1496.

Pardo Bazán

2404. Kronik, J.W. "Emilia Pardo Bazán and the Phenomenon of French

Decadentism." *PMLA* 81(1966):418-27.

Parini

2405. Petrini, Domenico. "La poesia e l'arte di Giuseppe Parini," 28-245 in *Dal Barocco al Decadentismo*. Studi de Letteratura. Raccolti da Vittorio Santoli. Vol. I. Firenze: Le Monnier, 1957.

Pascoli

2406. De Castris, A. Leone. "Il decadentismo pascoliano e la poetica del reale." *EPo* 9-11(1957):38-53.

2407. Fabio, Franco. *Giovanni Pascoli*. Vol. 2. Napoli: Libreria scientifica ed., 1972. 180 pp.

2408. Giannangeli, Ottaviano. "Le fonti spagnuole del Pascoli." *Dimensioni* 15,iii-iv(1971):17-77.

2409. ———. *Svolgimento della poetica e della poesia pascoliana*. Pescara: Quaderni di Dimensioni, 1972. 169 pp.

2410. Passaglia, Mario. "Figure metriche pascoliane:Inovenari di Castelvecchio." *LeS* 7(1972):47-80.

2411. Petrucciani, Mario, Marta Bruscia, and Gianfranco Mauriani,eds. *Materiali critici per Giovanni Pascoli*. Roma: Edizioni dell'Ateneo, 1971. 266 pp.

See also 1481.

Pasternak

2412. Jackson, Robert L. "The Symbol of the Wild Duck in *Dr. Zhivago*." *CL* 15(1963):39-45.

2413. Plank, Dale Lewin. "The Composition of Pasternak's Lyric, 1912-1932:A Study of Sound and Imagery." *DA* 24(1963):303(U. of Wash.).

2414. Vickery, Walter. "Symbolism

Aside:*Doktor Živago*." *SEEJ* 17 (1959):343-48.

2415. Wilson, Edmund. "Legend and Symbol in *Doctor Zhivago*." *Encounter* 12,vi(1959):5-16. [Also in *Nation* 188(1959):363-73.]

2416. ——. "Leggenda e simbolo nel *Dottor Zivago*." *TPr* 5(1960): 129-42.

Pater

2417. Hidden, Norman. "Walter Pater: Aesthetic Standards or Impressionism?" *UES* 2(1968):13-18.

2418. L'Homme, Charles E. "The Influence of Walter Pater:A Study on the Making of the Modern Literary Mind." *DA* 29(1969):2715A (Columbia).

2419. Monsman, Gerald. "Pater's Aesthetic Hero." *UTQ* 40(1971):136-51.

2420. Schuetz, Lawrence F. "Pater's *Marius*:The Temple of God and the Palace of Art." *ELT* 15(1972):1-19.

2421. Shmiefsky, Marvel. "A Study in Aesthetic Relativism:Pater's Poetics." *VP* 6(1968):105-24.

2422. Stavros, George. "Pater, Wilde and the Victorian Critics of the Romantics." *DAI* 33(1972):2344A (Wis., Madison).

See also 289, 1587, 1818, 2775.

Péladan

2423. Anon. "Les Rose + Croix:Col por Connaissance." *Arts* 210(Aug 1969):30.

2424. Jollivet de Castelot, F. "Livres: *L'occulte catholique*." *La Plume* 241(mai 1899):312.

2425. Lazare, Bernard. "Les livres: *Typhonia* par Joséphin Péladan." *Entretiens politiques et littéraires* 34 (janv 1893):41-44. [Rev. art.]

2426. Lethève, J. "Le Sar Péladan et les salons de la Rose+Croix." *Jardin des arts* (juin 1965):49-57.

See also 549, 799, 1097.

Perse

2427. Abel, Richard O. "The Relationship Between the Poetry of T. S. Eliot and Saint-John Perse." *DAI* 31 (1971):6041A(So. Calif.).

2428. Holban, Adela. "Rolul simbolului în poezia lui Saint-Jean Perse." *AŞUI* 15(1969):47-55. [Sum. in Fr.]

2429. Little, Roger. "Language as Imagery in Saint-John Perse." *FMLS* 6(1970):127-39.

2430. Soos, Emese M. "The *Anabase* of Saint-John Perse." *DAI* 32(1972): 5808A(Wis.).

2431. Sutherland, Donald. "Le haut et le pur." *Parnassus* 1,i(1972):47-56. [Rev. art.]

2432. Yoyo, Emile. *Saint-John Perse et le conteur*. Paris: Bordas, 1972. 112 pp.

See also 650, 1421, 1577, 1599.

Pessanha

2433. Lemos, Esther de. *A Clepsidra de Camilo Pessanha:Notas e reflexões*. Porto: Livraria Tavares Martins, 1956. 188 pp.

2434. Martins, António C. "Subsidios para o estudo da poética simbolista: O decassilabo de Camilo Pessanha," in Vol. I, *Coloquio internacional de estudos luso-brasileiros.* Lisboa, 1959.

2435. Miguel, Antonio Dias. *Camilo Pessanha—Elementos para o estudo da sua biografia e da sua obra*. Lisboa: Ocidente, 1956. 197 pp.

Pessoa

2436. Carvalho, Joaquim de Montezuma

de. " 'Tabacaria', um poema de Fernando Pessoa e as corrientes filosóficas do secolo XX." *Ocidente* 82(1972):129-38.

2437. Frias, Eduardo. *O nacionalismo místico de Fernando Pessoa.* Braga: Editora Pax, 1971. 102 pp.

2438. Lind, Georg R. "Fernando Pessoa perante a Primera Guerra mundial." *Ocidente* 82(1972):11-23. [Foll. by unpub. poems by P in Eng. tr., 24-30.]

2439. Nunes, Benedito. "Os outros de Fernando Pessoa." *BEPIF* 31(1970): 335-58.

See also 1171, 2161.

Philippide

2440. Cioculescu, Șerban. "Poetul Al. Philippide—Teoretician literar." *RoLit* 22 June(1972):7.

2441. Ivanescu, Cezar. "Poezia lui Al. Philippide." *Luc* 26 Aug(1972):3.

2442. Muntean, George. "Al. Philippide, poet și eseist." *RITL* 21(1972): 651-63.

Pica

2443. Ragusa, Olga. "Vittorio Pica, First Champion of French Symbolism in Italy." *Italica* 35(1958): 255-61.

Picasso

2444. Blunt, Anthony, and Phoebe Pool. *Picasso, the Formative Years.* Greenwich, Conn.: New York Graphic Society, 1962. 32 pp.

2445. Daix, Pierre, and George Boudaille. *Picasso, 1900-1906.* Neuchâtel: Eds. Ides et Calendes, 1966. 348 pp. [Tr. Phoebe Pool. Greenwich, Conn: N.Y. Graphic Soc., 1967.]

Poe

2446. Alexander, Jean. *Affidavits of Genius:French Essays on Poe from Forgues to Valéry.* Port Washington, N.Y.: Kennikat, 1971. 246 pp.

2447. ——. "Poe's *For Annie* and Mallarmé's *Nuit d'Idumée.*" *MLN* 77 (1962):534-36.

2448. Antcliffe, H. "Edgar Allen Poe and Music." *Chesterian* 25(1951): 60-64.

2449. Bandy, William T. *The Influence and Reputation of Edgar Allan Poe in Europe.* Baltimore: Edgar Allan Poe Society, 1962. 15 pp.

2450. Baudelaire, Charles P., *Edgar Allen Poe:Sa vie et ses ouvrages.* Bandy, William T., ed. Toronto, Buffalo: U. of Toronto P., 1973. 128 pp.

2451. Brie, Hartmut. "Die Theorie des poetischen Effekts bei Poe und Mallarmé." *NS* 21(1972):473-81.

2452. Cambiaire, C.P. "The Influence of Edgar Allan Poe in France." *RR* 17 (1926):319-37.

2452a. Carlson, Eric W., ed. *The Recognition of Edgar Allen Poe: Selected Criticism Since 1829.* Ann Arbor: U. of Mich. Press, 1966. 316 pp. [Repr. essays and arts. by var. hands, incl. Mallarmé, Baudelaire and W.B. Yeats *inter alios.*]

2453. Dieckmann, Liselotte. "E.T.A. Hoffmann und E.A. Poe:Verwandte Sensibilität bei verschiedenem Sprach- und Gesellschaftsraum," 273-80 in Victor Lange and Hans-Gert Roloff,eds. *Dichtung, Sprache, Gesellschaft:Akten des IV. Internationalen Germanisten-Kongresses 1970 in Princeton.* Frankfurt: Athenäum, 1971. 635 pp.

2454. Eliot, T.S. "From Poe to Valéry." *HudR* 2(1949):327-42.

2455. Evans, May G. *Music and Edgar Allan Poe:A Bibliographical Study.*

Baltimore: Johns Hopkins Press, 1939. 97 pp.

2456. Françon, M. "Poe et Baudelaire." *PMLA* 60(1945):741-59.

2457. Gogol, John M. "Two Russian Symbolists on Poe." *PN* 3(1970): 36-37.

2458. Jones, P. Mansell. "Poe and Baudelaire:The Affinity." *MLR* 40(1945): 279-83.

2459. ———. "Poe, Baudelaire and Mallarmé." *Lettres*(spec. issue 1948):69-78.

2460. ———. "Poe, Baudelaire and Mallarmé:A Problem of Literary Judgment." *MLR* 39(1944):236-46.

2461. Julien-Caim, L. "Edgar Poe et Valéry." *MdF* 304(mai 1950):81-94.

2462. Karátson, André. *Edgar Allan Poe et le groupe des écrivains du "Nyugat" en Hongrie.* (Fac. des Lettres et Sciences Humaines de l'Univ. de Clermont-Ferrand, Deuxième Sér., Fasc. 30.) Paris: Presses univs., 1971. 190 pp.

2463. Lemonnier, Léon. "L'influence d'Edgar Poe sur les conteurs français symbolistes et décadents." *RLC* 13 (1933):102-33.

2464. ———. "L'influence d'Edgar Poe sur Villiers de l'Isle-Adam." *MdF* (sept 15 1933):605-19.

2465. Marks, Emerson R. "Poe as Literary Theorist:A Reappraisal." *AL* 33 (1961):296-306.

2466. Oelke, Karl E. "The Rude Daughter:Alchemy in Poe's Early Poetry." *DAI* 33(1972):2388A(Columbia).

2467. Parks, Edd W. *Edgar Allan Poe as Literary Critic.* Athens: U. of Ga. P., 1964. 114 pp.

2468. Patterson, A.S. *L'influence d'Edgar Poe sur Charles Baudelaire.* Grenoble: U. of Grenoble, 1903. [Diss.]

2469. Rhodes, S.A. "The Influence of Poe on Baudelaire." *RR* 18(1927): 329-33.

2470. Samuel, Dorothy J. "Poe and Baudelaire:Parallels in Form and Symbol." *CLAJ* 3(1959):88-105.

2471. Schinzel, E. *Natur und Natursymbolik bei Poe, Baudelaire und den französischen Symbolisten.* Düren: n.p., 1931.

2472, Seylaz, Louis. *Edgar Poe et les premiers symbolistes français.* Lausanne: Imprimerie La Concorde, 1923. 183 pp.

2473. Staats, Armin. *Edgar Allan Poes symbolistische Erzählkunst.* (Beihefte zum Jahrbuch für Am Amerikastudien, 20.) Heidelberg: Carl Winter, 1967. 180 pp.

2474. Swigget, Glen L. "Poe and Recent Poetics." *SR* 6(1898):150-66.

2475. Timmerman, John. "Edgar Allan Poe:Artist, Aesthetician, Legend." *SDR* 10,i(1972):60-70.

2476. Veler, Richard P.,ed. *Papers on Poe:Essays in Honor of John Ward Ostrom.* Springfield, Ohio: Chantry Music Press at Wittenberg U., 1972. 236 pp.

2477. Wyld, Lionel D. "The Enigma of Poe:Reality vs. *L'Art Pour L'Art.*" *LHB* 2(1960):34-38.

See also 61, 261, 1045, 1119, 1219, 1220, 1286, 1316, 1540, 1644, 1645, 1646, 1682, 1804, 1852, 1925, 2136, 2161, 2289, 2796, 2823, 2843, 2960, 3023.

Pound

2478. Schneidau, Herbert N. *Ezra Pound:The Image and the Real.* Baton Rouge: La. State U. P., 1969. 210 pp.

2479. ———. "Pound and Yeats:The Question of Symbolism." *ELH* 32 (1965):220-37.

2480. Sechi, Giovanni. "*Decadenza* e *Avanguardia* in Ezra Pound." *NC* 5-6 (1956):184-96.

See also 458, 2335.

Praga

2481. Bouffard, Jean-Claude. "Un disciple de Baudelaire, Emile Praga." *RLC* 45(1971):159-79.

Prati

2482. Vogliolo, Giulano. *Decadenza e tramonto di Giovanni Prati*. Trento: Società de studi trentini de scienze storiche, 1971. 95 pp.

Proust

2483. Cohn, Robert G. "Proust and Mallarmé." *FS* 3(July 1970):262.

2484. Lerner, Michael G. "Edouard Rod et Marcel Proust." *FS* 25(1971): 162-68.

2485. Schneider, Marcel. "Proust et la musique:Fervent défenseur de Pelléas." *NL* (11 juin 1971):9. [Spec. issue on Proust.]

Puvis de Chavannes

2486. "Album des poètes." *La Plume* 138(janv 1895):54-61. [Poems in honor of P.]

2487. "Le Banquet." *La Plume* 138 (janv 1895):46:54. [Collection of speeches on P's works by others.]

2488. Cordey. "La grande peinture." *La Plume* 235(fév 1899):89-91.

2489. Durand-Tahier, H. "Puvis de Chavannes." *La Plume* 138(janv 1895): 27-37.

2490. Duvachel, Léon. "Ave, Picardia nutrix!" *La Plume* 138(janv 1895): 38-40.

2491. Germain, Alphonse. "Anecdotes sur Puvis de Chavannes." *La Plume* 138(janv 1895):41-45.

2492. Jean, René. *Puvis de Chavannes*. Paris: Librairie Félix Alcan, 1914. 167 pp.

2493. Marthold, Jules de. "Sainte-Geneviève." *La Plume* 138(janv 1895):37-38.

2494. Régnier, Henri de. "Puvis de Chavannes." *Entretiens politiques et littéraires* 3(juin 1890):87-89.

2495. Riotor, Léon. "Le 'Pauvre Pêcheur'." *La Plume* 138(janv 1895): 40-41.

2496. Saunier, Charles. "Le paysage dans l'oeuvre de Puvis de Chavannes." *La Plume* 138(janv 1895): 45-46.

2497. Vachon, Marius. *Puvis de Chavannes*. Paris, 1895. 170 pp.

See also 730, 757, 822.

Quasimodo *See* 616.

Rakič

2498. Kočsutič, Vl.R. "Les Parnassiens et les Symbolistes chez les Serbes:Les influences sur Milan Rakić." *FP* 3-4 (1964):143-84.

Rambosson

2499. Merrill, Stuart. "Yvanhoë Rambosson." *La Plume* 167(avril 1896): 208-10.

Raynaud

2500. Bourguignon, Jean. "A propos de 'La tour d'ivoire'." *La Plume* 256(déc 1899):783-84.

2501. " 'La tour d'ivoire' et la critique." *La Plume* 253 (nov 1899):781-19.

Ravel

2502. Lichtenthaler, Friederike. "Bertrand und Ravel:Eine Studie zum Gaspard de la nuit." *Oesterreichische Musikzeitschrift* 32,vi(1967):325-34.

See also 2131.

Redon

2503. Ashton, Dore, Harold Joachim, and John Rewald. *Odilon Redon Gustave Moreau, Radolphe Bresail.* New York: Museum of Modern Art, 1962.

2504. Bacou, Roseline. *Odilon Redon.* Vol. I:*La vie et l'oeuvre. Point de vue de la critique au sujet de l'oeuvre.* Vol. II:*Documents divers. Illustrations.* Genève: Pierre Cailler, 1956. 290 + 59 pp. + 107 illus.

2505. Berger, Klaus. *Odilon Redon:Fantasy and Colour.* Tr. Michael Bullock. New York, Toronto, London: Mc Graw Hill, 1968. 244 pp.

2506. Bersier, J. E. "Odilon Redon et nous." *Etudes d'Art* 13(1957-58): 47-54.

2507. Coquiot, Gustave. "Exposition Odilon Redon." *La Plume* 271(août 1900):480.

2508. Eigeldinger, Alfred. "L'imagination mythique d'Odilon Redon." *L'Art* 66(1958):21-28.

2509. Leclère, Tristan. "Notes d'art." *La Plume* 237(mai 1903):544-45.

2510. *Lettres d'Odilon Redon 1878-1916.* Publiées par sa famille avec une préface de Marius et Ary Leblond. Paris, Bruxelles: G. Van Oest, 1923. 142 pp.

2511. Mellerio, André. *Odilon Redon: Peintre, dessinateur et graveur.* Paris: Henri Floury, 1923. 215 pp.

2512. Mullay, Terence. "Odilon Redon and the Symbolists." *Apollo* 66 (1957):181-85.

2513. Redon, Odilon. *A soi-même.* Paris: H. Fleury, 1922. 178 pp.

2514. Roger-Marx, Claude. "Le conscient et l'inconscient chez Odilon Redon." *RdP* 64(jan 1957):97-101.

2515. ———. "Odilon Redon, peintre et mystique." *Oeil* 17(1956):21-27.

2516. Sandstrom, Sven. *Le monde imaginaire d'Odilon Redon.* New York:

G. Wittenborn, 1955; Lund: Gleerup, 1955.

2517. Werner, A. "Dream World of Odilon Redon." *American Artist* 34 (Nov 1970):40-42.

See also 732, 753a, 798, 802, 834.

Régnier

2518. Anon. "Régnier on Young Poets." *Commercial Advertiser* 21 Mar(1900).

2519. Arnauld, Michel. "Henri de Régnier: *Les amants singuliers (Mercure de France)*." *Revue Blanche* 26 (1901):477-78. [Rev. art.]

2520. Boisson, Madeleine. "Apollinaire et 'La galère' d'Henri de Régnier." *RLM* 276-79(1971):99-104.

2521. Delior, Paul. "Les romans." *La Plume* 371(mai 1905):443-47.

2522. Dérieux, N. "L'oeuvre romanesque de M. Henri de Régnier." *MdF* 110(1914):433-67.

2523. Golberg, Mécislas. "Deux poètes: Henri de Régnier et Jean Moréas." *La Plume* 356(fév 1904):161-85.

2524. Jarry, Alfred. "Le Périple." *La Plume* 335(avril 1903):423-24.

2525. Jean-Aubry, G. "Henri de Régnier." *MdF* 89(1911):719-32.

2526. Léautaud, P. "H. de Régnier." *MdF* 49(1904):577-613.

2527. Leblond, M-A. "Henri de Régnier et la critique 'décorative'." *MdF* 41 (1902):577-96.

2528. Morand, Paul. "Longues moustaches à Venise." *NL* (11 mars 1971):7.

2529. "Poèmes anciens et romanesques, par H. de Régnier." *L'Ermitage* 1 (1890):303-09.

2530. Retté, Adolphe. "M. Henri de Régnier:Aréthuse." *La Plume* 143 (avril 1895):152-53.

2531. Saint-Jacques, Louis de. "Expertises:Les 'Jeux rustiques et divins' de

M. Henri de Régnier." *La Plume* 192 (avril 1897):247-51.

2532. ——. "M. Henri de Régnier." *La Plume* 201(sept 1897):553-56.

2533. Van Dijk, T.A. "Het symbol en de semantische dieptestruktuur:Een Fragmentarische interpretate van Henri de Régnier, 'Le vase'." *LT* 273 (1970):753-66.

2534. Viguié, P. "Sur Henri de Régnier." *MdF* 172(1924):608-20.

See also 1039, 1097.

Renoir

2535. Hanson, Lawrence. *Renoir:The Man, the Painter, and His World*. New York: Dodd, Mead & Co., 1968. 332 pp.

2536. Natanson, Thadée. "De M. Renoir et de la Beauté." *Revue Blanche* 21 (1900):370-77.

2537. Perruchot, Henri. *La vie de Renoir*. Paris: Hachette, 1964. 377 pp.

Retté

2538. Degron, Henri. "Paysageries littéraires:Adolphe Retté." *La Plume* 352(déc 1903):651-60.

2539. Saint-Jacques, Louis de. "Adolphe Rette:A propos de la forêt bruissante et des critiques que l'on en fit." *La Plume* 173(juillet 1896):515-18. 515-18.

2540. ——. "Expertises:'Campagne première' de M. Adolphe Retté." *La Plume* 195(juin 1897):349-53.

2541. ——. "Expertises:Les 'Aspects' de M. Adolphe Retté." *La Plume* 191(avril 1897):212-16.

See also 585, 1031.

Ricardo

2542. Coelho, Nelly Novaes. "Cassiano Ricardo e 'Os sobreviventes'." *MGSL* 8 Jan(1972):8-9.

Rilke

2543. Allemann, Beda. 'Rilke und Mallarmé:Entwicklung einer Grundfrage der symbolistischen Poetik," 63-82 in Käte Hamburger,ed. *Rilke in neuer Sicht*. Stuttgart: Kohlhammer, 1971.

2544. Batterby, Kenneth A. *Rilke and France:A Study in Poetic Development*. London: Oxford U.P., 1966. 198 pp.

2545. Bémol, Maurice. "Rilke et les influences à propos d'un livre récent." *RLC* 27(1953):169-81.

2546. Bollnow, Otto F. *Rilke, poeta del hombre*. Madrid: Taurus Ediciones, S.A., 1963. 536 pp.

2547. Breen, Gerald M. "Mythology in Selected Poems of Rainer Maria Rilke (1875-1926)." *Unitas* 41 (1968):482-535.

2548. Brewster, Robert R. "Visual Expression of Musical Sound in Rilke's Lyric Poetry." *Monatshefte* 43 (1951):395-404.

2549. Bucher, Jean Marie F. "A Critical Appreciation of Valéry's Influence on Rilke." *DA* 28(1967):1389A (Brown).

2550. Buddeberg, E. "Spiegel-Symbolik und Person-Problem bei Rainer Maria Rilke." *DVLG* 24(1950):360-86.

2551. Cassou, Jean, and Edmond Jaloux. "Dialogue sur Rainer-Maria Rilke." *Revue de Genève* 21 (1930):21-26. [Interview.]

2552. Champagne, Marieluise K. "Rilke und der Jugendstil:Zur Entwicklung des gedanklichen und sensitiven Bezugssystem in der Stilkunst Rainer Maria Rilkes." *DAI* 33(1972): 1162A(Tulane).

2553. Dédéyan, Charles. *Rilke et la France*. 4 vols. Paris: Sedes, 1961.

2554. Ekner, Reidar. "Rilke, Obstfelder

och *Malte Laurids Brigge*." *Edda* 53 (1966):204-321.

2555. Goth, Maja. "The Myth of Narcissus in the Works of Rilke and Valéry." *ConL* 7(1966):12-20.

2556. Grossmann, Dietrich. *R.M. Rilke und der französische Symbolismus*. Jena: U. of Jena, 1938. [Diss.]

2557. Hell, Victor. *Rainer Maria Rilke: Existence humaine et poésie orphique*. Paris: Plon, 1965. 191 pp.

2558. Hermann, Rosemarie. *R.M. Rilke und der französische Geist*. Tübingen: U. of Tübingen, 1947. [Diss.]

2559. Hoeniger, F.D. "Symbolist Pattern in Rilke's 'Duino Elegies'." *GL&L* 3(1949-50):271-83.

2560. Kohlschmidt, Werner. "Rilke und Obstfelder," 458-77 in *Die Wissenschaft von deutscher Sprache und Dichtung:Methoden, Probleme, Aufgaben:Festschrift für Friedrich Maurer zum 65. Geburtstag am 5. Januar 1963*. Stuttgart: Klett, 1963.

2561. Kroger, E.P. "Rilke und die Französ. Lit." *Neue Schweizer* 22(1929):73-79.

2562. Kunz, Marcel. *Narziss:Untersuchungen zum Werk Rainer Maria Rilkes*. Bonn: Bouvier, 1970. 146 pp.

2563. Kyritz, Heinz-Georg. *Rilkes Auffassung von der Kunst und dem Künstler vor Duino (1896-1912)*. Montreal: McGill U., 1961. [Diss.]

2564. Lang, Renée. "Ein fruchtbringendes Missverständnis:Rilke und Valéry." *Symposium* 13(1959):51-62.

2565. ———. "Rilke and His French Contemporaries." *CL* 10(1958):136-43.

2566. ———. *Rilke, Gide et Valéry*. Boulogne-sur-Seine: Edition de la Revue Prétexte, 1953. 78 pp.

2567. Mágr, Clara. *Rainer Maria Rilke und die Musik*. Wien: Awandus, 1960. 228 pp.

2568. Mason, Eudo C. *Lebenshaltung*

und *Symbolik bei Rainer Maria Rilke*. (Literatur und Leben, Bd. 3.) Weimar: n.p., 1939.

2569. Müller, Franz W. "Rilke und die französische Dichtung." *Prisma* 1(1946-48):22-26.

2570. Neumann, Alfred R. "Rilke and His Relation to Music." *SGB* 20,iv (1960):25-28.

2571. Nolte, Fritz. *Der Todesbegriff bei R.M. Rilke, H. von Hofmannsthal und Thomas Mann*. Heidelberg: U. of Heidelberg, 1934. [Diss.]

2572. Peters, H.F. "The Space Metaphors in Rilke's Poetry." *GR* 24 (1949):124-35.

2573. Petzsch, Christoph. "Musik:Verführung und Gesetz (aus Briefen und Dichtungen Rilkes)." *GRM* 10(1960):65-85.

2574. Rapin, René. "Rilke, Jacobsen et Rodin." *Revue de Genève* 11(1925): 1734-43.

2575. Rickman, H.P. "Poetry and the Ephemeral:Rilke's and Eliot's Conceptions of the Poet's Task." *GL&L* 12(1959):174-85.

2576. Rolleston, James. *Rilke in Transition:An Exploration of His Earliest Poetry*. (YGS 4.) New Haven: Yale U.P., 1970. 246 pp.

2577. Rosa, António Ramos. "Rilke e 'o espaço interior do mundo'." *Colóquio* 10(1972):25-31.

2578. Saalmann, Dieter. "Die symbolistische Grundlage von Rainer Maria Rilkes *Die Aufzeichnungen des Malte Laurids Brigge* unter besonderer Berücksichtigung der äusseren Form des Werkes." *DAI* 31(1971): 3562A(Wash. U.).

2579. Shaw, Priscilla W. *Rilke, Valéry and Yeats:The Domain of the Self*. New Brunswick, N.J.: Rutgers U.P., 1964. 278 pp.

2580. Sheets, J.M. "Symbols and Salvation:Rilke and Machado in Spain." *CL* 23(1971):346-58.

2581. Sojcher, Jacques. "Une pensée

dépossédante." *CIS* 15-16(1967-68): 71-91.

2582. Stahl, August. *'Vokabeln der Not' und Früchte der Tröstung':Studien zur Bildlichkeit im Werke Rainer Maria Rilkes.* (AUS 8.) Heidelberg: Winter, 1967. 164 pp.

2583. Strauss, Walter A. "The Reconciliation of Opposites in Orphic Poetry:Rilke and Mallarmé." *CentR* 10(1966):214-36.

2584. Thorlby, Anthony. "Rilke and the Ideal World of Poetry." *YFS* 9(1952):132-42.

2585. Wais, Karin. *Studien zu Rilkes Valéry-Übertragungen.* Tübingen: Niemeyer, 1967. 164 pp.

2586. Webb, Karl E. "Rainer Maria Rilke and the Art of Jugendstil." *CentR* 16(1972):122-37.

2587. Weigand, Elsie. "Rilke and Eliot: The Articulation of the Mystic Experience." *GR* 30(1955):198-210.

See also 261, 1317, 1360, 1708, 1724, 1805, 2378, 2824, 2834, 2856.

Rimbaud

2588. Ahearn, Edward J. " 'Entends comme brame' and the Theme of Death in Nature in Rimbaud's Poetry." *FR* 43(1970):407-17.

2589. Ardennais, Pierre l'. "Le poète Arthur Rimbaud." *La Plume* 26(mai 1890):90.

2590. Arnoult, P. *Rimbaud.* Paris: Albin Michel, 1943.

2591. Ascione, Marc, and Jean-Pierre Chambon. "Les 'zolismes' de Rimbaud." *Europe* 529-30(1973):114-32.

2592. Bachelard, Gaston. "Rimbaud enfant," 150-56 in *Le droit de rêver.* Paris: Presses Univs. de France, 1970.

2593. Baróti, Dezsö. "Rimbaud és a magjar költeszet." *PIMÉ* 9(1971-72):181-95. [Rimbaud and Hungarian poetry.]

2594. Baudry, Jean-Louis. "Le texte de Rimbaud (fin)." *TelQ* 36(1969):33-53.

2595. Beaunier, A. "Arthur Rimbaud." *RdP* (1 sept 1900):202-24.

2596. Béraud, H. "Sources d'inspiration du 'Bateau ivre'." *MdF* 153(1922):103-10.

2597. Bergen-Le-Play, Louis. *Villon revient et Rimbaud insolite.* Paris: La Belle Cordière, 1969. 65 pp.

2598. Bérimont, Luc. "Une enfance hypertrophiée." *Europe* 529-30(1973):42-47.

2600. Boulestreau, Nicole. "Préliminaires à la biographie." *Europe* 529-30(1973):151-70.

2601. Briet, Suzanne. "Centenaire des débuts littéraires d'Arthur Rimbaud." *La Grive* 147-148(1970):85.

2602. Bruller-Dauxois, Jacqueline. "Assassin d'un poète." *Europe* 529-30(1973):54-57.

2603. Chadwick, Charles. "The Dating of Rimbaud's Word List." *FS* 23(1969):35-37.

2604. Charolles, Michel. "Le texte poétique et sa signification:Une lecture du poème intitulé 'Mouvement' *(Illuminations)* et de quelques commentaires qui en ont été donnés." *Europe* 529-30(1973):97-114.

2605. Chauvel, Jean. *L'aventure terrestre de Jean-Arthur Rimbaud.* Paris: Seghers, 1971.

2606. Chisholm, A.R. "Two Exegetical Studies." *ECr* 9(1969):28-36.

2607. Clément, Marilène. "L'homme aux semelles de vent." *Europe* 529-30(1973):26-32.

2608. Coquet, Jean-Claude. "Combinaisons et transformation en poésie (Arthur Rimbaud:*Les Illuminations*)." *Homme* 9(1969):23-41.

2609. Coulon, Marcel. *Le problème de Rimbaud.* Paris: G. Crès, 1923. 309 pp.

2610. ——. *La vie de Rimbaud et de son oeuvre*. Paris: Mercure de France, 1929. 357 pp.

2611. Davies, Margaret. "Rimbaud and Melville." *RLC* 43(1969):479-88.

2612. Delouze, Marc. "Les 'beaux *r*' de Rimbaud (rêve, révolte, révolution)." *Europe* 529-30(1973):36-41.

2613. Dhôtel, André. "Autour du chapeau haut-de-forme d'Arthur Rimbaud." *Europe* 529-30(1973): 48-54.

2614. Dontchev, Nicolaï. "Rimbaud en Bulgarie." *Europe* 529-30(1973): 147-50.

2615. Etiemble, René. "Bibliographie analytique du mythe de Rimbaud en hongrois." *RLC* 43(1969):361-79.

2616. ——. *Le mythe de Rimbaud*. 2 vols. Paris: Gallimard, 1952.

2617. ——. "Le mythe de Rimbaud en Hongrie." *CLS* 6(1969):361-79.

2618. Fischer, Jan O., and Vladimír Stupka. "Rimbaud, poète de la vision poétique moderne." *PP* 6(1969):59-74.

2619. Follain, Jean. "L'immense détresse enflammée de Rimbaud." *Europe* 529-30(1973):3-4.

2620. Forestier, Louis. "Rimbaud en son temps." *Europe* 529-30(1973): 4-21.

2621. ——. *Rimbaud. Poésies*. Paris: Gallimard, 1973.

2622. Fowlie, Wallace. *Rimbaud's Illuminations:A Study in Angelism*. New York: Greenwood Press, 1969. 231 pp.

2623. Frohock, W.M. "Rimbaud's Poetics:Hallucination and Epiphany." *RR* 46(1955):192-202.

2624. Gabriel, Roger. "Rimbaud, ou la poursuite du rêve." *Revue Nationale* 42(1970):129-32.

2625. Gaubert, E. "Une explication nouvelle du sonnet de voyelles d'Arthur Rimbaud." *MdF* 52(1904): 551-53.

2626. Gaucheron, Jacques. "Rimbaud et Rimbaud." *Europe* 529-30(1973):21-25.

2627. Gaultier, J. de. "Le lyrisme physiologique et la double personnalité d'Arthur Rimbaud." *MdF* 170 (1924):289-308.

2628. Gengoux, Jacques. *Le symbolique de Rimbaud:Le système, ses sources*. Paris: La Colombe, 1947. 219 pp.

2629. Gilbert-Lecomte, Roger. *Arthur Rimbaud*. Montpellier: Fata Morgana, 1972. 64 pp.

2630. Graaf, Daniel A. de. "Arthur Rimbaud en de muziek." *Mens en Melodie* 7,viii(1952):252-57.

2631. Hackett, C.A. "Rimbaud and the 'splendides villes'." *ECr* 9(1969):46-53.

2632. Héraut, H. "Du nouveau sur Rimbaud." *NRF* (1 oct 1934):602-08.

2633. Houston, John P. "Rimbaud, Mysticism, and Verlaine's Poetry of 1873-74." *ECr* 9(1969):19-27.

2634. Hubert, Renée R. "The Use of Reversals in Rimbaud's *Illuminations*." *ECr* 9(1969):9-18.

2635. Jude, Stéfan. "Rimbaud et/ou Mallarmé." *NRF* 20(sept 1972):120-24.

2636. Juin, Hubert. "Lecture de Rimbaud." *Europe* 529-30(1973):61-68.

2637. Kahn, Gustave. "Arthur Rimbaud." *Revue Blanche* 16(1898): 592-601.

2638. Karátson, André. "Rimbaud en Hongrie." *Etudes Finno-Ougriennes* 4(1967):148-75.

2639. Kloepfer, Rolf, and Ursula Oomen. *Sprachliche Konstituenten moderner Dichtung. Entwurf einer deskriptiven Poetik. Rimbaud*. Bad Homburg v.d.H.: Athenaum Verlag, 1970. 231 pp.

2640. Lombreaud, R. "Arthur Rimbaud et l'un de ses commentateurs anglais:Arthur Symons." *RLC* 29 (1955):88-91.

2641. Lukács, Georg. "Allegoria e simbolo." *Belfagor* 24(1969):125-26.

2642. Mallarmé, Stéphane. "Arthur Rimbaud." *Chap Book* 5(15 May 1896):8-17.

2643. Manca, Marie A. "Harmony and the Poet:Six Studies in the Creative Ordering of Reality." *DAI* 32 (1972):26417A(Yale.). [W.H. Crane, Shakespeare, Rimbaud, Char, Dante.]

2644. Meschonnic, Henri. "Ni Rimbaud ni Mallarmé." *NRF* 20(sept 1972): 125-27.

2645. Miller, Henry. *Le temps des assassins.* Honfleur: Pierre Jean Oswald, 1970. 161 pp.

2646. Nielsen, Laus S. "L'anti-conte chez Rimbaud à travers quelques-unes de ses *Illuminations.*" *RevR* 4(1969):61-62.

2647. "Notes et notules." *Entretiens politiques et littéraires* 22(janv 1892):43-48. [About letters on R.]

2648. Orsi, Agusto. *Arthur Rimbaud, poète et aventurier.* Addis Ababa: Ist. Italiano di Cultura, 1972. 31 pp.

2649. Piscopo, Ugo. "Les futuristes et Rimbaud." *Europe* 529-30(1973): 133-46. [Tr. Bernadette Morand.]

2650. Reboul, Yves. "Rimbaud dans le théâtre de Claudel: I. *Tête d'Or.* II. *L'oeuvre chrétienne.*" *Littératures. Annales publiées par la Faculté des Lettres et Sciences de Toulouse* 16(1969):79-106; 17(1970):33-53.

2651. Rebourcet, Gabriel, and Alain Sancerny. "Le haleur, ou l'épreuve terminée (Essai sur les *Illuminations*)." *Europe* 529-30(1973):76-97.

2652. Retté, Adolphe. "Aspects:Un amateur." *La Plume* 166(mars 1896):189-91.

2653. Richer, Jean. "Gautier en filigrane dans quelques *Illuminations.*" *Europe* 529-30(1973):69-76.

2654. Rickword, Edgell. *Rimbaud, the Boy and the Poet.* Londres: Heinemann, 1924. 234 pp.

2655. Riva, Ubaldo. "La musica di Rimbaud." *La Scala* 62(1955): 60-64,120-22.

2656. Rivière, J. "Rimbaud." *NRF* (1 juillet 1914):3-48; (1 août 1914): 209-30.

2657. Ruchon, François. *Jean-Arthur Rimbaud, sa vie, son oeuvre, son influence.* Paris: Champion, 1929. [Repr. Genève: Slatkine, 1970. 365 pp.]

2658. Soissons, S.C. de. "Jean Arthur Rimbaud." *ContempR* 81(1902): 867-76.

2659. Soupault, Philippe. "Sur les traces de Rimbaud." *Europe* 529-30 (1973):33-36.

2660. Starkie, Enid. *Arthur Rimbaud.* New York: New Directions, 1961. 491 pp.

2661. "Sur Rimbaud." *Entretiens politiques et littéraires* 20(déc 1891): 185-88.

2662. Symons, Arthur. "Arthur Rimbaud." *Saturday Review* 85(28 May 1898):706-07. [Repr. in his *Symbolist Movement in Literature.*]

2663. Ullmann, Fabrice. "L'environment pictural de Rimbaud." *Europe* 529-30(1973):57-60.

2664. Verlaine, Paul. "Arthur Rimbaud." *Senate* 2(Oct 1895):373-76.

2665. ———. "Nouvelles notes sur Rimbaud." *La Plume* 158(nov 1895): 503-04.

2666. Whibley, Charles. "A Vagabond Poet." *Blackwood's Magazine* 165 (1899):402-12.

See also 107, 127, 436, 549, 650, 651, 799, 1107, 1226, 1233, 1276, 1323, 1425, 1459, 1632, 1999, 2154, 2224, 2268, 2771, 2793, 2925, 2926, 3033, 3100.

Rivière

2667. Cook, Bradford. "Jacques Rivière

and Symbolism." *YFS* 9(1952):103-11.

2668. Raymond, Marcel. *Etudes sur Jacques Rivière*. Paris: Corti, 1972. 215 pp.

Rod

2669. Lerner, Michael G. "Edouard Rod and the *Naturistes.*" *NFS* 10(1971): 67-73.

2670. ———. "Edouard Rod et l'Angelterre." *RLMC* 24(1971):127-32.

2671. ———. "Edouard Rod's Last Novel:*La vie.*" *NFS* 9(1971):71-80.

2672. ———. "The Unpublished Manuscripts of Edouard Rod's *La course à la mort* and His Departure from Zola's Naturalism." *SFr* 15(1971): 68-77.

Rodenbach

2673. *L'amitié de Stéphane Mallarmé et de Georges Rodenbach*. Préf. de Henri Mondor. Lettres et textes inédits, 1887-1898, publiés avec une introd. et des notes par François Ruchon. Genève: Cailler, 1949. 169 pp.

2674. Bodson-Thomas, Anny. *L'esthétique de Georges Rodenbach*. Liège: H. Vaillant-Carmanne, 1942. 208 pp.

2675. González Martínez, Enrique. "Interpretacíon del gran poeta belga Jorge Rodenbach." *Nivel* 101 (1971):1-2. [Repr. of lect. pub. 1918 by Editorial Cultura.]

2676. Kies, A. "Baudelaire et Georges Rodenbach." *LR* 4(1950):217-36.

2677. Lo Curzio, Guglielmo. "Un parnassiano dei simbolisti," in *Rimbaud e altri pellegrinaggi*. Palermo: A. Palumbo, 1950.

2678. Muival, José. *Le poète du silence:Georges Rodenbach*. Bruxelles: Conférences et Théâtres, 1940.

2679. Segard, Achille. "Georges Rodenbach." *La Plume* 168(avril 1896): 238-39.

Rodó

2680. Esquenazi-Mayo, Roberto. "Revaloración de Rodó," 263-69 in *Actas del Primer Congreso Internacional de Hispanistas*. Frank Pierce, and Cyril A. Jones,eds. Celebrado en Oxford del 6 al 11 de septiembre de 1962. Oxford: Dolphin Book Co. Ltd. for the Internat. Assn. of Hispanists, 1964. 494 pp.

2681. Magariños Demello, Mateo J. "José Enrique Rodó. Hänen sanomansa merkitys ja pysyvyys." *Aika* 3(1972):26-34.

2682. Rey, José. "Homenaje de Colombia a José Enrique Rodó (El mensaje de Ariel)." *Nivel* 113(1972):5,8-10.

Rojas, Ricardo

2683. Kolb, Glen L. "Simbolismo y universalidad en el *Ollantay* de Rojas." *Hispania* 46(1963):328-32.

Rops

2684. Alexandre, Arsène. "Rops: Rustique, satirique, luxurieux." *La Plume* 172(juin 1896):454-55.

2685. Bailly, Edmond. "La musique dans l'oeuvre de Félicien Rops." *La Plume* 172(juin 1896):436-43.

2686. Champsaur, Félicien. "Deux portraits de F. Rops." *La Plume* 172 (juin 1896):447-52.

2687. Demolder, Eugène. "Etude partonymique sur Félicien Rops." *La Plume* 172(juin 1896):428-36.

2688. Detouche, Henry. "F. Rops: Ouvrier d'éternité." *La Plume* 172(juin 1896):456-57.

2689. "Félicien Rops et l'école de gravure en Belge." *La Plume* 172(juin

1896):468-71. [Extrait de *l'Art Moderne.*]

2690. Formentin, Ch. "Félicien Rops intime." *La Plume* 172(juin 1896):457-62.

2691. "F. Rops jugé par les Catholiques." *La Plume* 172(juin 1896): 453-54. [Extrait de *Journal de Bruxelles* 22 juin 1890.]

2692. "Hommage poétique à Félicien Rops." *La Plume* 172(juin 1896): 472-76.

2693. Huysmans, J.K. "Félicien Rops," *La Plume* 172(juin 1896):387-401.

2694. Lemonnier, Camille. "Une tentation de Saint Antoine de Félicien Rops." *La Plume* 172(juin 1896): 444-47.

2695. Maillard, Léon. "Félicien Rops graveur." *La Plume* 172(juin 1896): 499-504.

2696. Mirbeau, Octave. "Félicien Rops." *La Plume* 172(juin 1896): 487-92.

2697. "L'oeuvre de Félicien Rops." *La Plume* 172(juin 1896):506-14. [Incl. titles, descrips., dedications, etc.]

2698. Péladan, Joséphin. "Les maîtres contemporains." *La Plume* 172(juin 1896):413-28.

2699. Pica, Vittorio. "Félicien Rops à l'étranger:Italie." *La Plume* 172(juin 1896):462-64.

2700. Pontaury,Jacques. "Poisson rare." *La Plume* 172(juin 1896):505.

2701. Pradelle, J. "Rops naturien et féministe." *La Plume* 172(juin 1896):401-12. [With facsim.]

2702. Ramiro, E. "Beaux-Arts." *La Plume* 181(nov 1896):685-89.

2703. Rodrigues, Eugène. "Félicien Rops peintre." *La Plume* 172(juin 1896):477-78.

2704. Rops. F. "Lettres de Félicien Rops." *La Plume* 172(juin 1896):492-97.

2705. Saunier, Charles. "Félicien Rops:Le pendu." *La Plume* 172(juin 1896):478-79.

2706. Uzanne, Octave. "Félicien Rops par la plume et le crayon." *La Plume* 172(juin 1896):480-87.

2707. Verhaeren, Emile. "Salon des XX." *La Plume* 172(juin 1896):443.

2708. Zilcken, Philippe. "Félicien Rops à l'étranger:Hollande." *La Plume* 172(juin 1896):464-68

Rouault

2709. Courthion, Pierre. *Georges Rouault*. London: Thames and Hudson, 1962. 489 pp.

Rulfo

2710. Rodríguez-Luis, Julio. "Algunas observaciones sobre el simbolismo de la relación entre Susana San Juan y Pedro Páramo." *CHA* 270(1972): 584-94.

Saint-Pol Roux

2711. Amiot, Anne-Marie. "Les fondements mystiques de la poétique de Saint-Pol Roux," 89-111 in *Approches:Essais sur la poésie moderne de langue française.* (Annales de la Fac. des Lettres et Sciences Humaines de Nice 15.) Paris: Les Belles Lettres, 1971. 171 pp.

Samain

2712. Bocquet, Léon. *Albert Samain, sa vie, sou oeuvre*. Paris: Mercure de France, 1921. 283 pp.

2713. ———. *Autour d'Albert Samain*. Paris: Mercure de France, 1933. 244 pp.

2714. Cordiè, Carlo. *Due epigoni del simbolismo francese:Albert Samain e Louis Le Cardonnel*. Milano:Paideia, 1951. 272 pp.

2715. Denise, L. "Albert Samain." *MdF* 36(1900):5112.

2716. Ferdinand, Gohin. *L'Oeuvre*

poétique d'Albert Samain. Paris: Garnier, 1919. 85 pp.

2717. Kahn, Gustave. "Albert Samain." *La Plume* 273(sept 1900):531.

2718. Quillard, P. "Albert Samain." *MdF* 9(oct 1893):97-102.

2719. Rousseau, R. "La pensée poétique d'Albert Samain." *MdF* 143(1920):289-315.

Sánchez Ferlosio

2720. Schraibman, José, and William T. Little. "La estructura simbólica de *El Jarama*." *PQ* 51(1972):329-42.

Sartre

2721. Edwards, Michael. "*La Nausée*—A Symbolist Novel." *Adam* 343-45(1970):9-21.

Schönberg

2722. Brinkmann, Reinhold. "Schoenberg und George:Interpretation eines Liedes." *Archiv für Musikwissenschaft* 26,i(1969):1-28.

2723. Ehrenforth, Karl. *Ausdruck und Form:Schönbergs Durchbruch zur Atonalität in den George-Liedern Op. 15*. Bonn: Bouvier, 1963. 161 pp.

See also 1536.

Schopenhauer *See* 936.

Scriabin

2724. Bower, Faubion. *Scriabin*. Tokyo, Palo Alto: Kodansha, 1970.

2725. Swan, Alfred. *Scriabin*. Westport, Conn.: Greenwood Press, 1970. 119 pp.

Séguin

2726. Denis, Maurice. "Notes d'art." *La Plume* 141(mars 1895):118-19.

Seurat

2727. Dorra, Henri, and John Rewald. *Seurat:L'oeuvre peint, biographie, et catalogue critique*. Préf. de Georges Wildenstein. Paris: Les Beaux-Arts, 1959. 311 pp.

See also 793.

Shaw, G.B.

2728. Adams, Elsie B. *Bernard Shaw and the Aesthetes*. Columbus: Ohio State U.P., 1972. 193 pp.

Silva, J.A.

2729. Meyer-Minnemann, Klaus. "*De sobremesa* von José Asunción Silva: Ein lateinamerikanischer Roman des Fin de Siècle." *RJ* 24(1973):330-58.

2730. Roberts, Jack. "Life and Death in the Poetry of José Asunción Silva." *SoQ* 10(1972):137-65.

See also 1232.

Sitwell

2731. Hassan, Ihab H. "Edith Sitwell and the Symbolist Tradition." *CL* 7(1955):240-51.

See also 129, 1011.

Sluchevski

2732. Makocskij, Sergej. "K. Slučevskij, predteča simvolizma." *NovŽ* 59(1960):71-92.

Sologub

2733. Bristol, Evelyn. "Feodor Sologub as a Lyric Poet." *RusR* 30(1971):268-76.

2734. Field, Andrew. "*The Created*

Legend: Sologub's Symbolic Universe." *SEEJ* 5(1961):341-49.

2735. Holthusen, Johannes. *Fedor Sologubs Roman-Trilogie (Tvorimaja legenda) aus der Geschichte des Russischen Symbolismus.* (Musagetes, IX.) 'sGravenhage: Mouton, 1960.

2736. Struc, Roman S. " 'Petty Demons' and Beauty:Gogol, Dostoevsky, Sologub," 61-82 in Peter U. Hohendahl, Herbert Lindenberger, and Egon Schwartz,eds. *Essays on European Literature in Honor of Liselotte Dieckmann.* St. Louis, Mo.: Washington U.P., 1972. 254 pp.

Soloviev

2737. Florovskij, Prot. Georgij. "Ctenija po filosofii religii magistra filosofii V.S. Solov'eva." *Orbis Scriptus* 92(1966):221-36.

2738. Lager, Robert J. "Vladimir Soloviev:Symbolist Poet." *DAI* 31 (1970):2389A(Georgetown).

2738a. Lavrin, Janko. "Vladmir Soloviev and Slavophilism" *RusR* 20(1961): 11-18.

2739. Müller, Ludolf. "Der Text der 'Drei Gespräche' von Vladimir Solov'ev." *WSL* 4(1959):329-65.

2740. Stammler, Heinrich. "Vladimir Soloviev as a Literary Critic." *RusR* 22(1963):68-81.

See also 694.

Stevens, W.

2742. Benamou, Michel. "The Structures of Wallace Stevens' Imagination." *MArt* 1(1967):73-84.

2743. ———. "Sur le prétendu *symbolism* de Wallace Stevens." *Critique* 175(déc 1961):1029-45.

2744. ———. "Wallace Stevens and the Symbolist Imagination." *31(Mar 1964):35-63.*

2745. ———. *Wallace Stevens and the Symbolist Imagination.* Princeton: Princeton U.P., 1972. 154 pp.

2746. Blessing, Richard. "Wallace Stevens and the Necessary:A Technique of Dynamism." *TCL* 18(1972): 251-58.

2747. Bloom, Harold. "Death and the Native Strain in American Poetry." *SocR* 39(1972):449-62.

2748. Burtner, H.W. "The High Priest of the Secular:The Poetry of Wallace Stevens." *ConnR* 6,i(1972):34-45.

2749. Caldwell, Price. "Metaphoric Structures in Wallace Stevens' 'Thirteen Ways of Looking at a Blackbird'." *JEGP* 71(1972):321-35.

2750. Gaughan, Gerald C. "Wallace Stevens and Stéphane Mallarmé:A Comparative Study in Poetic Theory." *DA* 27(1967):3453A (Northwestern.).

2751. Kessler, Edward. *Images of Wallace Stevens.* New Brunswick, N.J.: Rutgers U.P., 1972. 267 pp.

2752. Litz, A. Walton. *Introspective Voyager:The Poetic Development of Wallace Stevens.* New York: Oxford U.P., 1972. 326 pp.

2753. McFadden, Georges. "Probings for an Integration of Color Symbolism in Wallace Stevens." *MP* 58 (1961):186-93.

2754. Riddel, Joseph N. "Stevens on Imagination:The Point of Departure," 55-85 in O.B. Hardison,Jr.,ed. *The Quest for Imagination:Essays in Twentieth Century Aesthetic Criticism.* Cleveland and London: The Press of Case Western Reserve U., 1971. 286 pp.

2755. Sheehan, Donald. "The Whole of *Harmonium:*Poetic Technique in Wallace Stevens," 175-86 in Warren French,ed. *The Fifties:Fiction, Poetry, Drama.* With Introd. DeLand, Fla.: Everett/Edwards, 1970. 316 pp.

2756. Simons, Hi. "Wallace Stevens and Mallarmé." *MP* 43-44(1947):235-59.

See also 1973, 1981, 2258.

Strindberg

2757. Ahlström, Stellan. " 'Mademoiselle Julie' de Strindberg et le wagnérisme." *MSpr* 62(1968):65-66.
2758. Allen, James L.,Jr. "Symbol and Meaning in Strindberg's 'Crime and Crime'." *MD* 9(1966):62-73.
2759. Block, Haskell M. "Strindberg and the Symbolist Drama." *MD* 5(1962):314-22.
2760. Daniel-Rops. "Strindberg et le génie du nord." *Revue de Genève* 14 (1927):575-95.
2761. Raphael, Robert. "Strindberg and Wagner," 260-68 in Carl F. Bayerschmidt, and Erik J. Friis,eds. *Scandinavian Studies:Essays Presented to Dr. Henry Goddard Leach on the Occasion of His Eighty-fifth Birthday*. Seattle: U. of Wash. P., 1965.
2762. Stockenström, Göran. *Ismael i öknen:Strindberg som mystiker.* (Acta Univ. Upsaliensis Historia Litterarum 5.) Uppsala, 1973. 547 pp.
2763. Wittrock, Ulf. "Strindberg och sekelslutets symbolism." *OB* 7(1962): 409-14.

See also 1378, 1574, 3106.

Stukenberg

2764. *Viggo Stukenberg–Sophus Claussen:En brevvexling*. (KDVS 40,ii.) Copenhagen, 1964.

Suarès

2765. Busi, Frederick. "Suarès et Villiers de l'Isle-Adam." *RLM* 346-50(1973):85-93.
2766. Cellier, Léon. "Suarès et Mallarmé." *RLM* 346-50(1973):61-84.

2767. Doherty, Thomas W. "Suarès et deux musiciens de son temps:Wagner et Debussy." *RLM* 346-50(1973): 105-23.
2768. Favre, Yves-Alain. "Musique du mot chez Suarès:*Lais et Sônes*." *RLM* 346-50(1973):183-200.
2769. George, Rambert. "Suarès et Verlaine." *RLM* 346-50(1973):41-60.
2770. Liger, Christian. "Le symbolisme ambigu d'André Suarès." *RLM* 346-50(1973):127-82.
2771. Pinguet, Maurice. "Suarès et le 'mystère' de Rimbaud." *RLM* 346-50(1973):13-39.
2772. Robichez, Jacques. " 'Ou tout moi, ou pas moi . . .':A propos d'un projet de représentation des *Pélerins d'Emmaüs*." *RLM* 346-50(1973):95-103.

Swinburne

2773. Crawford, Donald A. "Imagistic-Structural Design in Swinburne's Poetry." *DAI* 32(1972):5177A (N.Y.U.).
2774. Sypher, Francis J.,Jr. "Swinburne and Wagner." *VP* 9(1971):165-83.

See also 1226, 1242, 1266, 1539, 1600, 2925.

Symons

2775. Garbáty, Tomas J. "An Appraisal of Arthur Symons by Pater and Mallarmé." *N&Q* 7(1960):187-88.
2776. Goodman, John F. "Arthur Symons and French Symbolism:The Critical Theory." *DAI* 30(1970): 5408A(Wis.).
2777. Munro, John M. "Arthur Symons as Poet:Theory and Practice." *ELT* 6(1963):212-22.
2778. Peters, Robert L. "The *Salome* of Arthur Symons and Aubrey Beardsley." *Criticism* 2(1960):150-63.

2779. Stern, Carol S. "Arthur Symons's Literary Relationships, 1882-1900: Some Origins of the Symbolist Movement." *DA* 29(1969):2282A-83A (Northwestern).

2780. Thombreaud, Roger A. "Arthur Symons' Rendering of Mallarmé." *PULC* 20(1959):89-102.

See also 522, 1308, 1566, 1923, 2640, 3178.

Synge

2781. Rabuse, George. "J.M. Synges Verhältnis zur französischen Literatur und besonders zu Maeterlinck." *Archiv* 174(1938):36-53.

See also 1869, 3106.

Tailhade, Laurent

2782. Boisjolin, J. De. "La poésie aristophanesque chez M. Laurent Tailhade." *La Plume* 202(sept 1897): 570-72.

2783. Essebac, Achille. "Hommage à Laurent Tailhade." *La Plume* 303(déc 1901):924.

2784. Lavigne, Paul. "Laurent Tailhade." *La Plume* 39(déc 1890):225.

2785. Lazare, Bernard. " 'Vitraux' par Laurent Tailhade." *Entretiens politiques et littéraires* 22(janv 1892): 37-39. [Rev. art.]

2786. "Le procès Tailhade." *La Plume* 301(nov 1901):878-80.

2787. Zola, Emile. "A propos du procès Tailhade." *La Plume* 303(déc 1901): 924.

2788. Séverine. "Toast à Lèon Tailhade." *La Plume* 301(nov 1901):880-81.

See also 1031.

Tolstoi, L.

2789. Headings, Philip R. "The Ques-

tion of Exclusive Art:Tolstoy and T.S. Eliot's *The Waste Land*." *RLV* 32(1966):82-95.

2790. Nag, Marin. "Tolstoj, Ibsen; Bjørnson." *Edda* 53(1966):270-76.

2791. Trahan, Elizabeth. "L.N. Tolstoj's *Master and Man*—A Symbolic Narrative." *SEEJ* 7(1963):258-68.

Toorop

2792. Knipping, J.B. *Jan Toorop*. Amsterdam: H.J.W. Brecht, 1947. 59 pp.

Trakl

2793. Grimm, Reinhold. "Georg Trakls Verhältnis zu Rimbaud," 271-313 in *Zur Lyrik-Diskussion*. Darmstadt: Wissenschaftliche Buchgesellschaft, 1966.

Trismégiste

2794. Johansen, Sven. "D'un symbolisme ésotérique ... dont parle Hermès Trismégiste en son *Pimandre*." *OL* 25(1970):281-85.

Turgenev, I.

2795. Cadot, M. "Un problème de collaboration littéraire:I.S. Tourguéniev et Louis Viardot," 603-08 in Banašević, Nikola,ed. *Actes du Ve Congrès de l'Association Internationale de Littérature Comparée, Belgrade 1967*. Belgrade: U. de Belgrade; Amsterdam: Swets & Zeitlinger, 1969.

2796. Delaney, Joan. "Edgar Allan Poe and I.S. Turgenev." *SSASH* 15 (1969):349-54.

2797. Šatalov, S.E. *Problemy poètiki I.S. Turgeneva*. Moscow: Prosveščenie, 1969.

Tyutchev

2798. Du Feu, Veronica M. "Tiutcheff,

premier symboliste russe." *Langue et littérature* [6](1962):330-31.

Ujević

2799. Stamać, Ante. "Ujević i Baudelaire." *ForumZ* 20(1970):183-213.

Unamuno

2800. Cortés. Luis. "Unamuno y Machado." *CCU* 16-17(1967):93-98.
2801. Metzidakis, Philip. "Unamuno frente a la poesía de Rubén Darío." *RI* 25(1960):229-49.
2802. Ribbans, G.W. "Unamuno and Antonio Machado." *BHS* 34(1957): 10-28.

See also 653, 1517.

Ungaretti

2803. Anselmi, Luciano. "L'ancora del poeta." *RdC* (3 giugno 1972):3.
2804. Bigongiari, Piero. "Il sillabato ungarettiano." *FI* 6(1972):183-206.
2805. Cambon, Glauco. "Appunti per *La morte meditata* di Ungaretti." *FI* 6(1972):232-43.
2806. Contorbia, Franco. "Ungaretti e Proust." *LdProv* 2,1v(1971):3-11.
2807. Di Bella, Nino. "I quattro *ventenni* di Ungaretti:Tra crepuscolarismo ed ermetismo." *Parole e il libro* 51(1968):179-80.
2808. Frattarolo, Renzo. "Materiali per uno studio su Guiseppe Ungaretti." *ABI* 39(1971):379-409.
2809. Gutia, Joan. "Ungaretti e Mallarmé. *RLMC* 3(1952):254-59.
2810. Mander, Luciano. "La luce di Ungaretti." *Messagero* 11(maggio 1972):3.

See also 616.

Valéry

2811. Arnold, A. James. *Paul Valéry* and His Critics:A Bibliography. French-Language Criticism 1890-1927. Pub. For the Bibliog. Soc. of the U. of Va. Charlottesville: U.P. of Va., 1970. 617 pp. [Photo-offset of typed MS.]
2812. Basted, Ned. "*La symbolique des images dans l'oeuvre poétique de Valéry*. (Travaux et Mémoires, 24.) Aix en Provence: Publ. des Annales de la Faculté des Lettres d'Aix en Provence, 1962.
2813. ——. "Valéry et la clôture tragique." *AJFS* 8(1971):103-19.
2814. Bellemin-Noël, Jean. "Le narcissisme des 'Narcisses' (Valéry)." *Lit* 6(1972):35-55.
2815. Borges, Jorge. "Valéry como símbolo." *Paul Valéry* 14(Oct 1945): 30-32.
2816. Brombert, Victor. "Valéry:The Dance of Words." *HudR* 21(1968): 675-86.
2817. Crow, Christine M. *Paul Valéry: Consciousness and Nature*. London: Cambridge U.P., 1972. 271 pp.
2818. Doisy, Marcel. *Paul Valéry:Intelligence et poésie*. Paris: Cercle du livre, 1952. 241 pp.
2819. Downes, Gladys. *Paul Valéry en face du Symbolisme et du Surréalisme*. Paris: U. of Paris, 1953. [Diss.]
2820. Dresdin, Samuel. *L'artiste et l'absolu:Paul Valéry et Marcel Proust*. Academisch proefschrift Amsterdam. Amsterdam: Assen, Van Gorcum & Comp., 1941.
2821. Duchesne-Guillemin, Jacques. "Les dialogues de Paul Valéry." *CAIEF* 24(1972):75-91.
2822. ——. "Paul Valéry et la musique." *Revue musicale* 210 (1952):113-21.
2823. Erickson, John D. "Valéry on Leonardo, Poe and Mallarmé." *ECr* 13(1973):252-59. [Rev. art.]
2824. Eschmann, Ernst W. "Valéry und

Rilke. Fragmente eines Vergleichs." *Neue Schweizer Rundschau* 16,iii (July 1948):179-87.

2825. Fabre, L. "Au sujet du Valéry de M. Thibaudet." *NRF* (1 déc 1923): 662-76.

2826. Fabureau, Hubert. *Paul Valéry*. Paris: Eds. de la Nouvelle revue critique, 1937. 251 pp.

2827. Geen, Renée. "Valéry et Swedenborg." *FS* 20(1966):25-32.

2828. Genette, Gérard. "Valéry et la poétique du langage." *MLN* 87(1972): 600-15.

2829. Golea, Antoine. "Musik und Tanz transzendieren Poesie:'L'Ame et la Danse' von Paul Valéry." *Neue Zeitschrift für Musik* 123(Nov 1962): 518-19.

2830. Huber, Egon. "P. Valérys Metaphorik und der französische Symbolismus." *ZFSL* 67(1957):168-201; 68(1958):165-86; 69(1959):1-21.

2831. Jones, Rhys S. "Hegel and French Symbolism. Some Observations on the 'Hegelianism' of Paul Valéry." *FS* 4(1950):142-50.

2832. Köhler, Hartmut. *Poésie et profondeur sémantique dans "La jeune Parque" de Paul Valéry*. Nancy: Impr. U. Idoux, 1965. 48 pp.

2833. Larbaud, Valéry. "Paul Valéry." *RdP* (1 mars 1929):49-69.

2834. Latimer, Dan R. "Problems in the Symbol:A Theory and Application in the Poetry of Valéry, Rilke, and Yeats." *DAI* 33(1973):631A(Mich.).

2835. Lawler, James R. *Form and Meaning in Valéry's "Le cimetière marin."* Melbourne: Melbourne U.P.; London: Cambridge U.P., 1960. 41 pp.

2836. ———. " 'Existe' . . . 'Sois enfin toi même . . .'." *AJFS* 8(1971):146-74.

2837. ———. *Lecture de Valéry:Une étude de* Charmes. Paris: Presses univs., 1963. 269 pp.

2838. ———. "Lucide, phoenix de ce vertige . . ." *MLN* 87(1972):616-29.

2839. ———. "Valéry et Claudel:Un dialogue symboliste." *NRF* 16(sept 1968):239-61.

2840. Lefevre, Frédéric. *Entretiens avec Paul Valéry*. Paris: "Le Livre", 1926. 376 pp.

2841. Mathews, Jackson. "The Poïetics of Paul Valéry." *RR* 46(1955): 203-17.

2842. Mićević, Kolja. "O simbolici elemenata imitolosskoj figuraciji Pola Valerija." *KnijiNov* 402(1 Nov 1971):7.

2843. Ospina-Garcés de Fonseca, Helena. "Paul Valéry et Edgar Poe: L'influence de la théorie poétique de Poe chez Valéry," 3-13 in K.H. Mann,ed. *Anales del Departamento de Lenguas Modernas, Universidad de Costa Rica*. No. 1. Agosto 1972. San José: U. de Costa Rica. 112 pp.

2844. Paul, David. "Valéry and the Relentless World of the Symbol." *SoR* 6(1970):408-15.

2845. Planchart, Enrique. "Paul Valéry:Rioja y Valéry." *RNC* 7(1945):109-14.

2846. Prévost, J. "Sur une exégèse de Paul Valéry." *NRF* (1 fév 1926): 173-76.

2847. Régnier, Henri de. "La vie courante—hier et aujourd'hui—par Valéry vers Mallarmé." *Revue de France* 3(1923):642-45.

2848. Rey, Alain. "La conscience du poète:Les langages de Paul Valéry." *Lit* 4(1971):116-28.

2849. ———. "Monsieur Teste de haut en bas." *Poétique* 9(1972):80-88.

2850. Rivière, J. "Paul Valéry, poète." *NRF* (1 sept 1922):256-69.

2851. Souday, Paul. *Paul Valéry*. Paris: S. Kra, 1927. 144 pp.

2852. Valéry, Paul. " 'I Sometimes Said to Stéphane Mallarmé'." *MdF* 27(1965):94-112. [Tr. Malcolm Cowley.]

2853. ———. "Au sujet du 'Cimetiére marin'." *NRF* (1 mars 1933):399-411.

2854. Wahl, J. "Sur la pensée de Paul Valéry." *NRF* (1 sept 1933):449-63.

2855. Wais, Kurt, K. *Beiträge zur vergleichenden Literaturgeschichte.* Tübingen: Niemeyer, 1972. 406 pp. [Valéry and Baudelaire.]

2856. ———. "D.H. Lawrence, Valéry, Rilke in ibrer Auseinandersetzung mit den bildenden Künsten." *GRM* 2(1952):301-24.

2857. Whiting, Charles. "Femininity in Valéry's Early Poetry." *YFS* 9(1952):74-83.

2858. Wills, Ludmilla M. "Le regard contemplatif chez Valéry and Mallarmé." *DAI* 33(1972):1749A-50A (Rutgers).

2859. "Words and Silence in 'L'idée fixe'." *MLN* 87(1972):644-56.

See also 7, 261, 503, 907, 1025, 1084, 1107, 1233, 1241, 1272, 1274, 1483, 1582, 1598, 1615, 1771, 1779, 2075, 2120, 2151, 2170, 2193, 2194, 2224, 2454, 2461, 2549, 2555, 2564, 2566, 2579, 2585, 2920.

Valle-Inclán

2860. Díaz-Plaja, Guillermo. "Las estéticas de Valle-Inclán:Simbología y síntesis," 273 in Sánchez Romeralo, Jaime, and Norbert Poulussens,eds. *Actas del Segundo Congreso Internacional de Hispanistas.* Celebrado en Nijmegen del 20 al 25 de agosto de 1965. Nijmegen, Holland: Inst. Español de la U. de Nimega, 1967.

2861. Foster, David W. "La estructura expresionista en dos novelas de Valle-Inclán." *ExTL* 1,i(1972):46-63.

2862. González Lopéz, Emilio. *El arte dramático de Valle-Inclán (del decadentismo al expresionismo).* New York: Las Américas, 1967. 267 pp.

2863. ———. "La poesía simbolista de Valle-Inclán." *Grial* 23(1969):27-36.

2864. Mallo, Antonio E. "El símbolo de la rosa en Valle-Inclán." *Grial* 25 (1969):287-307.

2865. Tolman, Rosco N. "Symbolism in Valle-Inclán's *Sonata de primavera*," 166-69 in *Proceedings:Pacific Northwest Conference on Foreign Languages.* Walter Kraft,ed. Twenty-second Annual Meeting, April 16-17, 1971. Vol. XXII. Corvallis: Ore. State U., 1971. 306 pp.

Van Gogh

2866. Aigrisse, Gilberte. "L'évolution psychologique de Van Gogh étudiée à travers le symbolisme des éléments." *CIS* 8(1965):59-74.

See also 793.

Verhaeren

2867. Berger de Guevara, Viviane. "Le poète Emile Verhaeren." *RUCR* 36(1973):83-90.

2868. Delvaille, Bernard. "Du Symbolisme à l'Unanimisme:Notes sur Verhaeren." *Audace* 16,i(1970):91-104.

2869. Dozot, Marie-Hélène. "La vision intensive dans les *Villes tentaculaires* d'Emile Verhaeren." *CLIA* 1(1970):24-37.

2870. Estève, Edmond. *Un grand poète de la vie moderne:Emile Verhaeren.* Paris: Boivin, 1928.

2871. Fontaine, André. *Verhaeren et son oeuvre.* Paris: Mercure de France, 1929. 216 pp.

2872. González Martínez, Enrique. "Emile Verhaeren." *Nivel* 103(1972): 6,9,11. [Repr. of lect. pub. 1918 by Editorial Cultura.]

2873. Higgins, Ian. "Towards a Poetic Theater:Poetry and the Plastic Arts in Verhaeren's Aesthetics." *FMLS* 9(1973):1-23.

2874. Kahn, Gustave. "Emile Verhaeren:*Petites légendes* (Bruxelles, Deman)." *Revue Blanche* 24(1901): 479. [Rev. art.]

2875. Oechler, W.F. "The Reception of Emile Verhaeren in Germany:Some Unpublished Letters of Stefan Sweig." *MLN* 62(1947):226-34.

2876. Piérard, Louis. "Le tombeau de Verhaeren." *Revue de Genève* 13(1926):489-99.

2877. Pilon, Edmond. "Emile Verhaeren." *La Plume* 354(janv 1904): 33-44.

2878. Viélé-Griffin, Francis. "Emile Verhaeren." *La Plume* 143(avril 1895):141-42.

2879. ———. "A propos d'un livre de M. Emile Verhaeren." *Entretiens politiques et littéraires* 22(janv 1892): 15-19.

2880. Weld, Evelyn B.P. "Towards the Hours of Marthe." *DAI* 33(1972): 333A(Stanford).

2881. Zweig, Stefan. *Emile Verhaeren.* Paris: Mercure de France, 1910. 274 pp.

See also 893, 1031, 1039, 1075, 1268.

Verlaine

2882. Abraham, Claude K. "Verlaine: Etude d'une évolution poétique." *KFLQ* 10(1963):1-7.

2883. Anon. "Paul Verlaine." *Critic* 28 (18 Jan 1896):47.

2884. Anon. "Paul Verlaine the Symbolist." *Current Literature* 14(Oct 1893):212-13.

2885. Anon. "The Posthumous Verlaine." *Spectator* 87(22 Aug 1896):237-38.

2886. Anon. "Verlaine as Draughtsman." *Times*(London) 10 Mar (1896).

2887. Anon. "A Vindication of Verlaine." *Current Literature* 43(1907): 404-06. [Rev. art. on Lepelletier's *Paul Verlaine, sa vie, son oeuvre.*]

2888. Anon. "A Visit to Verlaine." *Literary Digest* 12(18 Apr 1896):732.

2889. Anon. "A Word about Paul Verlaine." *Literary Digest* 12(1 Feb 1896):403.

2890. Barrès, Philippe. "Barrès et Verlaine." *RDM* déc(1973):513-27.

2891. Batchelor, C.M. *Verlaine and Darío.* New Haven: Yale U., 1940. [Diss.]

2892. Baudot, Alain. "Poésie et musique chez Verlaine:Forme et signification." *EF* 4(1968):32-54.

2893. Belchior, Maria de Lourdes. "Verlaine e o simbolismo em Portugal." *Brotéria* 90(1970):305-19.

2894. ———. *Verlaine e o simbolismo em Portugal.* Lisboa: Edições Brotéria, 1970.

2895. Bernardelli, Giuseppe. "Un' eco di Banville nella 'Bonne chanson'." *RLMC* 25(1972):205-09.

2896. ———. "Verlaine e la maniera simbolista." *Aevum* 47(1973):125-46.

2897. Bronecque, J.-H. "Poème et poétiques:L'art poétique de Verlaine." *Dialogues* 4(Feb 1956):13-20.

2898. ———. *Verlaine.* Paris: Eds. du Seuil, 1966.

2899. Bury, Yetta Blaze de. "Paul Verlaine." *Cosmopolis* 1(1896):698-709.

2900. Carco, Francis. *Verlaine poète maudit.* Paris: Ed. Albin Michel, 1948. 236 pp.

2901. Carter, A.E. *Verlaine:A Study in Parallels.* (UTRFS 14.) Toronto: U. of Toronto P., 1969.

2902. Cartier, M. *La prose de Verlaine et de Mallarmé:Contribution à l'étude de la prose des symbolistes français. Quelques problèmes de langue et de stylistique.* Bern: Städt. Gymnasium, 1964.

2903. Cazals, F.A. "Paul Verlaine intime." *Senate* 4(Feb 1897):53-55; (June 1897):233-35.

2904. Chadwick, Charles,ed. *Sagesse.* London: Athlone, 1973. 103 pp.

2905. Chailley, Jacques. "Les goûts musicaux de Verlaine." *Revue de Musicologie* 35(1953):167.

2906. Chalupt, René. "Verlaine, ou:De la musique en toute chose." *Contrepoints* 6(1949):62-73.

2907. Chaussivert, J.S. "Saint-Beuve et les débuts littéraires de Verlaine," 282-83 [Abst.] in A.P. Treweek, ed. *Australasian Univs. Lang. and Lit. Assn.:Proceed. and Papers of the Twelfth Cong. Held at the Univ. of West Australia, 5-11 Feb. 1969.* [Sydney]: AULLA, 1970. 504 pp.

2908. Clodomir. "Correspondance étrangère:Verlaine en Allemagne." *La Plume* 137(janv 1895):25.

2909. Cuénot, Claude. "Un type de création littéraire:Paul Verlaine." *SFr* 12(1968):229-45.

2910. Degron, Henri. "Pour la statue de Paul Verlaine ou Variations sur un mufle considérable." *La Plume* 182 (nov 1896):736.

2911. Delille, Eugène. "The Poet Verlaine." *Fortnightly Review* 55 (1891):394-405.

2912. Diederichs-Maurer, Anna K. *Le thème de l'angoisse chez Verlaine.* Düsseldorf-Köln: Eugen Diederichs, 1971. 95 pp. [Diss., Zürich.]

2913. Dujardin, Edouard. "Verlaine." *Universal Review* 6(1890):412-24.

2914. Edwards, O. "About Paul Verlaine." *Daily Chronicle* (London) 17 Jan(1896).

2915. Emich, Isolde. "Zum Problem der deutschen Verlaine-übersetzungen." *FUF* 36(1962):52-55.

2916. Ermini, Filippo. *Paolo Verlaine e i poeti decadenti.* Torino: G.B. Paravia, 1896. 51 pp.

2917. Ferreres, Rafael. "Introducción de Paul Verlaine en España." *CHA* 260(1971):244-57.

2918. Fontaine, André. *Verlaine, homme de lettres.* Paris: Librairie Delagrave, 1937. 143 pp.

2919. Fortassier, Pierre. "Verlaine, la musique et les musiciens." *CAIEF* 12 (1960):143-59.

2920. Francavilla, Francesco. *Il simbolismo, con 12 tavole fuori testo.* Milano: Ultra, 1944. 67 pp.

2921. Gaucheron, Jacques. "Amour de la poésie." *Europe* (Feb-Mar 1962): 247-52.

2922. Gauss, Christian. "Paul Verlaine." *North American Review* 187(1908): 453-56. [Rev. art. on Lepelletier's *Paul Verlaine, sa vie, son œuvre.*]

2923. Germain, Andrè. "Verlaine et Huysmans." *Revue Européenne* 1 (May 1923):23-25.

2924. Gosse, Edmund. "A First Sight of Verlaine." *Savoy* 2(1896):113-16. [Repr. in *French Profiles.* London, 1905.]

2925. Graaf, Daniel. "L'influence de Swinburne sur Verlaine et Rimbaud." *RSH* 97(1960):87-92.

2926. ——. "Une source ancienne du symbolisme (Verlaine et Rimbaud débiteurs de Cyrano de Bergerac)." *MdF* 1094(Oct 1954):253-57.

2927. Grierson, Francis. "Paul Verlaine." *Critic* 43(1903):173-76.

2928. Griror'jan, K.N. "Verlen i russkij simvolizm." *RLit* 14,i(1971):111-20.

2929. Gsteiger, Manfred. "Grenzen der Nachdichtung:Verlaines 'Chanson d'automne' in der deutschen Literatur der Jahrhundertwende." *Sch-*

weizer Monatshefte für Politik, Wirtschaft, Kultur 48,iv(1968): 399-412.

2930. Ilie, Paul. "Verlaine and Machado:The Aesthetic Role of Time." *CL* 19(1963):261-65.

2931. Jean-Aubrey, Georges. "Paul Verlaine et les musiciens," 236-52 in *La musique française d'aujourd'hui*. Paris:Perrin, 1916.

2932. Kahn, Gustave. "Doumic contre Verlaine." *Revue Blanche* 24(1901): 256-59.

2933. Keary, C.F. "Paul Verlaine." *New Review* 16(1897):617-30.

2934. Kelly, M.J. "Paul Verlaine." *Monthly Review* 90(Dec 1897):153.

2935. Koven, Mrs. Reginald de. "Verlaine, a Feminine Appreciation." *Chap Book* 4(1896):285-89.

2936. Kronik, John W. "Clarín and Verlaine." *RLC* 37(1963):368-84.

2937. ———. "An Early Spanish Notice of Verlaine." *RomN* 12(1970): 110-13.

2938. Lachmann, Hedwig. "Paul Verlaine." *Entretiens politiques et littéraires* 56(déc 1893):508-17.

2939. Leclère, Tristan. "Les musiciens de Verlaine." *Revue Bleue* 72(14 nov 1903):633-35.

2940. Lemaître, Jules. "M. Paul Verlaine et les poètes symbolistes et décadents." *Revue Bleu* (7 Jan 1888):2-14.

2941. Lepelletier, Edmond A. *Paul Verlaine, His Life, His Work*. New York, 1909. [Tr. E.M. Lang. Orig. pub. Paris: Mercure de France, 1907.]

2942. Lethève, Jacques. "Quand Verlaine, Huysmans et Moréas partaient en guerre au nom des *poètes maudits*." *FL* 2(1959):6-11.

2943. Lyndon, Howard. "The Poet of Absinthe." *Bookman* 9(1899):440-44. [Rev. art. on Charles Donos, *Verlaine intime.*]

2944. MacCarthy, Desmond. "Paul Verlaine." *Albany Review* 1(Aug 1907): 593-600.

2945. Maillard, Léon. "Etude pour servir à l'iconographie de Paul Verlaine." *La Plume* 163(fév 1896):124-26.

2946. Manston, Augustus. "Verlaine." *Temple Bar* 108(1896):329-39. [Repr. in *Living Age* 210(1896): 501-07.]

2947. Mary, André. "Méditations sur Paul Verlaine." *L'Ermitage* 25(juillet 1902):27-41.

2948. M.B.M. "Verlaine, 'maître des poètes':Coppée and Other Candidates for the Succession." *Book Buyer* 13(1896):353.

2949. Micha, Alexandre. *Verlaine et les poètes symbolistes*. Paris: Larousse, 1943. 108 pp.

2950. Mourik, A. Van. "Verlaine in Holland." *LT* 181(1955):392-94.

2951. Nalyvajko, Dmytro. "Pol' Verlen po-ukrajinskiy." *Dnipro* 43,viii (1969):144-51.

2952. "Les Obsèques." *La Plume* 163 (fév 1896):117-22. [Facsim. of autograph letter from V.]

2953. "L'oeuvre de Paul Verlaine publiée." *La Plume* 163(fév 1896):126-30. [List of works with facsim. of autograph MS.]

2954. Pabst, Walter. "Góngora-Tone in Verlaines 'Wandteppich':Zum Ursprung des Sonetts *Allégorie* (1867)." *Archiv* 200(1963):102-07.

2955. Pilon, Edmond. "Verlaine." *L'Ermitage* 1(1896):59-62.

2956. "Résultats du Congrès des Poètes." *La Plume* 163(fév 1896):67-116. [Essays by var. poets on V.]

2957. Retté, Adolphe. "Paul Verlaine." *La Plume* 163(fév 1896):116-18.

2958. Richardson, Joanna. *Verlaine*. New York: Viking Press, 1971. 432 pp.

2959. Riessauw, A.M. "Verlaine en de

muziek." *Mens en Melodie* 21(Mar 1966):73-75.

2960. Roerchez, Jacques. "A propos de Verlaine:'Nevermore', *Bergamasques.*" *RSH* 118(1965):284-85.

2961. Ruck, Heribert. "Sprachliche Konstituenten in einem Gedicht von Verlaine." *NS* 21(1971):252-63.

2962. Safford, Irene A. "Verlaine's Dual Nature." *Critic* 32(26 Mar 1898): 220.

2963. Saint-Pol-Roux. "Origine de la famille Verlaine." *La Plume* 163(fév 1896):122. [Facsim. of V's "last" sonnet.]

2964. Sanborn, A.F. "The Vanity of Verlaine." *Bookman* 29(1909):390.

2965. Schaettel, Marcel. "Rythme et structure:Images formelles et dynamiques dans 'Clair de lune' de Verlaine." *RSH* 130(1968):259-66.

2966. Soissons, S.C. de. "Paul Verlaine." *Forum* 24(Oct 1897):246-56.

2967. Soulié, Paul. "Les clés de la perception poétique verlainienne d'après un commentaire de *Kaléidoscope.*" *IL* 24(1972):118-22.

2968. ———. "Le vague et l'aigu dans la perception verlainienne," 53-67 in *Approches:Essais sur la poésie moderne de langue française.* (Annales de la Fac. des Lettres et Sciences Humaines de Nice 15.) Paris: Les Belles Lettres, 1971. 171 pp.

2969. Stephan, P. "Decadent Poetry in 'Le chat noir':Verlaine's Langueur." *MLQ* 30(1969):535-44.

2970. ———. "Verlaine and Baudelaire: Two Uses of Obscured Lightings." *FR* 35(1961-62):26-35.

2971. Stickney, Joseph T. "Paul Verlaine." *Bachelor of Arts* 3(1896):18-36.

2972. Symons, Arthur. "The 'Invectives' of Verlaine." *Saturday Review* 82(26 Sept 1896):338-39.

2973. ———. "A Literary Causerie:On the 'Invectives' of Verlaine." *Savoy* 7(1896):88-90.

2974. ———. "M. Paul Verlaine." *Athenaeum* 3559(11 Jan 1896):54. [Also in *Critic* 28(25 Jan 1896):68.]

2975. ———. "Paul Verlaine." *National Review* 19(1892):501-15.

2976. ———. "Paul Verlaine." *Saturday Review* 81(11 Jan 1896):34-35.

2977. ———. "Verlaine's Confessions." *Saturday Review* 79(1 June 1895): 731-32.

2978. ———. "Verlaine's Latest Poems." *Saturday Review* 78(22 Dec 1894): 685-86. [On *Dédicaces.*]

2979. Ténib, Charles. "Psychologie:Défense de Paul Verlaine." *La Plume* 130(sept 1894):369-71.

2980. Thieme, Hugo P. "Paul Verlaine." *Inlander* 9(1899):352-58.

2981. Thompson, Vance. "Impressions of Verlaine." *M'lle New York* 1(15 Jan 1896).

2982. Trounoux, G.A. *Bibliographie verlainienne:Contribution critique à l'étude des littératures étrangères et comparées.* Leipzig: n.p., 1912.

2983. Underwood, Vernon P. *Verlaine et l'Angleterre.* Paris: Nizet, 1956. 510 pp.

2984. Van Westrum, Adrian S. "The King of the Poets." *Critic* 32(14 May 1898):324-27. [Rev. art. on Charles Donos, *Verlaine intime.*]

2985. Walker, Hallam. "Visual and Spatial Imagery in Verlaine's *Fêtes galantes.*" *PMLA* 87(1972):1007-15.

2986. Wilson, Alice L. "Shelley and Verlaine." *Poet Lore* 8(1896):406-20.

2987. Wright, Alfred J. "Verlaine and Debussy:*Fêtes galantes.*" *FR* 40 (1967):627-35.

2988. Yeats, W.B. "Verlaine in 1894." *Savoy* 2(1896):117-18.

2989. Zangwill, I. "Without Prejudice." *Pall Mall Magazine* 8(1896):654-56.

2990. Zimmerman, Eléonore M. *Magies de Verlaine.* Paris: Corti, 1967.

See also 385, 436, 451, 572, 585,

799, 966, 1084, 1104, 1168, 1191, 1226, 1247, 1268, 1471, 1500, 1505, 1696, 1697, 2042, 2370, 2633, 2769, 2777, 3033, 3100, 3133, 3159.

Verwey

2991. Delcour, Jean-Marie. "Verwey est-il un poète 'cérébral'?" *EG* 19 (1964):349-62.

2992. Kamerbeek, J.,Jr. *Albert Verwey en het nieuwe classicisme.* Groningen: Wolters, 1966. 124 pp.

2993. Kazemier, G. *Verwey en Gorter: Persephone en Mei.* Groningen: Noordhoff. [1965?]

2994. Jong, Martien J.G. de. " 'Dichters en der Schoonheid zonen':Albert Verwey en Stefan George." *SpL* 9(1966):272-80.

2995. Pannwitz, Rudolf. *Albert Verwey und Stefan George:Zu Verweys hunderstem Geburtstag.* Heidelberg: Schneider, 1965. 88 pp.

2996. Pauw, Wilfried de. *De vriendschap van Albert Verwey en Stefan George.* (Mededelings van die Univ. van S. Afrika 26.) Pretoria: U. of So. Africa, 1960. 57 pp. [Sum. in Fr.]

2997. Weevers, Theodor. "Albert Verwey and Stefan George:Their Conflicting Affinities." *GL&L* 22(1969): 79-89.

2998. ———. *Mythe en Vorm in de gedichten van Albert Verwey:Een inleiding tot zijn poëzie.* (Zwolse reeks van taal en letterkundige studies, 17.) Zwolle: Tjeeuk Willink, 1965.

Vielé-Griffin

2999. Beaunier, A. "Francis Vielé-Griffin." *MdF* 40(1901):577-610.

3000. Cours, Jean de. *Francis Vielé-Griffin:Son oeuvre-sa pensée-son art.* Paris: Champion, 1930. 242 pp.

3001. ———. "Un poéte symboliste:

Francis Vielé-Griffin." *MdF* 161 (1923):577-602.

3002. Hérold, A.-F. "Notes sur la 'Chevauché d'Yeldis'." *MdF* 8(juillet 1893):220-26.

3003. Keating, L.C. "Francis Vielé-Griffin and America." *Symposium* 14(1960):276-81.

3004. Kuhn, Reinhard C. "Vielé-Griffin and the Symbolist Movement." *DA* 18(1958):233(Princeton).

3005. ———. "Viélé-Griffin et les mouvements poétiques de son temps." *MdF* 335(1959):447-75.

3006. Nicolas, H. *La vie passionnée d'un poète symboliste et son évolution parallèle de son inspiration et de son art.* Paris: U. of Paris, 1958. [Diss.]

3007. Ogden, P. *A Study of the Aesthetics, Themes, Sources and Poetic Techniques of a Symbolist Poet.* Leeds: U. of Leeds, 1959-60. [Diss.]

3008. Retté, Adolphe. "Francis Viélé-Griffin." *La Plume* 96(avril 1893): 167-88.

3009. Scalamandrè, Raffaele. *Francis Vielé-Griffin e il simbolismo.* Vibo Valentia: M. Bonelli, 1950. 26 pp.

3010. Vielé-Griffin, F. "La désespérance du Parnasse." *MdF* 29(mars 1899): 577-81.

See also 1039.

Villiers de l'Isle-Adam

3011. Arnold, Ivor A. "Style and Structure in the Shorter Fiction of Villiers de l'Isle-Adam." *DAI* 32(1971): 954A(Toronto).

3012. Bailly, Emond. "Villiers de l'Isle-Adam." *L'Ermitage* 2(1892):161-70.

3013. Bordeaux, Henri. "Les premières poésies de Villiers de l'Isle-Adam." *Entretiens politiques et littéraires* 43 (mai 1893):440-51; 44(juin 1893): 511-19.

3014. Burguet, Frantz A. *Villiers de*

l'Isle-Adam. Paris: Mercure de France, 1965. 252 pp.

3015. Drougard, E. "Encore les *Elixirs du Diable*." *RLC* 15(1935):305-09.

3016. Friedman, M.J. "A Revaluation of *Axel*." *MD* (1959):236-43.

3017. Goldgar, Harry. "*Axel* de Villiers de l'Isle-Adam et *The Shadowy Waters* de W.B. Yeats." *RLC* 24 (1950):563-74.

3018. Jean-Marquerose. "Un mot de Villiers de l'Isle-Adam." *La Plume* 242(mai 1899):317.

3019. Lazare, Bernard. " 'Villiers de l'Isle-Adam' par Stéphane Mallarmé." *Entretiens politiques et littéraires* 32 (nov 1892):233-36. [Rev. art.]

3020. Noulet, Emilie. "Villiers de l'Isle-Adam y Stéphane Mallarmé." *Filosofía y Letras* 12(Oct-Dic 1943):291-300.

3021. Parks, Lloyd C. "The Influence of Villiers de l'Isle-Adam on W.B. Yeats." *DA* 20(1960):2784-85 (Washington).

3022. Raitt, A.W. "Villiers de l'Isle-Adam et l'illusionnisme des Symbolistes." *CAIEF* 12(1960):175-87.

3023. ———. *Villiers de l'Isle-Adam et le mouvement symboliste*. Paris: Corti, 1965. 421 pp. [Poe, Baudelaire, Dujardin, Gourmont, Mallarmé, Wagner.]

3024. Régnier, Henri de. "Notes dramatiques:Apropos d'*Axël* de Villier de l'Isle-Adam." *Entretiens politiques et littéraires* 36(fév 1893):138-40.

3025. Rose, Marilyn G. "*Axel*:Play and Hearsay." *CompD* 2(1968):173-84.

See also 436, 572, 1122, 1872, 2464, 2765, 3036, 3129, 3161.

Vinea

3026. Cioculescu, Şerban. "Despre universul poetic al lui Ion Vinea." *RoLit* 2Mar(1972):7.

Vivier

3027. Thiry, Marcel. "Robert Vivier, poète français de Belgique, sa place entre le symbolisme et le surréalisme." *PP* 15(1972):129-41.

Voronyj

3028. Holubenko, S. "Bat'ko ukrajins'koho modernizmu:Do 100-riččja narodžennja Mykoly Voronoho." *Moloda Ukrajina* 22,i(1972):2-4.

Wagner

3029. Anon. "Wagners invloed op de literatuur." *Mens en Melodie* 7(1952): 177-78.

3030. Beaufils, Marcel. *Wagner et le wagnérisme*. Paris: Aubier, 1947.

3031. Bertram, Johannes. *Mythos, Symbol, Idee in Richard Wagners Musik-Dramen*. Hamburg: Hamburger Kulturverlag, 1957. 336 pp.

3032. Carcassonne, E. "Wagner et Mallarmé." *RLC* 16(1936):347-66.

3033. Cœuroy, André. *Wagner et l'esprit romantique. Wagner et la France. Le Wagnérisme littéraire*. Paris: Gallimard, 1965. 380 pp.

3034. Corneau, André. "Nerthal:*L'anneau de Niebelung–L'or dans un drame wagnérien*." *Revue Blanche* 16(1898):157. [Rev. art.]

3035. Dauriac, Lionel. "L'esthétisme et le wagnérisme." *Grande revue* 11 (1899):582-603.

3036. Drougard, E. "Richard Wagner et Villiers de l'Isle-Adam." *RLC* 14 (1934):297-330.

3037. Evenepoel, Edmond. *Le wagnérisme hors d'Allemagne*. Paris: Fischbacher, 1891. 300 pp.

3038. Fiser, Emeric. *Le symbole littéraire:Essai sur la signification du symbole chez Wagner, Baudelaire,*

Mallarmé, Bergson et Marcel Proust. Paris: J. Corti, 1941. 223 pp.

3039. Friedlaender, A.H. von. "Der Wagner-Cultus in Frankreich." *Gegenwart* 58,xxxix(29 Sept 1900): 202-04.

3040. Gauthier-Villars. "Une nouvelle traduction de Wagner." *La Plume* 152(août 1895):252.

3041. Jäckel, Kurt. *Richard Wagner in der französischen Literatur.* 3 vols. Breslau:Priebatsch, 1931-32.

3042. Knust, Herbert. *Wagner, the King, and* The Waste Land. (Penn. State Studies 22.) University Park: Penn. State U. Comm. on Research, 1968.

3043. Lambert, L. Gary. "Richard Wagner vu par Charles Baudelaire," 38-45 in Walter C. Kraft,ed. *Proceedings: Pacific Northwest Conference on Foreign Languages.* Twenty-second Annual Meeting, April 16-17, 1971. Vol. 22. Corvallis:Ore. State U., 1971.

3044. Lassus, J. de. "L'influence wagnérienne sur le symbolisme français." *Vie des Peuples* (Dec 1925):673-87.

3045. Malvost, Henry de. "Lettre à M.C. Saint-Saens." *Entretiens politiques et littéraires* 54(nov 1893):411-18.

3046. Marinetti, F.T. "Mascagni contre Wagner." *La Plume* 284(fév 1901): 127-28.

3047. Robert, Gustave. "Richard Wagner et Max Nordau." *L'Ermitage* 2 (1894):81-86.

3048. Ruprecht, Erich. *Der Mythos bei Wagner und Nietzsche:Seine Bedeutung als Lebens- und Gestaltungsproblem.* Berlin: Junker und Dünnhaupt, 1938. 256 pp.

3049. Spigl, Friedrich. "Wagner et Debussy." *Revue Blanche* 27(1902): 517-33.

3050. Stein, H. von. *Dichtung und Musik im Werk Richard Wagners.* Berlin: de Gruyter, 1962. 323 pp.

3051. Stein, Jack M. *Richard Wagner and the Synthesis of the Arts.* Detroit: Wayne State U.P., 1960. 229 pp.

3052. Vanor, George. "L'art de Richard Wagner." *Entretiens politiques et littéraires* 59(sept 1893):197-201.

3053. ———. "Le drame wagnérien." *Entretiens politiques et littéraires* 36(fév 1893):167-74; 38(mars 1893):216-27.

3054. Welti, Heinrich. "Die Nachfolge Richard Wagners." *Cosmopolis* 1(mars 1896).

3055. Willy [Henry G.-V.]. "Wagner embêté par Nordau." *La Plume* 107 (oct 1893):406-07.

3056. ———. "Wagner et Godebski." *La Plume* 143(avril 1895):148-51. [Interview.]

3057. Woolley, Grange. *Richard Wagner et le symbolisme français:Les rapports principaux entre le wagnérisme et l'évolution de l'idée symboliste.* Paris: Presses univs, 1931. 180 pp.

3058. Wyzewa, Isabelle de. La Revue wagnérienne:Essai sur l'interprétation esthétique de Wagner en France. Paris: Perrin, 1934. 217 pp.

3059. Wyzewa, Teodor de. "La musique wagnérienne." *Revue wagnérienne* 6 (juillet 1886):183-93; 7(août 1886): 259-68.

See also 272, 379, 897, 936, 939, 947, 957, 1061, 1068, 1413, 1534, 2126, 2160, 2254, 2286, 2314, 2321, 2761, 2767, 2774, 3023, 3125.

Whitman

3060. Jones, P. Mansell. "Whitman and the Symbolists." *FS* 2(1948):54-67.

3061. Pongs, H. "Walt Whitman und Stefan George." *CL* 4(1952):289-322.

3062. Randall, H.F. "Whitman and Verhaeren—Priests of Human Brother-hood." *FR* 16(1942):36-43.

3063. Vielé-Griffin, Francis. "Autobio-graphie de Walt Whitman." *Entre-tiens politiques et littéraires* 25(avril 1892):166-69.

See also 292, 1658.

Wilde

3064. Baker, Houston A.,Jr. "A Trage-dy of the Artist:*The Picture of Dor-ian Gray.*" *NCF* 24(1969):349-55.

3065. Breugelmans, René. "Alienation, the Destiny of Modern Literature? Oscar Wilde and Stefan George." *Mosaic* 2,i(1968):18-28.

3066. ———. "The Reconciliation of Op-posites in the Mythopoesis of Wilde, George, and Hofmannsthal," 248-54 in Ralph W. Baldner,ed. *Proceedings: Pacific Northwest Conference on For-eign Languages*. Twenty-first Annual Meeting, April 3-4, 1970. Vol. 21. Victoria, B.C.: U. of Victoria, 1970.

3067. ———. "De Weerklank van Oscar Wilde in Nederland en Vlaanderen (1880-1960)." *SGG* 3(1961):53-144.

3068. Brontë, Diana. "The Influence of Oscar Wilde in the Life and Works of André Gide." *DAI* 30(1970):3425A-26A(N.C.,Chapel Hill).

3069. Carrillo, Gomez. "Comment Oscar Wilde rêva Salomé." *La Plume* 323 (oct 1902):1149-53.

3070. Clive, H.P. "Oscar Wilde's First Meeting with Mallarmé. *FS* 24 (1970):145-49.

3071. Fabbricatore, P. "Il trionfo dell'arte sulla vita." *LS* 12,ii(Mar-Apr 1963):17-23.

3072. Joost, Nicholas, and Franklin E. Court. "*Salomé*, the Moon, Oscar Wilde's Aesthetics:A Reading of the Play." *PLL* 8,supp.(1972):96-111.

3073. Jullian, Philippe. *Oscar Wilde*. New York: Viking Press, 1973. [Fr.

ed. Paris: Librairie académique Perr-in, 1967. 415 pp.]

3074. Lazare, Bernard. "Les livres." *Entretiens politiques et littéraires* 41 (avril 1893):282-84. [Rev. art.]

3075. Merrill, Stuart. "Pour Oscar Wilde:Epilogue." *La Plume* 161(janv 1896):8-10.

3076. Nassaar, Christopher S. "Into the Demon Universe:A Literary Explora-tion of Oscar Wilde." *DAI* 32 (1972):638A(Wis., Madison).

3077. Pappas, John J. "The Flower and the Beast:A Study of Oscar Wilde's Antithetical Attitudes Toward Na-ture and Man in *The Picture of Dorian Gray.*" *ELT* 15(1972):37-48.

3078. Recoulley, Alfred L.,III. "Oscar Wilde, the Dandy-Artist:A Study of Dandyism in the Life and Works of Oscar Wilde, With Particular Atten-tion Given to the Intellectual Bases of Wilde's Dandyism." *DAI* 30 (1969):290A(N.C., Chapel Hill).

3079. Régnier, Henri de. "Notes drama-tiques." *Entretiens politiques et lit-téraires* 38(mars 1893):236-38. [Rev. art.]

3080. Roditi, Edouard. *Oscar Wilde*. New York: New Directions, 1946. 256 pp.

3081. Schrickx, W. "Oscar Wilde in Bel-gium in 1879 and His Early Interest in Théophile Gautier." *RLV* 37 (1971):245-56.

3082. Souffrin, Eileen. "La rencontre de Wilde et de Mallarmé." *RLC* 33 (1959):529-35.

3083. Symons, Arthur. "Un artiste dans ses attitudes." *La Plume* 371(mai 1905):397-400.

See also 289, 1119, 1120, 1133, 1674, 1675, 1688, 1716, 1744, 2422.

Williams, W.C. *See* 1083.

Wyspiański

3084. Jakubowski, J.Z. *Stanislaw Wyspiański*. Warsaw: P.Z. Wyd. Szk., 1961.

3085. Kolbuszewski, Stanislas. "Stanislas Wyspiański et le théâtre polonais moderne." *ESl* 5(1961):131-52.

3086. ———. *Le théâtre de S. Wyspiański*. Warsaw: P.W.N. (1962).

3087. Łempicka, A. "Problemy wyzwolenia." *PL* 7(1961):301-38.

3088. ———. Wesele *we wspomnieniach i krytyce*. Cracow: Wyd. Literackie, 1961.

3089. Miodońska-Brookes, Ewa. "O kompozycyji czasu dramatycznego w utworach S. Wyspiańskiego:Na przykladzie *Achilleis.*" *RuchL* 12,iii (1971):141-48.

3090. Natanson, Wojciech. *Stanisław Wyspiański:Próba nowego spojrzenia*. Poznań: Wydawn. Poznańskie, 1966.

3091. Nowakowski, Jan. "Symbolizm i dramaturgia Wyspiańskiego." *PL* 53 (1962):423-50.

3092. ———. "Wyspiańskiego wizje historii." *ŻLit* 20(20 Dec 1970):6-7.

3093. Pszczołowska, Lucylla. "Wiersz–styl–dialog:Wokół dwóch redakcji 'Warszawianki'." *PL* 56,iv(1965): 439-64.

3094. Stokowa, Maria. *Kalendarz życia i twórczości Stanisława Wyspiańskiego*, T.I:*1869-1890*. Kraków: Wydawn. Literackie, 1971. 284 pp.

3095. Terlecki, Tymon. "Stanislaw Wyspianski and the Poetics of Symbolist Drama." *PolR* 15,iv (1970):55-63.

3096. ———. *Wyspiański i my*. London: B. Swiderski, 1957. 12 pp.

3097. ———. *Wyspiański in Two Perspectives*. Romae: Inst. Historicum Polonicum, 1971. 16 pp.

3098. Zimmer, Szczepan K. *Stanislaw Wyspiański, Biographical Sketch*. Tr. Halina Zimmer. Essen: n.p., 1959.

Wyzema

3099. Delsemme, Paul. *Theodor de Wyzema et le cosmopolitisme littéraire en France à l'époque du symbolisme.* 2 vols. Bruxelles: Presses Univs. de Bruxelles, 1967. 391 + 135 pp. [Vol. 2 bibliog.]

3100. Girolamo, Nicola di. *Teodor de Wyzema dall simbolismo al tradition, 1885-1887*. Bologna: Patròn, 1969. 190 pp.

See also 879.

Yeats

3101. Adlard, John. *Stenbock, Yeats and the Nineties:With an Hitherto Unpublished Essay by Arthur Symons and a Bibliography by Timothy Smith.* London: Cecil and Amelia Woolf. 1969. 113 pp.

3102. Allen, James L.,Jr. "Bird Symbolism in the Work of William Butler Yeats." *DA* 20(1960):117-22(U. of Fla.).

3103. ———. "William Butler Yeats's One Myth." *Person* 45(1964): 524-32.

3104. ———. "Yeats' Bird-Soul Symbolism." *TCL* 6(1960):117-22.

3105. Archibald, Douglas N. "Yeats's Encounters:Observations on Literary Influence and Literary History." *NLH* 1(1970):439-69.

3106. Barnes, T.R. "Yeats, Synge, Ibsen and Strindberg." *Scrutiny* 5(1936): 257-62.

3107. Block, Haskell M. "Some Concepts of the Literary Elite at the Turn of the Century." *Mosaic* 5 (1972):57-64.

3108. Cassidy, Robert L. "W.B. Yeats' Poetry and Prose:The Landscape of Art." *DAI* 33(1972):748A(W. Ontario).

3109. Cheadle, B.O. "Yeats and Symbolism." *ESA* 12(1969):132-50.

3110. Clarke, David R. "Yeats and the Modern Theatre." *Threshold* 4,ii (1960):36-56.

3111. Clark, David R., and George Mayhew,eds. *A Tower of Polished Black Stones:Early Versons of The Shadowy Waters*. Dublin: Dolmen Press, 1971. 71 pp. [Illus. by Leonard Baskin and drawings by Y.]

3112. Coltrane, Robert. "From Legend to Literature:W.B. Yeats and the Cuchulain Cycle." *LHR* 12(1971): 24-46.

3113. Colwell, Frederic S. "W.B. Yeats: The Dimensions of Poetic Vision." *DA* 27(1966):1053A(Mich. State).

3114. Cosman, Madeleine P. "Mannered Passion:W.B. Yeats and the Ossianic Myths." *WHR* 14(1960):163-71.

3115. Davis, Edward. *Yeat's Early Contacts with French Poetry*. (Communications of the Univ. of South Africa 29.) Pretoria: U. of So. Africa, 1961. 63 pp.

3116. Davray, Henry. "William Butler Yeats." *L'Ermitage* 2(1896):88-96.

3117. Domville, Eric. *A Concordance to the Plays of W.B. Yeats*. 2 vols. Ithaca, N.Y.: Cornell U.P., 1972.

3118. Donoghue, Denis,ed. *The Integrity of Yeats*. (The Thomas Davis Lectures.) Cork, Ireland: Mercier Press, 1964. 70 pp. [Essays by var. hands.]

3119. Donoghue, Denis. *William Butler Yeats*. New York: Viking, 1971.

3120. Donoghue, Denis, and J.R. Mulryne,eds. *An Honoured Guest:New Essays on W.B. Yeats*. London: E. Arnold, 1965. 196 pp.

3121. DuVall, Cecil H., and John B. Humma. "The Opening Phrase of Yeats' 'Leda and the Swan'." *RS* 40 (1972):131-32.

3122. Edwards, Michael. "Yeats and the Moon." *Adam* 334-336(1969):27-29.

3123. Ellmann, Richard. *The Identity of Yeats*. New York: Oxford U.P. 1954. 343 pp. [2nd ed., 1964.]

3124. ——. *Yeats:The Man and the Masks*. New York: Macmillan, 1948. 331 pp.

3125. Engleberg, Edward. "Picture and Gesture in the Yeatsian Aesthetic." *Criticism* 3(1960):101-20.

3126. ——. *The Vast Design:Patterns in W.B. Yeats's Aesthetic*. Toronto: U. of Toronto P., 1964. 224 pp.

3127. Fackler, Herbert V. "W.B. Yeats' *Deirdre*:Intensity by Condensation." *ForumH* 6(1968):43-46.

3128. Farrelly, James P. "Cuchulain: Yeats' 'Mental Traveller'." *HussR* 4 (1970):32-41.

3129. Faulkner, Peter. "Yeats as Critic." *Criticism* 4(1962):328-39.

3130. Friedman, Barton R. "Reflections of a Son of Talma:A Reading of *The Death of Cuchulain*." *ArQ* 27 (1971):308-20.

3131. Frye, Northrop. "The Top of the Tower:A Study of the Imagery of Yeats." *SoR* 5(1969):850-71.

3132. ——. "Yeats and the Language of Symbolism." *UTQ* 17(1947):1-7.

3133. Fullwood, Daphne. "The Influence on W.B. Yeats of Some French Poets (Mallarmé, Verlaine, Claudel)." *SoR* 6(1970):356-79.

3134. Green, J.T. "Symbolism in Yeats' Poetry." *Fort Hare Papers* 4,iii (1969):11-23.

3135. Haerdter, Michael. "William Butler Yeats—Irisches Theatre zwischen Symbolismus und Expressionismus." *MuK* 13(1965):30-42.

3136. Harrison, Dorothy G. "W.B. Yeats's Plays:The Ritual of a Lost Faith." *DAI* 32(1971):2091A (S.U.N.Y., Albany).

3137. Haydn, Hiram. "The Last of the Romantics:An Introduction to the Symbolism of W.B. Yeats." *SR* 15 (1947):297-323.

3138. Henn, Thomas R. *The Lonely Tower:Studies in the Poetry of W.B. Yeats.* London: Methuen, 1950. 362 pp.

3139. Hoffman, Daniel G. *Barbarous Knowledge:Myth in the Poetry of Yeats, Graves, & Muir.* N.Y.: Oxford U.P., 1967. 266 pp.

3140. Jeffares, A. Norman, and K.G.W. Cross,eds. *In Excited Reverie:A Centenary Tribute to William Butler Yeats, 1865-1939.* London and New York: Macmillan, 1965. 353 pp.

3141. Kayser, Wolfgang. "W.B. Yeats: Der dichterische Symbolismus übersetzt und erläutert," 239-48 in *Gestaltung-Umgestaltung:Festschrift zum 75. Geburtstag von Hermann August Korff.* Leipzig: Koehler und Amelang, 1957.

3142. Killen, A.M. "Some French Influences in the Works of W.B. Yeats at the End of the Nineteenth Century." *CLS* 8(1942):1-8.

3143. Klimek, Theodor. *Symbol und Wirklichkeit bei W.B. Yeats.* (AKML 45.) Bonn: Bouvier, 1967. 223 pp.

3144. Levine, Bernard. *The Dissolving Image.* Detroit: Wayne State U.P., 1970. 180 pp.

3145. Linebarger, James M. "Yeats' Symbolist Method and the Play:*Purgatory*." *DA* 24(1964):3750-51 (Emory).

3146. Maxwell, D.E.S., and S.B. Bushrui,eds. *W.B. Yeats, 1865-1965:Centenary Essays on the Art of W.B. Yeats.* Ibadan: Ibadan U.P., 1965. 252 pp.

3147. Melchiori, Giorgio. *The Whole Mystery of Art:Pattern into Poetry in the Work of W.B. Yeats.* London: Routledge and K. Paul, 1960. 360 pp.

3148. Moore, John R. "Evolution of Myth in the Plays of W.B. Yeats." *DA* 17(1957):1556-57(Columbia).

3149. ———. *Masks of Love and Death: Yeats as Dramatist.* Ithaca: Cornell U.P., 1971. 361 pp.

3150. Napoli, Joanne L. "The Meaning of the Dancer in the Poetry of William Butler Yeats." *DAI* 33(1972):2945A(Mass.).

3151. O'Brien, James. "Yeats' Discoveries of Self in 'The Wild Swans at Coole'." *CLQ* 8(1968):1-13.

3152. O'Donnell, James P. Sailing to Byzantium:*A Study in the Development of the Later Style and Symbolism in the Poetry of William Butler Yeats.* Cambridge: Harvard U.P. 1939. 95 pp.

3153. Orel, Harold. *The Development of William Butler Yeats:1885-1900.* Lawrence: U. of Kan. Pubs., 1968. 104 pp.

3154. Parkinson, Thomas. *W.B. Yeats, Self-Critic:A Study of His Early Verse [and] The Later Poetry.* 2 vols. in 1. Berkeley: U. of Calif. P., 1971 [1972]. [New printing, in one vol. of books prev. pub.]

3155. Pauly, Marie Hélène. "W.B. Yeats et les symbolistes français." *RLC* 20 (1940):13-33.

3156. Piggott, Jan R. "The Context of Yeats's 'Sailing to Byzantium'." *DAI* 32(1972):3962A(Calif., Davis).

3157. Rajan, B. "W.B. Yeats and the Unity of Being." *Nineteenth Century and After* 146(Sept 1949):150-61.

3158. Ransom, John C. "Yeats and His Symbols." *KR* 1(1939):309-22.

3159. Revard, Stella. "Verlaine and Yeats's 'A Dialogue of Self and Soul'." *PLL* 7(1971):272-78.

3160. ———. "Yeats, Mallarmé, and the Archetypal Feminine." *PLL* 8,supp. (1972):122-27.

3161. Rose, Marilyn G. "Yeats's Use of *Axël*." *CompD* 4(1970):253-64.

3162. Savage, D.S. "The Aestheticism of W.B. Yeats." *KR* 7(1945):118-34.

3163. Schrickx, W. "William Butler

Yeats: Symbolist cn visionair Dichter." *VlG* 49(1965):380-96.

3164. Seiden, Morton I. *William Butler Yeats:The Poet as a Mythmaker, 1865-1939.* East Lansing: Mich State U.P., 1962. 397 pp.

3165. Slattery, M.P. "*Deirdre*:The Mingling of Contraries in Plot and Symbolism." *MD* 11(1969):400-03.

3166. Spender, Stephen. "La crise des symboles." *France Libre* 7(15 jan 1944):206-10.

3167. Spivak, Gayatri C. "A Stylistic Contrast Between Yeats and Mallarmé." *Lang&S* 5(1972):100-07.

3168. Tindall, William Y. "The Symbolism of W.B. Yeats." *Accent* 5 (1945):203-12.

3169. Tsukimura, R. "The Language of Symbolism in Yeats and Hagiwara." *DA* 28(1968):3689A(Ind.).

3170. Unger, Leonard. "Yeats and *Hamlet*." *SoR* 6(1970):698-709.

3171. Ure, Peter. *Towards a Mythology: Studies in the Poetry of W.B. Yeats.* Liverpool: Univ. Press of Liverpool; London: Hodder & Stoughton, 1946. 123 pp.

3172. Verhulst, Margaret M. "Myth and Symbol in the Plays of William Butler Yeats." *DAI* 30(1970):3028A (Texas, Austin).

3173. Watanabe, Junko,ed. *The Symbolism of W.B. Yeats:His Doctrine of 'The Mask'.* (Collected Essays by the Members of the Faculty, 11.) Kyoritsu, Japan: Kyoritsu Women's Junior College, 1968.

3174. Watts, Harold H. "Yeats and Lapsed Mythology." *Renascence* 3 (1951):107-12.

3175. Webster, Brenda A.S. "Dream and the Dreamer in the Works of W.B. Yeats." *DA* 28(1968):4192A(Calif., Berkeley).

3176. ———. "Yeats' *The Shadowy Waters*:Oral Motifs and Identity in the Drafts." *AI* 28(1971):3-16.

3177. Wilson, F.A.C. *Yeats's Iconography.* New York: Macmillan, 1960.

3178. Witt, Marion. "A Note on Yeats and Symons." *N&Q* 7(1960):467-69.

3179. Youngblood, Sarah. "Yeats and the Symbolists." *SCB* 28(1968):82.

3180. Yun, Chang S. "The Tragic Theatre:The Nō and Yeat's Dance Plays." *DAI* 33(1973):3608A-09A(Princeton.).

See also 289, 905, 1000, 1011, 1050, 1857, 1926a, 2315, 2479, 2579, 2747, 2834, 2988, 3017, 3021.

Zamyatin

3181. Proffer, Carl R. "Notes on the Imagery in Zamjatin's *We*." *SEEJ* 7(1963):269-78.

Żeromski

3182. Paszek, Jerzy. "Symbol naczelny 'popioløw' Żeromskiego." *PL* 62,iii (1971):51-84.

Author Index

A. J. 2379
Aarnes, Asbjorn 1210
Abastado, Claude 2109
Abbatte, F. 718
Abel, Richard O. 1577, 2427
Abeles, Sally 924
Abramov, A. 2076
Abraham, Claude K. 2882
Adam, Paul 1, 194, 1347
Adams, Elsie B. 2728
Adéma, Pierre M. 1173
Adlard, John 3101
Admussen, Richard L. 1177
Adriani, Bruno 1211
Aggeler, William F. 1212
Agosti, Stefano 2110
Aguado-Andreut, Salvador 1489

Aguirre, J.M. 2030
Ahearn, Edward J. 2588
Ahlström, Stellan 2757
Aigrisse, Gilberte 2866
Ajalbert, Jean 383
Albers, Josef 1930
Albers, N.B. 1846
Albert, Henri 334, 1787, 1867
Albornoz, Aurora de 1897
Albrecht, Hellmuth F.G. 335, 1805
Alewyn, Richard 1806
Alexander, Jean 2446, 2447
Alexander, Paul J. 1113
Alexandre, Arsène 2684
Allard, R. 964
Allemann, Beda 2543
Allen, James L., Jr. 2758, 3102, 3103, 3104

Allen, Rubert C.   1647, 1648, 1649, 1898

Allinger, Erich   1666

Alonso, Amado   1490

Alvard, J.   719

Alvim, Tereza C.   384

Aman-Jean, Francois   385

Amaya, Mario   720, 721, 722

Ames, Russell   1578

Amiot, Anne-Marie   2711

Amsinck, Hanne   1200

Ancey, Georges   1868

Anderson, Harry   1434, 1435, 1436

Anderson, David D.   1454

Anderson, R. R.   386

Angelloz, J.   1667

Angers, Pierre   2

Anselmi, Luciano   2803

Antcliffe, H.   2448

Antignani, Gerardo   390

Antoine, Emile   966

Antrim, Harry T.   1579

Antunes, Manuel   391

Apetroaie, Ion   392

Apollinaire, Guillaume

Apollonino, Mario   393

Apostel, Léo   6

Aprea, Vincenzo   1466

Araujo, Murillo   394

Arbogast, Hubert   1668

Arbbour, Romeo   7

Archibald, Douglas N.   3105

Ardennais, Pierre l'   2589

Argan, Guilio C.   1931

Argüello, Santiago   1491

Arland, M.

Armstrong-Wallis   724

Arnaud, Noël   881

Arnauld, Michel   8, 967, 2519

Arnauld, R.   9

Arnold, A. James   2811

Arnold, Ivor A.   3011

Arnold, Paul   1213

Arnoult, P.   2570

Arnoux, Alexandre   1443

Ascione, Marc   2591

Asfar, Gabriel V.   1769

Ashmurst, A.W.   1492

Ashton, Dore   725, 2503

Asmus, V.   657

Atal, G.   706

Aubéry, Pierre   10, 395

Audard, Jean   2112, 2188, 2196

Auriant   2113

Aurier, G.-A.   726, 1661

Austin, Lloyd J.   21, 1114, 1214, 1215, 2114, 2115, 2116, 2117, 2118, 2119, 2120, 2121

Austin, William W.   915

Auty, R.   1798

Avila, Affonso   396

Axelrod, Steven   1216

Ayda, A.   2122

Azevedo, Leodegário A. de, filho   397

Babcock, James C.   1849

Bachelard, Gaston   2592

Bachrach, A.G.H.   1217

Backès, Jean-Louis   968

Baconsky, Rodica   642

BAcou, Roseline   12, 2504

Bailbé, Joseph-Marc   1896

Bailly, Edmond   2685, 3012

Bajomée, Danielle   1972

Baju, Anatole   398, 399, 400

Baker, Houston A., Jr.   13, 3064

Balakian, Anna   14, 15, 16, 401

Balasov, Nikolai   402

Baldick, Robert   778, 1850

Baldner, Ralph W.   3066

Balotă, Nicolae   336

Balseiro, José A.   1493

Baltag, Cezar   1187

Banasević, Nikola   713, 1391

Bancroft, David   1413

Bandy, L.J.   969

Bandy, William T.   1218, 1219, 1220, 1221, 1222, 2449, 2450

Banjanin, Milica E.   1223

Bänsch, Dieter   373

Barata, Mário   1148

Barbey d'Aurevilly, J.A.   882

Barbier, Carl   2123

Barea, José Antonio   17

Barilli, Renato   727, 728

Bàrnes, T.R.   3106

Barnett, Pat   1324

Baróti, Dezsö   2593

Barre, André   18

Barrès, Maurice   2326

Barrès, Philippe   2890

Barth, E.   1224
Barthals, Joseph   337
Baruk, Henri   19
Barzel, Hillel   707
Baskin, Leonard   3111
Basler, Adolphie   1348
Basted, Ned   2812, 2813
Bastos, C. Tavares   403
Bataille, Henry   20
Batchelor, C.M.   2891
Bathari, Jane   1533
Bathilliat, Marcel   1404
Batterby, Kenneth A.   2544
Battisti, Eugenio   729
Baudelaire, Charles P.   21, 2450
Baudot, Alain   2892
Baudry, Jean-Louis   2594
Bauer, Sibylle   1832
Bautista, Juan   411
Bayerschmidt, Carl F.   2761
Bayón, Damian C.   1650
Bays, Gwendolyn   22
Bazalgette, Léon   2048
Beatty, R.C.   23, 274
Beaubourg, Maurice   883
Beaufils, Marcel   3030
Beaujon, Georges   404
Beaunier, André   405, 406, 970, 2595,
    2999
Beausire, Pierre   2124
Becker, Aimé   1414
Becker, Carl   407
Becker, W.   1669
Bedwell, Carol E.B.   338
Beebe, Maurice   24
Beery, Judith A   1580
Béguin, Albert   1115
Behrens, Ralph   1632
Belchior, Maria De Lourdes   2893, 2894
Bell, S.M.   25
Bell, W.M.L.   25
Bellemin Noël, Jean   2306, 2814
Bellot, Etienne   26
Belmás, Antonio O.   1494
Bely, Andrei   27, 1331
Belyj, Andrej   27, 1331
Bémol, Maurice   2545
Benamoux, Michel   28, 1973, 2125,
    2742, 2743, 2744, 2745
Benda, Julien   2126

Bénédite, Léonce   730, 731
Benet, Rafael   731a
Benet Aurell, Jorge   731a
Benton, Rita   951
Béraud, H.   2596
Berberove, Nina   101
Berchan, Richard   1415
Bercovitch, Sacvan   275
Berendsohn, Walter A.   1807
Bérenger, Henry   884
Bergen-Le-Play, Louis   2597
Berger de Guevara, Viviane   2867
Berger, Klaus   732, 2505
Bergonzi, Bernard   276
Bergsten, Staffan   1581
Bergstrøm-Nielsen, Carl   339
Bérimont, Luc   2598
Berkov, P.N.   1395
Bernac, Pierre   916
Bernard, Jean-Marc   408
Bernard, Suzanne   2127
Bernardelli, Giuseppe   409, 2895, 2896
Berry, R.M.   410
Bersier, J.E.   2506
Berthelot, Ph.   29
Bertocci, Angelo   1225
Bertram, Johannes   3031
Bertran, P.   411
Betz, Dorothy K.M.   1226
Beyette, Thomas K.   227
Bianchi, Ruggero   1553, 2024
Bianquis, Geneviève   1808
Bigley, B.M.   1869
Bigongiari, Piero   412, 2804
Billy, André   413
Binder, Alois   1670
Binet, Alfred   971
Binni, Walter   414
Bird, Edward A.   2128
Bjørnsen, Johan F.   2397
Blake, Patricia   2077
Blanchart, Paul   2049
Blanchot, Maurice   1100
Blanco Aguinaga, Carlos   1183
Blank, Bernard   1671
Blessing, Richard   2746
Blisset, William F.   2314
Block, Haskell M.   278, 972, 973, 1809,
    2129, 2130, 2759, 3107
Blok, Aleksandr   658, 1361

Blok, W. 1448
Bloom, Harold 2747
Bloy, L. 415
Blum, Jean 975
Blunt, Anthony 2444
Bly, Robert 279
Bo, Carlo 1467, 1899
Bocarov, M.D. 2078
Bocquet, Léon 2712, 2713
Bocsi, J. Peter 1495
Bodart, Roger 2050
Boes, A. Karl 30
Böschenstein, Bernhard 340
Bodson-Thomas, Anny 2674
Bohmer, Helga 2131
Boisdeffre, Pierre de 1741
Boisjolin, J. De 2782
Boissière, Albert 733
Boisson, Madeleine 2520
Bollier, E.P. 1582
Bollnow, Otto F. 2546
Bonenfant, Jean-Charles 2360
Bonfantini, Mario 1227, 2017
Bonneau, Georges 31, 416
Bonnefoy, Yves 32
Bonnet, Henri 2132
Bonomo, Dario 1468
Bordeaux, Henri 976, 3013
Borel, Jacques 33, 1116, 1885
Borges, Jorge 2815
Bornecque, Jacques-Henri 34, 417
Bornmann, Bianca M. 1672, 1673
Bornstein, Paul 1117, 1118
Borowitz, Helen 1119
Bosch, Rafael 1088
Boschot, Adolphe 418, 2133
Bose, Mme. Das 35
Bote, Lidia 419
Boudaille, George 2445
Bouffard, Jean-Claude 2481
Bouhélier, Saint-Georges de 420
Boulestreau, Nicole 2600
Boulez, Pierre 917, 1932
Bounoure, Gabriel 2134
Bourde, P. 645
Bourguignon, Jean 2500
Boussard, Léon 1770
Boutet, Henri 734
Boutique, Alexandre 36
Bouview, E. 37

Bouyer, Raymond 735, 1622
Bower, Faubion 2724
Bowra, C. Maurice 38, 39, 40
Boyle, Robert S.J. 1844
Braak, S. 977, 2395
Brachin, Pierre 341
Braet, Herman 421
Brandt Corstius, Johannes C. 342
Brandt, Torben 1437
Brasil, Assis 422, 423, 424, 2135
Bray, René 41
Breen, Gerald M. 2547
Brench, Angela D. 1228
Bresson, Leo 1438
Breugelmans, René 1674, 1675, 3065,
    3066, 3067
Brewster, Robert R. 2548
Brie, Hartmut 2136, 2451
Briel, Henri de 1228
Briet, Suzanne 2601
Brieu, Jacques 42
Bright, William 918
Brinkmann, Reinhold
Brinkmann, Richard 43, 978
Bristol, Evelyn 2733
Briusov, V. 659
Brockett, Oscar G. 1870
Broderman, Ramón E. 2292
Brodeur, Leo A. 1416
Brodsky, N.L. 664
Brody, Elaine 1534
Brom, Gerard 343
Brombert, Victor 2157, 2816
Brontë, Diana 3068
Bronecque, J.-H. 2897, 2898
Brostrøm, Torben 1439
Brotherston, Gordon 2046
Brotman, D. Bosley 1583
Brown, C. 1633
Brown, Calvin S. 44, 919, 2137
Brown, Eleanor G. 1229
Brückler, Silke 1810
Brulez, Raymond 1759
Bruller-Dauxois 2602
Brun, J. 45
Brunetière, Ferdinant 46, 47, 425, 426
Brunnemann, Anna 1230
Bruns, Gerald L. 2138
Bruscia, Marta 2411
Bruum, Ursula 280, 1089

Bruyr, José   1231, 2051
Bucarelli, Palma   1933
Buccellato, M.   1101
Bucher, Jean Marie F.   2549
Buddeberg, E.   2550
Buet, Charles   1851
Bukáček, Josef   1021
Bulgin, Kathleen   1742
Bullock, Michael   2505
Burch, Francis F.   1444
Burger, Hilde   1811, 1812, 1813
Burger, P.   2373
Burguet, Frantz A.   3014
Burkhart, Charles J.   2315
Burkhart, Gagmar   1332
Burne, Glenn S.   1760
Burns, C.A.   427
Burssow, B.   1558
Burtner, H.W.   2748
Bury, Yetta Blaze de   48, 2899
Bus, L.M.R.   1496
Bushrui, S.B.   3146
Busi, Frederick   2765
Buss, Alcides   1171
Butler, John D.   2327
Butler, Philip F.   1269, 2193
Butor, Michel   2139
Buurman, Henk   1570
Buysse, Cyriel   736
Caccese, Neusa Pensard   428
Cadot, M.   2795
Caldwell, Price   2749
Calid, Piet   2006, 2375
Cambiaire, C.P.   2452
Cambon, Glanco   1584, 2805
Campos, Augusto de   1964
Campos, C.L.   2140
Campos, Haroldo de   2079
Campos, Mario   1497
Camurati, Mireya   1792
Cândido, Antonio   1149
Cansinos Asseüs, Rafael   1120
Canudo, Ricciotto   885
Caramaschi, E.   1761
Carcassonne, E.   3032
Carco, Francis   2900
Carden, Poe   429
Cargo, Robert T.   1231a
Carilla, Emilio   2031
Carlson, Eric W.   2025, 2452a

Carlyle, Thomas   49
Carmody, Francis   50, 430, 1927
Carré, Jean-Marie   2052
Carrel, F.   2141
Carreño, Mada   1498
Carreter, Fernando-Lázaro   1900
Carrier, Warren   1232
Carrillo, Gomez   3069
Carter, A.E.   431, 2901
Carter, Boyd G.   1783
Carter, Thomas P.   51
Cartier, M.   2902
Carton de Wiart, Henry   432
Carvalho, J.G. Herculano de   433
Carvalho, Joaquim de Montezuma de
   2436
Cary, Joseph B., Jr.   979
Casella, Georges   52
Cassidy, Robert L.   3108
Cassirer, Ernest   53, 54
Cassou, Jean   434, 1934, 2551
Castelo, J. Aderaldo   435
Castex, Pierre-Georges   436, 1233, 2142
Castro, E.M.   437
Castro, Silvio   438
Castro Leal, Antonio   2022
Catraro, Atanasio   1469
Cattaui, Georges   1233, 2142
Caussy, Fernand   1102
Cazals, F.E.   2903
Cazamain, Louis   980
Celant, Germano   439
Cellier, Léon   1090, 1234, 2766
Čeremin, G.   2080
Cevasco, G.A.   1852
Chadwick, Charles   55, 2143, 2603, 2904
Chailley, Jacques   2905
Chairi, Joseph   1585
Chalon, Jean   56
Chalupt, René   2906
Chambon, Jean-Pierre   2591
Chamorro, Alejandro H.   1499
Champagne, Marieluise K.   2552
Champagne, Paul   2309
Champigny, Robert   57, 981, 1974
Champsaur, Félicien   2686
Chantovoine, H.   982
Charlsworth, Barbara   282
Charolles, Michel   2604
Charpentier, John   58, 1236

Chasca, Edmundo de   1500
Chassé, Charles   59, 737, 1121
Chast, Denyse   440, 2144
Chastel, André   2145
Chaussivert, J.J.   2907
Chauvel, Jean   2605
Cheadle, B.O.   3109
Chérix, Robert-Benoit   441
Chiari, Joseph   60, 61, 442
Chicoteau, Marcel   62
Child, Theodore   983
Chisholm, A.-R.   283, 2146, 2147,
    2148, 2149, 2150, 2151, 2152,
    2153, 2154, 2606
Chiusano, Italo Alighiero 886
Christa, Boris   1362
Christalder, Martin   284
Christophe, Jules   738
Christophe, Lucien   63, 443
Ciaffé, Gesualdo   1470
Cidade, Hernani   984
Cigada, Sergio   1471
Ciobanu, Valeriu   445
Cioculescu, Barbu   1188
Cioculescu, Šerban   446, 1157, 1356,
    2440, 3026
Cioran, Samuel   1333, 1334, 1335
Ciplijauskaité, Biruté   1771
Čiževskij, Dmitrij   660
Cladel, Léon   1237
Clancy, James H.   1870
Claretie, Jules   65
Clark, Philip F.   1238
Clarke, David R.   3110, 3111
Claudel, Paul   985
Clay, Julien   1935
Clément, Marilène   2607
Clerget, Fernand   2354
Clive, H.P.   3070
Clodomir   2908
Closset, F.   344
Clouard, Henri   447
Cobb, Carl W.   2032
Cobos, Pablo de A.
Coelho, Jacinto de Prado   448, 1391
Coelho, Nelly Novaes   449, 2542
Coeuroy, André   66, 920, 921, 922,
    1044, 3033
Coffman, Stanley K., Jr.   1455
Cohen, Gustave   923

Cohen, J.   2155
Cohn, Adolphe   450
Cohn, Robert G.   67, 2165, 2157,
    2158, 2159, 2483
Collaer, Paul   924, 925
Collet, Georges-Paul   1567, 2316
Colleville, Vicompte de   451
Collie, Michael   1975
Coltrane, Robert   3112
Colum, Padriac   285
Colwell, Frederic S.   3113
Cone, Eduard T.   927
Contorbia, Franco   2806
Cook, Bradford   2667
Cook, Douglas B.   1239
Cooke, Deryck   928
Cooper, Martin   929
Cooperman, Hasye   2160
Coppée, François   739
Coquet, Jean-Claude   2608
Coquiot, Gustave   2507
Corbin, Henry   68
Cordey   2488
Cordiè, Carlo   452, 2714
Corneau, André   3034
Cornell, Kenneth   69, 453, 454
Correa, Gustavo   1651, 1652, 1653
Corrèa, Manuel T.   2161
Cortés, Luis   2800
Cortés, René   455
Cosman, Madeleine P.   3114
Costanzo, Luigi   1501
Costaz, G.   887
Coulon, Marcel   1182, 2002, 2304,
    2328, 2329, 2330, 2609, 2610
Cours, Jean de   3000, 3001
Coursange, Emile   2355
Court, Franklin E.   3072
Courthion, Pierre   740, 2709
Cousturier, Edmond   741
Coutant, Gaston   1103
Coutuvrat, G.   456
Coutuvrat, J.   456
Cowley, Malcolm   2852
Cox, David   930
Crane, R.S.   187
Crawford, Donald A.   2773
Creed, Howard   1459
Crepet, Jacques   1240
Crespa, Angel   457

Cressot, Marcel 1853
Crispoiti, Enrico 70
Crist, Bainbridge 931
Cristea, Dan 1189
Crohanǎlniceanu, Ovid S. 444
Cross, K.G.W. 3140
Crow, Christine M. 2817
Cruickshank, John 2140
Cuadrado, Eduardo G. 2034
Cuénot, Claude 1104, 2909
Czerny, Zygmunt 1154
Daemmrich, Horst S. 1122
Daffner, Hugo 1123
D'Agostino, Nemi 458
Dahmen, Hans 1676
Daix, Pierre 2445
Dakin, Laurence 1560
Dam, C.F. van 1571
Daniel-Rops 2760
Daniels, May 888
Darmángeat, Pierre 2035
Darroch, Ann B. 1502
Dauriac, Lionel 3035
David, Claude 1677, 1678
Davidson, Angus 200
Davidson, Arthur 1586
Davies, Gardner 2162
Davies, L. 932
Davies, Margaret 2611
Davignon, Henry 1620, 2015
David, Edward 3115
Davis, Eugene 986
Davray, Henry D. 742, 889, 987,
    1325, 3116
Davy Charles 988
Daxhelet, Arthur 71, 459
Debauve, J.-L. 1976
Debicki, Andrew P. 1772
DeBrousse, J.-R. 1997
De Castris, A. Leone 2406
Décaudin, Michel 72, 73, 460, 461,
    462, 463, 464, 465, 1124, 1125,
    1172, 1173, 1174, 1175, 1176,
    2053, 2337

Decker, Henry 1241
Dédéyan, Charles 466, 2553
Degron, Henri 989, 2301, 2403, 2538,
    2910
Deguy, Michel 74, 990
Delany, Joan 2796

Delaroche, Achille 75
Delattre, Floris 1242
DeLaura, David J. 1587
Delcour, Jean-Marie 2991
Delfel, Guy 2163
Delille, Eugène 2911
Delior, Paul 1970, 2164, 2331, 2521
Delouze, Marc 2612
Delsemme, Paul 2356, 3099
Delvaille, Bernard 467, 468, 991, 1995,
    2868
Demedts, A. 2054
De Michelis, Cesare G. 660a
DeMichelis, Euralio 469
De Montera, V. 1472
Demolder, Eugène 2687
Denis, Maurice 470, 743, 744, 745,
    746, 2726
Denise, L. 2715
D'Entremont, Eléne 1854
Dérieux, Henry 471, 1243
Dérieux, N. 2522
Derungs, Werner 1814
Deschamps, Léon 471, 992, 1139
Desmoineaux, Auguste 1871
De Tommasco, Vincenzo 1503
Detouche, Henry 2688
Deutsch, Max 1936
Devaille, Bernard 1995
Devillers, Hippolyte 747
De Waelhens, Alphonse 76
Dhôtel, André 473
Diaz, David S. 1797
Diaz-Plaja, Guillermo 1901, 2860
Di Bella, Nino 2807
Dickson, Ronald J. 1654
Dieckmann, Liselotte 345, 2453
Diederichs-Maurer, Anna K. 2912
Diehl, O. 346
Dimier, Louis 748
Dimov, Georgi 701
Dimov, Leonid 1190
Dinar, André 77
Divoire, Fernand 78
Doherty, Thomas W. 2767
Doisy, Marcel 2818
Dolembreux, Jacques 79
Domaradzki, Ghéodore F. 2390
Dombille, Eric 3117
Donchin, Georgette 661, 662, 663
Doneux, Guy 2055

Donkersloot, N.A.   2007
Donoghue, Denis   1588, 3118, 3119, 3120
Dontchev, Nicolaï   2614
Dorazio, Piero   1937
Dorfles, Gillo   749
Dornis, Jean   474
Dorra, Henri   2727
Doucet, J.   1244
Doumic, R.   2056
Downes, Gladys   2819
Dozot, Marie-Hèléne   2869
Dragmirescu, Samuel   2820
Dragomirescu, M.I.   1158
Dragone, Angelo   750
Dresdin, Samuel   2820
Dresse, Paul   80
Drewska, Hèléne   1126
Drieu la Rochelle, Pierre   81, 82
Drimba, Ovidiu   475, 2029
Droguett cz., Iván   476
Drougard, E.   1872, 3015, 3036
Duarte, Paulo   1149
Dubarle, Father   1417
Dubos, Charles   1245
Dubus, Edouard   477
Duchesne-Guillemin, Jacques   1821, 1822, 2821, 2822
D'Udine, Jean   1623, 2345
Du Feu, Veronica M.   2798
Duffy, John J.   1561
Dujardin, Edouard   83, 933, 993, 2913
Dumont-Wilden, Louis   2057
Dumur, Louis   84
Dupin, Jacques   1938
Duployé, Pie   1855
Durand, Gilbert   85, 86, 87, 88, 994, 1186
Durand, René L.   1504
Durand, Yves   89
Durand-Tahier, H.   2489
Durgnat, Raymond   90
Durzak, Manfred   1697, 1680, 1681, 1682, 1683
Duschak, A.G.   934
Duthie, Enid Lowry   347, 1684
Duvachel, Léon   2490
Duvakin, V.D.   2081

Du Vall, Cecil H.   3121
Dyserinck, H.   478
Eckart-Bäcker, Ursula   935
Edel, Léon   1922
Edeline, Francis   995
Edwards, Michael   1743, 2721, 3122
Edwards, O.   2914
Eguia, Ruiz C.   479
Ehrenforth, Karl   2723
Eide, Roar   1968
Eigeldinger, Alfred   2508
Eitel, Wolfgang   526, 1274
Eimermacher, Karl   664
Ekner, Reidar   348, 2554
Eliassen-De Kat, Martha H.   1449, 1752
Eliot, T.S.   996, 1246, 2454
Eliot, Valerie   1589
Ellis, J.R.   1261
Ellis, Keith   589, 1526
Ellmann, Richard   2318, 3123, 3124
Elwert, W. Theodor   997
Emerson, Ralph W.   998
Emich, Isolde   2915
Empson, William   1590
Engel, Claire-Elaine   91
Engel, Eduard   480
Engelberg, Edward   999, 3125, 3126
Engelen, Bernard   481
Engels, Edouard   92
Engelson, Moïse   93
Engelstad, Carl F.   1969
Eon, Henry   751
Epstein, Edna S.   2165
Erickson, John D.   1856, 2823
Ermini, Filippo   2916
Ermite, Pierre L.   94
Ernoult, C.   2166
Ernst, Fritz   355
Eršov, P.   1363
Erwin, John F., Jr.   1418, 2167
Es, G. van   1753
Eschmann, Ernst W.   2824
Escorailles, Albert de   482
Esquenazi-Mayo, Roberto   2680
Essebac, Achille   2783
Estève, Edmond   2870
Estienne, Charles   1939
Etiemble, René   2615, 2616, 2617

Eustachiewicz, Leslaw 1788
Evans, Calvin H. 890, 1815, 2058, 2168
Evans, May G. 2455
Evans, Patrick 1664
Evenpoel, Edmond 3037
Ewbank, Inga-Stina 1873
Fabbricatore, P. 3071
Faber du Faur, Curt von 1685
Fabio, Franco 2407
Fabre, L. 2825
Fabureau, Hubert 2826
Fackler, Herbert V. 286, 3127
Fagus 96, 483, 484, 752, 1624
Faillet, Georges 96, 483, 484, 752, 1624
Farmer, Albert J. 286a
Farrelly, James P. 3128
Fauchereau, Serge 2391
Fauconnier, Jean 1247
Faulkner, Peter 3129
Faurie, Marie-Josèphe 485, 486
Fausset, Hugh l'Anson 97
Faustino, Mário 2135
Favre, Robert 98
Favre, Yves-Alain 2768
Feder, Lillian 1000
Fehr, A.J.A. 487
Feidelson, Charles 287
Fein, John M. 1408
Feldman, David 488
Ferdinand, Gohin 2716
Fernández Retamar, Roberto 489
Ferran, André 1248
Ferreres, Rafael 490, 2917
Ferro, Tulio R. 1392
Feuerlicht, Ignace 1249
Fezzi, Elda 753
Fiber, L.A. 1505
Fiechterner, H.A. 1816
Field, Andrew 1971, 2734
Figueiredo, Fidelino de 1127
Finke, Ulrich 753a
Finn, Kay 1786
Fiumi, Annamaria B. 1591
Fischer, Jan O. 2021, 2618

Fiser, Emeric 3038
Fixler, M. 1857
Flam, Léopold 99
Fletcher, J.G. 2026
Fletcher, Ian 281, 288, 491
Flora, Francesco 492, 493
Florovskij, Prot. Georgij 2737
Flower, B.O. 2382
Focillon, Henri 754
Fogelquist, Donald F. 1506
Foldenauer, Karl 1817
Folejewski, Zbigniew 2082
Follain, Jean 2619
Fongaro, Antonio 2169
Fontainas, André 100, 101, 755, 1250, 1350, 2170, 2296
Fontaine, André 2871, 2918
Forcadas, Alberto 1507
Foreman, Dorothy Z. 494
Forestier, Louis 146, 1462, 2392, 2393, 2394, 2620, 2621
Formentin, Ch. 2690
Formigari, Lia 102, 1001
Formont, Maxime 1002
Forryan, Barbara 843
Foster, David W. 2861
Forster-Hahn, Françoise 756
Fortassier, Pierre 1629, 2919
Fowlie, Wallace 103, 104, 495, 496, 497, 1251, 1419, 1773, 2171, 2172, 2173, 2174, 2175, 2323, 2622
Fox, Charles J. 1923
Fox, E. Inman 105
Fox, Steven J. 289
Francavilla, Francesco 2920
France, Anatole 645, 2332
Françon, M. 2456
Frandon, I.-M. 1252
Frank, Heinz G. 1003
Franzbach, Martin 1464
Frattarolo, Renzo 2808
Frattini, Alberto 498
Frederiksen, Emil 1915, 1916
Freedman, Ralph 1091
French, Warren 2755

Fretet, Jean   2176
Frias, Eduardo   2437
Friedlaender, A.H. von   3039
Friedman, Barton R.   3130
Friedman, Melvin J.   278, 973, 3016
Friedrich, Hugo   1004
Friis, Erik J.   2761
Frohock, W.M.   2623
Frommel, G.   1686
Frye, Northrup   106, 927, 3131,
   3132
Fuente, Carmen de la   2023
Fuller, F.   758
Fullwood, Daphne   3133
Fumet, Stanislas   107
Furst, Lilian R.   108
Fussell, Paul   1592
Futrell, Michael   1364
Gabibbe, G.   499
Gabriel, Roger 2624
Gadoffre, G.F.   1303, 2264
Gaede, Edouard   2177
Gagnon, Lysiane   2363
Gaiser, Konrad   2187
Gale, A.L.   290
Gáldi, L.   1357
Galliard, J.-J   2059
Gallico, Claudio   1253
Galloti, Monola de   759
Gallwitz, Klaus   1940
Ganz, Peter F.   362
Garbáty, Thomas J.   291, 2775
García-Abrines, Luis   1508
Gardner, W.H.   1845
Garfîas, Francisco   1902
Gaskell, Ronald   1974
Gates, Norman T.   1147
Gaubert, Ernest   52, 2625
Gaucheron, Jacques   2626, 2921
Gaudefoy-Demombynes, J.   500
Gaughan, Gerald C.   2750
Gaultier, Jules de   109, 760, 2627
Gautier, F.   1254
Gauss, Christian   2922
Gauthier-Villars   3040
Gauvain, Jean   1361
Geen, Renée   2827
Geiser, Christoph   2291
Gellynck, H.   349

Genette, Gérard   2828
Gengoux, Jacques   110, 2178, 2628
George, Rambert   2769
Georgescu, Paul   1160
Georgin, René   2333
Gerasimov, Ju. K.   1365
Gerhard, Melitta   1687
Gerhardt, D.   230
Germain, Alphonse   111, 761, 762,
   763, 2491
Germain, Andrè   2923
Gevaert, H. Fiérens   764
Ghéon, Henri   1005, 1535, 1886,
   1887, 2334
Ghil, René   112, 501, 502
Ghypa, Matila   503
Giannangeli, Ottaviano   2408, 2409
Giannesci, Ferdinando   504
Giannoni, Robert   1146
Gibbons, K.G.   1554
Gicovate, Bernardo   505, 1793, 1794,
   1903
Gide, André   113, 1255
Giedion-Welcker   1941
Gielen, J.G.   936, 2179
Gierszynski, Stanislas   1351
Gilbert-Lecomte, Roger   2629
Gill, Austin   2180, 2181, 2182, 2183
Gille, Jean-Charles   937
Gille, Valère   506
Gillouin, René   2335
Gindin, S.I.   1396
Girard, Marcel   507
Girolamo, Nicola di   3100
Glendinning, Nigel   1509
Glur, Guido   1688
Gömöri, George   1142
Goes, Fernando   508
Goff, Penrith   350, 1818, 1819,
   1820
Gogol, John M.   2457
Goić, Cedomil   1510
Goldberg, Mécislas   2523
Goldfarb, Russel M.   1562, 1563
Goldgar, Harry   3017
Goldsmith, Ulrich K.   1689, 1690,
   1691, 2184
Golea, Antoine   2829
Gonzáles, Muela Joaquín   1774

Gonzáles Martínez, Enrique   2675, 2872
González-Gerth, Miguel   1511, 1795
González Lopéz, Emilio   2862, 2863
González-Rodas, Rubio   1512
Goodman, John F.   2776
Gorbunov, V.D.   2083
Gordon, Jan B.   114, 1564
Goriély, Benjamin   2084
Gorren, Aline   509
Gosse, Edmund   2185, 2924
Gossez, A.M.   1007
Got, Maurice   891
Goth, Maja   2555
Gothot-Mersch, Claudine   1178
Gottschalk, Hilde   1692
Goudeau, Emile   115
Gourmont, J. de   2336
Gourmont, Rémy de   116, 510, 511,
   512, 1006, 1105
Graaf, Daniel A. de   513, 1256, 2186,
   2630, 2925, 2926
Grandmont, Elio de   2364
Grandpré, Daruty de   1257
Grappe, G.   117
Grassi, Ernesto   2187
Gravier, Maurice   1201
Gray, Camilla   665
Green, J.T.   3134
Greene, E.J.H.   1977
Greet, Anne H.   1177
Gregh, Fernand   514, 515
Gregory, Horace   1555
Greiff, Otto de   1513
Greimas, Algirdas J.   2197
Gresset, Michel   516
Grey, M.A.R.   1821
Grierson, Francis   2927
Griffiths, R.M.   517
Grigor'yan K.   666
Grimm, Reinhold   382, 1849,
   2060, 2793
Grin, Micha   1445
Gringoire, Pedro   518
Grinke, Paul   765
Griror'jan, K.N.   2928
Grojnowski, Daniel   118, 766, 1978,
   1979
Groot, Maria de   2008
Gross, Harvey

Grossmann, Dietrich   2556
Grossman, L.   1397
Gsteiger, Manfred   351, 1258, 1259,
   2929
Guérin, Joseph   1663
Guerra, E. Carrera   2085
Guerra, Manuel H.   892
Guerrand, Roger H.   767
Guex-Gaslambide   519
Guggenheim, Susanna   520
Guichard, Léon   521, 938, 939, 1980
Guitte, Robert   522
Guiguet, Jean   1456
Guillory, Daniel L.   2324
Guimbretière, André   119, 1009
Guiraud, Pierre   120
Gullace, Giovanni G.   1473
Gullón, Ricardo   523, 1514, 1904,
   2036, 2037, 2038
Gumilev, Nikolai   667
Gunter, Richard   1846
Gutia, Joan   2809
Gutierrez-Girardot, R.   2039
Gzovskaja, O.   1366
Haasan, I.H.   1260
Hackett, C.A.   2631
Hadar, Tayitta   2061
Haerdter, Michael   3135
Hagen, Fredéric   2188
Hahl-Koch, J.   668
Hahn, Erika   1822
Hajek, Edelgard   352
Hakanson, B.   121
Hale, Edward E.   2383
Halévy, Daniel   1420, 2317
Hall, Donald   32
Hall, James H.   940
Hamann, Richard   353
Hambly, Peter S.
Hamburger, Käte   2543
Hamburger, Michael   1010
Hamel, A. van   524
Hanganu, George   1191
Hanighen, F.C.   1858
Hannevik, Arne   2398
Hannum, Hunter G.   1130, 1693
Hanson, Howard L., Jr.   2298
Hanson, Lawrence   2535
Harding, Brian R.   292

Hardison, O.B., Jr. 225, 2754
Hargrove, Nancy D. 1594
Harmer, Ruth 1875
Harris, Wendell V. 293, 1092
Harrison, Dorothy G. 3136
Harrison, John Wm. 1411
Hart, Pierre R. 1336
Hassan, Ihab H. 1011, 2731
Hatzfeld, Helmut A. 525
Hauser, O. 1262
Hautecoeur, Louis 1550
Havard, Robert G. 1655
Haydn, Hiram 3137
Hayman, David 1924
Hays, H.R. 1981
Hayward, Max 2077
Headings, Philip R. 2789
Healey, Eleanor C. 294
Healy, J.J. 295
Heckmann, Harald 960
Hédiard, Germain 1625
Hell, Victor 2557
Hellens, Franz 893
Heller, Erich 1595
Henderson, John A. 894
Henel, Heinrich 123, 1012
Henessy, Helen 196
Henn, Thomas R. 3138
Henry, Geritt 768, 769
Henry, Marjorie L. 2299
Hense, Anton 770
Héraut, H. 2632
Hermand, Jost 353, 354
Hermann, Friedrich 1694
Hermann, Rosemarie 2558
Hérold, A.-F. 3002
Heyen, William 297
Hidden, Norman 2417
Higginbotham, Virginia 1656, 1657
Higgins, Ian 2873
Hildebrandt, Kurt 1695
Hina, Horst 526
Hinck, Walter 895
Hinz, Evelyn J. 1457
Hirst, Desirée 124
Hittle, Gervasse G. 1263
Hobohm, Freya 1696, 1697
Hodin, J.P. 2359
Hönnighausen, Lothar 1565

Hösle, Johannes 355, 526, 1274
Hoeniger, F.D. 2559
Hoffman, Daniel G. 3139
Hoffman, Frederick J. 298
Hoffman, E. 771
Hofmannsthal, Hugo von 1823
Hofstätter, Hans H. 773, 774
Hogarth, Janet E. 2384
Hohendahl, Peter U. 2736
Holban, Adela 2428
Holdsworth, Carole A. 527
Holm, Søren 125
Holten, Ragnar von 2346, 2347
Holthusen, Hans Egon 1013
Holthusen, Johannes 669, 670, 2735
Holton, Milne 1458
Holubenko, S. 3028
Homann, Roger 1131
Hoog, Armand 2302
Hoope, Manfred 1824
Hoorweg, C.M. 356
Horányi, Mátyá 1515
Horodincǎ, Georgetta 1161, 1162,
    1163, 1164, 1165, 2190
Horry, Ruth N. 1421
Hough, Graham 2318
Houston, John P. 2633
Houston, Robert W. 1459
Howarth, Herbert 1596, 1597
Huber, Egon 2830
Hubert, Judd D. 126, 1264, 1265
Hubert, Renée R. 2634
Hultman-Boye, Hans 2018
Humbert, Agnès 775
Humma, John B. 3121
Huon, Y. 127
Hurley, E.A. 128
Husain, F.N. Yusuf Jamal 129
Huysmans, J.-K. 776, 1859, 2693
Hyslop, Francis E., Jr. 1265a, 1265b,
    1265c, 1265d, 1265e, 1265f
Ibáñez, Roberto 1516
Ibarra, Fernando 1796
Ibels, André 528
Iengo, Francesco 130
Ilie, Paul 2930
Ilsley, Marjorie H. 2191
Ireson, John C. 896, 1928, 2181
Isaacs, Joseph 1014

Issacharoff, Michael 1860
Itterbeck, Eugene van 131
Ivanescu, Cezar 2441
Ivanov, Vyacheslav 1881
Jackson, Holbrook 301
Jackson, S.B. 910
Jackson, Robert L. 2412
Jacobsen, R. 2009
Jäckel, Kurt 3041
Jaeger, Hans 1698
Jakubowski, J.Z. 3084
Jalink, J.M. 2010
Jaloux, Edmond 132, 2551
Jammes, F. 1888
Jamot, P. 1551
Jansonius, F. 1754
Jarema, Ja. Ja. 1635
Jarry, Alfred 2524
Jasper, Gertrude 897
Jaśzi, Andrew O. 133
Jaudon, Pierre 1352, 2192
Jaworska, Wladyslava 1664
Jean, René 2492
Jean-Aubrey, Georges 302, 1266,
 1982, 2525, 2931
Jean-Marquerose 3018
Jean-Nesmy, Claude 1999
Jechová, Hana 671
Jeffares, A. Normon 3140
Jensen, Kjeld B. 672
Jeske-Choinski, Teodor 673
Jiménez, Juan R. 1905
Joachim, Harold 2503
Johansen, Svend 529, 2794
Johnson, Lee M. 1267
Jolles, F. 1699
Jollivet de Castelot, F. 134, 135, 2424
Jolly, Cynthia 959
Jones, A.R. 303
Jones, Cyril A. 2680
Jones, Percy Mansell 530, 1268,
 1269, 2458, 2459, 2460, 3060
Jones, Rhys S. 2193, 2194, 2831
Jones, R.F. 304
Jones, W. Glynn 1917, 1918
Jong, Martien J.G. de 357, 2011,
 2994
Joost, Nicholas 3072
Joset, Jacques 136, 531

Josez, Virgile 1353
Joshi, B.N. 1847
Jost, Dominik 1700
Jost, François 380, 1621
Jouanny, Robert A. 2337, 2337a
Jourdain, Louis 2195
Joyce, James 1876
Jude, Stéfan 2635
Juden, Brian 1270
Juin, Hubert 532, 1634, 2086, 2636
Julén, Björn 2019
Julien-Caim, L. 2461
Jullian, Gustave 137
Jullian Philippe 137, 777, 778, 779,
 1474, 1475, 2312, 2313, 3073
Jullien, Adolphe 1626
Jur'eva, Zoja 1367
Just, Klaus G. 1701
Kaech, René 1422
Kahn, Gustave 138, 139, 140, 533,
 780, 898, 1015, 1405, 1983, 2338,
 2637, 2717, 2874, 2932
Kahnweiler, Daniel-Henry 2196
Kaire, Alexandre 1271
Kalfus, Richard M. 1803
Kalitin, N. 2087
Kamerbeek, J., Jr. 141, 1360, 2012,
 2992
Kandinsky, Nina 1943
Kandinsky, Wassily 781
Karátson, André 708, 2462, 2638
Karig, Sara 959
Karl, Frederick R. 1441
Karlinsky, S. 674
Kärnell, Karl-Åke 1574
Kaufman, J. Lee 1556
Kayser, Wolfgang J. 142, 534, 3141
Kazemier, G. 2993
Kearns, E.J. 1016
Keary, C.F. 2933
Keating, L.C. 3003
Keefer, Lubov 1749
Kelly, M.J. 2934
Kerbrat, Georges 782
Kermode, Frank 1017
Kern, Peter C. 1825
Kessler, Edward 2751
Kester, Garyl 1784
Kesting, Marianne 941, 2062

Keuchel, Ernst 1337
Kies, A. 1272, 2676
Killen, A.M. 3142
King, William W. 1273
Kirby, Michael S. 535
Kirillova, Irina 1798
Kirsop, Wallace 1394
Kisch, Sir Cecil 1368
Kiss, S. 1143
Kjetsaa, Geir 1412
Klemperer, Victor 143, 359, 536
Klimek, Theodor 3143
Klingsor, Tristan 783, 942, 1093
Kloepfer, Rolf 2639
Klomp, Henri 1755
Kluge, Rolf-Dieter 675
Klussmann, Paul Gerhard 1702
Knipping, J.B. 2792
Knowles, Dorothy 899
Knust, Herbert 3042
Ko Won 144
Kobel, Erwin 1826
Kobylinskij, L. 676
Kočutič, Vl.R. 2498
Köhler, Hartmut 1274, 2832
Kohlschmidt, Werner 2560
Kojève, A. 1944
Kolb, Glen L. 2683
Kolbuszewski, Stanislas 3085, 3086
Kolmogorov, A.N. 2088
Konev, Ilija 701
Kooij, J.G. 1450
Kondratov, A.M. 2089
Kopeczi, B. 1145
Kopp, Karl Caton 305
Koskimies, Rafael 360
Kosutitch, V. 677
Kotzin, Michael 784
Koven, Mrs. Reginald de 2935
Kraft, Walter C. 2865, 3043
Krawitz, Henry 145
Kriek, I. 1369
Kristeva, Julia 2197
Kroger, E.P. 2561
Kron, Wolfgang 978
Kronegger, M.E. 1094, 1925
Kronik, John W. 2404, 2936, 2937
Kugel, James L. 146
Kuhn, Reinhard C. 3004, 3005

Kunz, Marcel 2562
Kurth, Lieselotte E. 1131
Kurylenko, J.M. 1636
Kyritz, Heinz-Gerog 2563
Kzocsa, Sándor 1275
Labat, Louis 1389
Lacaze-Duthiers, Gérard de 785
Lachmann, Hedwig 2938
Laffitte, Sophie 1370
Laforgue, Jules 1276
Lafue, Pierre 537
Lager, Robert J. 2738
Lalou, René 538
Lam, Andrzej 678
Lambert, L. Gary 3043
Lamberti, M. Mimita 786
Lamont, R. 1128
Landmann, Georg P. 1703
Lang, E.M. 2941
Lang, Renée 2564, 2565, 2566
Lange, Victor 1719, 2453
Langer, W. 1704
Langlois, Walter G. 2157
Lankheit, Klaus 1945
Lannes, Roger 2198
Lanson, Gustave 539, 1018, 2199
Lapauze, Henry 540
Lappalainen, Pekka 1641
Laran, Jean 2349
Larbaud, Valéry 2833
Larsen, Finn Stein 1919
Lassus, J. de 3044
Last, Jef 1744
Latimer, Dan R. 2834
Lattard, François 2003
Laubenthal, Penne J. 1658
Laurent, Emile 541
Lavaud, Guy 147
Laver, James 1861
Lavigne, Paul 2784
Lavrenëv, B. 2090
Lavrin, Janko 2738a
Lawler, James R. 542, 1106, 1423,
    1598, 2835, 2836, 2837, 2838, 2839
Lawrenson, T.E. 1303, 2264
Lazare, Bernard 148, 149, 2063, 2425,
    2785, 3019, 3074
Lazarowicz, Klaus 978
Leblond, Ary 2510

Leblond, Marius   2510
Le Blond, Maurice A.   1019, 1020, 1889, 2527
Lebois, André   150, 1388
Le Breton, A.   1890
Le Cardonnel, G.   151
Le Cardonnel, Louis   543
Leclère, Tristan   1406, 2509, 2939
Lecomte, George   787
Lefebve, Maurice-Jean   152, 153, 1021
Lefevre, Frédéric   2840
Legrand, Francine-Claire   788, 789, 1963
Lehmann, A.G.   154, 155, 544
Lehmann, Peter L.   1705
Leiris, Alan de   2357
Leite, Lígia C. Moraes   545
Lejeune, Claire   156
Lemaître, Henri   546
Lemaître, Jules   2940
Lemonnier, Camille   2694
Lemonnier, Léon   1277, 2463, 2464
Lemos, Esther de   2433
Lempicka, A.   3087, 3088
Lepelletier, Edmond   2941
Lepetit, Jules   1278
Leppien, Jean   1946
Lerner, Michael G.   2484, 2669, 2670, 2671, 2672
LeRouge, Gustave   547
Leroy, Amélie Claire   1316
Lescure, Jean   1022
Lesdaine,Pierre   159
Lester, John A., Jr.   306
Lethève, Jacques   160, 548, 790, 791, 1129, 2426, 2942
Levcenko, Myxajlo   2091
Levin, Harry   550
Levin, V.I.   1371
Levine, Bernard   3144
Levy, Kurt L.   589, 1526
Lewis, Jack   510
Lewitter, L.R.   1798
L'Homme, Charles E.   2418
Lichtblau, Charlotte   792
Lichtenthaler, Friederike   2502
Liger, Christian   2770
Lind, Georg R.   2438

Lindenberger, Herbert   2736
Lindsay, Kenneth C.   1947
Lindsay, Marshall   1745
Lindsttöm, Göran   1642
Linebarger, James M.   3145
Linke, Hansjürgen   1706
Linssen, H.   1756
Lioure, Michel   1424
Lira Osvaldo, SS. CC.   1906
Lisboa, Henriqueta   1780
Little, Roger   1599, 2429
Little, William T.   2720
Litvak de Pérez de la Dehesa, Lily   551
Litz, A. Walton   2752
Litz, Norman   1517
Liui, François   1862
Lobner, Coriana del Greco   1476
Lockerbie, S.I.   1179
Lockspeiser, Edward   943, 944, 1538, 1539, 1540, 1541, 1542, 1543, 2200
Lo Curzio, Guglielmo   2677
Loevgren, Sven   793
Lohner, Edgar   1130
Lombardo, Agostino   307, 308
Lombreaud, R.   2640
Lombroso, Cesare   2385
Lopes, João A.   1150
López, Tele Porto Ancona   1151
Losereit, Sigrid   552
Lossky, N.O.   679
Lote, G.   1023
Loudet, René   1518
Lucas, Fábio   1152
Lucie-Smith, Edward   795
Lukács, Georg   2641
Lund, Hans P.   2201, 2202
Luszeznski, Walter R.   1279
Luzi, Mario   162, 163, 2203
Lyndon, Howard   2943
MacCarthy, Desmond   2944
Macchia, Giovanni   1280
MacCombie, John   1425
MacKendrick, Louis K.   309
Macrí, Oreste   164, 553
Magariños Demello, Mateo J.   2681
Magidoff, R.   1379
Magliola, Robert R.   1281
Mágr, Clara   2567

Maia, João   554
Maier, Hans A.   1707
Maillard, Léon   796, 2695, 2945
Maione, Italo   1708
Maire, G.   1282
Makocskij, Sergej   2732
Mallarmé, Stéphane   1026, 2642
Mallo, Antonio E.   2864
Malmstad, John Earl   1338
Malpique, Cruz   1393
Malvost, Henry de   3045
Manca, Marie A.   2643
Mander, Luciano   2810
Mann, K.H.   2843
Mannoni, O.   2204
Manston, Augustus   2205, 2946
Manu, Emil   1192
Marcazzan, M.   165
Marchiori, Giuseppe   797, 798, 1948
Mariano, Emilio   1467, 1477
Marie, Aristide   166
Marinetti, F.T.   3046
Maritain, Jacques   1027
Marjoux, Jean-Jacques   555
Marinello, Juan   2293
Markov, Vladimir   1198
Markovitch, Milan   1398
Marks, Emerson R.   2465
Marshall, Robert   1600
Marthold, Jules de   2493
Martin-Crosa, Ricardo   1028
Martin, Graham   1603
Martin, Mildred   1601
Martin, Wallace   281, 310
Martino, Pierre   167
Martins, António C.   2434
Martins, Heitor   1965
Mary, André   1283, 2947
Marzot, Guilo   556
Masbic-Nerov I.   680, 1372
Masing, I.   1373
Masini, Lara V.   800
Maslenikov, Oleg A.   681, 1339, 1799, 1800
Mason, Eudo C.   2568
Mathauser, Zdněk   2092
Mathews, Andrew J.   557
Mathews, Jackson   2841
Matthieu, Pierre-Louis   2350

Matich, Olga   1801
Matlaw, R.E.   682
Mattenklott, Gert   1326
Matthews, W.K.   709
Mauclair, Camille   558, 559, 801, 1984
Maumoff, Alice R.   1966
Mauriano, Gianfranco   2411
Maurice-Amour, Lila   1284
Maurras, Edouard   2358
Maxwell, D.E.S.   3146
Mayhew, George   3111
Mayor, Avelino H.   1519
Mayoux, J.J.   168
Mazel, Henri   169, 1386
M.B.M.   2948
McClain, William H.   1131
McClelland, John   1024
McFadden, Georges   2753
McFarlane, I.D.   896
McFarlane, James W.   2399
McKulick, Benjamin Max   2047
McLaren, James C.   1025
McLuhan, Marshall   2206
Meckier, Jerome   1602
Medvedev, P.N.   1374
Meessen, Hubert J.   1709
Meeuwesse, Karl
Meier, Peter P.   1863
Mein, Margaret   1285
Melchiori, Giorgio   3147
Melin, Lars   1920
Mellerio, André   2511
Mendès, Catulle   1029, 1030
Menduini, Agosto   361
Mercier, Alain   560, 1791
Merlet, J.-F. Louis   1891
Merrill, Stuart   170, 1031, 1032, 1033, 1034, 2499, 3075
Meschonnic, Henri   2644
Messer, Thomas J.   1949
Messina, Maria G.   802
Metzger, Erika A.   1710
Metzger, Michael M.   1710
Metzidakis, Philip   2801
Meunier, Dauphin   2339
Meyer, Franz   1950
Meyer, Leonard D.   945
Meyer-Minnemann, Klaus   2729

150

Meylan, Pierre 946
Mićević, Kolja 2842
Micha, Alexandre 2949
Michalski, André S. 1797
Michanek, Germuud 1643
Michaud, Guy 171, 172, 173, 561,
1035, 1132, 2207, 2208
Michaud, Régis 1286
Michelet, Victor-Emile 1059
Michell, Joyce 947
Mickel, Emanuel 1231a, 1287
Mickelsen, David J. 1095
Mickiewicz, D. 683
Micu, Dumitru 1166
Middleton, J.C. 362
Miguel, Antonio Dias 2435
Milch, Werner 363
Milicia, Joseph, Jr. 1557
Miller, Henry 2645
Miller, Philip L. 948, 1036
Millerio, André 803
Milner, John
Minkowski, Eugène 175
Mintcheff, Kina 1864
Mioc, Simion 1193
Miodonśka-Brooks, Ewa 3089
Miomandre, Francis de 1985, 2297
Mirbeau, Octave 2696
Miropol'ski, A.L. 659
Mirvaldová-Janatová, Hana 684
Missac, Pierre 2112, 2188, 2196,
2209
Mistry Freny 1827
Mitchell, Bonner 176
Mitescu, Adriana 1194
Mittenzwei, Johannes 177
Mitterand, Henri 178
Mix, Katherine C. 311
Mockel, Albert 179, 562
Mocul'skij, K. 1329
Mohrenschildt, D.S. von 685
Moises, Maussaud 563
Monas, Sidney 1340
Mondor, Henri 2210, 2211, 2212,
2213, 2214
Mondrone, Domenico 2093
Money, Agnes T. 1907, 2229
Monférier, Jacques 564
Monsman, Gerald 2419

Montenegro, Abelardo F. 1464a
Monterde, Francisco 2374
Monuio, Luis 1521
Moore, A.K. 1037
Moore, Harry T. 1990
Moore, John R. 3148, 3149
Mor, Antonio 565
Morais, Frederico 1153
Morand, Bernadette 2649
Morand, Paul 2528
Morawska, Ludmilla 1107, 1108
Moréas, Jean 645, 2215
Moreau, Pierre 180, 181, 1038
Morice, Charles 566, 1354, 2216
Morier, Henri 1039
Morino, L. 911
Morgan, Charles 182
Morgan, M.T. 346
Morrissette, Bruce A. 183, 312
Morsiani, Giovanna 1588
Moser, Charles A. 2094
Mossop, Deryk, J. 1039a
Moulin, L. 1892
Mouloud, Noël 184
Mounin, Georges 1109
Mourey, Gabriel 567, 805, 1040
Mourik, A. van 2950
Muche, Georg 1951
Mühler, Robert 1828
Müller, Franz W. 2569
Müller, Ludolf 2739
Muival, José 2678
Mullay, Terence 2512
Muller, Joseph-Emile 806
Mulryne, J.R. 3120
Munch, Jean 185
Muner, Mario 186
Munier, Roger 1041
Munro, John M. 1566, 2777
Munro, T. 2217
Muntean, George 2442
Muricy, Andrade 1465
Muricy, J.C. 568
Museux, E. 807
Myers, B. 808
Myers, Rollo H. 949, 950
Nag, Martin 686, 2790
Nagy, Péter 710
Nakov, Andrée B. 810

Nalyvajko, Dmytro 2951
Napoli, Joanne L. 3150
Nardis, L. de 2064
Naremore, James 313
Nassaar, Christopher S. 3076
Natanson, Thadée 811, 2536
Natanson, Wojciech 3090
Naumann, Walter 1042
Neapes, Erwin 1521
Neddermann, Emmy 1908, 1909
Negru, Svetlana 1967
Nelli, René 1043
Nelson, James G. 314
Nerval, Gérard de 1044
Neumann, Alfred R. 2570
Neumann, Gerhard 2218
Nicholas, Henry 2219, 3006
Nicolescu, Basarab 1204
Nicoletti, G. 2386
Niebuhr, Walter 1829
Nielsen, Laus S. 2646
Nikola, Banašević 2795
Nilsson, Nils Ake 687
Nishida, Hideho 1952
Noda, Misashi 711
Nöel, Jean 2319
Noguez, Dominique 1746
Noisay, M. de 2340
Nolte, Fritz 2571
Nordau, Max 2387
Norton, R.C. 1830
Noske, Frits 951
Noszlopy, George T. 1180
Noulet, Emilie 1045, 1046, 2220,
    2221, 2222, 2223, 2224, 3020
Novotny, Fritz 880
Nowakowski, Jan 3091, 3092
Nozick, Martin 2320
Nugent, R. 1290
Nunes, Benedito 2439
Nyman, Alf Tor 1047
Oberholzer, Otto 1330
Oblomievskij, D. 569
O'Brien, James 3151
Ockenden, Raymond C. 1713,
    1714
O'Donnell, James P. 3152
Oechler, W.F. 2875
Oeuel, Mildred 1426

Oelke, Karl E. 2466
Ogden, P. 3007
Olinto, Antônio 570
Oliveros-Delgado, Rafael 1522
Olson, E. 187
Olson, Paul R. 1910, 1911
Oomen, Ursula 2639
Orel, Harold 3153
Orlandini, Marisa V. 812
Orliac, Antoine 571
Orsi, Agusto 2648
Ortigues, Edmond 188
Osborn, Catherine B. 1291
Osmont, Anne 572
Ospina-García de Fonseca, Helena 2843
Oswald, V.A. 1715 , 1716
Oswald, Werner 1427
Oswaldo, Angelo 573
Otten, Michel 2310
Ousterhout, Polly B. 2065
Ovcharenko, Maria 1637
Ourousof, Prince A. 1292, 1293, 1294
Oxenhandler, Neal 1295, 2225
Pabst, Walter 2954
Pacheco, Léon 574
Pachmuss, Temira 1802
Pachón Padilla, Eduardo 575
Pádua, Antônio de 189
Pagnini, Marcello 315, 316
Pajman, A. 1375
Paladilhe, Jean 2351
Palleske, Siegwalt O. 2066
Palmiery, R. 2344
Panayotopoulos, J.M. 712
Panizza, Oskar 364
Pannwitz, Rudolf 2995
Paolazzi, G.V. 1478
Pappas, John J. 3077
Papu, Edgar 1167
Paratore, Ettore 1479
Parent, Monique 997
Parkinson, Thomas 3154
Parks, Edd W. 2467
Parks, Lloyd C. 3021
Paslick, Robert H. 365
Passaglia, Mario 2410
Pasternak, Boris 2095
Paszek, Jerzy 3182
Paterson, Gary H. 317

Patri Aimé 2226, 2227
Patterson, A.S. 2468
Paul, David 2844
Paul, Fritz 1877
Paulin, Hillewi 2020
Paulsen, W. 366
Pauly, Marie Hélène 3155
Pautasso, Sergio 576, 577
Pauw, Wilfried de 2996
Pavel, Toma 1205
Paxton, Norman 110, 2228
Paz, Octavio 1177, 2229
Pearson, Gabriel 1603
Peković, Slobodanka 1804
Péladan, Joséphin 813, 2698
Péladan, Sor 2352
Pellegrini, Carlo 578, 1398
Pelletier, Abel 579
Pensa, Mario 1717
Perez de la Dehesa, Rafael 2067
Peregrino, Joao, Junior 580, 581
Perl, Walter H. 1155, 1156
Perrin, Henri 2305
Perruchot, Henri 2305
Perruchot, Henri 1665, 2537
Perry, T.S. 191
Perticucci Bernardini, Ada 192
Pestalozzi, Karl 1048
Peters, H.F. 2572
Peters, Robert L. 318, 2778
Petersen, Lise B. 1440
Petit, Jacques 1428
Petrini, Domenico 2405
Petrini, Enzo 582
Petroveanu, Mihail 1195, 1206
Petrucciani, Mario 583, 2230, 2411
Petzsch, Christoph 2573
Pevel, H. 2231
Peyre, Henri 192a, 1265f, 1747, 1987
Pfannkuch, Karl 193
Pfeiffer, Jean 1049
Pflanzl, Jutta 1341
Philippide, Al 2232
Philips, C. Henry 1544
Philonenko, Monique 2233
Pica, Vittorio 2699
Picco, F. 584
Picon, Gaëtan 1954
Piemme, Michèle 2016

Piérard, Louis 2876
Pierce, Frank 2680
Pierre, José 2351
Piggott, Jan R. 3156
Piguiet, Jean-Claude 952
Pillat, Dinu 1207, 1208
Pilon, Edmond 585, 815, 1893, 1929,
    1988, 2877, 2955
Pincus-Witton, Robert 816, 817
Pinguet, Maurice 2771
Pino, Frank, Jr. 2041
Pinto, Vivian De S. 1050
Piru, Alexandru 1168
Piscopo, Ugo 2649
Piselli, Francesco 2234
Placer, Xavier 586
Planchart, Enrique 2845
Plank, Dale Lewin 2413
Platz, Hermann 1296
Plowert, Jacques 194
Pontaut, Alain 2365
Podraza-Kwaitkowska, Maria 195, 688
Poggioli, Renato 689, 2235
Point, Armand 196
Poirion, Daniel 1297
Poizat, Alfred 587, 588
Polak, Bettina Spaanstra 197, 367
Polanšćak, Antun 1298
Pollack, Seweryn 690
Pollak, I. 1718
Pollard, Arthur 276
Pollmann, Leo 1429
Pongs, Hermann 198, 3061
Pontaury, Jacques 2700
Pontaut, Alain 2365
Pontiero, Giovanni 589
Pool, Phoebe 2444, 2445
Pope, Isabel 954
Popo, E. 2236
Popov, R.N. 2096
Porter, Laurence M. 1177
Porter, Michael 1831
Postic, Marcel 2069
Poulet, Geroges 1299
Pouillart, R. 1390
Poulussens, Jaime 2860
Poulussens, Norbert 2860
Poÿlo, Anne 1996
Pozzi, Giani 590

Pradal-Rodriguez, G.   2237
Pradelle, J.   2701
Praz, Mario   200, 316, 1605
Predmore, Michael P.   1912
Predmore, Richard L.   1659
Prete, Antonio   1299a
Previtali Morrow, Giovanni   1782
Prévost, J.   2846
Printz-Pahlson, Göran   368
Proffer, Carl R.   3181
Proust, M.   1300
Prunier, Francis   1878
Pszczolowska, Lucylla   3093
Pucciani, Oreste   201
Purves, A.C.   202
Queiroz, Maria J. de   591
Quennell, Peter   1301
Quillard, P.   2342, 2718
Quillard, R.   1894
Rabbin, Marcelle   2238
Rabuse, Geroge   2781
Radian, Sanda   1169
Radley, Hilton   1051
Ragusa, Olga M.   592, 593, 2402, 2443
Raitt, A.W.   594, 3022, 3023
Rajan, B.   3157
Rambosson, Yvanhoé   818, 819, 820,
   821, 822, 823, 1328
Ramiro, E.   2702
Ramnoux, Clemńce   203
Ramos, Feliciano   1410
Ramos, Pericles Eugenio de Silvio   595
Ramsey, Warren   319, 1628, 1987,
   1989, 1990, 2239
Randall, A.W.G.   369
Randall, H.F.   3062
Ransom, John C.   320, 3158
Rantavaara, Irma   713
Raphael, Robert   2761
Rapin, René   2574
Rapsilber, E.   370
Rasch, Wolfdietrich   900, 1719
Rauhut, F.   953
Raymond, Marcel   204, 1052, 2668
Raynal, Maurice   824
Raynaud, Ernest   205, 206, 207,
   208, 596, 825, 912, 1053, 1302
Read, Herbert   1955
Reade, Brian E.   1327

Reavy, George   2077
Rebell, Hugues   826, 1054, 1631
Reboul, Yves   2650
Rebourcet, Gabriel   2651
Recoulley, Alfred L., III   3078
Redon, Ari   12
Redon, Odilon   2513
Redonnel, Paul   827
Reed, John R.   321
Rees, Garnet   896, 1214, 1303
Rees, Thomas R.   1606, 1762
Reeve, F.D.   1342, 1376, 1377, 1400
Régie, José   1055
Régnier, Henri de   209, 1304, 1568,
   1865, 1879, 2240, 2241, 2492, 2847,
   3024, 3079
Rehder, Helmut   43
Réja, Marcel   1355
Renna, Pamela S.   1463
Retté, Adolphe   210, 597, 598, 828,
   913, 1056, 1057, 1111, 1552, 1866,
   1998, 2242, 2243, 2244, 2245, 2530
   2652, 2957, 3008
Revard, Stella   3159, 3160
Revel, Jean-François   1480
Reverseau, J.P.   599
Rewald, John   600, 829, 2503, 2727
Rexroth, Kenneth   322
Rey, Alain   2848, 2849
Rey, José   2682
Rey, William H.   1832
Reyes, Alfonso   2246, 2247
Reynold, Gonzaque de   1306
Rheims, Maurice   830
Rhodes, S.A.   2469
Rian, Eivind   2400
Ribbans, Geoffrey W.   2042, 2802
Ribeiro, João   601
Ricardo, Guillan   2043
Rice, Martin P.   1401
Richard, Jean-Pierre   2249
Richard, Noël   211, 602, 603, 2004
Richardson, Edgar P.   831
Richardson, Joanna   2958
Richer, Jean   2307, 2653
Rickman, H.P.   2575
Richtofen, Erich von   212
Richword, Edgell   2654
Ricoeur, Paul   213

Riddel, Joseph N. 2754
Rieder, Dolly S. 1177
Riessauw, A.M. 2959
Rieger, Er2in 1833
Rieux, Lionel des 1058
Rimanelli, Giose 604
Riotor, Léon 832, 2495
Ripellino, Angelo Mario 2097
Riva, Ubaldo 2655
Rivière, Jacques 1307, 2656, 2850
Rocahe, J. 1308
Robert, Gustave 3047
Roberts, Keith 833, 1384
Roberts, Jack 2730
Robichez, Jacques 901, 902, 2028,
  2772
Rod, Eduard 605
Roditi, Edouard 834, 3080
Rodrigues, Eugène 2703
Rodrigues, Urbana Tavares 606
Rodrigues-Luis, Julio 2710
Roedig, Ch. F. 1309
Roerchez, Jacques 2960
Roger-Marx, Claude 2514, 2515
Roinard, Paul-Napoléon 1059
Rolland de Reneville, André 607
Rolleston, James 2576
Roloff, Hans-Gert 1719, 2453
Romains, Willy P. 2070
Romani, Bruno 608, 2027
Romano, Salvatore 609
Romeralo, Sánchez 2860
Romero, Hector R. 1184
Rondault, Jean 1763
Ronse, Henri 1096
Rookmaaker, H.R. 835
Rops, F. 2704
Rosa, António Ramos 2577
Rose, Marilyn Gaddis 1133, 3025,
  3161
Rose, William J. 691
Rosehaupt, Hans W. 371
Rostand, Claude 924
Rota, V. 1481
Rouge, Gustave Le 836
Rouge, Jean de 837
Rousseau, André 903
Rousseau, R. 2719
Roussel, Georges 1482

Rousselot, Jean 2000
Rousset, Lucien 214
Royère, J. 1310
Rubio, D. 610
Ruchon, François 1991, 2657
Ruck, Heribert 2961
Rudler, Madeleine 215
Ruff, Marcel 1265f
Rukalski, Z. 611
Rull, Enrique 1523
Rümke, Henricus C.
Ruprecht, Erich 372, 373, 3048
Russell, Dora Isella 1403
Russi, Antonio 612
Rusu, Liviu 1621
Rutten, M. 613
Rzewuska, E. 2303
Saalmann, Dieter 2578
Sabršula, J. 2021
Safford, Irene A. 2962
Saint-Antoine 216, 904
St. Aubyn, Frederick G. 1834, 2250
Saint-Jacques, Louis de 1140, 1385,
  1992, 2071, 2251, 2300, 2531, 2532,
  2539, 2540, 2541
Saint-Paul, Albert 1720
Saint-Pol-Roux 2963
Saintsbury, George 2388
Sáinz y Rodriguez 614
Saix, Guillot de 615, 2072
Salazar, Adolfo 954
Salinas, Pedro 1524
Samson, Jean Noël 2366
Samuel, Dorothy J. 2470
Sanborn, A.F. 2964
Sancerny, Alain 2651
Sánchez, Ernesto M. 1525
Sandblad, Nils Gosta 838
Sandstrom, Sven 2516
San Lazzaro, Clementina di 1721
Santilli, Tommaso 616
Santoli, Vittorio 1722
Saraiva, Arnaldo 617
Saramandu, N. 1196
Šarykin, D.M. 1378
Šatalov, S.E.
Saunier, Charles 839, 840, 1627, 2353,
  2496, 2705
Saurat, D. 2252

Saruo, Antoine 1060
Savage, Catherine 1748
Savage, D.S. 3162
Scalamandrè, Raffaele 3009
Schade, George D. 1511
Schaeffner, André 1311, 1540
Schaettel, Marcel 2965
Schaumann, G. 2098, 2099
Scheffer, Robert 1097
Scheiwiller, Vanni 647
Schelling, Friedrich W.J. von 841
Scher, Steven 955
Schérer, Jacques 2253
Scherer, Robert 217
Schinz, Albert 618
Schinzel, E. 2471
Schlesinger, Max 218
Schlumberger, J. 2343
Schmid, Martin E. 1835
Schmidt, Albert-Marie 219, 619,
 1430, 1723
Schmidt, Tatyana 1199
Schmidt-Garre, Helmut 956, 1545,
 1546, 2254
Schmitz, Victor A. 1724
Schneidau, Herbert N. 2478, 2479
Schneider, G. 1956
Schneider, Marcel 620, 2485
Schnitzler, O. 1836
Schonauer, Fritz 1725
Schonthal, Aviva H. 621
Schoolfie.d, C.C. 2401
Schopfer, Jean 842
Schrader, Ludwig 220, 1526
Schraibman José 1720
Schrickx, W. 3081, 3163
Schuchard, Ronald 1607
Schüssler, Margarethe 1837
Schuetz, Lawrence F. 2420
Schulman, Ivan A. 622, 2294
Schultz, H. Stefan 1726, 1727
Schultze, Jürgen 843
Schwartz, Paul J. 2255
Schwarz, Egon 1130, 2736
Schwermer, J. 957
Schwerte, Hans 374
Séailles, Gabriel 1407
Secchi, Giovanni 623, 2480
Secretan, Philibert

Seeba, Hinrich C. 1838
Ségalen, V. 222
Segard, Achille 1141, 2679
Segui, Shinichi 1957
Seguin, M. 1312
Seiden, Morton I. 3164
Seillière, E. 375
Sells, C. 843a
Selz, Peter 844
Sen, Jyoti P. 1608
Sengle, Friedrich 1728
Senior, John 1134
Serra-Lima, Federico 1527
Séverine 2788
Severini, G. 223
Seylaz, Louis 2472
Sharter, I. Martin 905
Shaw, Priscilla W. 2579
Sheehan, Donald 2755
Sheets, J.M. 2580
Sheppard, Richard 1609
Sherard, Robert H. 2256
Shmiefsky, Marvel 2421
Siciliano, I. 2257
Siebenmann, Gustav 624
Siefken, H. 1839
Sigele, Rizel Pincus 1514
Silva, Wilson Melo da 1781
Silvera, Tasso da 625
Silvestre, Armand 845
Silvo, Castro R. 626
Simões, João G. 627, 628
Simón Diáz, José 629
Simon, John 846
Simons, Hi 2756
Simonsen, Sofus E. 1202
Sinfelt, Frederick W. 2321
Singh, Brijraj 323
Sincim 1061
Sior, Marie-Louise 1729
Skvoznikov, V.D. 2100
Skyrme, Raymond 1528
Slattery, M.P. 3165
Slavutych, Yar 1638
Slonim, Marc 692, 693
Smeets, Albert 847
Smith, Grover 1610
Smith Harold J. 2259
Smith, James, M. 630, 631

Smith, M.H. 2260
Smorodin, A. 2101, 2102
Sobejano, Gonzalo 1514
Sötomann, A.L. 2013, 2014
Soissons, S.C. 1658, 1966
Sojcher, Jacques 848, 2581
Sokel, Walter H. 376
Sokolsky, Anatole A. 2103
Sommavilla, Guido 224, 1559
Sommers, P.B. 1630
Somville, Pierre 225
Sonnenfeld, Albert 1446, 1993
Soos, Ermese M. 2430
Sorrento, Luigi 1062
Sőtés, István 1145
Souchon, Paul 2005
Souday, Paul 2851
Souffrin, Eileen 3082
Soulairol, Jean 2261
Soulié, Paul 2967, 2968
Soupault, Philippe 2659
Soupault-Niemeyer, R. 1958
Souriau, Paul 226
Souza, R. de 1063
Spagnoletti, Giacento 227
Specovius, Günther 1343
Spender, Stephen 32, 3166
Spenlé, Jean-Edouard 1730
Spies, Lina 2376
Spigl, Friedrich 3049
Spillebeen, Willy 2377
Spinucci, Pietro 1611
Spire, A. 1064, 1065, 1313
Spitzer, Leo 632
Spivak, Gayatri C. 3167
Staats, Armin 2473
Stacy, Robert H. 1882
Stählin, Wilhelm 229
Stäuble, Michele 1315
Stahl, August 2582
Stahl, E.L. 377
Stamać, Ante 2799
Stammler, Heinrich 2740
Stanford, Derek 324
Stanic, Sharman Elsa 2367
Stark, Bernice S. 633
Starkie, Enid 325, 634, 1314, 2660
Starr, Doris 378
Stavros, George 2422

Steffen, Hans 1840
Steffensen, Eigil 1344
Steffensen, Steffen 1731
Stein, H. von 3050
Stein, Jack M. 1066, 3051
Steiner, Herbert 635
Steland, Dieter 2262
Stepan, F. 230
Stephan, Philip 231, 1067, 2969, 2970
Stéphane, N. 1612
Stepun, Fiodor Avgustovich 694
Stergiopoulos, Kostos 714
Stern, Carol S. 2779
Stern, James 1823
Stern Tanya 1823
Stevens, Mary Anne 137
Stickney, Joseph T. 2971
Stimson, Frederick S. 1185
Stockenström, Gōran 2762
Stokowa, Maria 3094
Stormon, E.J. 1613
Stowell, H. Peter 1883
Strakhovsky, Leonid I. 695
Strauss, George 1732
Strauss, Walter A. 2263, 2583
Strelka, Joseph P. 124
Strémoonkhoff, D. 696
Strich, Fritz 232, 379
Stromberg, Roland 233
Struc, Roman S. 2736
Struve, Gleb 702, 1345
Stuart, Esmè 1316
Stuckenschmidt, H.H. 1959
Stuiveling, Garmt 1451
Stupka, Vladimír 2618
Stutfield, Hugh W. 2389
Suarès, André 958
Subrahmanian, Krishnaswami 234
Suckling, Norman 1067a
Sugar, Charlotte de 1317
Sulloway, Alison G. 1848
Suško, Mario 698
Sutcliffe, F.E. 1303, 2264
Sutherland, Donald 2431
Sutton, Denys 849, 850, 851
Swan, Alfred 2725
Swift, Bernard C. 1098, 2264
Swigget, Glen L. 2474

Symons, Arthur   237, 238, 636, 853,
2265, 2662, 2972, 2973, 2974, 2975,
2976, 2977, 2978, 3083
Sypher, Francis, J., Jr.   2774
Syre, Sivert   1880
Szabolcsi, Bence   959
Szabolcsi, Miklos   715
Szymański, Wiesław P.   699
Tahier-Durand, H.   854
Taillandier, Yvon   855
Tamayo Vargas, Augusto   1529
Taranovsky, Kiril   1379
Tarizzo, Domenico   238a
Tate, Allen   1614
Taupin, René   326, 327, 1135, 1764
Taylor, John R.   856
Taylor, S.W.   857
Taylor, Terry O.   1785
Teles, Gilberto Mendonça   449, 637
Temple, Ruth   328
Ténib, Charles   858, 2979
Terenzio, Vincenzo   1547
Terelecki, Tymon   3095, 3096, 3097
Theile, Wolfgang   700, 1739, 1740
Thévenin, Léon   1768
Thibaudet, Albert   239, 2266, 2267,
2268, 2269, 2270
Thieme, Hugo P.   240, 2980
Thiry, Marcel   3027
Thomas, Henri   1447
Thombreaud, Roger A.   2780
Thompson, Vance   241, 242, 638, 1068,
2981
Thorel, Jean   639
Thorlby, Anthony   2584
Thys, Walter   380
Tiedemann-Bartels, Hella   1318
Timmerman, John   2475
Timofeev, L.   1380, 1381
Timofeeva, V.V.   2104, 2105
Tindall, William Y.   243, 1926, 3168
Todoran, Eugene   1358
Tolman, Rosco N.   2865
Tomassoni, Italo   859
Tomić, Josip   2295
Torrens, James   1615
Torres Bodet, Jaime   1530
Tortel, Jean   2271
Toscano, Bruno   861

Tosi, Guy   640, 1472, 1483, 1484
Touny-Lérys   1895
Trahan, Elizabeth   2791
Traverso, Leone   1485
Treweek, A.P.   1373, 2907
Tricht, H.W. van   1452
Trier, Eduard   862
Trounoux, G.A.   2982
Trueblood, Alan S.   1531
Tschiżewskij, Dimtrij   670, 1346
Tsukimura, R.   3169
Tukh, B.   1402
Turnell, Martin   1319
Turquet-Milnes, Gladys R.   1320
Twart, Koenraad W.   641
Uitti, Karl D.   1099, 1765
Ulibarri, Sabine R.   1913
Ullmann, Fabrice   2663
Ulner, Arnold R.   1750
Underwood, Vernon   2893
Ungaretti, Giuseppe   2272
Unger, Leonard   3170
Urban, George R.   1733
Ure, Peter   3171
Uzanne, Joseph   863
Uzanne, Octave   2706
Vachon, G.-André   2369
Vachon, Marius   2497
Vaida, Mircea   642, 1170
Vaillant, Annette   864
Valdén, Nils Gösta   1575
Valente, José A.   1532
Valentinov, Nikolay   702
Valeri, Diego   643, 1486
Valéry, Paul   244, 245, 1069, 1070,
2273, 2852, 2853
Valeton, D.   1181
Valette, Alfred   246
Valin, Pierre   868, 906
Valkhoff, P.   381
Vallas, Léon   1548
Vallier, Dora   1960
Vallmy, Jean   1071
Valsecchi, Marco   247
Van Bever, Pierre   248
Vandelpÿl, Fritz   1573
Van Dijk, T.A.   2533
Van Nuffel, Robert O.   644
Van Roosbroeck, Gustave L.   249

Van Westrum, Adrian S.   2984
Vanier, Léon   645
Vanor, Georges   869, 3052, 3053
Varga, József   1144
Vargas, Maria F.   1431
Vaucaire, Maruice   1136
Valčev, Velicko   701
Vėbrienė, Genovaitė   2308
Vecchi, Vittorio   2106
Vecchioni, Mario   1487
Vedia, Léonidas de   250
Vejdle, V.   1382
Veler, Richard P.   2476
Vellay, Charles   151, 543
Vendelfelt, Erik   1644, 1645, 1646
Verdin, Simone   1072
Vereno, Matthias   250a
Vergniol, Camille   1321
Verhulst, Margaret M.   3172
Verhaeren, Emile   1073, 2707
Verhoeff, J.P.   2274
Verlaine, Paul   2664, 2665
Vérola, Paul   1387
Vertpré   646
Vestdijk, S.   1322
Vettori, Vittorio   1488
Vezér, Erzsébet   1145
Vial, Fernand   1432
Vianu, Tudor   1209
Viazzi, Glauco   647
Vickery, John B.   278, 973
Vickery, Walter   2414
Vidal, Hernán   2073
Vieillard, Roger   1961
Vielé-Griffin, Francis   251, 252,
    253, 254, 255, 256, 870, 1074,
    1075, 1076, 1077, 1078, 1079,
    1112, 1569, 2275, 2276, 2344,
    2878, 2879, 3010, 3063
Vigée, Claude   257, 1080, 1775,
    1776, 1777, 1778
Vigié-Lecocq, E.   1081
Viguié, P.   2534
Vinaver, Eugène   1214
Vinding, Ole   1921
Visan, Tancrède de   258, 259, 648
Vitaletti, G.   1137
Vivier, Robert   2311
Vlasto, A.P.   1798

Vogel, Lucy   1383
Vogliolo, Giulano   2482
Volboudt, Pierre   1962
Vomperskij, V.P.   2107
Vonessen, Franz   259a
Vornicu, Mihai   1197
Vortriede, Werner   260, 1734, 1735,
    2267, 2278, 2279, 2396
Vossler, K.   649
Vultur, Smaranda   1359
Wahl, J.   2854
Wais, Karin   2585
Wais, Kurt   261, 355, 650, 1138,
    2074, 2075, 2280, 2281, 2855, 2856
Walch, J.   1082
Waldemann, Emil   872
Walker, Hallam   2895
Wallon, Simone   960
Walzer, Pierre   651
Wangson, Otto   1789
Warmoes, J.   873
Warnach, W.   1841
Wasserstrom, William   2325
Watanabe, Junko   3173
Watson, Harold   1433
Watts, Harold H.   3174
Wautier, André   652
Weatherhead, Andrew   1083
Webb, Karl E.   2586
Weber, Alfred   1616
Weber, Horst   1842
Weber, Jean-Paul   1084
Webster, Brenda A.S.   3175, 3176
Weevers, Theodor   2997, 2998
Weigand, Elsie   2587
Weigand, W.   331
Weil, Irwin   1751
Weinberg, Bernard   263
Weinberg, Kerry   1617
Weinberg, Kurt   1790
Weinhandl, Ferdinand   264
Weintraub, Stanley   329, 330, 1329
Welch, Cyril   1323
Welch, Liliane   1323, 2282, 2283
Weld, Evelyn B.P.   2880
Welleck, Albert   961, 962, 1085
Welleck, René   265, 266
Wells, Benjamin W.   1086
Welti, Heinrich   3054

Wenguerow, Zinaide 703
Wenk, Arthur B. 1549
Wenseleers, Lucas 2378
Wernaer, Robert M. 267
Werner, A. 2517
West, James 704
West, Rebecca 268
Weston, Neville 874
Wheat, Linda R. 1994
Wheelwright, P. 269
Whibley, Charles 2666
White, Clyde P. 2322
Whiting, Charles 2857
Whitmore, Donnell R. 963
Whittet, G.S. 875
Whittick, A. 876
Wiedemann, Conrad 1840
Wiegner, Kathleen 331
Wijkmark, Carl-Henning 1576
Wilenski, R.H. 877
Williams, Thomas A. 2284, 2285
Wills, Ludmilla M. 2858
Willy, Henry G.V. 3055, 3056
Wilson, Alice L. 2986
Wilson, Edmund 269a, 2415, 2416
Wilson, F.A.C. 3177
Wilson, Jean 1087
Wimsatt, W.K. 1618
Wind, E. 878
Winge, Mette 1203
Winkel, Joseph 2286
Winkler, Michael 1736
Winters, Yvor 332
Winzberger, Karl-Heinz 178
Witt, Marion 3178
Wittrock, Ulf 2763
Wolff-Windegg. joô´ 1926a
Wolters, Friedrich 1737
Won, Yo 716
Woolley, Grange 2287, 3057
Woudenberg, Gerda van 1453
Wright, Alfred J. 2987
Wright N. 1619

Wulf, Lippman 1315
Wunberg, Gotthart 2843
Wyczynski, Paul 270, 271, 2370, 2371, 2372, 2373
Wyld, Lionel D. 2477
Wytrzens, G. 1640
Wyzema, Teodor de 272, 879
Wyzewa, Isabelle de 3058
Wyzewa, Teodor de 3059
Yamada, Shoi Chi 1766
Yannella, Philip R. 1460
Yeats, W.B. 2988
Yelton, Donald C. 1442
Ynduráin, Domingo 2044
Ynduráin, Francisco 1914
Yoder, Albert C., III 333
Young, Howart T. 653
Youngblood, Sarah 3179
Yoyo, Emile 2432
Yun, Chang S. 3180
Zabeltitz, Max Zobel von 1738
Zajcev, V.A. 2108
Zamfir, Mihai 654
Zangwill, I. 2989
Zardoya, Concha 1779
Zarev, Pantelej 701
Zayed, Georges 2288
Zeitler, Rudolf 880
Zerbe, L.R. 273, 655
Zérèga-Fombona, A. 656
Zilcken, Philippe 2708
Zillmer, Herman L. 907
Zimbardo, R.A. 1660
Zimmer, Szczepan 3098
Zimmerman, Eléonore M. 2289, 2990
Zirmunskij, Viktor M. 705
Žmegač, Viktor 382
Zola, Emile 2787
Zolnai, Béla 717
Zubiria, Romón de 2045
Zuckerkandi, Frédéric 2290
Zweig, Paul 2001
Zweig, Stefan 2881